Inner Hebrides
Including Mull, Iona, Islay, Jura and more

the Bradt Travel Guide

Katie Featherstone

edition
1

www.bradtguides.com

Bradt Travel Guides Ltd, UK
The Globe Pequot Press Inc, USA

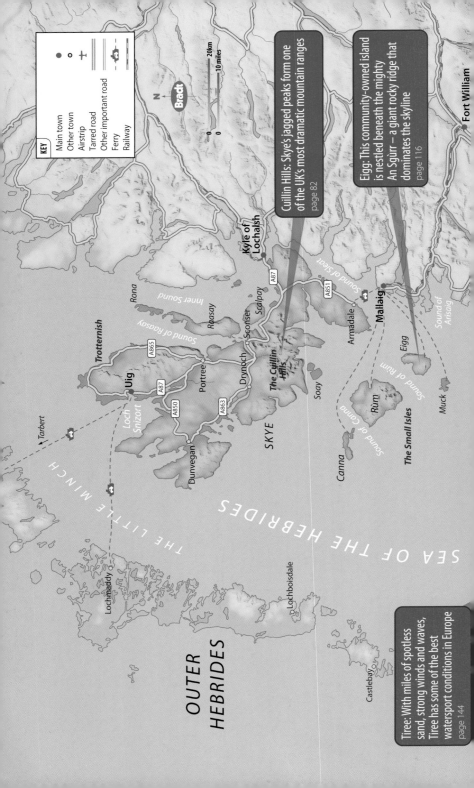

KEY

- ● Main town
- ○ Other town
- ✈ Airstrip
- ━━ Tarred road
- ─── Other important road
- ⇄ Ferry
- ┼┼┼ Railway

Bradt

N

0   20km
0   10 miles

Cuillin Hills: Skye's jagged peaks form one of the UK's most dramatic mountain ranges
page 82

Eigg: This community-owned island is nestled beneath the mighty An Sgùrr – a giant rocky ridge that dominates the skyline
page 116

Tiree: With miles of spotless sand, strong winds and waves, Tiree has some of the best watersport conditions in Europe
page 144

Fort William

Kyle of Lochalsh

A87

A851

Mallaig

Armadale

Sound of Sleat

Rona

Inner Sound

Raasay

Sound of Raasay

Scalpay

Sconser

Trotternish

A865

Uig

A87

Portree

A850

Drynoch

A863

The Cuillin Hills

SKYE

Loch Snizort

Dunvegan

Soay

Eigg

Sound of Rum

Sound of Canna

Canna

Rum

Sound of Arisaig

Muck

The Small Isles

▲ Tarbert

THE LITTLE MINCH

SEA OF THE HEBRIDES

Lochmaddy

OUTER HEBRIDES

○ Lochboisdale

Castlebay

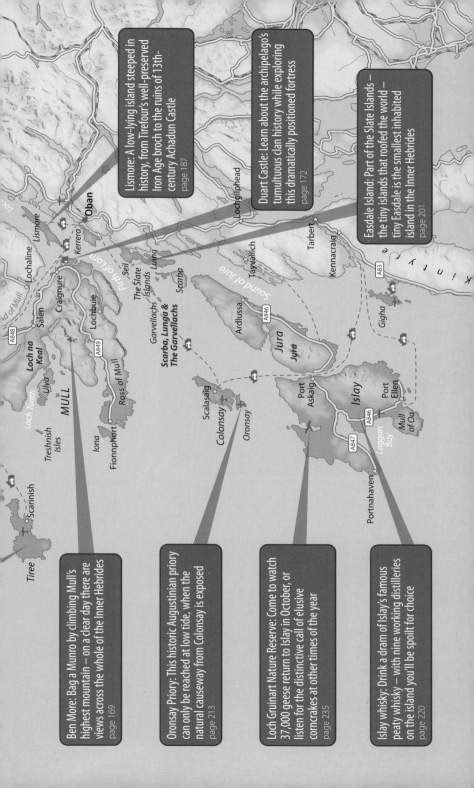

Lismore: A low-lying island steeped in history, from Tirefour's well-preserved Iron Age broch to the ruins of 13th-century Achadun Castle
page 187

Duart Castle: Learn about the archipelago's tumultuous clan history while exploring this dramatically positioned fortress
page 172

Easdale Island: Part of the Slate Islands — the tiny islands that roofed the world — tiny Easdale is the smallest inhabited island in the Inner Hebrides
page 201

Ben More: Bag a Munro by climbing Mull's highest mountain — on a clear day there are views across the whole of the Inner Hebrides
page 169

Oronsay Priory: This historic Augustinian priory can only be reached at low tide, when the natural causeway from Colonsay is exposed
page 213

Loch Gruinart Nature Reserve: Come to watch 37,000 geese return to Islay in October, or listen for the distinctive call of elusive corncrakes at other times of the year
page 235

Islay whisky: Drink a dram of Islay's famous peaty whisky — with nine working distilleries on the island you'll be spoilt for choice
page 220

Oban
Lochaline
Salen
Craignure
Lochbuie
Kerrera
Lismore
Firth of Lorn
Seil
The Slate Islands
Luing
Scarba
Garvellachs
Scarba, Lunga &
The Garvellachs
Lochgilphead
Taynuilt
Tarbert
Kennacraig
A83
Ardlussa
A846
Sound of Jura
Jura
Jura
Gigha
MULL
Loch na
Keal
Loch Tuath
Ulva
Treshnish
Isles
Iona
Fionnphort
Ross of Mull
A849
A848
Scarinish
Tiree
Colonsay
Scalasaig
Oronsay
Port
Askaig
Islay
Port
Ellen
A846
Mull
of Oa
Laggan
Bay
Portnahaven
A847
Sound of Mull
Kintyre

Inner Hebrides
Don't miss...

Puffins
From May until August,
watch puffins nesting
on the Treshnish Isles or
Sanday
(PT/VS) pages 185 and 125

Climb Mull's highest peak
Take in panoramic views from the
top of Ben More on Mull
(m/S) page 169

Geese migration
Visit Islay in mid-October to witness over 30,000 geese returning to the island
(SS) page 235

Canna
Explore the tiny island of Canna with its population of just 20
(SS) page 122

Picture-perfect settlements
Taste island specialities or pick up local crafts on your wanderings through the towns and villages of the Inner Hebrides. Pictured here colourful Tobermory.
(SV/S) page 161

Inner Hebrides
in colour

above   Skye's pretty capital Portree is the Inner Hebrides' most populous settlement (NH/S) page 58

left   Nestled below the mighty Paps, life on Jura is centred around Craighouse, the island's largest township (PT/VS) page 243

below   Whisky is the mainstay of Islay's economy — there are nine distilleries across the island (TWS/S) page 220

above	The small passenger ferry between Point on Lismore and mainland Port Appin only takes 10 minutes (EQ/S) page 189
below left	Island culture and history is preserved in the islands' excellent heritage centres and small museums; pictured: Skye Museum of Island Life (FB/S) page 72
bottom left	Highland dancing, pipe bands and Herculean feats of strength all feature in the islands' Highland Games and summer fèis events (SS) page 44
below right	A ferry operator's dog rides between Seil and Luing in the Slate Islands (KF) page 203

above left   St Edward's Church, Sanday, with Rùm's dramatic cliffs behind (NN/S) page 126

top right   Iona Abbey now attracts pilgrims from all over the world (Ch/S) page 184

above right   In 1598 on Islay, the MacLeans were burnt to death in Kilnave Chapel (4/S) page 235

below left   The ruins of a 13th-century chapel at Kirkapol on Tiree (KF) page 150

bottom left   West Highland grave slabs depict warriors, swords and crosses, each stone telling the story of the person it commemorates (KF) page 20

below right   On Seil, Kilbrandon Church is famous for its dramatic stained-glass windows designed by Dr Douglas Strachan (KF) page 201

AUTHOR

Katie Featherstone is a history graduate with a specific interest in remote places and under-represented people. After studying the impact of Norsemen on Islay at university, she seized the chance to research the Inner Hebrides more broadly for this guide, applying the same level of scrutiny and breadth of sources throughout the process.

Although this is her first book, Katie has been writing on the website **w** featherytravels.com since 2012, covering everything from how to navigate public transport through Peru's Central Highlands to explaining the refugee situation in Calais in 2016 and, more recently, trying to prepare hikers for conditions in the Icelandic mountains, where she still works during the summer months. You can follow her on Facebook, Twitter and Instagram via @featherytravels.

AUTHOR'S STORY

Having holidayed around the Inner Hebrides every year since I was born, I spent my first decade of adulthood getting as far away from the UK as possible, writing a lot and trying to learn how to use a camera. Sometime around Christmas 2016 I reconsidered and decided that, actually, I found hiking in horizontal rain somewhat more exciting than lying under palm trees – and I haven't been able to shake the idea since.

My obsession with islands comes from the idea of isolated communities; tiny kingdoms separated by savage seas and the plentiful coastline surrounding them. My family seem to share this enthusiasm and, although their reasons are their own, have moved to Islay permanently; I continue to live here, there and everywhere, but always return to the Hebrides – drawn back by the wilderness and miles of rugged coastline still to explore.

This is my first book and, desperate to make a good job of it, I began by researching wildly, in as much detail as I physically could, in every direction. I scoured old books, poured over Historic Environment Scotland's map (**w** canmore.org.uk) and questioned locals relentlessly. On each island, I drove down every side road, poked my head into countless en suites, and tramped around the countryside looking for ancient monuments, beaches and beautiful views. At some point, I realised that I had done enough research to write a book ten times longer than this one, and that somehow I now needed to battle this information on to the page. I hope this guide will help others discover what makes the Inner Hebrides so special: the islands' most spectacular sights and some of their more secret spots.

First edition published September 2020

Bradt Travel Guides Ltd
31a High Street, Chesham, Buckinghamshire, HP5 1BW, England
www.bradtguides.com
Print edition published in the USA by The Globe Pequot Press Inc,
PO Box 480, Guilford, Connecticut 06437-0480

Text copyright © 2020 Katie Featherstone
Maps copyright © 2020 Bradt Travel Guides Ltd; includes map data © OpenStreetMap contributors; contains Ordnance Survey Data © Crown copyright and database right 2020
Photographs copyright © 2020 Individual photographers (see below)
Project Managers: Claire Strange, Emma Gibbs and Anna Moores with thanks to Sarah Dickinson
Cover research: Marta Bescos

ISBN: 978 1 78477 644 2

British Library Cataloguing in Publication Data
A catalogue record for this book is available from the British Library

Photographs
Dreamstime.com (DT): Nigel Hoy (NH/DT); Katie Featherstone (KF); Mary-Anne Featherstone (MF); iStock.com (iS): alex_west (AW/iS), Shaiith/iStock (S/iS), Wild & Free (WF/iS); Shutterstock.com (S): 4 season backpacking (4/S), Erik AJV (EA/S), Francesco Bonino (FB/S), Mark Caunt (MC/S), Chanonry (C/S), Charlesy (Ch/S), Richard Darby (RD/S), Erni (E/S) FrontlitPhotography (F/S), Giedriius (G/S), Nataliya Hora (NH/S), Inspired By Maps (IBM/S) Mark Medcalf (MM/S), AlanMorris (AM/S), mountaintreks (m/S), Nicol Nicolson (NN/S), Martin Prochazkacz (MP/S), EQRoy (EQ/S), Spumador (Sp/S), Kevin Standage (KS/S), Elizabeth O' Sullivan (EOS/S), Tyler W. Stipp (TWS/S), Stefano_Valeri (SV/S); SuperStock (SS); Visit Scotland (VS): Kenny Lam (KM/VS), Paul Tomkins (PT/VS)
Front cover Highland cow (S/iS)
Back cover The approach to Iona (EOS/S)
Title page A replica of a Celtic cross, Iona Abbey (AM/S); Islay geese (SS); The Cullins, Skye (KM/VS)

Maps David McCutcheon FBCart.S

Typeset by Ian Spick
Production managed by Jellyfish Print Solutions; printed in India
Digital conversion by www.dataworks.co.in

Acknowledgements

They say it takes a village to raise a child and for now we can consider this my baby. Firstly of course, I must thank Bradt for giving me the opportunity to write this book; I'm rarely short on adjectives, but they all sound hollow in comparison to what this means to me. To Sue Cooper for coaxing me through the initial stages, Rachel Fielding for her enthusiasm and encouragement, Emma Gibbs and Anna Moores for helping me pull it all together, David McCutcheon for his wonderful maps, and Claire Strange for always somehow making it sound like 100 alterations were *overall* a positive thing. It would have taken very little to crush me at any stage of the process, but I've left each communication feeling more positive than before it started. If every business could conduct itself in a similar manner, the working world would be a much happier place. On the subject of Bradt, I must also mention Mark Rowe who firstly, thankfully, did not want to write this book himself. His *Outer Hebrides*, now a companion to this guide, has been a hard act to follow. I have carried it with me as a prop, point of reference and talisman of what could be achieved. Thanks too to James Lowen for his excellent natural history section.

I am also most grateful to Bonnie Wood for her energy, enthusiasm and support, as well as connecting me with the following invaluable organisations: Wild About Argyll, Explore Islay & Jura, Visit Mull & Iona, Road to the Isles, Oban & Lorn Tourism Alliance, and Skye Connect. Thank you also to all those who invited me to stay or eat – this book would not exist without your support, to everyone who shared their local knowledge or accepted my eleventh-hour requests to poke around their B&Bs, and to CalMac for providing my ferry journeys.

Thanks to my family, friends and those I don't know in person who have encouraged me to keep writing w featherytravels.com for so many years; to Bryony Welburn for your last-minute rescue, to Janet and Rod de Maine for their enthusiasm, support and the gift of Percy the VW Polo who has worn through four new tyres in the process. Thank you to my lovely Nan, Pauline Short, for always being on my side. Thank you to my family whose Hebridean enthusiasm puts mine to shame: to my sister Jenny for sharing my first adventures and my mum Mary-Ann for teaching me to appreciate beautiful places. Thank you to my dad Nick for passing on his cynicism, desire to investigate and haphazardly applied perfectionism, not to mention, more seriously, for his countless hours of proofreading; really, I wrote this book for you.

Finally and most of all, thanks to Dan for accompanying me on this journey and sharing some of the load. Without you I would have withered away; I hope we might finally have time to get married now it's finished.

Contents

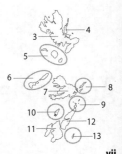

Introduction **vii**

PART ONE GENERAL INFORMATION 1

Chapter 1 **Background Information** **3**
Geography 3, Geology 4, Climate 5, Natural history and conservation 5, Archaeology and physical history 13, History 13, Government and politics 16, Economy 17, People 18, Language 18, Religion 18, Education 19, Culture 19

Chapter 2 **Practical Information** **23**
When to visit 23, Highlights 24, Suggested itineraries 25, Tour operators 25, Tourist information 26, Maps, tides and weather 26, Red tape 27, Getting there and away 27, Health 30, Safety 32, Women and LBGTQ travellers 33, Travellers with disabilities 33, Travelling with children 33, Travelling with a dog 34, What to take 34, Money and budgeting 35, Getting around 36, Accommodation 40, Eating and drinking 42, Public holidays and festivals 44, Shopping 45, Arts and entertainment 46, Outdoor activities 46, Media and communications 48, Cultural etiquette 49, Travelling positively 49

PART TWO THE GUIDE 51

Chapter 3 **Skye (An t-Eilean Sgitheanach)** **53**
History 53, Getting there and away 56, Getting around 57, Tourist information and tours 57, Events 58, Portree and the Braes 58, Uig and the Trotternish Peninsula 63, Edinbane, Dunvegan and the Duirinish and Waternish Peninsulas 74, Minginish and the Cuillin Hills 82, Broadford and Elgol 85, Sleat, Kyleakin and the southeast 88

Chapter 4 **Raasay (Ratharsair)** **97**
History 97, Getting there and away 98, Getting around 98, Where to stay, eat and drink 98, Shopping and galleries 99, Other practicalities 100, What to see and do 100

Chapter 5	**The Small Isles** History 105, Getting there and away 107, Other practicalities 108, Events 108, Rùm 109, Eigg (Eige) 116, Canna (Canaigh) and Sanday (Sandaigh) 122, Muck (Muc) 129	**105**
Chapter 6	**Coll (Cola) and Tiree (Tirodh)** History 134, Getting there and away 135, Coll 137, Tiree 144	**134**
Chapter 7	**Mull (Muile) and Iona (Ì Chaluim Chille)** Mull 155, Isle of Ulva (Ulbha) 179, Iona 179	**155**
Chapter 8	**Lismore (Lios Mòr) and Kerrera (Cearara)** Lismore 187, Kerrera 193	**187**
Chapter 9	**The Slate Islands** Getting there and away 196, Tourist information 197, Other practicalities 197, Events 197, Seil (Saoil) 197, Easdale Island (Eilean Èisdeal) 201, Luing (Luinn) 203	**196**
Chapter 10	**Colonsay (Colbhasa)** Getting there and away 207, Getting around 207, Where to stay 208, Where to eat and drink 209, Shopping 209, Sports and activities 209, Other practicalities 210, Events 210, What to see and do 210	**207**
Chapter 11	**Islay (Ìle)** History 214, Getting there and away 218, Getting around 218, Sports and activities 220, Events 221, Bowmore, Bridgend and the northeast 221, Port Ellen, the Oa and the southeast 226, The west 233	**214**
Chapter 12	**Jura (Diùra)** Getting there and away 238, Getting around 239, Tourist information 240, Where to stay 240, Where to eat and drink 241, Shopping 241, Other practicalities 241, Events 242, What to see and do 242	**238**
Chapter 13	**Gigha (Giogha)** History 249, Getting there and away 252, Getting around 252, Tourist information 252, Where to stay 253, Where to eat and drink 253, Shopping 253, Other practicalities 254, Events 254, What to see and do 255	**249**
Chapter 14	**Gateway Towns** Oban 259, Mallaig 263, Other ports and connections 265	**259**
Appendix 1	**Glossary**	**266**
Appendix 2	**Further Information**	**269**
Index		**274**
Index of advertisers		**279**

MAP LIST

Bowmore	222	Mull	156–7
Canna & Sanday	124	Oban	260
Coll	138	Port Ellen	227
Colonsay & Oronsay	208	Portree	61
Eigg	117	Raasay	96
Ferry routes	29	Ross of Mull	174
Firth of Lorn	188	Rùm	110
Gigha	250	Skye	54–5
Inner Hebrides	1st colour section	Sleat	90
Iona	180	The Slate Islands	198–9
Islay	216–17	The Small Isles	106
Jura	239	Tiree	146
Kerrera	194	Tobermory	162
Lismore	190	Trotternish	64
Mallaig	263	Uig	73
Muck	130		

FEEDBACK REQUEST AND UPDATES WEBSITE

At Bradt Travel Guides we're aware that guidebooks start to go out of date on the day they're published – and that you, our readers, are out there in the field doing research of your own. You'll find out before us when a fine new family-run hotel opens or a favourite restaurant changes hands and goes downhill. So why not write and tell us about your experiences? Contact us on ☎ 01753 893444 or e info@bradtguides.com. We will forward emails to the author, who may post updates on the Bradt website at w bradtguides.com/updates. Alternatively, you can add a review of the book to w bradtguides.com or Amazon.

Introduction

Splintering off Scotland's west coast, the Inner Hebrides is a loosely scattered archipelago that includes all the islands from Skye in the north to Islay and Gigha in the south; they stretch as far west as Tiree and cut into the mainland to the east, with Lismore and Kerrera sitting in the Firth of Lorn. Romantically remote and relatively accessible to varying degrees, this book covers 21 islands, but these are just the places with a year-round population of more than ten, at least one place for a visitor to stay and regular boat services; there are countless other islands of varying sizes within the archipelago.

Surrounded by miles of intricate coastline, with vast swathes of wilderness inland, the Inner Hebrides is a haven for wildlife and a particularly important habitat for coastal birds and marine mammals. Sightings of seals are almost guaranteed, while even luckier or more patient visitors have a chance to spot otters, basking sharks and even minke whales.

With Scotland's 'right to roam', well-prepared hikers have infinite possibilities on the islands. Large areas of each map remain uninhabited and there is a high likelihood of being able to enjoy Mull's dramatic rock formations or Jura's Paps without the interruption of another person in sight.

The islands' modern-day charms and gentle demeanour give little indication of their turbulent past: Irish monks and Viking invasions, the creation of the Lords of the Isles' kingdom and subsequent clan warfare. These long-lost civilisations left behind ruined castles, intricate carvings and crumbling chapels, sprinkling the islands with fascinating archaeology.

The 19th-century Clearances hit the Inner Hebrides hard and the bumpy road to recovery through the 20th century and into the 21st is still far from over. Reclaiming an identity, through cèilidh dances and music, their native Gaelic language and traditional industries, remains an ongoing struggle but, despite having fewer than 20,000 people living across the whole region, each of the islands has a distinctive history, character and culture. Pious Iona, Islay with its whisky and Canna, where the village shop still has an honesty box, all have their own individual charm. Whichever islands you choose to visit, you can be sure to feel a world apart from mainland Great Britain.

AND A SPECIAL THANKS

We were able to proceed with this new edition – at a time when the Covid-19 pandemic had hit independent travel publishers very hard – in part due to the extraordinary generosity of David Hananel. Thank you again, David.

SYMBOLS Sights, accommodation, places to eat and drink and shops marked ♿ indicate that they are wheelchair accessible and that any available toilets are suitable for people with disabilities.

In accommodation listings, hotels, B&Bs and hostels are marked with a 🏠, self-catering weekly rentals with 🏚 and campsites by ▲. In eating and drinking listings, restaurants are marked with a ✖, cafés and takeaways with a 🍴 and bars with a ♟.

In *What to see and do* sections, suggested walks are marked with 🚶, while cycle rides with 🚲. These walks/cycle rides are indicated on the maps using the same symbols. Where scale allows, the routes have also been plotted.

AUTHOR'S FAVOURITES Finding genuinely characterful accommodation or that unmissable off-the-beaten-track café can be difficult, so the author has chosen a few of her favourite places throughout the country to point you in the right direction. These 'author's favourites' are marked with a ✻.

PRICE CODES Throughout this guide we have used price codes to indicate the cost of those places to stay and eat listed in the guide. For a key to these price codes, see page 41 for accommodation and page 44 for restaurants.

MAPS
Keys and symbols Maps include alphabetical keys covering the locations of those places to stay, eat or drink that are featured in the book. Note that regional maps may not show all hotels and restaurants in the area: other establishments may be located in towns shown on the map.

Grids and grid references The Skye map uses gridlines to allow easy location of sites. Map grid references are listed in square brackets after the name of the place or site of interest in the text, with page number followed by grid number, eg: [54 D4].

Tag us in your posts and share your adventures using this guide with us – we'd love to hear from you.

🄵 BradtGuides & featherytravels
🐦 @BradtGuides & @featherytravels
📷 @bradtguides & @featherytravels
🅟 bradtguides
▶ bradtguides

Part One

GENERAL INFORMATION

THE INNER HEBRIDES AT A GLANCE

Location Islands off the west coast of Scotland

Neighbouring regions Outer Hebrides, Argyll and the Highlands

Size/area (km²) A combined landmass of 1,594 square miles

Climate Mild oceanic climate; plenty of wind and rain

Population 20,000

Main towns Portree, Tobermory

Economy Agriculture, tourism, fishing, whisky distilling

Languages English and Scottish Gaelic

Religion Christian: mainly Church of Scotland, Free Church of Scotland and other Protestant denominations. Increasing numbers of inhabitants are atheist or agnostic.

Currency Pound sterling (Scotland has its own banknotes, but English notes are also accepted)

Exchange rate (Jul 2020) US$1 = £0.79; €1 = £0.89

International telephone code +44

Time GMT+1 (Oct–Mar), GMT+1 (Mar–Oct)

Electrical voltage 230V

Weights and measures Road signs in miles; elsewhere both metric and imperial units are widely used

Flag The UK's Union Jack. Scotland's flag is the 'St Andrew's Cross' or 'Saltire', which has a white cross diagonally set on a blue background. Some islands also have their own flag such as Tiree's Bratach Thiriodh, which depicts ears of barley forming a sun on a green background.

National sports Highland Games, football, rugby, shinty

Public holidays The same as mainland Scotland: 1 January (New Year's Day), 2 January, Good Friday, early May bank holiday (first Monday in May), spring bank holiday (last Monday in May), summer bank holiday (first Monday in August), 30 November (St Andrew's Day), 25 December (Christmas Day), 26 December (Boxing Day)

Background Information

GEOGRAPHY

Looking at a map of Scotland, the Inner Hebrides crumble off the west coast at a point where the mainland appears so intricately broken by lochs and coastline that it is often difficult to tell which parts of land are islands and what is attached. This is a scattered archipelago, spanning 150 miles north to south and around 50 miles east to west. While over 20 of the islands are inhabited, a countless number have no human residents at all; from Scarba, at 6 square miles, to hundreds of rocky islets that are left to nature as some of the UK's most precious areas of wilderness.

Spread across a combined landmass of 1,594 square miles (4,130km²), the definition of the Inner Hebrides is somewhat hazy even to the people who live there. During the course of researching this book, I was often asked by residents which islands was I going to include. Does Seil still count as an island even though it is only separated from the mainland by the tiniest, bridged channel and, in that case, what about Skye? This guidebook includes both Seil and Skye, as well as all the inhabited islands up the Firth of Lorn into Loch Linnhe, where the Hebridean definition gets a little stretched.

Scattered as they are, the islands are defined by the stretches of water surrounding them. For centuries these seas would have been impassable for most inhabitants and in high winds that can still be the case today.

The most northerly of the islands is Skye, separated from the Outer Hebrides by the Little Minch, while more temperate Islay and Gigha are the most southerly. The other islands are spread out between them: some, like Seil and Kerrera, so close to the mainland that they are almost still part of it; while, in the far west of the region, low-lying Coll and Tiree are exposed to the full force of the Atlantic Ocean.

POPULATION Around 20,000 people currently call the Inner Hebrides home. Half of the archipelago's population live on the biggest island, Skye, which is 639 square miles (1,656km²), and around another 6,000 are split between the second and third largest islands, Mull and Islay. However, aside from those three islands, geographical size and population have very little correlation here, with the fourth largest island (Jura) having fewer than 200 inhabitants and Tiree, the sixth largest island, home to over 700 inhabitants; Seil, which ranks 16th in size, has over 500 inhabitants.

Although each island has its own 'capital', Skye's Portree, with fewer than 5,000 residents, is the largest town in the archipelago; Tobermory on Mull is the second biggest settlement, being home to around 1,000 people. The vast majority of townships are little more than hamlets, with few houses and no amenities at all.

GEOLOGY

With craggy coastlines and sandy beaches, bleak moorland, mountains and fertile glens, one of the Inner Hebrides' greatest delights is the sheer variety of its landscapes. To understand them better, it is necessary to look at the islands' geology, which varies greatly across the archipelago.

The oldest rocks in the region (as well as in the UK) are those of Lewisian gneisses, which take their name from Lewis in the Outer Hebrides and date from around 2,500 million years ago, during the Archean Eon. These can be found on northern Raasay, Rùm, Coll, Tiree, Iona and the southeastern coast of Skye's Sleat Peninsula.

Also on the Sleat Peninsula, northeastern Rùm and Raasay are layers of red Torridonian sandstones, sedimentary rocks that settled around 1,000 million years ago. Around Ord and the head of Loch Slapin on Skye there are also a variety of sedimentary rocks from the Cambrian and Ordovician periods, deposited in a shallow sea around 550 to 450 million years ago.

In contrast, but from a similar time period, the Slate Islands (unsurprisingly, perhaps) were formed from metamorphic slate; the export of the characteristic blue-grey slates once held up the economy of these islands.

More sedimentary rocks were deposited by rivers and shallow seas during the Mesozoic Era (around 245 to 90 million years ago). These are of particular interest for the evidence they left behind of life during the Triassic, Jurassic and Cretaceous periods: Jurassic dinosaur footprints can be seen at An Corran on Skye (page 69); and on Camas Mòr on Muck (page 132), layers packed with fossilised shells are exposed on the foreshore. Sedimentary rocks from this period can also be found on Raasay, Eigg and Rùm.

The Palaeogene Period (66 to 23 million years ago) left signs of volcanic complexes from a time when northwest Europe began to split from North America, creating the North Atlantic. Arguably the most dramatic mountain range in Britain, the Cuillin Hills (page 82) on Skye are remnants of the roots of one such early Palaeogene volcanic centre.

Over the last 2 million years, the main geological activity across the Inner Hebrides has been the shaping of existing rocks and landscapes by moving ice. Various ice ages have swept across Scotland, the most recent of which peaked about 18,000 years ago. After their creation as volcanic complexes, both the Skye and Rùm Cuillins were later eroded by the build-up and withdrawal of glaciers. On Jura, Sgriob na Caillich (see box, page 245) is thought to be a medial moraine, a narrow strip of debris deposited between two streams of the Devensian ice sheet as they collided. Trotternish Ridge in northern Skye continued to see landslides long after the disappearance of the glaciers, resulting in amazing rock formations such as the Storr (page 67) and Quiraing (page 69).

The islands' geology has resulted in often dramatically different ecosystems and undoubtedly affected human communities and industry. Rùm, with its savage peaks, and waterlogged Jura have always had relatively small populations as vast swathes of their land are simply uninhabitable. In contrast, Lismore is based on metamorphosed limestone and particularly fertile; this has affected life on the island for both wildlife and people. Islay's peat bogs have long been harvested for fuel and used in the process of whisky making, while quarrying has taken place on most islands in the region: slate on the Slate Islands (page 196), iron ore on Raasay (page 97), limestone on Lismore (page 187) and pink Ross of Mull granite (page 178) are just a few examples.

CLIMATE

The islands' proximity to the Atlantic Ocean gives it a mild oceanic climate with cool temperatures. In winter, the north of Skye averages around 6°C, whereas temperatures in Islay and Gigha are closer to 8°C; in summer, Skye sees averages of 15°C and the more southerly islands are a degree or two warmer than that. Tiree is known as one of the sunniest places in the UK, but there is nothing to protect you from the savage Atlantic winds there. Apart from on the loftiest peaks, the islands generally receive very little snow and they are said to be kept warmer by the Gulf Stream; none of this is a great comfort in the long winter months, however, in the face of howling winds and biting rain.

Thought to be already affecting the behaviour of certain species of wildlife, there are major concerns about how **climate change** will affect the future of the Inner Hebrides. Warmer temperatures, rising sea levels and even more unpredictable weather would make the Inner Hebrides increasingly inhospitable for both wildlife and human inhabitants.

NATURAL HISTORY AND CONSERVATION

Many different parts of the Inner Hebrides are recognised as unique and protected under various conservation areas. Loch na Keal National Scenic Area, which is protected from 'inappropriate' development because of its exceptional landscapes and coastline, covers much of western Mull and all the small islands out to the Treshnish Isles. The new Argyll Coast and Islands Hope Spot (w argyllhopespot. scot) includes the north and east of Jura, the Slate Islands, Lismore, Kerrera and the Sound of Mull; it is said to be rivalled only by St Kilda in terms of biodiversity in Scotland. There are two RSPB reserves on Islay (pages 230 and 235), one on Coll (page 144) and almost the entirety of Rùm is run as a nature reserve by Scottish Natural Heritage. Countless other small reserves, such as Ballachuan Hazelwood (see box, page 201) on Seil, protect specific locations and species.

PLASTIC POLLUTION

Aside from climate change, the biggest human-inflicted environmental threat to species in the Inner Hebrides is undoubtedly plastic pollution. The archipelago's exposed beaches, in a prime location to receive accidental unbiodegradable litter from Scotland, Ireland and the Atlantic Ocean, receive a new haul of debris with every storm. Although some of this is everyday food packaging, bathroom waste and balloons, the depressing majority here comes from the fishing industry. Nets, plastic straps, fish boxes, floats and buoys are a common sight on the islands' shorelines; the once scenic additions of round glass floats or fraying rope made from biodegradable materials such as heather have changed to plastic tangles, perfectly designed to trap fish and equally destructive to birds and larger marine mammals such as whales, who can eat it by mistake. The visible evidence of this problem is only the tip of the proverbial iceberg; microplastics, tiny scraps that can be eaten by small fish and enter the food chain, are said to be as omnipresent as ten million pieces per square kilometre.

While in the Inner Hebrides, consider collecting litter when you visit the beaches and disposing of it when you find a large enough public bin.

1

HABITATS AND HIGHLIGHTS Like many isolated islands, the Inner Hebrides have developed their own very specialised ecosystems. Although, excluding deer and goats, they are generally low in species of land mammal, this is over-compensated with birds and marine wildlife. The occasional arrival of invasive hedgehogs and non-native species is something of a mystery, which raises much confusion and can cause a great deal of damage. The Tiree machair complex is particularly noteworthy as one of the few examples of rabbit-free machair in Scotland; elsewhere, such as on Canna, you can immediately see the erosive damage of their burrowing.

Sandy beaches and the machair
Machair is a Gaelic word for a fertile low-lying grassy area. It is used to describe the habitat formed as strong wind blows crushed shells up from the shore and this sandy base is colonised by grasses and plants. One of the least common habitats in Europe, the calcium-rich shell sand supports a fragile ecosystem, parts of which can easily be destroyed by careless boots or, significantly worse, off-road driving. On sandy beaches, curlews, oystercatchers, ringed plovers and other wading birds feed at the water's edge and nest further up the tide line. With relatively small numbers of land predators, ground-nesting birds are common and successful. It is particularly important to keep dogs under control in spring when seabirds might be nesting; sharp-beaked Arctic terns and predatory skuas are likely to dive-bomb you if you get too close.

Rocky shorelines and cliffs
On rocky coasts, the area between high and low tide lines supports a fascinating array of species. Small fish and prawns get caught in rock pools, while sea urchins and starfish cling to the rocks. By carefully investigating under thongs of seaweed, you can discover sheltering crabs, frilly sea slugs and colourful shells. The coastline of the Inner Hebrides is fringed by an intricate network of peninsulas and partially protruding rocks, which form sanctuaries for otters and seals. Protecting their eggs from potential land and sea predators, including humans, cliffs can host huge colonies of nesting seabirds: guillemot, fulmar, kittiwake, shags and gulls; puffins nest in a couple of specific places on the Treshnish Isles (see box, page 185) and Sanday (page 125).

Kelp forests
The kelps are a set of large, brown seaweeds, which grow exceptionally fast and can reach lengths of up to 260ft in the right conditions. Providing the coast with some degree of protection in storms, kelp forests are both food and shelter for many marine creatures. A strong, claw-like 'holdfast' anchors each plant on to

---

GROUND NESTING BIRDS

In May and June, beaches with pebbles and sand can be nest sites for seagulls, terns, oystercatchers, ringed plovers and other wading birds. During the spring and summer, grassland, moorland, heather and peat habitats might hide the nests of game birds such as pheasants and grouse, as well as snipe and small birds like skylarks, meadow pipits and lapwings.

Birds will usually alert you to their presence with plenty of noise, but you should always look where you step and it is important to keep dogs on a lead or under very close control as they can disturb birds off their nests and even eat the eggs.

If you are walking on an RSPB reserve, it's best to check their specific recommendations as these might vary throughout the year.

THE HEBRIDEAN WHALE TRAIL

While I was on Mull, I managed to interview Karl Stevens from the Hebridean Whale and Dolphin Trust about their new project, the Hebridean Whale Trail (w whaletrail.org). Visibly brimming with enthusiasm, he is a great champion for Scotland's marine mammals.

'We just want people to know that they should look,' Karl said, impulsively glancing over his shoulder to the window out on to Tobermory Harbour from our table in the bakery. 'Even if they just sit for an extra 5 minutes; it's about slowing people down. These islands are one of the best places in Europe for land-based marine mammal watching, but not many people realise that yet.'

Karl went on to explain how one-quarter of the world's whale and dolphin species are found off the west coast of Scotland. Resident populations of bottle-nosed dolphin can be seen in Tobermory Harbour itself and the region is one of the best places to see porpoise in Europe. Coll and Tiree are known for their basking sharks and minke whales, especially between April and October before the basking sharks move to deeper waters and minke whales migrate further south. Each year a very lucky few people manage to see killer whales.

The Hebridean Whale Trail, stretching between Cape Wrath (the most northwesterly point of mainland Scotland), St Kilda (in the Outer Hebrides) and Arran, encompasses the Inner Hebrides and aims to make cetacean spotting as accessible as possible. To report your sightings, you can download the Hebridean Whale and Dolphin Trust's app or create an account on their website (w whaletrack.hwdt.org).

Even more excitingly, there is a possibility to join the team on board the *Silurian* (w hwdt.org/silurian), receiving training in marine research and sailing, to work alongside the HWDT crew as a field biologist.

a rock; the tiny caves and tunnels created by this feature typically host between 30 and 70 different species per plant.

The high seas   With fierce currents, crashing waves and Corryvreckan whirlpool, the seas surrounding the Inner Hebrides do not always feel like a habitable environment but, despite depleted fish stocks, the area is still an excellent place to spot the UK's largest and most exciting species: whales, dolphins, basking sharks and large numbers of seals.

Peat bogs   The Inner Hebrides are rich in peat bogs. Peat is formed as the ground becomes waterlogged and plant matter is unable to decompose properly. Although it only supports a small number of species, mostly *Sphagnum* bog mosses, cotton grasses and some small carnivorous plants such as sundew, as well as birds such as merlin, golden plover and dunlin, this habitat is of global environmental importance for its ability to trap huge quantities of carbon. The carbon dioxide that is absorbed and converted by plants during photosynthesis is trapped under anaerobic conditions beneath the water and stored underground for an infinite length of time.

Accumulated peatland also provides an unusual opportunity to examine the entire history of an ecosystem's development; as a form of archive, it stores pollen grains and plant remains (macrofossils), making it possible to reconstruct an idea of past landscapes and climatic periods; in the case of UK peatlands, this is as far back as 10,000 years.

Farmland When managed sympathetically, something that the RSPB and other organisations are working hard to promote, low-intensity farming can work alongside wildlife. Islay's choughs (page 11), for example, feed on insects and larvae found under cowpats. Corncrakes are only found in small pockets of the mainland, but changes in farming methods have increased populations in certain parts of the Hebrides where they stay between April and September before migrating to Africa for the winter. Towards the end of April into the beginning of May, Coll (page 144) is one of the best places in the UK to hear their distinctive 'crex-crex' call. Whether they are appreciated or not, barnacle and white-fronted geese swamp farmers' fields every autumn, the most dramatic display being found on Islay (page 235).

Woodland The Inner Hebrides are not known for their forests, but there are some magical exceptions including the woodland around Craignure on Mull (page 173), near Inver on Raasay (page 103) and Bridgend Woods on Islay (page 225). Ancient woodland – those that have existed since before 1750 – supports a unique variety of delicate lichens, ferns, fungi and even the elusive pine marten in places. Native broad-leaved trees are the perfect habitat for many small birds including redstart, wood warbler and tree pipit and although evergreen conifer plantations are generally considered to be less scenic, especially when they have to be felled, they do support good populations of the certain species which thrive, siskin and goldcrest for example.

Lofty peaks The Skye Cuillins are the Inner Hebrides' most imposing mountain range, with 3,254ft Sgùrr Alasdair being the highest peak; Jura, Rùm, Mull and Islay all have substantial hills and most of the islands have some variation in altitude. These peaks are important habitats for golden eagles and, in the case of Rùm, Manx shearwater, which arrive in their thousands to breed. On Mull in particular, you might see golden and white-tailed or sea eagles flying together. It is important not to publicise their nesting sites online, as unfortunately there is still a black market for eggs.

FLORA AND FAUNA *with James Lowen*

Among visitors with even a smidgeon of interest in nature, few depart the Inner Hebrides anything other than wowed. The waters between the islands are arguably the UK's finest for spotting whales and dolphins, while rocky coastlines and interpolating bays are frequented by otters and seals. Boat trips offer a near-guarantee of close views of white-tailed eagle, while the closely related golden eagle soars on uplifts of air above. Feathered throngs of geese and seabirds delight in winter and summer respectively, while the latter season can be one of plenty for colourful orchids, rare bumblebees and stunning butterflies and moths.

Land mammals The most iconic mammal inhabiting the Inner Hebrides is one that blurs the boundaries between land and water: the **otter**. Equally at home in lochs, ditches and seaweed-strewn, rocky bays, this member of the weasel family is rather common on many islands. Seeing it is another matter, usually requiring either persistence or luck. Early morning and late evening are best, particularly – for coastal animals – on an incoming tide. Chances are highest on calm days, when it is easier to spot the distinctive V-shaped furrow made by a swimming otter. Tiree (including Loch Bhasapol), Mull (Calgary Bay), Skye (Milovaig) and Rùm (Kinloch) are probably your best bets.

Rivalling the otter for top spot is **red deer**, the UK's largest wholly land-dwelling mammal, which inhabits several islands. Typically, animals spend the summer on high moorlands, but descend to the lowlands in winter. The most exciting time of year to see them is autumn, when males engage in 'rutting' – a visceral, antler-clacking display of dominance that decides which individuals secure the rights to sire that year's offspring. Jura is thought to mean 'deer island', and perhaps 7,000 individual deer live there, while the red deer of Rùm have been studied intensively since 1953 – one of the longest-running and most comprehensive studies of any animal anywhere in the world.

The most obvious land mammal on Islay and Tiree is the **brown hare**, while **mountain hares** have been introduced to islands including Mull, Skye and Raasay. The latter is less rangy than the more familiar former species, with shorter ears. Mountain hares on Mull, at least, originated from Ireland, which makes them **Irish hares** – a subspecies that originally colonised Ireland during the last Ice Age.

Two other iconic British mammals owe their unexpected presence to human activity. **Hedgehogs** were covertly introduced to Tiree, where they now roam lowland grasslands and machair. Meanwhile, the opening of the Skye Bridge has enabled **pine martens** to cross from mainland Scotland on to Skye. They have now spread throughout the south and west of the island. Less clear is how pine martens reached Mull during the Noughties. The most plausible theory suggests that the original arrivals were stowaways aboard timber-laden ships.

Marine life

Like otters, seals confuse the distinction between land and marine mammals. But whereas the otter is essentially a landlubber that may feed at sea, the UK's two seals are fundamentally sea-dwelling creatures that come ashore to breed and lounge. Both **grey seal** and **harbour** (aka **common**) **seal** are readily seen around the coasts of many islands. Distinguishing the two can be difficult. Grey typically has a Roman nose on a flat head, unlike the rather squished-in face and round head of harbour. One of the UK's largest colonies (or 'rookeries') of grey seal is on the Treshnish Isles. Good places to see harbour seal are the southeast coast of Islay, and the bays of Vaul and Salum on Tiree.

According to mammal expert Richard Moores, 'the seas of the Inner Hebrides, being rich in food, are undoubtedly one of Britain's best areas for watching whales and dolphins'. Even more excitingly, they are relatively easy to see thanks to regular boat trips organised by local companies. Scotland's most common species, **harbour porpoise**, occurs year-round and is particularly abundant in the sounds of Mull and Jura. A small resident pod of **bottle-nosed dolphins** inhabits waters around Mull and has become a firm favourite among tourists. This species – the quintessential dolphin – tends to stick close to shore; favoured spots include Tobermory and Dervaig bays.

Waters between Mull, Coll and Tiree can be good for seeing **common dolphins** during the summer (until mid-August). According to the Hebridean Whale and Dolphin Trust (HWDT), sightings have increased 20-fold since 2004. Coll and the Small Isles are best for the thickset **Risso's dolphin**, which is most frequently seen in autumn. The Small Isles also offer the greatest chance of **orcas** (aka **killer whales**). A single pod is known from the area, and scientists have tracked it widely through the waters of west Scotland.

If you have never seen a whale, you can do no worse in the UK than join a vessel exploring the seas of the Inner Hebrides. A highlight of summer boat trips in the deep waters around the Small Isles, Mull or Coll is **minke whale**, which can be ten yards long and weigh ten tonnes. Typical views can be frustratingly brief – a quick roll of the back and a flash of dorsal fin as the whale surfaces to breathe – but occasional animals amaze by performing acrobatic leaps out of the water.

The second-largest fish in the world's seas – behind only the whale shark of tropical waters – is the **basking shark**. The Inner Hebrides is one of the best places *anywhere* to see this marine behemoth. Seen from above water, the telltale signs are an equilateral dorsal fin, followed a few feet later by a smaller isosceles triangle – the tail fin – piercing the calm sea. Observations start in May, peak between June and August, and end in October. Waters around Tiree and Coll appear to be the shark's favourite, although the Small Isles and west of Mull are also good. Boat trips enable close views but animals can often be seen from land too.

Birds There is only one contender for the title of the Inner Hebrides' most famous bird: the **white-tailed eagle**. Following six decades of absence from the UK, the island of Rùm was selected as the location for a groundbreaking reintroduction programme. Not only did this return the 'flying barn door' to the country, but it has also boosted the local economy: eagles are thought to contribute £5 million annually to the coffers in Mull. You have a chance of spotting a 'sea eagle' along the coastlines of any island, but Mull and Skye are arguably the best, with perhaps 15 pairs on the latter. On the former, Loch na Keal is probably the best spot: eagles sit for hours on Scarisdale Rocks. On Skye, you could do worse than taking a boat trip from Portree, from where boat trips run each morning with captains proffering fish to hungry raptors.

Skye, Mull and Islay are among the best islands for **golden eagle**. Seeing this large raptor, which looks longer winged and longer tailed than its heftier relative, typically involves scanning the skyline through binoculars. Good areas to search are Glen More (on Mull) and the Cuillins (Skye). Whatever you do, make sure you don't mistake a **buzzard**; birdwatchers and locals alike dismissively call these 'tourist eagles' in view of over-eager misidentifications. Other predatory birds for which it is worth keeping an eye out include **hen harriers** (especially on Islay), **merlins** (particularly Coll), **peregrines** (along coasts or near concentrations of ducks) and **short-eared owls** (in moorland glens).

Wintering geese are an internationally renowned feature of Islay, Tiree and Coll, where vast flocks can fill field and sky alike. Alongside perhaps 6,000 **Greenland white-fronted geese**, over 30,000 **barnacle geese** throng on Islay. Few birds' names have such a curious etymology as this piebald waterbird. For several hundred years, it was believed to grow underwater in goose barnacle shells attached to driftwood before emerging on to land in autumn. Nowadays, there is conflict between the geese and Islay residents. Scottish Natural Heritage recompenses farmers for damage to pasture and crops caused by browsing geese – and, in 2015, authorised an annual cull that has seen 8,200 geese shot across three winters.

The sea is a good place to look for other large birds. Duck such as **eider** and **red-breasted merganser** are present year-round, being joined in winter by **scaup** and the globally threatened **long-tailed duck**. Three species of diver feed offshore during the colder months with one, **red-throated diver**, moving to moorland lochans on Jura, Islay and Skye in order to breed.

The Hebrides harbours plenty of true seabirds, which congregate in discrete breeding colonies on long-favoured cliffs. The commoner species, which you could equally well bump into while on a ferry or boat trip, include **fulmar**, **shag**, **guillemot** and **razorbill**. The UK's largest seabird, the **gannet**, is routinely seen feeding offshore, as are **kittiwakes** (a rapidly declining and now globally threatened gull) and **Arctic terns** (the avian world's most extreme migrant). The suave-looking **black guillemot** – colloquially known as 'tystie' – is a Scottish speciality; Port Askaig (Islay) is a particularly good place to bump into one. **Puffins** nest on the Treshnish Isles, while the mountains of Rùm host the world's largest colony of **Manx shearwaters**, meaning this ocean wanderer can be easily seen in surrounding waters. The UK's southernmost **Arctic skuas** – an aerial pirate that harries other seabirds to release their catch – breed on Jura.

Two species of grouse inhabit upland areas of certain islands. **Red grouse** favours heather-rich moorland while its mountaineer cousin, **ptarmigan**, frequents stony ground at higher altitudes, notably in the Cuillins (Skye). Lowlands, particularly seasonally flooded grasslands and (on Tiree and Coll) machair, are nationally important for breeding waders. **Lapwings**, **oystercatchers** and **redshanks** are the most prominent, attracting attention with their strident cries, but the diligent should also be rewarded with **curlews**, **dunlins** and **snipes**.

Occupying similar terrain, but usually concentrated in dense cover such as iris beds or hayfields, is the **corncrake**. This odd-looking and rare rail arrives in April to spend the summer on fortunate islands (Coll, Tiree, Iona and Islay). A reclusive bird, it is usually detected by voice – a loud, double-note rasp uttered incessantly day and night. Tiree's thriving population comprises one-third of the UK quotient – testament to years of conservation-sensitive farming from local crofters.

Another charismatic feathered creature sought by visiting birdwatchers is the **chough**. This red-billed ragamuffin is a crow essentially restricted to Britain's western coast, where it probes soft turf for invertebrates. An unabashed aeronaut, groups float in the wind before dive-bombing the ground, only to pull out at the last moment. Islay is the best place to see it. **Rock doves** also occur here – and more widely along clifftop grasslands and seacliffs. This is the wild ancestor of the ubiquitous feral pigeon that blights our cities – an avian indication that you are treading through wilderness.

Other animals Among life in cold blood, the **common toad** is relatively uncommon and poorly distributed, whereas the **common frog** is widespread and increasingly frequent. **Palmate newts** are a feature of acidic watercourses, including on Mull. **Adders** – our sole venomous snake – are regularly encountered in sheltered moorland on Islay, Mull and Skye.

The islands are rather too windy for visitors to readily see butterflies, but calm sunny days can see flower-rich meadows and machair come alive with these winged wonders. **Small tortoiseshell**, **green-veined white**, **small heath** and **meadow brown** are common and widespread. On the dunes, **grayling** sit with their wings snapped shut, their superbly camouflaged form revealed only when you tread too close and flush them into the air. **Small pearl-bordered fritillary**, a blaze of orange embroidered with black, is a feature of damp grasslands during June and July. **Common blue** – the males of which are scintillatingly neon – adorns the machair, and migrant **painted lady** and **red admiral** add variety in certain summers.

Excitingly, the Inner Hebrides is host to some of the UK's rarest butterflies and moths. As its name suggests, the gorgeous **marsh fritillary** resides in damp grassland on parts of Islay (such as The Oa), Jura and Mull. Adults nectar at the lilac-bloomed devil's-bit scabious from mid-May to mid-July, while the caterpillars build large, easily noticeable webs during August and September. The **pearl-bordered fritillary** has declined dramatically across the UK, and now only a single colony remains in this region – in southern Mull.

This same island is graced by some remarkable and very scarce day-flying moths. In spring, **narrow-bordered bee hawk-moths** buzz over flowers like tiny hummingbirds. Come June and July, two dramatic and very localised species of

1

black-and-red burnet moth buzz around wild thyme-covered coastal grassland. In the UK, **slender Scotch burnet** is known only from a handful of sites on Mull (notably Glengorm) and Ulva, while **transparent burnet** occurs at several locations on Mull, plus Lismore and north Jura. Other famous day-flying Hebridean moths include the Barbour-green **forester**, the bizarre **belted beauty** (whose female is flightless and rather resembles a raisin covered in belly fluff), the caramel-coloured and decidedly scarce **dew moth**, the stunning, pink-fringed **clouded buff** and the dramatic **emperor**, whose wings display eye-like spots to terrify wannabe predators.

The Inner Hebrides host a small range of dragonflies and damselflies, which typically hawk, flurry and fluster around freshwater pools, particularly in boggy areas. The mightiest – indeed the largest in the UK – is the **golden-ringed dragonfly**, which scuds scarily in search of inattentive prey. A couple of steps down in size are the darters and chasers. The **four-spotted chaser** is the first to emerge, on the wing from late May. In July and August, it is followed by the striking **black darter** and **common darter** of a Scottish-exclusive form known as 'Highland' darter. Damselflies are the smallest and weediest of the lot – with the **blue-tailed damselfly** being widespread but the **common blue damselfly** favouring large lochs.

Nine species of bumblebee thrive on the flower-festooned machair and pastures of Tiree and Coll, where they provide the indispensable ecological function of pollination. **Moss carder bee**, with its burnt-orange upper body and yellow lower body, is a striking and common sight. But the star is the **great yellow bumblebee** – a large, bright-yellow insect that has declined by 80% nationwide in the last century. Another machair speciality is the **short-necked oil beetle**, thought extinct in the UK until 2008 but which is now known to be doing well on Coll. This beetle is a rather gruesome parasite. Once the eggs have hatched, larvae wiggle on to vegetation then hitch a lift on a passing solitary bee. Upon being transported to the bee's nest, the larvae both eats its host's eggs and devours the protein-rich pollen brought back by the adult, before emerging as an adult beetle the following spring.

Plants Conservation body Plantlife has identified eight distinct 'Important Plant Areas' on the Inner Hebrides, a notable density for a relatively small landmass. One of the richest is Ardmeanach Peninsula (Mull), which supports 400 species of plant, including nationally scarce species such as **hairy stonecrop**, **alpine cinquefoil** and **mountain avens**. Small lochs on Coll and Tiree support one of the UK's most important populations of **slender naiad**. The machair of those two islands, plus Colonsay, bursts into bloom in May and reaches its peak in July. Spring's primroses cede to the sun-yellow of **buttercups**, **bedstraw** and **trefoils** which, in turn, are supplanted by the whites, blues and purples of **pansies**, **vetches**, **ragged robin** and **gentians**. Steep basalt seacliffs on Eigg support **roseroot**, **sea campion** and alpine-arctic species such as **yellow saxifrage**, **Arctic sandwort** and **alpine willowherb**.

Perhaps the most readily appreciated plants of the Inner Hebrides are its orchids. Tiree, Coll, Islay and Mull are probably the best islands for these showy plants. **Heath spotted**, **northern marsh** and **heath fragrant orchids** can be locally abundant. On meadows, you can easily see **greater butterfly orchid** and **common twayblade**, but a sharp pair of eyes will be needed to spot the smaller **frog orchid** and **small white orchid**. Damp upland areas are the domain of **bog orchid** and the tiny **lesser twayblade**. But perhaps the most desirable of all Hebridean orchids is **Irish lady's-tresses** – a delicate ivory whirl of a plant. For this you must head to Coll, Colonsay or Oronsay – and be prepared to search diligently. Not all the natural specialities of the Inner Hebrides are as showy as bottle-nosed dolphins or white-tailed eagles...

ARCHAEOLOGY AND PHYSICAL HISTORY

Although there is an astounding wealth of archaeology across the Inner Hebrides, the majority of it requires a little perseverance to discover and some imagination to appreciate. There are some notable exceptions: impressive medieval castles such as the restored Duart on Mull (page 172) and Dunvegan on Skye (page 80), as well as more ruinous and atmospheric structures like Raasay's Brochel (page 102), Gylen on Kerrera (page 195) and Lismore's Castle Coeffin (page 192); religious buildings including the impressive Oronsay Priory (page 213) and the heavily restored Iona Abbey (page 184); plus Islay's Finlaggan (page 225), once the central power base for the Lords of the Isles.

Anyone with an interest in archaeology or history should familiarise themselves with the incredible map provided by Historic Environment Scotland (w canmore. org.uk/map/about; select 'view all sites' & zooming in on the area of interest). Keen archaeologists or detectorists will most likely be aware of Scotland's Treasure Trove policy (w treasuretrovescotland.co.uk), which states that any finds belong to the Scottish government. Artefacts should be reported directly to Treasure Trove unless they include human remains, in which case, the police should be made aware immediately.

HISTORY

There seems to be a common assumption that because the Hebrides are on the edge of our current civilisation they must have been among the last places to be settled. Looking at the types of archaeological evidence present, this theory is quickly blown out of the water, but more recent documentation also proves the islands were not always at the fringes; their surrounding waterways often put them central to control of the nearby Scottish mainland.

PREHISTORY
Mesolithic era Around 11,500 years ago, the glaciers of the last Ice Age melted away and the Mesolithic era began as humans were able to live in the Inner Hebrides. From c9,000–3,000BC, hunter gatherers roamed the islands, predominantly leaving traces of their presence behind in middens or as arrow heads.

Neolithic era This era (c4,000–2,000BC) marked the adoption of farming. People began to settle on the islands, leaving behind burial sites in the forms of cairns and cists, as well as mysterious standing stone monuments.

The Bronze and Iron ages
The development of metalworking technology marked the beginning of the Bronze Age around 2,000BC, which then ran into the Iron Age (800BC–AD100). The Inner Hebrides has many roundhouses from these periods and, from the Iron Age, a collection of brochs.

The Picts
From AD100 onwards, the Picts – a civilisation that spoke an early Celtic language called Pictish – inhabited eastern and northern Scotland, including the northern islands of the Inner Hebrides. A transitional era between archaeology and history, our knowledge of this mysterious civilisation is predominantly informed by carved stones and later writings.

DÁL RIATA AND THE CONVERSION OF THE PICTS
The Scots, or Scotti, of Dál Riata were a Gaelic-speaking, Irish kingdom who emigrated across to modern-day

Scotland's western seaboard at an unknown date in the centuries before the year AD500. During this time, monks from Ireland – including the famous St Columba and his contemporary St Moluag – established religious centres on Iona and Lismore and began the somewhat unclear process of converting the Picts to Christianity. By the 8th century, Dál Riata's empire extended from Ardnamurchan to the Mull of Kintyre and included the islands from Coll and Tiree to Bute and Arran, with possible colonies on Skye and Raasay too. There is evidence of some struggle between the Picts and the Scots of Dál Riata, but it seems to have been a gradual takeover by the Scots. By 843, Kenneth, son of Alpin, had become king of the Picts as well as Dál Riata and the Picts faded away into history.

From the middle of the 7th century, there were three ruling family groups: Cenél nÓengusa (kindred of Oengus) on Islay; Cenél nGabráin governed Kintyre, Cowal and Bute (possibly also Gigha, Jura and Arran); and Cenél Loairn had Lorn, Colonsay, Ardnamurchan, Mull, Coll and Tiree. This was the beginning of the Kingdom of Scotland, with Argyll deriving from the Gaelic *Airer Goidel* (coastline of the Gael).

THE NORSE For obvious geographic reasons, the islands stretching from Shetland around the western coast of Scotland were among the first and most affected by Viking invasions. Their advanced shipbuilding techniques and maritime skills far outmatched any existing power in the area. With Ireland, the Isle of Man and Norway all being part of the Norse kingdom, the Hebrides were far from the remote and scattered hideaway we imagine today and instead part of a busy nautical highway. As early as 795, Skye was attacked and, from this time onwards, Iona was subject to numerous raids and massacres (though somehow a small community of zealous monks persisted until the 11th century).

The Norse used the Hebrides as stepping stones, relatively inconsequential parts of an ever-expanding movement across England, Ireland, mainland Europe, Russia, Iceland and eventually as far as North America.

For most individual Norsemen, it was a very different story. Along with the generally accepted pillaging, many so-called Vikings were not warriors but farmers and fishermen, searching for fertile lands to inhabit. The density of Norse names for settlements decreases the further south in the region you look while the proportion of them referring to topographical features rather than farms increases, suggesting that they did not settle for long. Although there is endless historical debate, it seems relatively conclusive that there was more intermingling than previously assumed. Crosses carved and buried among Viking graves, recordings of Irish-Norse names and the simple fact that both Norse and Gaelic existed simultaneously all the way through until the 13th century show that the relationship between cultures was more nuanced. During this period, a title of Lord or 'King' of the Isles developed, an unspecific and complicated title that echoed on until the end of the 15th century, long after the influence of the Norwegian crown had faded, and one that is actually still held by the Prince of Wales.

Although Norse dominion strengthened through Godred Crovan's establishment of a dynasty covering the' Hebrides and the Isle of Man, his granddaughter later went on to marry Somerled of Argyll and thus the power of his genetics outlasted that of Norwegian control in the region.

Somerled, the Lord of Argyll, was a new breed of sea king with appropriately mixed heritage: part Gaelic, part Norse. He died while invading the mainland in 1164, but his influence in the Hebrides was monumental and his ancestors continued to rule the western seaboard as 'Lords of the Isles' until 1266, when the Kingdom of Scotland took the Hebrides and Isle of Man under the Treaty of Perth.

CLAN RULE The Lords of the Isles continued as a crown dependency of Scotland until the latter half of the 15th century when a series of ill-advised power scuffles forced the King of Scotland to remove their lands. Other clans such as the MacLeods, MacDonalds and MacKinnons increased their hold on the islands and retained their power until the 18th century. With the Treaty of Union in 1707, the Inner Hebrides became part of the new Kingdom of Great Britain, but their remote location allowed them to continue much as before. However, after several clan chiefs came out in support of the Jacobite rebellions in 1715 and 1745 (attempts by Charles Edward Stuart – Bonnie Prince Charlie – to regain the British throne for his father James Francis Edward Stuart), their autonomy was diminished.

POPULATION GROWTH AND DECLINE IN THE 18TH AND 19TH CENTURIES The kelp industry (in which the ash of seaweed kelp – rich in iodine and alkali – is used in the production of glass) boomed in the 18th century and up until the end of the Napoleonic Wars in 1815. In combination with grain being sold at high prices and the introduction of the potato from the mid 18th century, the islands' populations continued to grow until the 1820s. The subsequent decades, however, were filled with misery and famine as the grain market collapsed owing to cheaper imports, kelp ceased to be profitable, fish stocks failed and potatoes caught a blight, causing failed crops and mass hunger. Many people left the islands by choice, but many more were forced out in the infamous Clearances as tenants were replaced by more profitable sheep.

Between 1820 and 1900, the population of the Inner Hebrides was cut in half, with all islands affected and some, such as Rùm and Muck, losing their entire populations. People left to try and make a living in other parts of Scotland, or were given 'assisted passage' as far as Canada, Australia and the United States. While some reportedly prospered, others died of disease or were unable to scratch a living in foreign lands; without the technology to communicate, whether they survived or not would never have been known to those who were left behind. The Inner Hebrides are littered with the remains of these lost communities' settlements, with the descendants of the people that used to inhabit them scattered across the globe.

The Clearances are a dark period of history for Scotland's Highlands and islands, but also more complex than the popular narrative often suggests. As a general overview, the old, traditional landowners, often the clan families, became more integrated with society elsewhere in the UK and less involved with their tenants. This mingling also introduced them to ways of life they were previously unexposed to: building fashionable houses, sending their children away to expensive schools, paying large expenses for their sons' army careers and travelling more – all of which put a strain on their finances. Although crofters' rights were eventually established after the Battle of the Braes (page 56) and the investigation under the Napier Commission in 1886, populations on the islands continued to dwindle until recent decades when some of them have slowly begun to recover.

THE WORLD WARS Like all of the UK, the Inner Hebrides were gravely affected by both World Wars. War memorials and military graveyards, found all across the region, are sombre reminders of how many lives were lost. A number of disastrous shipwrecks off the islands' treacherous coastlines resulted in heroic rescue attempts from the islanders and their involvement in the traumatic process of retrieving and identifying the bodies of those who did not survive; the enormous American Monument on Islay (page 218) is a visible testament. In the north, Raasay became the unlikely location of a prisoner of war camp as well as mining iron ore needed for submarines (page 98). Used as a base for military communications (page 135) during World War II, Tiree is the Inner Hebridean island that's possibly the most visibly altered by its military past.

THE INNER HEBRIDES TODAY While island populations are still only a fraction of their pre-Clearances numbers, gradual improvements to transport links, increased amenities and the Scottish Land Reform Act of 2003 – which made it easier for communities to buy out the land they live on – have given island residents more control over their lives. According to Brendan O'Hara, who represents the Scottish National Party in Argyll and Bute, 'physical and digital connectivity and depopulation' remain among his constituents' major concerns, with bad road conditions and a lack of high-speed broadband being the most frustrating topics. Although job prospects have increased (see opposite), a seasonal imbalance between the abundance of work and availability of affordable housing still make it hard for young people to settle. Many islanders have multiple jobs to support themselves.

GOVERNMENT AND POLITICS

Split between the two councils, which also include far greater swathes of mainland, it is difficult to talk generally about politics in the Inner Hebrides. The Highland council includes Skye, Raasay and the Small Isles, as well as a huge area of northwestern Scotland, while Argyll and Bute encompasses all the islands further south. While mainland Argyll and the more southerly Hebrides seem to work cohesively, facing a lot of similar issues and needing the same solutions, Skye's high numbers of visitors sets it apart from the rest of the Highlands and many inhabitants believe they would be better served with more autonomy or by joining the Outer Hebrides.

At Scotland's independence referendum in 2014, both areas reflected the national vote by voting against independence (Argyll and Bute 58.52%, Highland 52.92%); the last few UK-wide general elections have seen the region vote in MPs from the Scottish National Party (SNP). In 2016, the UK voted to leave the EU in another historic referendum. Although across the UK the 'leave' vote was victorious at 51.9%, every council area in Scotland voted 'remain' overall. At the time of writing, Brexit was only just beginning – how the next few years will pan out, and the effect it will have on the Inner Hebrides, and Scotland as a whole, remains to be seen.

On a more localised level, decision-making processes vary greatly between islands. One factor that comes into this system of management is land ownership. Large areas of land across the Inner Hebrides are still privately owned, as they have been for centuries, and although crofting laws allow tenants more rights and security than they had back in clan times, several of the same families have retained ownership throughout many generations (most notably, the MacLeods of Dunvegan who still own large parts of Skye). Since the economic troubles in the 1800s, the majority of islands and areas of land have been split or sold to new owners. Eigg, Gigha and more recently Ulva have been bought by the communities themselves, whereas in other places people have come together to organise their own development programmes for local improvements: South Islay Development (f), the Tiree Community Development Trust (w tireetrust.org.uk) and the Isle of Canna Community Development Trust (w theisleofcanna.com) are notably successful examples of this, but there are many others.

ECONOMY

Although tourism is ever-growing in the Inner Hebrides, traditional industries such as crofting, fishing and whisky distilling continue. Whisky is currently booming on Islay, with new distilleries opening and providing good jobs for locals. Crofting and fishing continue to be a struggle here, though some entrepreneurs have created successful businesses off the back of these traditional employments by offering boat trips, accommodation on their crofts or through selling high-quality produce.

Much of the available work is part time, meaning that many people have more than one job or supplement their income with a small side business. Owing to tourism, the majority of work also falls over the summer, meaning that many people either try to earn their annual salary in under five months or travel elsewhere to find jobs in the off season. The unreliability of tourism is a problem, but even more so is the lack of accommodation for the necessary workforce during summer months, compounded by it being more profitable to rent property to visitors. It is not at all uncommon to see caravans and mobile homes hidden around the back

FISH FARMS

The Inner Hebrides has over 70 fish farms. Once hailed as a sustainable solution to lessen any further impact on the UK's severely depleted fish stocks, fish farms have subsequently come under scrutiny for a different set of environmental concerns. According to a report from the Scottish Environment Protection Agency in 2018, almost one out of every five salmon farms in Scotland failed to meet statutory environmental standards and there are a variety of associated problems.

Open-net pens placed in sheltered coastal waters close to the shore can hold tens of thousands of fish. Although this system is 'good' for the farmed fish themselves, allowing water to flow freely around them, extreme levels of pollutants are also uncontained, suffocating the underlying seabed in faeces and uneaten food and releasing chemical treatments and medicines directly into the surrounding waters. Intensive farming of any sort makes animals susceptible to disease and parasites, most commonly in this case sea lice, which are a health risk not only to the farmed fish themselves, but also to nearby wildlife.

Nets are also a danger to other species, particularly predators such as seals, dolphins and porpoises that can become entangled while attacking seemingly easy pickings. To try and prevent this problem, as well as the resulting damage to nets and loss of fish, Acoustic Deterrent Devices (ADDs) are used by salmon farms to try and scare away predators with noise. Seemingly a neat solution, an output of over 179 decibels is enough to deafen porpoises, dolphins and whales, driving them away from their feeding grounds and potentially causing them to starve. Licensed shooting of seals is also used to protect farmed fish.

Although the environmental consequences seem damning, the stable source of employment and job creation by fish farms is enticing and, in some cases, essential in order to provide a livelihood for young people wishing to remain on the islands. Initiatives such as Gigha Halibut (see box, page 254), which farms fish on land, and double-layered nets can be implemented to lessen environmental impact.

1

of hotels; more often than not, this is staff accommodation. According to the most recent (2011) census figures, 70% of people of working age in the Inner Hebrides are classed as 'economically active'.

PEOPLE

The inhabitants of the Inner Hebrides are a diverse mix of long-standing residents and visitors who have fallen in love with the archipelago and decided to move to one of the islands permanently. Whereas the statistics for the entirety of Scotland suggest that 62.4% of people identify their nationality as 'Scottish only', in Argyll and Bute this figure is reduced to 57.4% and in Highland 61.5%. Looking at the islands more specifically, the picture is complicated and not as you might expect: in the south of Mull only 31.8% identify as only Scottish, 39.4% on northeast Coll and 41% on Iona; on the other hand, in Portree it is 71.6%, Gigha 66.9% and northern Islay 63.7%. The majority of those who do not see themselves as purely Scottish are from other parts of the UK, particularly England.

LANGUAGE

Apart from in the Outer Hebrides, the council areas of Argyll and Bute and Highlands have the highest percentage of Scottish Gaelic speakers in Scotland: somewhere between 1% and 10%. Once widely spoken across the region, with the disintegration of traditional communities in the 18th and 19th centuries Gaelic fell out of fashion with the ruling classes and began to decline. Although it seems unlikely that the language will ever recover to its previous strength, Gaelic culture has been making a revival in recent years and is celebrated in festivals, music and through various centres of heritage and education. Visitors should have no trouble making themselves understood in English, but strong Scottish regional accents can take some time to get used to.

RELIGION

Christianity, mainly Church of Scotland, Free Church of Scotland and other Protestant denominations including Baptist, is still by far the main religion, although the number of people who do not identify as religious has also increased

FINDING YOUR INNER HEBRIDEAN ANCESTORS

Inhabitants of the Inner Hebrides whose ancestors have lived there for many generations are few and far between, while those with island family links are spread across the globe. Poverty and the Clearances (page 15) forced large percentages of each island's population to find a life for themselves elsewhere, whether this was in other parts of Scotland, the UK or as distantly as the USA, Canada and Australia. For members of this diaspora who are looking to find out more about their families, individual island heritage centres should be a first port of call. Many of these centres hold an archive or are at least likely to have knowledgeable volunteers to point you in the right direction where information is available.

Scotland Births Deaths and Marriages (w sctbdm.com) is a free resource for researching genealogy and Scottish family history.

COMMON GAELIC WORDS AND PHRASES

VERY BASIC PLEASANTRIES

Hello/welcome	Fàilte (fahl-tche)
Goodbye	Beannachd leat (benn-ichk let)
Please	Ma's e do thoil e (mass eh doh holl eh)
Thank you	Tapadh leat (ta-pa let)

COMMON WORDS IN PLACE NAMES

Beag	Small	Dùn	Fort
Beinn	Mountain	Eaglais	Church
Bhaile	Town/village	Eilean	Island
Bùth	Shop	Mar	Sea
Chlach	Stone	Mòr	Big
Cnoc	Hill	Taigh	House
Dubh	Black	Tràigh	Beach

in recent years. Across Scotland the percentage of people who state their religion as Christian is around 50%; in the Highland council area it is closer to 54%, whereas it rises to nearly 70% in Argyll and Bute, with some of the islands even higher. Around a third of people identify as Church of Scotland across the country, but this number rises to 40% in Argyll and Bute and as high as 60% on Tiree. However, the numbers of Roman Catholics are generally much lower than across the rest of Scotland.

EDUCATION

Having enough resident children to support a primary school is a matter of much concern in many rural communities, but even more so on the islands; ask almost anyone who they would like to move to their island and they will most likely say that they need young families or couples who are likely to have children. Although island-based primary schools are seemingly idyllic, with a wealth of interesting local trips and small class sizes, the majority of islands (excluding Islay, Mull, Skye and Tiree) do not have a large enough population or enough funding to support a secondary school. While some children do a weekly ferry commute, staying on the mainland Monday to Friday, other families decide against this; one of the main causes of island depopulation is that when children reach the age where they would otherwise have to go away and board, the whole family decides to move to the mainland with them. Parents may return once their children are fully fledged, but there is usually a notable lack of teenagers and people in their twenties on the islands. Improvements in technology including remote learning, are making gradual improvements in the options for young adults.

CULTURE

With long, dark winters, dramatic weather and historically isolated communities, each of the islands has its own distinct culture. While some subtleties might not be apparent to a first-time visitor, architectural differences set the islands apart and their residents' creative work is represented across a huge variety of disciplines and styles.

ARCHITECTURE Tiny croft houses nestled in dramatic scenery are synonymous with Scotland and the Inner Hebrides have no lack of these. Mull, Skye, Eigg and Canna are a photographer's dream in this respect, but by far the most striking examples of traditional buildings are the blackhouses on Tiree. Low, whitewashed buildings, some of which are still thatched, but now more frequently seen with striking black felt roofs, these dwellings were built with double dry-stone walls, packed with earth and without chimneys, so smoke was supposed to simply drift up through the thatch. Once home to both animals and people, they might look romantic now but would have been a cramped and eye-watering abode, particularly challenging through the long winter months. While most blackhouses are still in use, or rented out as holiday cottages, the Skye Museum of Island Life (page 72) gives visitors a chance to see how blackhouses were traditionally lived in.

Colourful or whitewashed seaside villages are another iconic sight, with Mull's Tobermory being the most famous example, but Portree is also cheerfully painted, with each house different from the next. Portnahaven, with its rows of small white cottages and grey slate roofs, could have been taken straight off the pages of a children's picture book, while there are countless other examples on the Slate Islands, Coll and Gigha.

Modern architecture is uncommon, with An Turas (page 149) being the most obvious example, and the islands' most striking buildings are often either ruined castles or churches; arguably the prettiest examples of the latter can be found in Dervaig on Mull (page 168), Canna (page 125) and the round church overlooking Bowmore (page 221).

ART The Inner Hebrides have a long and varied artistic tradition. During the time of Columba (page 14), Iona was a great centre of learning, producing a specific style of decoratively carved crosses and possibly Ireland's gloriously decorative national treasure, the Book of Kells, a couple of centuries later. The majority of medieval art remaining on the islands is carved into stone as West Highland grave slabs, depicting warriors, swords and crosses, each stone telling the story of the person it commemorates.

Duart (page 172), Dunvegan (page 80) and Kinloch (page 112) castles are brimming with invaluable artwork; portraits of clan chiefs and tumultuous seascapes preserved for generations to come. In 1831 J M W Turner was commissioned by Sir Walter Scott's Edinburgh publisher, to illustrate the *Poetical Works of Sir Walter Scott*, a job which took him to Loch Coruisk (Loch Coriskin) on Skye and Fingal's Cave on Staffa, two spectacular locations, made only more dramatic in Turner's interpretation.

These days, the island art scene is thriving and the majority of islands have at least one gallery; real enthusiasts could spend a whole holiday on Skye discovering them and still manage to miss a few. While there are a few established exhibition spaces to be found in the islands' main villages, the majority are hidden down long farm tracks, in somebody's shed or taking up the best room in the house. Despite these impromptu settings, the quality of work displayed is usually very impressive, representing the islands' high concentration of artists who've either grown up inspired by their surroundings, or moved to the Inner Hebrides especially.

CRAFTS Craft shops are perhaps even more prevalent than art galleries, and often likely to be a coalition of several craftspeople. Knitting and weaving are perhaps some of the most highly regarded crafts on the islands and buying something made from local wool is one of the best ways you can support the local economy. There are only a few small, family businesses and individuals creating woven goods on Skye and Islay, but in some ways this allows more creative freedom; the delicate, modern designs on show at the Ellishadder Gallery (page 66) and the pedal-powered loom at Skye Weavers (page 76) are great examples. Knitting and crochet are more widespread, with a locally made warm woolly hat being one of the most treasured and practical souvenirs you can find.

LITERATURE With plenty of space to think, an emotive setting and everyday battles with the forces of nature, it is perhaps unsurprising that the Hebrides have been home to an array of writers or the setting for their work. House of Lochar (page 209) are a small publishers and bookseller based on Colonsay, who specialise in local interest books.

Martin Martin's book *A Description of the Western Islands of Scotland* (1703) and Samuel Johnson's *A Journey to the Western Islands of Scotland* (1775), which describes his 83-day journey through the Hebrides with his younger friend James Boswell, describe the islands from an outsider point of view, recording their

CHILDREN'S LITERATURE, FILM AND TV

The islands have inspired countless children's stories, many of which have beautiful accompanying pictures.

The intricately illustrated story books by Benedict Blathwayt, who has spent most of his life on Mull, are a feast for imaginative children. I grew up reading *Tig and Tag*, the adventures of two Scottish blackface sheep, but he has other books such as *Bear's Adventure* (set in Tobermory), *Ferry* and *Little Seal*, aimed at children aged three to five.

Despite the somewhat repetitive theme song, the CBeebies TV series *Balamory* had a very devoted following. Set somewhere strikingly similar to Mull's Tobermory (and filmed there; page 161), children aged between three and five might be excited to see the colourful harbour in real life.

Katie Morag is the title character in a series of illustrated children's books set on Struay, a fictional island inspired by Coll where the author and illustrator Mairi Hedderwick has lived for long periods. Katie is a determined and independent child, perfectly at home on the island. The books are aimed at children aged five to eight, and a TV series was made for CBeebies in 2013–15 (and still shown on repeat).

Successful Scottish writer and illustrator Debi Gliori created both *The Tobermory Cat*, set on Mull, and *A Hebridean Alphabet*, detailing all the things you might hope to see in a day on one of the islands. They are aimed at children aged around five to seven.

The Hill of the Red Fox by Allan Campbell McLean, for children aged from ten to younger teenagers, is a spy thriller written in 1955. Living in the time of the Cold War, the 13-year-old protagonist gets entangled in a dangerous situation while on his long summer holiday on Skye.

The Secret of Kells is a beautifully animated film directed by Tomm Moore. Although it is set in Kells, Ireland, the Viking invasions of the Hebrides are central to the story as 'master illuminator' Brother Aidan arrives with the Book of Kells, or Book of Iona, after the Vikings attacked his monastery on Iona. It is a gentle film, aimed at children, but adults with an interest in illustration, animation or Celtic mythology are also likely to enjoy it.

perceived peculiarities as remote and obscure fringes of the map. Many of the places they describe are still recognisable.

Published in 1949, the most famous novel to come out of the Inner Hebrides was *Nineteen Eighty Four*, which George Orwell wrote mostly at Barnhill, in the wilderness north of Jura (see box, page 248), little changed to this day.

Of course, historically, the main language on the islands was Gaelic. The seminal poet Sorley MacLean (1911–96) grew up on Raasay. His immensely popular poem *Hallaig*, published in 1954, reflects on the Clearances, referring to a deserted township (page 102) on the island's southeast coast.

MUSIC AND DANCING Local pipe bands, bards and Gaelic choirs still exist on many of the islands. While certain groups, such as the Isle of Skye Pipe Band (page 60) have a long-standing tradition, others have formed in recent years as part of an ongoing cultural revival. Modern cèilidhs are traditional social gatherings, with Gaelic folk music, usually held in village halls and other community buildings. They are organised more formally than the old spontaneous gatherings, but will generally include amateur performances of traditional music, singing and dancing. Visitors are welcome, especially if they join in with the Highland dancing.

To find local events once you have arrived on the islands, buy a copy of the local paper or newssheet. The frequency of concerts and celebrations dramatically increase during the island fèis (festival; page 44).

In classical music, *The Hebrides*, also known as *Fingal's Cave* after the famous rock formation on Staffa (see box, page 185), is an overture written by the German composer Felix Mendelssohn in 1830. The iconic 'Skye Boat Song', written in the 1870s about Flora MacDonald and Bonnie Price Charlie (page 56) and more recently adapted for recital on bagpipes, is one of Scotland's most easily recognised tunes.

Perhaps the best-known musicians to come from the islands in recent years are the Celtic rock band Skerryvore, who were formed on Tiree in 2004, taking their name from the majestic lighthouse visible from the south of the island. Runrig, an earlier band of a similar genre, formed on Skye in 1973.

TV AND FILM While the islands provide a scenic backdrop for several films and TV series, their most popular on-screen appearances are undoubtedly in British nature documentaries. The BBC's *Hebrides – Islands on the Edge* (2013) was a popular series, while the islands also regularly feature on the BBC's *Springwatch*, *Autumnwatch*, *Winterwatch*, and *Coast*.

SPORT Sport is a big deal on the islands and, whether it is the local team's 'at home' rugby match or the annual Highland Games, fans and supporters will usually show up in force. The biggest Highland Games in the region is held near Portree at the beginning of August (w skye-highland-games.co.uk), but there are other events on different islands throughout the summer (see opposite). A team game played with sticks and a ball, shinty is a traditional Highland game, which has some comparisons to hockey or lacrosse; it's only occasionally played now.

2

Practical Information

WHEN TO VISIT

As with any destination, but possibly more than most, your impression of the Inner Hebrides will be greatly affected by the weather. Beautiful and unspoilt in sunshine, it suddenly becomes all too apparent when it rains that the smaller islands are severely lacking a coffee shop. To add to the adventure, seasonal conditions are totally impossible to predict in advance, with clear bright days in winter being just as common as whole weeks of rain in July. Then there's also daylight hours: the summer solstice on 20 June sees 18 hours of daylight on Skye while the shortest day of the year (21 December) lasts for just 6 hours and 37 minutes. However, with the right mindset, clothing and interests any time of year can be enjoyable, but there are a few general trends to bear in mind.

SPRING (MARCH TO MAY) As hours of daylight increase around March and the year opens out into spring, the islands begin to emerge from their winter slumber. Although few visitors take advantage of these months, they are arguably the most rewarding. Temperatures are still relatively low in March, but April, generally known in the UK for its showers, is actually often a sunny time on the islands. Even if it rains, you will see a wonderful show of wildflowers as well as many species of birds returning from their winter migration. The midges don't tend to come out in force until around 20 May, making spring a good time to avoid them.

One downside of coming early is that seasonal attractions, cafés and places to stay do not generally open until the middle of April and sometimes stay closed until June; that said, it is a perfect time to visit the most popular natural attractions, such as Skye's Old Man of Storr, as the majority of visitors will not arrive until the summer.

Seabirds start nesting on the cliffs in March, but the few places with breeding puffins are best visited from the beginning of May until August.

SUMMER (JUNE TO EARLY SEPTEMBER) Most people visit the Inner Hebrides in summer and there are several enticing reasons for visiting at this time of year. Nights are at their shortest in late June and the following couple of months are the best time to see basking sharks and marine mammals such as porpoise, dolphins and minke whale.

Summer is also the main time to attend festivities including fèis events of traditional Gaelic arts and culture (page 44), Highland Games, agricultural shows and other local traditions. Accommodation generally needs to be booked in advance and the most popular attractions are likely to be busy but, if you get off the beaten track or just walk a little further you'll likely find that the majority of places are still free to explore in solitude.

AUTUMN (SEPTEMBER TO NOVEMBER) The summer stretches into September before starting to fade away into autumn, with a higher likelihood of storms and temperatures beginning to drop. With geese returning in their thousands, stags rutting and broad-leaved trees in their golden and copper finery, autumn is a great time for nature lovers.

Many places close in October, their owners catching up with creative projects or maintenance work; this can make it increasingly difficult to find places to eat out or visit (aside from those that are outside or open access). Accommodation options are more limited, but those that do stay open often cut their rates significantly.

WINTER (NOVEMBER TO FEBRUARY) Serious hiking and many other outdoor activities start to become infeasible in November and December, with short hours of daylight, snow on high mountaintops and unpredictable weather. Although the long winter nights are perfect for being cosy by the fireplace, in clear weather the cold nights are also great for stargazing; with so little light pollution, the sky puts on an incredible display and it's sometimes even possible to see the northern lights.

Christmas and Hogmanay (New Year's Eve) are festive celebrations with hearty food and drink, best spent at home with family or at the local pub.

If not before, almost everywhere closes in January and February, and the now seemingly endless winter drags on with storms, freezing temperatures and occasional, glorious respite. Few people choose to visit at this time of year, but those that do often have the feeling of having an island to themselves.

HIGHLIGHTS

With the greatest joy coming from accidental otter spotting, strolling across empty expanses of sand and finding hidden archaeology among overgrown heather, the Inner Hebrides is really a region to discover your own highlights. That said, there are of course some things that should not disappoint.

All the islands have great wildlife-watching opportunities, but excursions to see **puffins** on the Treshnish Isles (see box, page 185) or Sanday in the Small Isles (page 125) at the right time of year are undoubtedly one of the most guaranteed and rewarding experiences. Witnessing **37,000 geese returning to Islay** around early to mid-October (page 235), visiting the teeming **seabird cliffs on Colonsay** (page 212) or the **Manx shearwaters on Rùm** (see box, page 114) are welcome reassurance about the natural world.

Mountaineers will find their best options in **Skye's Cuillins**, but hikers and hillwalkers will love **Ben More on Mull** (page 169), **Jura's Paps** (page 243) and the huge nature reserve of **Rùm** (page 109). On Coll and Tiree particularly, visitors are spoilt for choice over **deserted sandy beaches** (page 134), but Islay, Mull, Gigha and Colonsay all have more than their fair share.

Islay is known primarily for its **whisky** and visiting some of its distilleries will undoubtedly be a highlight for enthusiasts. **Portree** (on Skye; page 58) has the best variety of places to eat and drink, while colourful **Tobermory** (Mull; page 161) is a fun place to spend an afternoon whatever the weather.

The restored splendour of the imposing fortress of **Duart Castle** (page 172) and **Iona Abbey**, with its connection to Columba and huge collection of carved medieval grave slabs (page 184), are some of the most interesting and impressive historical sites across the islands. Equally important, but slightly less well known, are the **priory on Oronsay** (page 213) and Islay's **Finlaggan** (page 225).

SUGGESTED ITINERARIES

If I can convey one message through this book, it is that these islands should not be rushed and, while they are all different, you will get more enjoyment from a two-week trip to just one or two islands than you possibly could from trying to visit seven within the same period. That said, the smaller and more accessible islands – the Slate Islands, Lismore, Kerrera and Gigha – can be visited on short trips of **a couple of days**.

One week could easily be spent on any of the islands, but you could also visit a couple in the same area: some of the Small Isles; the Slate Islands and Lismore; Islay and Jura or Colonsay; or Coll and Tiree.

Two weeks will give you enough time to relax and explore some of the large islands like Skye, Mull or Islay at a more leisurely pace. Within two weeks, you could also comfortably visit all of the Small Isles or hopscotch from Oban to Colonsay to Islay and then over to Jura.

Those who have **longer than two weeks** and want to explore more of the region should first look at the map of ferry connections (page 29) and see which islands are linked together. Unlike the Outer Hebrides, which are essentially strung out in a long strand, travelling between the Inner Hebrides is a stop-start affair that involves multiple trips to the mainland.

Visiting every island in this book at a relaxed pace takes around **three months** (trust me) and should ideally be planned to coincide with the seasons: Skye is much further north than Gigha, for example, and gets cold earlier in autumn and warms up later in spring.

TOUR OPERATORS

Although the Inner Hebrides are easy to navigate independently, those who are not confident driving on single-track roads, want to meet like-minded people or have the hassle removed from trip planning might prefer to opt for a tour. Day trips and guided walks are best found more locally, but the following companies offer multi-day trips across several islands.

If it is simply trip planning and organisation you require, there are various self-drive or self-guided options, whereas other companies offer the added reassurance, information and entertainment provided by a guide.

Highland Experience \0131 285 3314; w highlandexperience.com. Bus & minibus tours visiting Skye, Mull & Iona. Depart from Glasgow, Edinburgh or Inverness.

Imagine Alba m 0772 5302307; w imaginealba.com. Luxury tours & self-drive itineraries. Oban based.

McKinlay Kidd \0141 308 8009; w mckinlaykidd.com/scotland. Various self-drive, car-free & guided tours with the option of tailor-made trips.

Rabbies \0131 226 3133; w rabbies.com. Small group minibus trips. Depart from Glasgow,

Edinburgh, Inverness, London & Manchester.

Roaming Scotland \01259 752728; w roamingscotland.com. 'Tour & walk' multi-day trips on the Small Isles, Mull, Iona & Skye, including small hikes & ancient sites. Departing from Edinburgh & Glasgow.

Scottish Routes \0131 347 8886; w scottishroutes.com. Minibus whisky tours with multi-day trips to Islay, departing from Edinburgh.

Wilde Tours m 07974 451615; w wilde-tours. com. 3-day private tours to Mull & Skye departing from Edinburgh.

BOAT TRIPS AND COASTAL WILDLIFE WATCHING The majority of boat trips can be found in the individual island chapters: there are quick seal-spotting excursions, trips to uninhabited islands such as the Treshnish Isles and Staffa (see box, page 185) or out to Skerryvore lighthouse (page 153), as well as whale-watching excursions.

Arisaig Marine 01687 450224; w arisaig. co.uk. Trips out to Eigg, Muck & Rùm, with the aim of seeing wildlife en route, & some hours ashore. Trips depart from Arisaig.

Basking Shark Scotland m 07975 723140; w baskingsharkscotland.co.uk. Trips from Coll as well as a 4-day 'Spring Basking Shark & Inner Hebrides Exploration' starting in Oban. There's a possibility to snorkel with seals, see puffins & watch white-tailed eagles depending on the season.

Coastal Connections m 07919 615210; w coastal-connection.co.uk. Regular trips to Mull

as well as private charters to any of the islands between Muck & Islay. Based in Oban.

Minch Adventures m 07437 670212; w minchadventures.co.uk. Trips to the Small Isles & Skye, 4x4 access to Rùm, drop-off to remote hiking locations & luxury seafood lunches. Based in Mallaig.

Selkie Explorers 01687 462692; w selkie-explorers.com. Sailing adventures around the Small Isles & further afield on a small boat carrying max 9 passengers including crew. Trips depart from Mallaig, but the organisation is based on Eigg.

SMALL-SCALE CRUISES Far from the stereotypical image of enormous ships docking in too-small harbours, these companies offer trips for between six and 50 people.

Hebridean Island Cruises 01756 704704; w hebridean.co.uk. The *Hebridean Princess* carries 50 passengers in 30 luxury cabins. Trips all over the Hebrides for 4–10 nights, departing from Oban.

The Majestic Line 01369 707951; w themajesticline.co.uk. Small group or private tours on retired fishing boats & custom-built vessels. Departing from Oban with options covering most of the Inner Hebrides.

St Hilda Sea Adventures m 07745 550988; w sthildaseaadventures.co.uk. Sailing from Oban, cruises have fewer than 12 passengers aboard an ex-tall ship, Norwegian ferry or cruising lifeboat. Options include sailing around Islay, Jura, Mull, Skye, the Small Isles & the Slate Islands, with wildlife watching & distillery visits.

TOURIST INFORMATION

There are few tourist information offices in the Inner Hebrides, but many islands have community centres or shops that provide an unofficial service. Most individual islands or smaller groups also have their own websites. See page 271 for full listings.

Visit Scotland w visitscotland.com. Scotland's national tourist board runs 3 iCentres in the Inner Hebrides: Portree on Skye (Bayfield Hse, Bayfield Rd, IV51 9EL; 01478 612992), Craignure on Mull (The Pier, PA65 6AY; 01680 812377) & Bowmore on Islay (The Square, Main St, PA43 7JP; 01496 305165); as well as one in Oban (North Pier, PA34 5QD; 01631 563122) on the mainland. These information centres offer free advice, maps &

leaflets. Staff are usually knowledgeable locals & will help you book tours, find transport & accommodation where possible, although it is often better to do most of this in advance if your trip depends on it.

Wild About Argyll w wildaboutargyll.co.uk. Lots of inspiration & information about the Inner Hebridean islands that fall under the county of Argyll.

MAPS, TIDES AND WEATHER

MAPS Mapping Great Britain since 1791, **Ordnance Survey** (w ordnancesurvey. co.uk) have occasionally been known to confuse Gaelic, Old Norse and English place names, but remain an infinite source of information. They are now also available digitally and can be purchased from the Ordnance Survey website. For driving, long-distance cycling and trip planning, the OS Landranger series of 1:50000 scale maps should be detailed enough, but if you are walking, mountain biking or travelling off-road, you will find the Explorer 1:25000 scale more useful. OS maps are now available on- and offline in the form of a paid subscription app (w ordnancesurvey.co.uk/shop/os-maps-online.html), which can be very useful for day walks. Do be wary that phones and Scottish weather are not always compatible, and for longer walks in wilderness areas it's important to have backup in the form of a GPS or paper map and compass.

Harveys Maps (w harveymaps.co.uk) work particularly well for the Cuillins on Skye, as they are designed specifically for walking with easy-to-read colours and clear contour lines, plus, most importantly, they are waterproof.

As well as online, you can often buy locally relevant maps from shops on the islands themselves, as well as at Waterstones in Oban (📞 01631 571455; w waterstones.com) and specialist book and map shops such as Stanfords (w stanfords.co.uk) in London and Bristol. It is always best to call ahead to check the shop has the particular map you need in stock.

TIDES Tide times can be estimated at w tides.willyweather.co.uk, but it is always best to check with someone once you arrive, as there can be local differences to account for.

WEATHER The islands are known for their tendency to experience all four seasons in one day; while it is always a good idea to check the weather forecast, it's also sensible to keep waterproofs and a spare woolly hat on hand at all times. The wind direction can give some indication as to which parts of the coastline will be more exposed or sheltered on that particular day. For the best weather forecasts, check w metoffice.gov.uk or BBC Weather (w bbc.com/weather).

RED TAPE

The Inner Hebrides are part of the UK, so visitors from the EU do not currently need a visa. However, now that the UK has left the European Union, documentation requirements for EU citizens may change – especially once the transition period has ended in January 2021; check before travelling at w gov.uk/visit-uk-holiday-family-friends. People coming from the United States, Canada, Australia and other countries should follow the same procedures as entering the UK elsewhere.

EMBASSIES While many countries have consulates based in Edinburgh or Glasgow, their main embassies are in London; all major nations are fully represented by embassies or High Commissions (for Commonwealth members). A full list of contact details can be found at w gov.uk/government/publications/foreign-embassies-in-the-uk.

GETTING THERE AND AWAY

The Inner Hebrides range from relatively remote to quite accessible depending on your choice of destination. While it might take 4 hours to reach Tiree from the mainland, or you could have to wait a couple of days to catch a ferry to Canna, driving across to Seil or Skye takes a matter of minutes. In all cases, the journey should be considered a part of your trip, as mainland Argyll and the Highlands are beautiful parts of Scotland and ferry journeys provide great wildlife-watching opportunities in the open sea.

Note that it's not necessary to have a car to visit the Inner Hebrides, but – with the exception of Skye and Seil where some buses run directly over the bridge – in order to reach the islands by public transport you will generally have to change and get on to the ferry on foot.

BY BUS AND TRAIN The best place to check all public transport routes and times within Scotland is w travelinescotland.com.

Most visitors travelling by bus or train from elsewhere in the UK, including from Edinburgh or London, are likely to have come through **Glasgow**. Buses leave from Buchanan Bus Station for Kennacraig, Tayinloan, Oban and Fort William (where you can change for Mallaig), with the most useful operators being Citylink (◊ 0141 352 4444; w www.citylink.co.uk), West Coast Motors (◊ 01586 552319; w westcoastmotors.co.uk) and Stagecoach (◊ 01463 233371; w stagecoachbus.com).

Trains to Oban, Mallaig, Arrochar and Tarbet (the last two for bus connections towards Kennacraig and Tayinloan) leave from **Glasgow Queen Street**. Times and fares can be checked via w scotrail.co.uk.

The journey from Glasgow to Oban by both bus and train takes just over 3 hours (costing around £30 on the train and between £10 and £25 on the bus), with departures every couple of hours throughout the day. Travelling to Mallaig takes just over 5 hours with only a couple of departures each day and the possibility of needing to change in Fort William. By train, this route costs about £37, with the journey by bus likely to be around £30.

It takes just over 3 hours to reach Kennacraig, for connections to Islay, by Citylink bus and costs around £19, whereas travelling to Tayinloan (for Gigha) adds a further 30 minutes and a couple of pounds more; there are departures a few times a day.

If you know your travel plans, it is usually worth booking tickets in advance. Citylink, for example, offer a 50% discount.

Travelling between mainland port towns on public transport can be a longer process than you might hope. Transport routes are set up on the assumption that passengers will be travelling in and out of port towns to/from the islands rather than between towns and, although there are connecting routes, there are usually several changes to make.

BY SEA The word 'ferry' in the Inner Hebrides may refer to anything from a six-seat, independently run passenger boat to a multistorey car ferry. Possibly the most important thing to know about travelling by ferry around the Inner Hebrides is that while foot passengers do not need to book tickets in advance, the opposite applies for vehicle tickets. Bicycles travel for free where space is available. There are a few quieter or more frequent routes that are an exception to the pre-booked vehicle rule: Sconser to Raasay; Tayinloan to Gigha; North Cuan to South Cuan (Luing). On these, it is not possible to book space in advance, so you just show up and join the (vehicle) queue.

Arriving in a vehicle at the larger ferry ports, there are usually staff in high-visibility jackets who will direct you into the correct lane; on less busy routes the normal procedure is generally to just drive to the back of the queue and wait for further instruction.

For foot passengers and vehicle tickets that cannot be booked in advance, there might be a ticket office and, if not, you can just pay on the ferry; this can

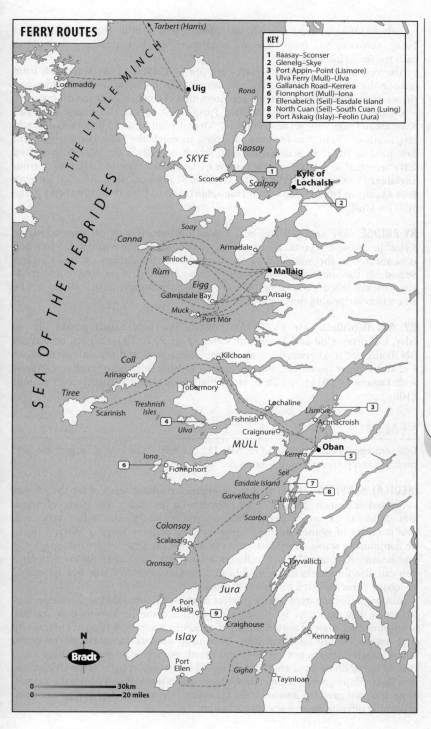

FERRY ROUTES

Tarbert (Harris)

THE LITTLE MINCH

Lochmaddy

Rona

Uig

KEY
1 Raasay–Sconser
2 Glenelg–Skye
3 Port Appin–Point (Lismore)
4 Ulva Ferry (Mull)–Ulva
5 Gallanach Road–Kerrera
6 Fionnphort (Mull)–Iona
7 Ellenabeich (Seil)–Easdale Island
8 North Cuan (Seil)–South Cuan (Luing)
9 Port Askaig (Islay)–Feolin (Jura)

Raasay

SKYE

Scalpay

Sconser

1

Kyle of
Lochalsh

2

Soay

Canna

Armadale

Kinloch

Rùm

Mallaig

Eigg

Galmisdale Bay

Arisaig

Muck

Port Mòr

SEA OF THE HEBRIDES

Coll

Arinagour

Kilchoan

Tiree

Tobermory

Scarinish

Treshnish
Isles

Lochaline

Lismore

3

Fishnish

Achnacroish

4

Ulva

Craignure

MULL

Iona

Kerrera

Oban

6

Fionnphort

5

Seil

Easdale Island

7

Garvellachs

8

Luing

Scarba

Colonsay

Scalasaig

Tayvallich

Oronsay

Jura

Port
Askaig

9

Craighouse

Islay

Kennacraig

N

Bradt

Port
Ellen

Gigha

Tayinloan

0 _____ 30km
0 _____ 20 miles

usually be done by card or cash, but some routes such as the short sailing to Luing, across to Jura from Islay and small passenger boats, can only be paid in cash (or sometimes cheque).

The vast majority of ferry services are run by **CalMac** (✆ 08000 665000; from outside the UK: +44 1475 650397; w calmac.co.uk). Check online or download their service status app, so you are kept informed of changes or cancellations.

Of the main port towns, **Mallaig** (page 263) serves the Small Isles and Skye; **Oban** (page 259) serves Mull, Coll, Tiree, Colonsay and Lismore; **Gallanach**, just south of Oban, has ferries to Kerrera; to reach the Slate Islands, you will first have to travel to **Seil**; **Kennacraig**, which is really little more than a shed ferry terminal in a large car park, serves Islay; and ferries to Gigha leave from **Tayinloan**. You can also travel to Raasay from **Sconser** on Skye; to Colonsay from **Port Askaig** on Islay; to Iona from **Fionnphort**; and to Ulva from **Ulva Ferry** (page 169) on Mull.

BY BRIDGE Skye and Seil can be accessed on foot, bus or car over a bridge. Kyleakin on Skye is connected to Kyle of Lochalsh on the mainland, while Seil is connected to the mainland by the 'Bridge Over the Atlantic' across Clachan Sound. At the time of writing, both of these crossings were free, but there is always some talk of reinstating the toll for the Skye Bridge, so that would not be an entirely surprising development.

BY AIR Hebridean Air (✆ 08458 057465; w hebrideanair.co.uk) fly to Islay, Colonsay, Coll and Tiree from Oban (page 259). These flights, on a small BN2B aircraft, run between one and three times a week and usually cost between £30 and £70 per passenger. You can also fly to Islay from Edinburgh or Glasgow with **Loganair** (✆ 0344 800 2855; w loganair.co.uk), which usually costs around £100.

HEALTH

In an **emergency** call ✆ 999 or ✆ 112. **NHS 111** can help if you have an urgent medical problem and you're not sure what to do; ✆ 111.

MEDICAL SERVICES Access to non-emergency medical services on the islands is limited and many places do not even have a pharmacy. For peace of mind, you should stock up on any medication you regularly need before your trip. The majority of islands do have some form of doctors' surgery, district nurse or community nurse. Hospitals are only located on Skye, in Portree (page 62) and Broadford (page 87), and in Bowmore on Islay (page 224); on the mainland you can also find them in Lochgilphead, Oban and Fort William, but serious or specialist cases are often flown to Glasgow.

Although this apparent lack of services might seem intimidating, it is important to realise that although health care might not come in a form that you are accustomed to, there is always a plan of action in place: well-trained community first responders are on call nearby, dispensing doctors can prescribe medicine where pharmacies are not available and health professionals generally have more time to spend on each patient than you would find in busier parts of the UK; brand-new defibrillators are also now attached to walls in many places across the islands. Note, too, that prescriptions are free in Scotland. Dentists are few and far between, often only offering emergency appointments.

DRINKING WATER You can happily assume that all water from kitchen taps is drinkable unless otherwise indicated. In special cases it may come reddish-brown from the tap; this is just caused by the water running through peat underground and is nothing to be concerned about.

For hikers, water from small streams in the hills is generally safe to drink as long as you are able to check far enough upstream to be sure that there is not a dead sheep or deer near the water; to be safe you can use a filtration system or tablets.

HARMFUL OR IRRITATING CREATURES Scotland does not have any large predators to worry about, but it is important to know how to deal with certain bites and stings. In the extremely unlikely event that you or a companion experience a severe allergic reaction, call ❧ 999 straight away and they will help you decide what to do next. Examples of a severe allergic reaction are: difficulty breathing; chest pain; fits or seizures; a swollen face, mouth or throat; severe bleeding; vomiting; light-headedness or loss of consciousness.

Ticks The most dangerous creature on the islands is actually the tiny tick. This small, blood-sucking parasite starts out as an almost invisible black dot and then grows as it fills itself with blood. Alone, it is no more than an irritation, causing itching and at worse an infection, but the problem is that the minuscule arachnids have now contracted Lyme disease and can occasionally pass this on to human hosts. Saying that, most ticks are harmless and simply need to be removed.

Ticks usually bite in late spring and summer. The best way to prevent getting bitten is to avoid walking through undergrowth with bare skin brushing the plants. Although it isn't very fashionable, tucking your trousers into your socks will stop them from climbing up your legs; boots are better than trainers for the same reason. Spend a moment checking yourself when you get back from a walk so you can remove the tick quickly if you find one.

Ticks should ideally be **removed** complete, and as soon as possible, to reduce the chance of infection. You can use special tick tweezers, which can be bought in good travel shops, or failing this with your finger nails, grasping the tick as close to your body as possible, and pulling it away steadily and firmly at right angles to your skin without jerking or twisting. Applying irritants (eg: Olbas oil) or lit cigarettes is to be discouraged since they can cause the ticks to regurgitate and therefore increase the risk of disease. Once the tick is removed, if possible douse the wound with alcohol (any spirit will do), soap and water, or iodine. If you are travelling with small children, remember to check their heads, and particularly behind the ears, for ticks. Spreading redness around the bite and/or fever and/or aching joints after a tick bite imply that you have an infection that requires antibiotic treatment. In this case seek medical advice.

Midges These tiny biting flies do not carry disease in Scotland or generally have any lasting effect, but they can be unbearably annoying. Especially troublesome when there's no wind to blow them away, they are common around marshy ground, bodies of water, dense undergrowth and forests. Although the relentless clouds are worst in late July and August, midges can come out as early as the middle of May and stick around until September.

There are various repelling sprays and creams, but your best defences are clothing and trying not to be outside around dusk, when they usually come out in force. Bizarrely, Avon's oily Skin So Soft moisturising spray is used as a repellent by Royal Marine Commandos as well as some locals.

Adders Black and brown, with a zigzag and diamond pattern, adders are Scotland's only venomous snake. Although they are not aggressive, they can bite when they feel threatened or are accidently trodden on. Common on heather moorland, look out for them on sunny summer days when they might be basking in the sun; if you are walking through undergrowth, it can be a good idea to hit the plants in front of you with a stick to alert them of your presence. In the unlikely event that you get bitten, try to remember what the snake looked like as doctors will need a positive identification before they can administer an antidote, stay calm and still, loosen any constricting jewellery or clothing and call ✆ 999 immediately. Bites are usually painful, but not deadly.

Jellyfish and other sea creatures Most stings from British sea creatures are not dangerous and can be treated without the help of a medical professional. While weaver fish, sea urchins and jellyfish are all relatively common in the Inner Hebrides, the likelihood of getting stung is very low because the seawater is cold enough for most people not to stay in for long without a wetsuit. Wearing water shoes will protect you against weaver fish and sea urchins as well as sharp rocks. If you are stung, rinse the affected area with seawater, remove any spines from the skin using tweezers, soak the area in water as hot as can be tolerated for at least 30 minutes (a clean cloth soaked in hot water can also be used) and finally take regular-strength painkillers. Seek medical attention if you have continuous severe pain, or if you have been stung on your face or genitals.

SAFETY

In terms of both residents and visitors, the Inner Hebrides are very safe. Most inhabitants do not bother to lock their doors and if any criminal activity was to take place then the culprits could not get very far before being stopped at the ferry terminal; in many places, the honesty box shop is still a workable business model.

DRINK DRIVING AND TRAVELLING AT NIGHT Drink driving can still be a problem in the Inner Hebrides. Scotland's low alcohol limits (page 38) apply just as rigorously on the islands, but the rural and isolated nature of some communities can mean that some people, whether locals or distillery-visiting holidaymakers, feel that the law may be more flexible than elsewhere. Police checks do exist, but it is also important to drive, cycle or walk along roads with extra care at night.

OUTDOOR EMERGENCIES To reach **Mountain Rescue**, just call the normal emergency number (✆ 999 or 112) and ask for 'police, mountain rescue'. Do the same to call the **coastguard** and simply ask for 'coastguard'. You can also contact 999 via SMS text message, which might be easier in areas of poor network coverage, but it is easier for the emergency services if you have registered your phone in advance (w ngts.org.uk/how-to-use-ngt/contact-999-using-ngt.html); this service should only be used when a phone call is not possible.

The best way to avoid getting into trouble in the first place is to be well prepared and understand your own capabilities. Land- and seascapes that appear gentle in photos can turn out to be much more severe with the addition of Scotland's famously relentless weather. If you are unsure of your ability or a total beginner, don't try something new without being accompanied by a more experienced and trustworthy friend or guide.

Though **walking** is the most accessible activity on the islands – and one which many people can enjoy with appropriate clothing and a little forward planning – **navigation** becomes vital when hillwalking inland. Map-reading skills and a compass, along with the possible addition of a GPS device, are essential.

When **swimming in the sea**, it is important to be aware of rip tides. If you find yourself being dragged out, do not fight the current, but swim out sideways, parallel with the shore, to escape. Another obvious hazard can be waves. You should be able to tell if the sea looks too rough to swim in, but even on calmer days you can hurt yourself by being pushed on to the rocks at the side of a bay. Only very confident swimmers who are used to similar conditions should swim out of their depth when alone at the beach.

Kayaking and other small craft can be safe on lochs or in sheltered bays, but the open sea is a serious endeavour only suitable for those with experience or with a guide.

WOMEN AND LBGTQ TRAVELLERS

Although casual discrimination exists in the Inner Hebrides the same as anywhere else in the UK, it is unlikely to affect your trip. Women should not fear walking alone through towns at night and LBGTQ travellers are unlikely to raise eyebrows.

Akin to most parts of the country, there can be no guarantees against occasional drunken wolf whistlers on a Friday night outside the pub, but this uncouth behaviour is looked down upon by the community. Should you ever feel unsafe, don't be afraid to explain the situation to any member of staff or other local person and they will most likely take you under their wing. Period protection is widely available in even the smallest community shops, but the range of products on offer is generally more limited than in larger Scottish towns.

TRAVELLERS WITH DISABILITIES

Although things tend to move slowly in the Hebrides, communities are now making a real effort to be inclusive of people with disabilities. CalMac ferries offer a 25% discount on the price of a vehicle ticket for Blue Badge holders from EU countries, as well as arranging for you to park near the lift on larger ferries for hassle-free embarkation. Support dogs are also welcome in all passenger areas.

There is some form of wheelchair-accessible accommodation on most of the islands but, whatever your disability, it is always a good idea to phone ahead and explain your specific needs. Many places that are not officially adapted are still keen to try and accommodate or assist guests with disabilities in any way possible.

Unfortunately, properly wheelchair-accessible attractions are few and far between. Those islands that do not normally allow cars will usually make an exception for blue-badge holders if it is physically possible to bring a car over on the ferry.

An ever-growing resource for wheelchair users is w euansguide.com, and the Visit Scotland website is a good way to search for accessible accommodation (w visitscotland.com/accommodation/accessible). In addition, many of the individual island websites will be able to help you find suitable options (page 271).

TRAVELLING WITH CHILDREN

The Inner Hebrides is an excellent place to visit with children. There might not be such a wide-range of organised activities and attractions as available elsewhere, but the islands are the perfect setting to make your own fun. The majority of island accommodation is child friendly, but self-catering and camping options usually offer more freedom and value for money for families.

Children old enough to make sensible choices outdoors can enjoy a level of independence that has often been lost elsewhere. Swimming in the sea and scrambling on rocks are part of the adventure, but are always more risky if done alone; with patchy or non-existent phone signal, it isn't always easy to keep in touch.

Indoor activities for children can be a little more tricky to find across the islands, but Tobermory (page 161) is a rewarding destination, as is Port Charlotte's Islay Nature Centre (page 234); budding palaeontologists should visit the Staffin Dinosaur Museum (page 69).

TRAVELLING WITH A DOG

Well-behaved dogs can have a great holiday in the Inner Hebrides: they travel free on ferries and are even allowed to sit inside with their owners in certain parts of the ship; dogs are a talking point with locals throughout the islands; and there are plenty of places that they can run around. Special care needs to be taken around livestock (see box, page 47) and ground nesting birds in the spring (see box, page 6).

WHAT TO TAKE

You can expect local shops, on all but the most sparsely populated islands, to have basic essentials of food, cleaning products and toiletries, but if you have a preferred brand, it would be a good idea to pick up supplies on the mainland. With a few exceptions in Portree and Tobermory there are very few places to buy clothing or shoes, so it is always best to bring what you need with you.

At any time of year, wet or muddy ground usually means that without sturdy footwear you can't go anywhere outside of towns and villages without getting sopping wet feet. Waterproof walking boots are recommended, though if you only plan on doing very short walks wellies or rubber boots will also work. Regardless of your plans, a waterproof jacket is essential and anybody doing any walking will also want waterproof trousers. Putting aside their dubious fashion credentials, waterproof ponchos do not seem to work well in wind.

In general, the Inner Hebrides are places to wear practical and comfortable clothing; getting on and off ferries is not simple in high heels, and light, floaty dresses are likely to fly up in the wind, revealing your underwear at unfortunate moments. You can, of course, take a nicer outfit for evening meals out, but it is unlikely anyone will look twice if you don't.

Unlike many other places in Europe, the UK uses a 13-amp plug with three rectangular prongs arranged in a triangle. Coming from elsewhere, you will need an adaptor – it's advisable to buy one of these in advance of travelling out to the islands as they can be hard to get hold of.

Good binoculars are essential for wildlife enthusiasts, while the pocket version will always be useful to get a closer look at seals, a distant otter or eagle. Photographers will benefit from a high-quality zoom lens and tripod.

Those partaking in moderate **day hikes** should come prepared with:

- An OS map or Harvey map of the area (page 26)
- A compass and the ability to use it and/or GPS device and extra batteries
- Food, including a little extra, and filled water bottle or bladder
- Small first-aid kit

- Fully charged mobile phone (keep in flight mode to save battery)
- Waterproof jacket and trousers
- Walking boots
- Walking trousers
- Quick-drying T-shirt
- Micro-fleece/mid-layer warm top suitable for hiking in
- Gloves (preferably rainproof)
- A warm hat (whatever you are comfortable in; wool stays warmer when wet)

Optional extras:
- Gaiters (for protection against adders)
- Walking poles
- Thin neck warmer or scarf to pull over your face and protect against wind chill

Multi-day hikers in summer and shoulder seasons should add the following:

- A hiking backpack
- A strong tent. Take some extra strings, pegs and gaffer tape for emergencies.
- Sleeping bag. Look at the comfort rating (not the extreme rating) and be sure that it can go lower than 5°C in summer or to −5°C in spring or autumn.
- Cooking equipment: a small gas stove, several lighters and matches (protected from water), a pot, sharp knife and spoon at least
- Dry bags to keep your clothes and sleeping bag safe (several strong plastic bags are also workable)
- Waterproof bag cover (might come with your bag)
- Roll mat
- A charged power bank
- Wool/wool-blend socks (at least two pairs)
- Thick, warm jumper in wool/fleece or a down (type) jacket (for sitting down in the evenings)
- Hiking trousers (one or two pairs in total depending on quality of waterproof trousers)
- Long-sleeved base-layers
- Underwear
- Torch
- A strong needle and thread/dental floss for emergency fabric repairs
- Basic and minimal toiletries including hand sanitiser
- Suncream

Optional extras:
- A wind-breaker jacket
- Long thermal underwear (for evenings, sleeping or if you find that you are too cold while hiking)
- Binoculars
- Insect repellent (the best protection against midges might just be to hide in your tent)

MONEY AND BUDGETING

Pound sterling is the only currency accepted on the islands and, although Scotland has its own banknotes, both standard British and Scottish versions are accepted.

Excluding the largest and most populous islands, most places in the Inner Hebrides do not have their own bank. ATMs are few and far between, but people with UK bank cards can withdraw cash at some post offices. Some shops offer cashback with a purchase or have a fee-paying ATM of their own, but this isn't guaranteed. It is therefore always a good idea to take out some cash on the mainland before travelling.

UK bank cheques are occasionally accepted, but it feels like only a matter of time until this dies out. It probably does not need mentioning but travellers' cheques are now an outdated system and extremely unlikely to be recognised.

Accommodation can usually be paid for online in advance, but otherwise it is worth noting that B&Bs probably will not have a card machine on site, whereas hotels, larger campsites and hostels usually will. Similarly, restaurants will nearly always take cards, but cafés and small shops are likely to only take cash.

BUDGETING Campsites usually cost around £10 per person per night, so by sleeping in a tent combined with cycling, hitchhiking, walking or taking buses, and eating basic food from grocery stores, it would be possible to get by on about £20 per day or even less for the very determined.

Dorm beds are generally around £20, so without carrying camping equipment the bare minimum rises to around £30 a day; the sporadic placement of hostels means this sort of trip will require some planning and booking in advance.

A couple wanting a private room in a cheaper B&B will struggle to find anything less than £80 per night in most places, and unfortunately single people will often still be paying around £60. Considering most B&Bs will not have anywhere to cook, you will probably want to eat out at least once a day, making the total at least £120 a day for a couple or £80 a day for a single person.

The mid-range of B&Bs, hotels and restaurants will probably bring a couple up to £150–200 a day, but this can be dramatically reduced by renting self-catering accommodation and cooking your own food.

Luxury, high-end accommodation and places to eat may or may not exist depending on which island you are visiting; Skye has by far the widest range in this price bracket, with Islay coming in second for its accommodation, but lagging behind with top-end restaurant choices.

Eating and drinking out is comparable to elsewhere in the UK. You will usually find that prices seem cheap in comparison with Edinburgh or London, but are generally slightly more expensive than other rural parts of Scotland. In a pub, a main course will cost £8–20, a pint of beer around £4, while a dram of whisky upwards of about £3.50. A sandwich and hot drink from a café will set you back around £6.

The price of groceries is comparable to any small corner shop or village store in the UK. General examples include: a loaf of bread £1.40; a pint of milk about 60p; and a Mars bar 80p.

A souvenir shop will usually sell postcards for around 75p or a T-shirt for about £25. Fuel is generally about 10p a litre more expensive than on the mainland; a litre of petrol costs around £1.30.

GETTING AROUND

BY ROAD Almost all roads in the Inner Hebrides are paved and, excluding a few good stretches on Skye and a couple on Mull and Islay, the vast majority are single track. The condition of the roads is a point of much contention among locals who are accustomed to driving on narrow roads, but resent the inconvenience and damage caused by pot-holes.

You can generally expect the quality of roads to decrease in accordance with the size of the population and proximity to the mainland: although single track, Seil's roads are smooth and painless, whereas those on Skye's northern Waternish Peninsula, the west coast of Mull and towards the north of Raasay are more dubious.

Jura deserves a special mention for its only substantial road: the A846. The classification as an A road should not confuse visitors into assuming it will be well maintained – the northern section sees grass growing in the middle and in places the sides are so sunken that a small car is likely to occasionally graze the road with its undercarriage.

Driving on single-track roads
The only friction that regularly occurs between residents and visitors regards driving on single-track roads. Many good drivers coming from elsewhere in the UK or abroad will not have much previous experience driving on roads like this, but for locals it is second nature.

Single-track roads are those that are only wide enough for one car at a time; passing places dotted along the way allow vehicles to get past each other. You should always pull into a space on your left-hand side, unless you are passing a particularly slow and difficult-to-manoeuvre vehicle, such as a lorry or a tractor with a trailer, in which case it might be more sensible to pull over to the right. If you do need to pull over to the right, indicate well in advance to avoid confusion.

It is important to use the passing places for allowing both oncoming traffic to pass you and cars from behind to overtake you. If you are driving below the speed limit and somebody is driving behind you, you should pull in at the nearest convenient opportunity and let them overtake. With oncoming traffic, by far the least stressful way to use the passing places is to pull in first and wait for the other car to pass. (This usually provides a good opportunity to admire the view.)

Flashing headlights is often used by locals to indicate that they have stopped to let you pass, but it is worth noting that this effect can be accidentally replicated by a car with its lights on driving over bumps in the road.

Hazards
As well as driving on single-track roads, there are a few more hazards encountered when driving on the islands that visitors may not be used to. Sheep, cattle, deer and other animals frequently wander on to the road; slow-moving tractors, quad bikes and bicycles are common; and pot-holes or obstacles such as fallen branches or minor flooding might not be dealt with as quickly as elsewhere. If you come across unaccompanied farm animals on the road, drive slowly and carefully towards them, which usually gets them to move. Sheep are not particularly bright and it can be tempting to use your horn, but this tends to make them panic even more.

To reduce the risk of an accident, reduce your speed more than usual as you approach corners, minor junctions and turnings, so you are not taken by surprise. Although you may feel pressured to increase your speed by a hurried local driving behind you, it is always better to find somewhere to pull in and let them pass.

THE DRIVER'S WAVE

Across the Inner Hebrides, apart from on Skye and Mull, it is still customary to wave at other drivers as you pass them. This need not be more than a casual upright stretching of your fingers from the steering wheel, but is appreciated as a friendly gesture.

Parking Official car parks can be rather few and far between on the islands, and the unspoken 'common sense' rules about where parking is allowed are not always immediately obvious to visitors (myself included). Blocking passing places, gates or any kind of access is never allowed for obvious reasons.

Mull and Islay tend to have adequate if not explicitly marked car parks. The most popular tourist sites on Skye are sometimes overcrowded; in these cases, it is really frowned upon to park off the edge of the road, as heavy traffic destroys the ground quickly and ruins the area for everyone. On smaller or less populous islands, the parking situation is a little more ad hoc. In some very quiet places, it might be possible to park on ground by the side of the road, but be careful not to do so in front of houses or on fragile habitat such as machair (page 6). If you are unsure, simply ask any local and they will usually be very happy to explain.

Drink driving Scotland's drink-driving limits were reduced in 2014 and are now significantly lower than elsewhere in the UK; even one drink could be enough to put you above the limit. The cut-off measurements are: 22mcg of alcohol in 100ml of breath; 50mg of alcohol in 100ml of blood; and 67mg of alcohol in 100ml of urine.

Fuel The majority of islands that allow visiting cars also have some form of filling station, with the notable exceptions of the Slate Islands and Raasay; in these cases, make sure you fill up before heading over. Note that fuel is often slightly more expensive than on the islands.

Campervans Driving a small campervan around the islands is a real taste of freedom, but single-track roads can be a lot more difficult to negotiate in large vehicles. One idea to alleviate this headache is to bring or hire bicycles; leaving your campervan in a campsite for the day, you can then explore baggage-free and without having to worry about getting stuck. Campervan drivers on Skye should visit the community-run campsite Camping Skye (page 86), who are happy to provide information on road conditions across the island. Some of the smaller islands, such as Lismore, are particularly unsuitable for large vehicles and it is worth contacting a campsite in advance to ask for their advice.

Larger campsites and a few special community-run facilities allow you to dispose of toilet waste. These are all mentioned in the island chapters, and it is worth checking there is one in advance, as not all islands will have one.

Parking up for the night is a delicate issue and should be done with care. It is kinder to both residents and nature to use campsites, where they are available. Contrary to popular belief, the Scottish Outdoor Access Code (page 42), which allows wild camping in tents, does not apply to vehicles. If you are camping outside of campsites, make sure that you are well away from houses and somewhere where your vehicle is not causing any obstruction. Be sure not to park in passing places (whether for an hour or a night) and be aware as you drive that traffic might be stuck behind you – pull over when you can, even if that makes your journey slower.

Car hire You can hire cars locally on Skye, Mull and Islay (see the island chapters for details), plus in Oban from Hazelbank Motors (✆ 01631 566476; w obancarhire. co.uk) and Lochgilphead and Campbeltown from Kintyre Hire (✆ 01586 554480; w kintyrehire.com).

It is important to check that the car you hire has a spare tyre, as this is not standard on all models and it can truly ruin a holiday to have to wait for one to be delivered from the mainland. Also think carefully about ground clearance; the very smallest cars are not always easy to drive on more remote roads or those in poor condition. Personally, I did all the research for this book in a little VW Polo, but I also managed to burst four tyres and scraped the bottom of the car on numerous occasions.

Electric car charging points At the time of writing, the only public charging points in the Inner Hebrides are all on Skye, but new points are springing up so check the most recent situation on w greenerscotland.org/greener-travel/greener-driving/charge-point-map before planning any travel with an electric car.

BY BUS With a little forward planning, a holiday or trip around some of the Inner Hebridean islands by bus is perfectly possible and allows you the extra luxuries of being a little higher above the ground and not needing to watch the road, so you can relax and enjoy the scenery.

Bus services on the islands, though reliable, comfortable and convenient where they exist, have limited routes and timetables. Generally, schedules work around school times rather than the arrival of ferries, so there might be some wait between connections. On Sundays, services are dramatically reduced and often do not run at all.

Bus companies and fares vary from island to island. On Skye, Portree to Broadford (with Stagecoach) takes 40 minutes and costs £6.30; on Mull, Craignure to Tobermory (West Coast Motors) takes 50 minutes and costs £5.20; and on Islay, Bowmore to Port Ellen (Argyll and Bute Council/Islay Coaches) takes 20 minutes and costs £2.70. There are usually significant reductions on return tickets.

BY FERRY Routes between islands are more limited and less frequent than those between the islands and the mainland, making it impossible to explore the whole archipelago without intermittently visiting the mainland; fortunately, Argyll and the Highlands are both beautiful parts of Scotland, so this is really no hardship.

That said, it is possible to travel between some of the islands: Coll and Tiree; Islay to Jura and Colonsay; between some of the Small Isles; Seil to Easdale and Luing; Skye to Raasay; and Mull to Iona and Ulva.

For general information about ferries and routes, see page 28 and the map on page 29.

BY BICYCLE Cycling is a cheap, sustainable and healthy way to get around the islands. Apart from certain places on Skye, roads are rarely busy and, assuming the weather co-operates, it is a good way to see the scenery and wildlife. Most of the islands, keen to reduce traffic, welcome cyclists and often have at least one place offering bike hire; this usually costs between £15 and £20 a day, with reductions for longer periods and children. As long as there is space, bikes are carried for free on CalMac ferries.

When you are cycling on single-track roads, pull over into left-hand passing places or the side of the road to let cars pass.

HITCHHIKING As a sensible and cautious person, I would not usually recommend hitchhiking to the public, but I happily do so, even for solo women or young people, on the islands. Basic precautions such as talking to the driver briefly before you get in the car and not travelling at night still apply, but the main consideration is how long you might have to wait before someone is actually driving the way you're heading.

Accommodation in the Inner Hebrides is a wonderfully Scottish experience. You can stay in a homely B&B and be treated to a full Scottish breakfast with eggs from the back garden; sit by a roaring fire in a country house hotel; or rent an old crofter's cottage on a secluded stretch of coastline.

The quality of accommodation in each price bracket is generally very high, with the biggest 'problem' usually being slow Wi-Fi connection. In high season, many types of mid-range or higher-end accommodation will have a minimum two-night stay. Whereas some places close completely over winter, others will offer substantial discounts.

Excluding camping in your own tent, accommodation needs to be booked in advance during high season. On Skye in particular there are stories of people starting to look for somewhere to stay in Broadford and travelling all the way up to Trotternish without finding anywhere to sleep; a costly and upsetting mistake to make.

HOTELS Only around half of the islands featured in this book have a hotel. Far from impersonal chain establishments, hotels in the Inner Hebrides are distinctly individual, often owner-managed and run with great pride.

For those seeking old-fashioned Scottish luxury – high-ceilinged banquet halls, huge log fires and free-standing baths deep enough for wallowing – a scattering of high-quality accommodations have been established in buildings once called 'the big house'. These manor houses were once home to the laird, his family and their servants, but have since been made into hotels, providing employment for local people and a second life for historic buildings.

Other high-end hotels are more modern, often stunningly situated with panoramic views and serving excellent food. Generally, all hotels have rooms with en-suite bathrooms, offer breakfast and the option of eating dinner on site.

BED AND BREAKFASTS B&Bs make up the bulk of accommodation in the Inner Hebrides. Although the majority of them are in part of somebody's home, most are professionally managed, spotlessly clean and serve a hearty breakfast. The kitchen is not usually for guest use, but most B&Bs provide tea- and coffee-making facilities in your bedroom.

Owners are often keen to share their local knowledge and favourite spots. At the very top end, they might be similar to hotels, but smaller and more personal, with luxurious finishings and glorious views. The bulk of B&Bs cost between £80 and £100 a night; these do not fall in the 'luxury' bracket, but are generally clean, comfortable and serving a filling fried breakfast. Some of the true hidden gems fall under £80, simply because the building is too old to be modernised with en suites and the owner does not feel they can charge anything more.

GUESTHOUSES The definition of a guesthouse is somewhat obscure. Generally speaking, they are bigger than B&Bs, less likely to be in the owner's home and possibly with a lower staff presence. Accommodation is normally in private rooms rather than dormitory style, and there is unlikely to be a kitchen for guests' use.

HOSTELS AND BUNKHOUSES The definition between hostels and bunkhouses in the Inner Hebrides is very unclear. Originally, bunkhouses were more rudimentary converted farm buildings, with the word 'hostel' inferring a few more amenities and a higher level of comfort, but these distinctions do not really apply any more. These types of accommodation have predominantly shared dorm rooms but might have some affordable private rooms. They will also have a shared kitchen and bathrooms.

Even islands with a very small population, like those in the Small Isles, seem to have a bunkhouse, the best of which have a relaxed communal space and are sometimes in stunning locations.

Hostels and bunkhouses are often the best choice for independent travellers, and those who are looking to save money and meet new people. Older travellers should feel just as welcome to stay in them as twenty-somethings.

SELF-CATERING PROPERTIES Self-catering accommodation, where you rent an entire house or apartment, falls into a distinctly different category from hotels, B&Bs and hostels. Although you can sometimes book properties for a couple of nights during low season, it is more usual to have to book a whole week. For family holidays or groups of friends, this style of accommodation provides all the freedom and flexibility of having your own home. Often in more remote and scenic locations, you can find everything from a modernised blackhouse or old crofter's cottage to modern buildings with plenty of glass to show off the view.

All self-catering accommodation should have a kitchen and most will have free laundry facilities. You will not generally see much, if anything, of the owner, and can consider the house your own for the duration of your stay.

CAMPSITES Campsites in the Inner Hebrides range from very basic but picturesquely positioned pieces of land with little more than clean running water and toilets, to large holiday park sites with hardstanding areas for caravans, laundry facilities and electric hook up. The majority of staff are helpful and knowledgeable about the local area.

CARAVAN PARKS, GLAMPING AND PODS This is camping for people without their own tent. Ranging from insulated caravans with a small bathroom, kitchen and heating, to wooden shell 'pods', which may be nothing more than a dry place to put your own bedding, it is important to check exactly what facilities are provided in advance. Semi-permanent tents such as yurts and tipis also fall under this category. Location is particularly vital here: as tourism has increased in Scotland, pods have sprung up as a quick way to provide accommodation without the complication of

ACCOMMODATION PRICE CODES

The following codes are used to give a general indication of price bracket. They are based on the cost of one night in a double room, two people in a dorm or two sharing a tent in high season, and include breakfast where it is offered. You are likely, however, to find large seasonal discounts, reductions for single travellers or for longer stays. For self-catering properties, rather than giving a price code, the cost of a week during high season is used instead to avoid confusion.

Luxury	£££££	£200+
Upmarket	££££	£120–200
Mid-range	£££	£80–120
Thrifty	££	£50–80
Budget	£	up to £50

having to apply for planning permission. While waking up in a wooden hut on the shorefront can be invigorating, the same cannot be said for the edge of a 'busy' road, so it is a good idea to check the finer details before booking anything.

WILD CAMPING The Scottish Outdoor Access Code (w www.outdooraccess-scotland.scot) applies to people camping in tents or with bivvy bags rather than vehicles. It states that individuals or small groups may camp freely for less than three nights, as long as they are not disturbing local people or farm animals, and that they should be well out of sight of buildings or roads and away from enclosed fields. Care should be taken not to disturb deer stalking or grouse shooting and, most importantly, campers should 'leave no trace' of their campsite, litter or fires. Human waste should always be buried in an adequate hole and kept well away from water sources.

MOUNTAIN BOTHIES ASSOCIATION Official bothies in remote locations are cared for by volunteers from the Mountain Bothies Association (w mountainbothies.org. uk). These are disused buildings or houses that have been repaired or converted into free accommodation for passing walkers and hikers. Anyone is welcome to use them, but the same 'leave no trace' rules as wild camping are also very important here as guests rely on each other to keep the building and surroundings in a good condition. Some bothies have particular access rules as detailed on the website, but groups of six or more are never permitted and you should not stay longer than a couple of nights. Bothies are no longer a well-kept secret and you should embrace the idea of sharing with strangers and prepare to meet new friends.

EATING AND DRINKING

LOCAL PRODUCE AND SPECIALITIES Although there is more to Scottish cuisine than **haggis**, first-time visitors to Scotland should try to forget their preconceived notions and be prepared to try it. Traditionally held together in an animal's stomach, the tasty filling contains sheep's heart, liver and lungs, minced onion, oatmeal, suet, pepper and salt along with other spices. Unlike other depressing meat substitutes, vegetarian haggis is remarkably tasty; it usually includes beans, pulses and nuts in addition to the usual non-meat ingredients.

Look out too for **Cranachan**, a delicious dessert made from oats, cream, whisky and raspberries. For breakfast, **porridge** is a must; medium-ground oats are preferred and serving suggestions range from just a pinch of salt to sugar and a tot of whisky. Look out too for the square **Lorne sausage**, usually made from beef, which can be tried on the CalMac ferry, if not before.

Local **seafood** and **venison** are some of the islands' most luxurious abundances. You can also find free-range eggs, homemade jams or chutneys and other fresh produce sold from people's gateways and other unexpected places. Mull is particularly rich in honesty box shops, despite being one of the bigger and more frequently visited islands, and the excellent Mull and Iona Food Trail (w mullandionafood.co.uk) helps visitors locate these hidden gems.

EATING OUT Thirty years ago you would have been lucky to find a fish and chip shop on most Scottish islands, but the Inner Hebrides are now starting to gain international recognition for their quality ingredients and small collection of exceptional restaurants.

Loch Bay (page 75), on Skye's Waternish Peninsula, currently holds the Inner Hebrides' only **Michelin star**, but a further eight restaurants are listed in the

Michelin guide. Five of these are on Skye, mostly clustered in the northwest: The Three Chimneys (page 75); the Edinbane Inn (page 76); Scorrybreac (page 60); and Coruisk House (page 86). Three are on Mull: Pennygate Lodge (page 171), Highland Cottage and Ninth Wave (page 175). Of course, the Michelin Guide is not the be-all and end-all of fine dining, and many of the smaller islands also have excellent places to eat. There are also many relaxed mid-range restaurants and cosy pubs serving good food along the lines of hearty venison pies, local seafood and Aberdeen Angus steaks.

The variety of **vegetarian and vegan food** available on the islands is dramatically increasing every season. Many places are also beginning to offer gluten-free options and are usually happy to work around allergies wherever possible; in these cases it is usually a good idea to phone and ask in advance.

Fish and chip shops and vans can still be found in some of the larger townships, often serving Scottish specialities such as battered haggis or black pudding, and sometimes their vegetarian alternatives. Thankfully the fabled battered Mars bar does not often appear on the menu.

Cafés across the islands serve increasingly good coffee, with a couple of artisan coffee shops found on Skye. More homely establishments also sell inexpensive freshly baked cakes and sometimes light lunches such as soup or sandwiches. Homemade pastries and pies, usually made with plenty of butter, are generally good value and delicious where available.

DRINKS Many people travel to Scotland especially because of their love of whisky, and if you appreciate a peaty dram then there is no more rewarding destination than Islay (see box, page 220), which currently has nine working distilleries and rumours of others reopening or starting up soon. Many of the distilleries run tours, which allow you to see the inner workings of the process and try a few 'samples' along the way.

HARDY BREEDS

Highland cattle and blackface sheep are synonymous with the Scottish landscape and are, conveniently, often more willing to oblige for photos than more skittish wildlife species. Of course, farmers do not keep these animals around to be cute. Highland cattle, Luing cattle (page 203) and Aberdeen Angus, all bred predominantly for beef, and blackface sheep, recognisable by their curled horns, black faces and legs, are hardy breeds able to withstand ferocious Scottish storms, low temperatures and snow.

Keeping these robust animals allows farmers to make use of difficult land in the hills or along coastlines that would otherwise be impossible to cultivate. The conditions animals are kept in are the epitome of free range and you will often encounter them in dubious positions on the edges of cliffs or occasionally, unfortunately, as a woolly mess below.

Buying local beef and lamb supports more traditional farming methods, which have a much lower impact on the environment than industrial-scale operations elsewhere: animals are predominantly grass fed and buying local saves on emissions produced in transport and helps preserve a valued way of life by providing important jobs for young people in the community.

Of course, there are other ethical arguments against eating any meat at all, but this has to be some of the most guilt-free beef and lamb on the planet.

Jura, Skye, Raasay and Mull also all have their own whisky distilleries, so a grand tour of the Inner Hebrides or several shorter trips, with the aim of visiting them all, would be an interesting plan for enthusiasts.

Newer on the scene are artisan gins, craft ales and even rum; it is claimed that Colonsay is the smallest island in the world with its own brewery. You can try all of these, as well as whiskies, in local pubs and restaurants. In the 1970s, an Englishman visiting an island pub would have had difficulty ordering his normal pint of bitter and may have had to refer to it as 'a pint o' heavy', or maybe a 'half and a half pint' to be understood. These days drinks at the bar are international, but it is always worth asking the bartender if they serve anything local and they might even give you a little backstory about where it is made.

PUBLIC HOLIDAYS AND FESTIVALS

While winters are quiet apart from Christmas and Hogmanay, the summer is filled with sporting events like the Highland Games, agricultural shows and music or cultural festivals. These range from very small-scale individual village traditions to those that are internationally renowned.

PUBLIC HOLIDAYS

1 January	New Year's Day
2 January	New Year Holiday
Friday before Easter Sunday	Good Friday
First Monday in May	May Day
Last Monday in May	Spring Holiday
First Monday in August	Summer Holiday
30 November	St Andrew's Day
25 December	Christmas Day
26 December	Boxing Day

FESTIVALS

Fèis Simply meaning 'festival', fèis events are lively celebrations of Gaelic culture originating in Ancient Ireland. Including Highland dancing in traditional dress, music (such as piping, fiddles, flute playing, tin whistles and Gaelic singing), sports, theatre and other performances, these festivities are held in different parts of Scotland on different dates. The following are well-established annual fèis events in the Inner Hebrides, which welcome visitors:

May   Islay's Fèis Ìle centres largely around the whisky distilleries and is an extremely popular event with accommodation booked up to a year in advance; page 221.

July	
Fèis Eige (Eigg) and Fèis Thiriodh (Tiree).	
July/August	Fèis an Eilein on Sleat, Skye; six weeks of events.

Highland Games

Highland Games A long-held tradition, surviving from clan times or even earlier, spectators are welcome to cheer participants in 'heavy events', including hammer throwing, tossing the caber, and the shot. There are also often 'light events', such as running, cycling and tug of war. The festive atmosphere is kept alive with Highland dancing and music in the form of pipe bands and other performances with traditional instruments.

The biggest event of this type in the region is the Isle of Skye Highland Games in Portree (page 58), held in August; another is held in Tobermory on Mull in July (page 160), while in the same month the Small Isles Games is hosted by a different island each year (page 108).

Agricultural shows These annual events give farmers the opportunity to present their finest sheep and cows, including majestic Highland breeds of course. There may also be competitions in horseriding and dog showing, as well as baked goods, vegetables, flowers and crafts. They are family events, which are likely to have some children's entertainment, such as a bouncy castle or games.

The following have been running for some years and welcome visitors:

July	*August*
Lismore Agricultural Show (page 191)	**Bunessan Show** Mull (page 161)
Tiree Agricultural Show (page 148)	**Islay Show** (page 221)

CHRISTMAS AND EASTER These Christian celebrations are usually celebrated at home with family or in church. If you are staying on the islands at either time and would like to join the celebrations, check what services are being held in the local church. There might also be events for children such as Easter egg hunts.

HOGMANAY This celebration of the new year is held on 31 December and possibly derives from a Norse winter solstice, and also incorporates parts of the Gaelic celebration of Samhain. The turn of midnight is referred to as 'the bells' and there are a great many localised traditions, but the practice of first-footing, starting immediately after midnight, is common; the first person to cross the threshold in the new year brings symbolic gifts and luck to the household. You're more likely to come across this tradition by accident, though Hogmanay celebrations are held in many local pubs, hotels and restaurants, as well as outside in the form of fireworks and other festivities. Have a look on local noticeboards to see if any events are taking place while you're there.

SHOPPING

With the exception of the Co-op, which has grocery stores on all of the bigger islands, the Inner Hebrides are a stronghold of independent shops. You will not find anything resembling a shopping mall, there are no national chain clothing shops and many places still close for lunch. All of this is not to say that there is nothing to buy – far from it.

ARTS AND CRAFTS Anything handmade from local wool is likely to be high quality as well as supporting a struggling, traditional industry. Knitted jumpers, warm hats and gloves are obvious favourites, but you can also buy hand-loom woven scarves and throws, and even sheep skins.

You might be more surprised to find the elegant work of silversmiths and, in some parts of the Inner Hebrides, particularly on Skye, it feels like there is a tiny art gallery on every corner; discovering local artists and craftspeople is one of the best rainy-day pastimes you can find.

More modestly, a host of independent craft shops sell unique gifts or souvenirs, everything from homemade natural toiletries and candles to postcards from local wildlife photographers.

FOOD SHOPPING It was not so long ago that the process of food shopping on the islands involved pointing out cans of peas to a lady standing behind a counter; often only one type of bread was available: a depressing white sliced 'Scottish Loaf' from Mother's Pride. Although there are a few surviving examples from this time, the majority of local grocery stores have now been modernised. Considering that most of the islands have a population size barely large enough to be considered a village elsewhere in the UK, the quality and variety of their stock is quite remarkable and buying groceries in local stores is a great way to support the island's community.

Quickly catching on to environmental and health trends, you can often buy unpackaged seasonal vegetables and local free-range beef and lamb or venison from the surrounding hills. Freshly caught seafood is also a real highlight.

ARTS AND ENTERTAINMENT

Individual island websites (page 271), community noticeboards and local newspapers are a great way to find out what's on. Cèilidhs (community events with organised dancing) are still an integral part of society and are regularly held as celebrations across the region. Many islands also have their own pipe band, which usually perform at larger events. This is a long and proudly held tradition heralding back to clan times.

The Screen Machine (w screenmachine.co.uk), a fantastic mobile cinema, visits Raasay, Eigg, Mull, Coll, Tiree, Colonsay, Islay, Jura and Gigha. Mull also has its own theatre (page 166).

Local pubs often offer weekly, monthly or occasional traditional music nights; although the bagpipes are an acquired taste, they rarely feature, and you are more likely to come across the fiddle, tin whistle, accordion or singing.

OUTDOOR ACTIVITIES

With huge swathes of wilderness and seemingly endless miles of rugged coastline, the Inner Hebrides can feel like a giant adventure playground for those with the right expertise and equipment. Visitors who lack experience or can't bring their own kit also have ever-increasing opportunities to try new sports with a guide or to rent out equipment to use independently. You can book a rock-climbing session on Raasay (see box, page 100), hire mountain bikes on Eigg (page 116) or go kayaking with a guide along the coast of Skye (page 67 and 92) or Islay (page 220) for example. With miles of sandy coastline, a good swell and strong wind, Tiree is world famous for its watersports (page 147) and has great options for lessons and equipment hire.

For adults and children who love horses, there is nothing quite comparable to the thrill of cantering along the beach or trekking across open moorland. There are opportunities to join a group trek on Mull (page 166), Tiree (page 148) and Skye (page 77).

WALKING AND HIKING Slowly and on foot is arguably the best way to explore the Inner Hebrides. Moving quietly, you will notice wildlife and nothing will make you feel as connected with the landscape as getting a wet foot in a bog. You must be totally independent as nothing is waymarked and in many places there isn't even a path.

Scotland's Land Reform Act of 2003 gives everyone rights of access over land and inland water throughout Scotland, as long as they abide by the Access Code (w outdooraccess-scotland.com). These rights are known as the 'freedom to roam' and trust that people will respect landowners and others as well as the environment itself. In the Inner Hebrides, the majority of restrictions revolve around deer stalking (particularly on Jura, see box, page 242, and Islay, see box, page 219).

The Inner Hebrides have 13 Munros, Scottish mountains with a summit height of more than 3,000ft (914m), 12 of which are in Skye's Black Cuillins (page 85); these are generally considered to be the hardest of the Munros to 'bag', in some cases only accessible to serious mountaineers or rock climbers. In this case even good hikers should consider hiring a guide.

Mull's Ben More (page 169) is the final Munro in the archipelago and very much easier to climb. For serious hillwalkers, the Paps of Jura and the Rùm Cuillins also have rewarding climbs, while rough multi-day coastal walks can be an exciting challenge on Islay. Increasingly popular and taking in some of Skye's most incredible

WALKING AROUND LIVESTOCK

Walk or drive almost anywhere in the Inner Hebrides and you are likely to see either sheep or cows. Although they will generally just ignore you, there are a couple of things that are worth being aware of.

Sheep are particularly vulnerable while they are pregnant or with small lambs. This time in the spring, usually April or May, is called 'lambing' and extra care needs to be taken around them. 'Worrying' is a term used for disturbing sheep, making them get up or attempt to run away. Sadly, this can cause them to lose their lambs or even die. Worrying most commonly happens when sheep are chased by a dog and can actually happen as early as November when the ewes first become pregnant.

Farmers are understandably tetchy about the issue and generally ask that dog walkers go around fields with pregnant sheep or small lambs in them where possible. If it is impractical to walk around the whole field, keep dogs on a short lead and walk as far away from the sheep as you can, giving them at least 15yds of space. If there is somebody available to ask, it is always preferable to do so.

The same advice applies to **cows**, but remember that cows can also be aggressive when they have calves and there are sometimes bulls roaming free. At any time of year and regardless of whether you have a dog or not, it is always best to keep your distance so as not to disturb them, but there is no need to be frightened. Always avoid getting between a cow and her calf as this can cause distress; if they begin to approach you, walk away calmly as cows are more likely to get excited and chase you if you run.

If you find an animal in distress, maybe stuck in a fence or obviously suffering in some way, inform a local person, who is likely to know the farmer. Sheep occasionally get stuck on their backs, which is a very unnatural position for them and may ultimately result in their death; if you encounter this, the most helpful thing to do is to calmly approach and roll the sheep back over. Obviously it would be better to refer this job to a farmer if one is nearby.

landscapes, the Skye Trail (see box, page 94) is a 79-mile unofficial long-distance route that traverses most of the island.

SURFING The Inner Hebrides are not a popular destination for surfers as beaches are unguarded and there can be strong rip tides (page 33). However, for those who really know what they're doing, there are enough good waves to make taking a board worthwhile. Alone in the Atlantic with beaches facing every direction, Tiree is unsurprisingly the best place to find surf, but a few other spots are worth bearing in mind: Hogh Bay on Coll; Islay's Laggan, Machir and Saligo bays; the north end of Staffin Bay and Brother's Point on Skye; and occasionally Kiloran on Colonsay. Magic Seaweed (w magicseaweed.com) provides reliable forecasts and Stormrider Surf (w lowpressure.co.uk) have published a surf guide to Scotland that is available as an ebook.

MEDIA AND COMMUNICATIONS

MEDIA Some islands have their own newspapers, which are a great source of information regarding upcoming events, community projects and local businesses; the news section also gives an interesting insight into island life. Where available, these will be sold in community shops and might also be accessible online.

The *Ileach* (w ileach.co.uk) covers Islay and Jura, while the *West Highland Free Press* (w whfp.com) is a community-based, employee-owned newspaper based in Broadford on Skye. On Mull, you can find the monthly *Round and About* magazine (w roundandaboutmull.co.uk), while Tiree also publishes the fortnightly newsletter *An Tirisdeach* (w antirisdeach.com).

Argyll FM (w www.argyllfm.com; 106.5, 107.1 and 107.7FM) broadcasts to the west coast of Scotland, while BBC Radio Scotland (w bbc.co.uk/radioscotland; 92.4–94.7FM) is the national station. Generally, all British TV channels are available. Anyone learning Gaelic should watch BBC Alba (w bbc.co.uk/alba), a TV channel dedicated to the language; or tune into Radio nan Gàidheal (w bbc. co.uk/radionangaidheal; 103.5–105FM).

INTERNET There are very few internet cafés in the Inner Hebrides, with the Cyber Café in Port Ellen on Islay (page 228) being the only standalone example. Public-use computers in accommodation, community centres and libraries are more common.

Wi-Fi is widely available in accommodation and some cafés, but is often slow or temperamental. The situation is sporadic across the Inner Hebrides with certain places, on Rùm for example, having broadband speeds to rival any UK city, whereas the most rural parts of Skye and Islay sometimes struggle to connect at all. CalMac ferry terminals usually have Wi-Fi and so do the ferries themselves, but it rarely works for more than half an hour out of the port.

TELEPHONE Network coverage for mobiles is notably bad, especially in more rural areas. It's therefore always a good idea to check vital travel information before you leave the safety net of Wi-Fi or network coverage. Thankfully a lot of red telephone boxes are still in operation if you need to make an urgent call.

POST Post offices are widespread, but their opening hours can be extremely limited in more remote locations. Once posted, mail does not usually seem to take much longer to arrive than on the mainland. Visitors are always encouraged to post their postcards from rural post offices, where the threat of closure is a constant worry.

CULTURAL ETIQUETTE

OPENING TIMES Although I've included opening times for almost every establishment in this book, it seems almost inevitable that half of them will have changed by the time you visit. Opening times, particularly out of season, can vary depending on staff availability, the current ferry schedule or whether it happened to be busy that morning. Many shops close for lunch, restaurants stop serving dinner early and small art galleries are generally an extension of somebody's home, so it often just depends on whether they had something else to do that day.

If your plans are relying on something in particular, it is always best to phone ahead. On Sundays, many shops still close, and ferries and buses have dramatically reduced hours.

RELIGIOUS SITES Churches, chapels and graveyards are an integral part of the Inner Hebridean landscape and are often of interest for their historical or picturesque value. Although most locals welcome visitors to look around, be mindful that services might be in progress (usually indicated by cars parked outside) and adopt a suitably sombre demeanour when exploring.

TRAVELLING POSITIVELY

Often cold, windy and wet, somewhat lacking in famous 'attractions' and not always particularly easy to get to, the Inner Hebrides attract a certain type of person. If you're dreaming of deserted beaches, dramatic cliffs and rugged landscapes; of somewhere to disconnect or reconnect; or an honest experience among genuine people – you will not be disappointed. Treat the islands as your home, support the businesses you would like to thrive and enjoy the wilderness whatever the weather; you can always adjust your plans. Most importantly, take your time; only by travelling slowly will you discover the Inner Hebrides' true charm.

Part Two

THE GUIDE

3

Skye (An t-Eilean Sgitheanach)

With a mountainous interior dominated by the mighty Cuillin Hills, Skye's more romantic Gaelic name, Eilean a' Cheò ('the misty isle') refers to the lingering clouds that shroud its lofty peaks and cling to the valleys. The sea cuts into the land in the form of long, sheltered lochs, creating five enormous peninsulas and around 400 miles of rugged coastline to explore.

The second largest island in Great Britain, Skye's population of 10,000 is larger than those of the other Inner Hebridean islands combined and, with the added accessibility of a connecting bridge from the mainland, it also receives a significantly higher number of visitors. There is something to tempt most travellers here, from excellent restaurants to the wealth of outdoor activities; the island is also a haven for creatives, and stumbling across tiny galleries in unexpected places is one of its greatest joys.

While Skye is famous for a few 'honeypot' locations – the Old Man of Storr, the Fairy Pools, Dunvegan Castle, Neist Point and the Fairy Glen in particular – it's possible to still find more magical and atmospheric places elsewhere on the island (particularly if you favour solitude over crowds). The Trotternish and Minginish peninsulas have incredible hiking opportunities, some of which will satisfy even serious mountaineers, and there are plenty of other fantastic places to walk across the island.

Despite the crowds in a handful of places, the vast majority of the island is an uninhabited wilderness, home to some of Scotland's most exciting species, including sea and golden eagles, otters and minke whale, not to mention more plentiful seabirds, seals and mountain hares.

HISTORY

As a huge and somewhat disjointed island, Skye's past is tricky to surmise as a whole. At An Corran near Staffin is a Mesolithic hunter-gatherer shell midden that's thought to be over 9,000 years old, making it one of the oldest archaeological discoveries in Scotland. An Corran has been linked to a site at Applecross (on the mainland) by the tools made of baked Staffin mudstone that were found there. A number of other archaeological sites are visible to casual observers, including Neolithic cairns, such as the one at Rubh' An Dunain (page 84), several Iron-Age souterrains and a large concentration of strategically placed duns and brochs.

The Picts are thought to have inhabited Skye during the late Iron Age, but left little more than a few carvings, the easiest of which to find is the symbol stone Clach Ard at Tote (page 78). The island later came under the control of Dál Riata in the 7th century AD, followed by the Norse who obliterated previous place names, but left little further indication of their presence. The 'Viking canal' at Rubh' An Dunain (page 84) has been radiocarbon dated to the turn of the 12th century, an unsettled period after the decline of Norse control.

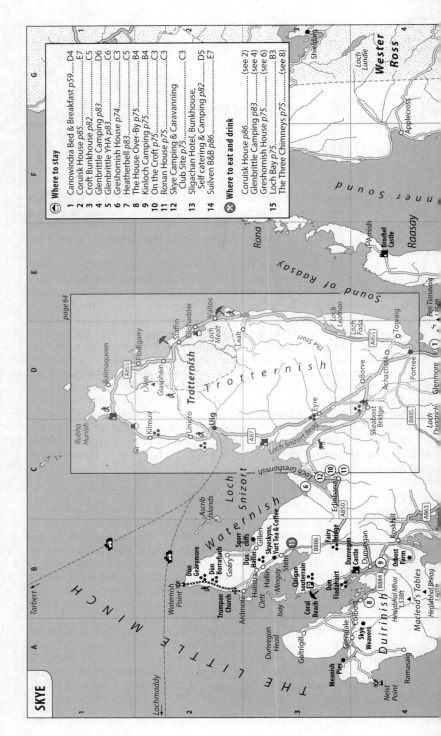

SKYE

ⓘ **Where to stay**

1	Canowindra Bed & Breakfast p59.....D4
2	Coruisk House p85.....E7
3	Croft Bunkhouse p82.....C5
4	Glenbrittle Camping p83.....D6
5	Glenbrittle YHA p83.....C6
6	Greshornish House p74.....C3
7	Heatherbell p83.....C5
8	The House Over-By p75.....B4
9	Kinloch Camping p75.....B4
10	On the Croft p75.....C3
11	Ronan House p75.....C3
12	Skye Camping & Caravanning Club Site p75.....C3
13	Sligachan Hotel, Bunkhouse, Self catering & Camping p82.....D5
14	Suliven B&B p86.....E7

❌ **Where to eat and drink**

	Coruisk House p86.....(see 2)
	Glenbrittle Camping p83.....(see 4)
	Greshornish House p75.....(see 6)
15	Loch Bay p75.....B3
	The Three Chimneys p75.....(see 8)

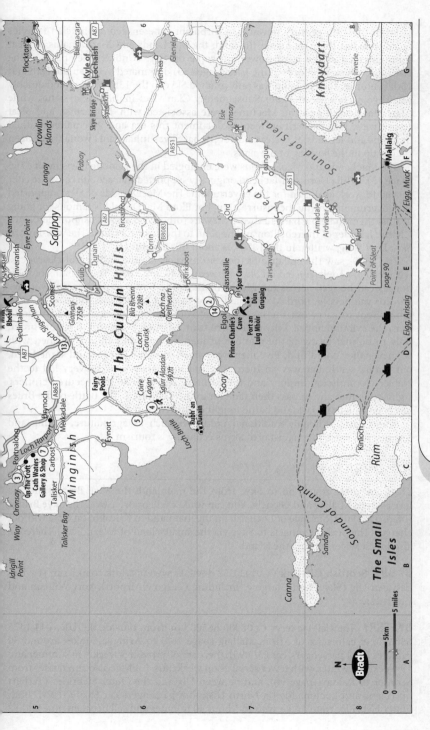

From the 13th century onwards, a turbulent time ensued as the clan families raced to assert their claims on the land; the MacLeods and MacDonalds of Sleat soon emerged as the most powerful people on Skye. Unlike other parts of the Hebrides, where the Lords of the Isles (page 135) dominated between the 12th and 15th centuries, the Lordship was only granted Skye in the 15th century and quickly lost it again a few decades later. Subsequently, Clan MacKinnon rose in status, while Clan MacNeacail and the MacInnes were associated with Trotternish and Sleat respectively. Limited written records document this era and it remains swathed in myths and legends; it is clear, however, that Skye's inhabitants would have been caught up in the feuding of the clans.

The MacLeods and MacDonalds were entangled in the Jacobite uprising of 1745 (page 15). While Norman MacLeod originally supported the Jacobite cause, he later turned to work against it for the government. The MacDonalds of Sleat supported the government during the insurrection, but Flora MacDonald is famous for going against them to help Charles Edward Stewart (otherwise known as 'Bonnie Prince Charlie'), leader of the rebellion and hopeful to the throne, escape. The well-known *Skye Boat Song*, written in the 1870s, is about this adventure.

The 1800s saw the collapse of the kelp market, famine and brutal clearances, with 30,000 people evicted off Skye between 1840 and 1880. The remains of their houses can be seen across the island. In 1882, the Battle of the Braes saw a rare win for the people: Lord MacDonald tried to evict his tenants, but the sheriff's officer sent to carry out the task was met with forceful resistance and made to burn the eviction notice. Fifty policemen from Glasgow were sent to restore order, only to be met by twice the number of men, women and children armed with whatever they could find. Five men were arrested, some injured and some fined, but public sentiment was on their side and ultimately their bravery led to the Napier Commission inquiry and the Crofters' Act of 1886 that secured crofters' rights to tenure and to pass their land on to their children. The Battle of the Braes has been called the last land battle fought on British shores.

These days, although traditional industries such as agriculture, fishing and forestry still exist, the mainstay of Skye's economy is tourism.

GETTING THERE AND AWAY

There are three routes on to Skye from the mainland: the Skye Bridge and the ferries from Mallaig and Glenelg. You can walk, cycle or drive over the **Skye Bridge** [map, page 90] from Kyle of Lochalsh on the mainland to Kyleakin on Skye without charge. (The bridge connects to Skye via the small island of Eilean Bàn.) There are also bus services serving the island.

BY BUS Scottish Citylink (❋ 0141 352 4444; w www.citylink.co.uk) run services between Uig (Skye) and Glasgow (including Glasgow Airport), Fort William and Inverness.

BY FERRY The **CalMac** ferry (❋ 08000 665000 or, from outside the UK, +44 1475 650397; w calmac.co.uk) from **Mallaig** (page 264) to Armadale takes around 30 minutes (foot passengers/car £3/9.95); there are 60 crossings weekly in summer and 19 weekly in winter, with fewer services on weekends. CalMac also run ferries from Sconser to Raasay (page 98), and between Uig and the Outer Hebrides (Tarbert on Harris and Lochmaddy on North Uist; foot passengers/car £6.50/31.65). Both Outer Hebrides routes take around 1 hour 40 minutes and sail between nine and 12 times weekly, depending on the time of year. Book in advance for all routes if you're travellng with a vehicle.

The last manually operated turntable ferry in Scotland, the *Glenachulish*, sails across beautiful Kyle Rhea from **Glenelg** (w skyeferry.co.uk; ⊕ Easter–Oct 10.00–18.00/19.00 daily; car £15).

MOORINGS

Broadford w isleofskyemoorings.co.uk	**Loch Dunvegan** w lochdunveganmoorings.com
Kyle Harbour w highland.gov.uk/info/1523/	**Portree** w portreemoorings.co.uk
transport_and_streets/102/harbours/5	

GETTING AROUND

BY BIKE Cycling is a great way to soak up Skye's scenery, though be aware that some of the roads are much busier than on other Inner Hebridean islands and cars drive particularly fast down the A87. Good options include: Sleat, Waternish, the Braes and the western parts of Minginish.

Bike hire

🚲 **South Skye Cycles** Westmans Pottery, Teangue IV44 8RE; 📞 01471 833484; w southskyecycles.co.uk

BY BUS The following operators run services on Skye. Check w traveline.info for listings of all stops, current timetables and fares. Some of these buses run less often than once a day.

🚌 **A MacDonald** (📞 01470 592733; cash only)
608: Portree–Fiskavaig
610: Portree–Peinchorran
6100: Dunvegan–Portree
6108: Trumpan–Dunvegan

🚌 **Stagecoach** (📞 01463 233371; w stagecoachbus.com)
50: Portree–Broadford–Kyle of Lochalsh
51: Kyle of Lochalsh–Broadford–Armadale
52: Portree–Broadford–Armadale
55: Glasnakillie–Elgol–Broadford–Kyle of Lochalsh

56/56X: Portree–Edinbane–Dunvegan–Glendale (Duirinish)
57A: Portree–'North End Circular' anticlockwise around Trotternish
57C: Portree–'North End Circular' clockwise around Trotternish
58: Portree Town Service

🚌 **Citylink** (w www.citylink.co.uk)
915/916: Uig–Kensaleyre–Portree–Broadford–Kyleakin
917: Portree–Broadford–Kyleakin

DRIVING Driving times on Skye should not be underestimated and neither should the strain of driving on single-track roads for unaccustomed visitors. Whatever your vehicle, you must be competent at reversing it around corners. Many of Skye's minor roads are unsuitable for large campervans, with small passing places, steep undulations or pot-holes.

TOURIST INFORMATION AND TOURS

Tourist information is available from Portree iCentre [map, page 61] (Bayfield Hse, Bayfield Rd, IV51 9EL; 📞 01478 612992; ⊕ 09.00–17.00 Mon–Sat, 10.00–16.00 Sun). Skye is a large island with lots to see and do so, if you are looking to tick off most of the major sights in a short space of time, booking a tour might be a more relaxing option than driving. There's also a wide range of options for outdoor activities. The following operators are all based on Skye:

MINIBUS AND PRIVATE TOURS

Isle of Skye Wildlife Tours Portree IV51 9LP; m 07972 260249; w skyewildlife.com. Minibus tours starting in Portree with the aim of spotting otters & eagles. Guide Andy is a local expert with many years' experience.

Skye History and Heritage Day Tours 01478 611915; w skyehistoryandheritagetours.com. A choice of trips visiting both famous & unknown historical sites. Also wild swimming days. Max 4 passengers.

Skye Luxury Tours 01599 537100; w skyeluxury.co.uk. Individually designed private tours in a long-wheelbase Jaguar XJ or luxury Mercedes people carrier.

Skye Minibus Tours Dunvegan IV55 8GT; 01470 521448; w skye-minibus-tours.co.uk. Tours begin in Portree & visit famous places on Skye including the Old Man of Storr & Fairy Pools.

Skye Scenic Tours Flodigarry IV51 9HZ; 01478 617006; w skyescenictours.com. Starting in Portree, these minibus day tours visit some of Skye's best-known sights.

BOAT TRIPS

Good places for boat trips include Elgol (page 87), Uig (page 72) & Portree (see below).

OUTDOOR ACTIVITIES

Skye Adventure m 07785 96239, 07810 660735; w skyeadventure.com. A wide range of guided outdoor activity sessions including climbing, hiking, canyoning & coasteering.

Skye Guides 3 Luib, Broadford IV49 9AN; 01471 8222116; w skyeguides.co.uk. Mountain guides for the Black Cuillin Ridge, plus abseiling, ice climbing, scrambling, rock climbing & alpine training courses. Mike, originally from Carlisle, has many years of expert experience & is recommended by local hikers.

South Skye Cycles Sleat (page 92). Cycling tours, as well as bike hire & repairs.

South Skye Sea Kayak Sleat (page 92). Kayak trips.

EVENTS

MARCH

Dunvegan 5km/10km [f] DunveganCastle10k; e graham@skye-events.co.uk. Running race starting at Dunvegan Castle.

JUNE

The Skye Food and Drink Festival w skyefoodanddrinkfestival.co.uk. A week of food markets & classes, plus a cèilidh.

Isle of Skye Half Marathon Portree; [f]

JULY

Fèis an Eilein/The Skye Festival w seall. co.uk/feis-an-eilein-skye-festival. Ten days of music, performances & events across Sleat.

AUGUST

Isle of Skye Highland Games The Lump, Portree; w skye-highland-games.co.uk. Held near the beginning of Aug, the Highland Games are the most iconic event on Skye. The event has taken place every year since 1877 with the only exceptions being during the 2 World Wars.

SEPTEMBER

Skye Live The Lump, Portree; w skyelive.co.uk. Music festival with a varied line-up including traditional Scottish acts & global electronic musicians.

CHRISTMAS AND HOGMANAY

Look out for possible fireworks & events hosted by Broadford & Strath Community Company (w broadfordandstrath.org).

PORTREE AND THE BRAES

Skye's small but bustling capital is home to nearly half the island's population. Clustered around a pretty harbour, at the mouth of three rivers, part of the town looks out towards Ben Tianavaig with other houses hidden behind a small, rounded peninsula called the Lump.

Southeast of Portree, the Braes Peninsula is rural and astonishingly unspoilt by tourism despite its proximity to the capital. The gentle coastline looks over the Narrows of Raasay to Clachan and Inverarish.

GETTING AROUND Although everything seems to be severely up- or downhill, Portree is small enough to explore on foot. The Braes, around 6 miles further southeast, isn't well served by public transport, so is easier to access with your own wheels.

By bus While Portree is well served by all three operators on Skye (page 57), A MacDonald operate the only route into the Braes (ending at Peinchorran), which runs once a day (Mon–Fri only) to fit the needs of schoolchildren travelling to and from Portree.

WHERE TO STAY *Map, page 61, unless otherwise stated*
Although Portree has the widest range of places to stay of anywhere in the Inner Hebrides, you will generally get less for your money than elsewhere. Booking in advance is essential in high season.

🏠 **Cuillin Hills** (39 rooms) Scorrybreac Rd, IV51 9QU; 📞 01478 612003; w cuillinhills-hotel-skye.co.uk; ♿. Grand 18th-century building set in large grounds on the northern edge of Portree (& thus slightly separate from the town). Recently extended & renovated, so little of the original building is left. It's worth paying the extra for a sea view. **£££££**

🏠 **The Marmalade Hotel** (34 rooms) Home Farm Rd, IV51 9LX; 📞 01478 611711; w marmaladehotel.co.uk; ♿. Boutique-style hotel in an attractive 19th-century Georgian house with a modern extension. Stylish interior incorporates some original features. Smaller rooms than Cuillin Hills. **£££££**

🏠 **Canowindra Bed & Breakfast** [54 D4] (4 rooms) Penifiler IV51 9LG; 📞 01478 613640; w canowindraskye.co.uk; ⊕ Mar–end Oct. A luxurious B&B with views of the Cuillins. In a peaceful location, 6mins' drive south from Portree towards the Braes. **££££**

🏠 **The Portree Hotel** (26 rooms) Somerled Sq, IV51 9EH; 📞 01478 612511; w theportreehotel.com. Historic building in centre of town with view over the square. Decorated in bold colours with tartan cushions. Friendly local staff, some of whom have been working in the hotel for 3 generations. **££££**

✳ 🏠 **Ben Tianavaig** (3 rooms) 5 Bosville Tce, IV51 9DG; 📞 01478 612152; w ben-tianavaig.

co.uk; ⊕ Apr–Oct. Large, light, en-suite rooms in 19th-century terrace house. Great views of the harbour & across to Ben Tianavaig, hence the name. Charlotte & Bill, originally from England, are friendly & helpful hosts who genuinely enjoy having people to stay. Excellent b/fast options with daily special. Charlotte also makes intricate one-off cowls, scarves & hats with locally dyed Scottish wool. Min stay 2 nights. Great value. **£££**

🏠 **Larchside Bed and Breakfast** [54 D4] (3 rooms) Achachork IV51 9HT; 📞 01478 611884; w larchsideskye.co.uk; ⊕ end Mar–Oct. Peaceful location, 2 miles north of central Portree in a small crofting township. Bedrooms have views of the Cuillins. Warm welcome, excellent service & receives impeccable guest reviews. **£££**

🏠 **Portree Youth Hostel** (53 beds) Lisigarry Ct, IV51 9EW; 📞 01478 612231; w hostellingscotland.org.uk/hostels/portree. Basic, busy single-sex dorms with small kitchen for the number of beds. High season & the Portree premium take this hostel into the next price bracket even for dorm rooms. **££**

🏠 **Portree Independent Hostel** (60 beds) Old Post Office, The Green, IV51 9BT; 📞 01478 613737; w hostelskye.co.uk. Bright yellow renovated post office building. Equally bright inside & slightly shabby, but large kitchen makes up for it, especially in comparison with the youth hostel. Helpful, knowledgeable staff. **£**

⚑ Torvaig Caravan Site [54 D4] Torvaig, IV51 9HU; 📞01478 611849; m 07900 293914; w portreecampsite.co.uk; ⊕ Apr–Oct; reception: 08.00–19.30. Campsite for tents, caravans & motorhomes, 1 mile north of Portree. No late arrivals. Paid Wi-Fi. **£**

✗ WHERE TO EAT AND DRINK *Map, opposite*

The choice and standard of eating options in Portree is excellent and is likely to be much appreciated by those who have been on extended Hebridean adventures.

✗ Scorrybreac 7 Bosville Tce, IV51 9DG; 📞01478 612069; w scorrybreac.com; ⊕ 17.00–21.00 Tue–Sat. Unimposing, intimate restaurant with only 8 tables. Elegant modern Scottish dishes, with French influence using quality, local, seasonal produce. Local favourite for very special occasions. **£££**

✗ Dulse & Brose at The Bosville 9–11 Bosville Tce, IV51 9DG; 📞01478 612846; w perlehotels.com/the-bosville/restaurant; ⊕ summer 07.30–09.30, noon–14.30 & 18.00–21.30, winter 18.00–20.30 daily. High-quality, seasonal menu focusing on Scottish ingredients. **££–£££**

✗ Cuillin Hills (page 59) Smart, fine-dining restaurant specialising in seafood, with large windows to enjoy the view while you eat. Special vegan menu. **££**

✗ The Rosedale Hotel Restaurant Beaumont Cres, IV51 9DF; 📞01478 613131; w rosedalehotelskye.co.uk/restaurant; ⊕ Mar–Oct 18.00–21.00 Mon–Sat. Delicately presented Scottish tapas dishes & local seafood. Unbeatable view across the harbour. **££**

✗ Sea Breezes 2 Marine Bldgs, Quay St, IV51 9DE; 📞01478 612016; w seabreezes-skye.co.uk; ⊕ Apr–Oct 17.30–21.00 Tue–Sun, Jul & Aug also noon–14.00. Fresh seafood with harbourfront view. Simply decorated in nautical theme. **££**

✗ The Chippy Armadale Hse, Bank St, IV51 9DA; ⊕ from 17.00 daily. Fish & chips, cooked in beef fat. Also pizza. Cash only. **£**

✗ Pizza in the Skye Howdens car park, Dunvegan Rd, IV51 9HF; m 07814 872421; 📘; ⊕ mid-Feb–Nov noon–19.00 Mon–Thu, noon–20.00 Fri & Sat. Inexpensive wood-fired pizza to takeaway. Also runs scheme to provide food for disadvantaged local youth. **£**

✗ Relish 1 Wentworth St, IV51 9EJ; 📞01478 613787; 📘; ⊕ 09.00–17.00 Mon–Fri, 09.00–15.00 Sat. Local favourite deli serving takeaway coffee, sandwiches, soup, homemade sausage rolls & pastries. Proper food to takeaway such as chilli & rice. **£**

☕ Bakery & Skyeworks Gallery The Old Woollen Mill, Dunvegan Rd, IV51 9HG; 📞01478 612669; ⊕ 10.00–17.00 Mon–Sat. Artisan baking & local art gallery. **£**

☕ The Red Brick Café Jans, 5–6 Broom Pl, IV51 9HL; 📞01478 613417; ⊕ 08.30–16.00 Mon–Sat; ♿. Despite its improbable location inside Jans hardware store, the Red Brick Café is a favourite with both locals wanting a fry up & visitors drawn in by the café's excellent reviews. B/fast, lunch, coffee & cake. **£**

ENTERTAINMENT AND NIGHTLIFE

🎭 Aros Community Theatre Viewfield Rd, IV51 9EU; 📞01478 613750; w aroscommunitytheatre.co.uk; ♿. Music, comedy, dance, opera, art exhibitions, talks & a year-round cinema programme.

🍷 Merchant Bar 9–11 Bosville Tce; 📞01478 612846; w perlehotels.com/the-bosville/restaurant; ⊕ 11.00–11.00 daily. Wide selection of Scottish gins & single malts, as well as Skye Brewery ales on tap.

🍷 The West Highland Bar The Portree Hotel (page 59). Live music most nights throughout summer & at w/ends during winter. Open fire, craft beer on tap & cocktail menu.

Isle of Skye Pipe Band 📘. Performances in Somerled Sq every Tue eve over summer.

SHOPPING
Arts and crafts

Highland Natural Accents The Green, Portree; 📞01478 611694; w highlandnaturalaccents.com. Small, high-end textiles gallery.

Skye Batiks The Green, IV51 9BY; 📞01478 613331; w skyebatiks.com; ⊕ 09.00–17.30 Mon–Sat, 10.00–17.00 Sun. Interesting Sri Lankan/Scottish-fusion colourful batiks & woven

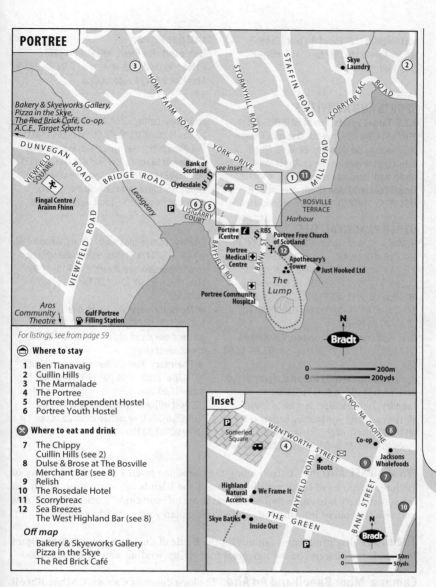

PORTREE

Bakery & Skyeworks Gallery,
Pizza in the Skye,
The Red Brick Café, Co-op,
A.C.E., Target Sports

Skye
Laundry

BOSVILLE
TERRACE
Harbour

Bank of
Scotland
Clydesdale

Portree
iCentre
RBS
Portree Free Church
of Scotland
Portree
Medical
Centre
Apothecary's
Tower
Just Hooked Ltd
The
Lump

Portree Community
Hospital

Aros
Community
Theatre
Gulf Portree
Filling Station

Fingal Centre /
Arainn Fhinn

For listings, see from page 59

Where to stay
1 Ben Tianavaig
2 Cuillin Hills
3 The Marmalade
4 The Portree
5 Portree Independent Hostel
6 Portree Youth Hostel

Where to eat and drink
7 The Chippy
  Cuillin Hills (see 2)
8 Dulse & Brose at The Bosville
  Merchant Bar (see 8)
9 Relish
10 The Rosedale Hotel
11 Scorrybreac
12 Sea Breezes
  The West Highland Bar (see 8)

Off map
  Bakery & Skyeworks Gallery
  Pizza in the Skye
  The Red Brick Café

Inset

Somerled
Square

Co-op

Jacksons
Wholefoods

Boots

Highland
Natural
Accents
We Frame It

Skye Batiks
Inside Out
THE GREEN

cotton including clothing & smocks, accessories &
homewares.
We Frame It Kings Hse, The Green, IV51 9BS;
w we-frame-it.co.uk; ⏷ winter 10.00–18.00
daily, summer 09.00–19.00 daily. Work from
Scottish/Skye artists & gifts.

Food shops
Co-op Bank St, IV51 9DA ☎ 01478 612855;
⏷ 07.00–23.00 daily; ♿); Woodpark Rd, IV51

9HQ ☎ 01478 612483; ⏷ 07.00–22.00 daily; ♿).
The Woodpark Rd branch is a large supermarket in
an industrial estate.
Jacksons Wholefoods Bank St, IV51 9EJ;
☎ 01478 613326; w highlandwholefoods.co.uk;
⏷ 09.00–17.00 Mon–Sat; ♿. An actual co-
operative selling health foods, wholefoods & other
uncommon groceries. Entrance & bottom floor
accessible to people in wheelchairs, but staff can
assist with goods upstairs.

Skye (An t-Eilean Sgitheanach) **PORTREE AND THE BRAES** 3

61

Just Hooked Ltd End of the pier, IV51 9BE; ⓕ; ☉ Apr–Oct flexible Tue–Sat. Fresh fish & seafood.

Outdoor gear
Inside Out The Green, IV51 9BY; ☎01478 611663; w inside-out-skye.com; ☉ 09.00–18.00 Mon–Sat. Hiking & outdoor shop.

SPORTS AND ACTIVITIES
A.C.E. Target Sports Struan Rd (B885), IV51 9EG; ☎01478 612081; w ace-skye.com. Archery, clay shooting, axe throwing, air rifle & Airsoft Arena. Uses renewable energy. Access along single-track road, may be impassable in winter.
Fingal Centre/Arainn Fhinn Viewfield Rd, IV51 9ET; ☎01478 614819; w highlifehighland.

com/fingal-centre; ☉ 07.00–21.00 Mon–Thu, 07.00–19.00 Fri, 09.00–16.00 Sat, 10.00–16.00 Sun. Swimming pool, gym, steam room & sauna.
Seaflower Skye Portree Harbour, Quay St, IV51 9DE; m 07342 622727; w seaflowerskye.com. Luxury day trips around Skye, Raasay & Rona, departing from Portree. Local seafood lunches.

OTHER PRACTICALITIES
$ Banks Bank of Scotland, Somerled Sq, IV51 9EH (☎01478 612438; ☉ 10.00–16.00 Mon–Fri); Clydesdale Bank, Somerled Sq, IV51 9EH (☎0800 345 7365; ☉ 09.15–16.30 Mon–Fri); RBS, Bank St, IV51 9BX (☎03457 242424, 03457 242424; ☉ 09.15–17.00 Mon–Tue & Thu–Fri, 10.00–17.00 Wed)
Fuel Gulf Portree Filling Station, Viewfield Rd, IV51 9EU; ☉ 07.30–21.00 Mon–Sat, 09.30–18.00 Sun
⊞ Portree Community Hospital Fancyhill (off Bank St), IV51 9BZ; ☎ 01478 613200
Laundry Portree Independent Hostel (page 59; coin operated); Skye Laundry, Budhmor Pl, IV51 9DJ (☎01478 612132; w skyelaundry.co.uk; ☉ 09.00–19.00 Mon–Fri, 10.00–18.00 Sat & Sun)

Library Portree Community Library, Viewfield Rd, IV51 9ET; ☎01478 614823; w highlifehighland. com/libraries/portree-library; ☉ 09.10–17.00 Mon, Wed & Fri, 09.10–20.00 Tue & Thu, 10.00–16.00 Sat
⊞ Medical centre Portree Medical Centre, Bank St, IV51 9BZ (☎01478 612013; w www. portreemedical.scot.nhs.uk; ☉ 08.00–18.00 by appointment only)
✚ Pharmacy Boots, 5 Wentworth St, IV51 9EJ; ☎01478 612100; ☉ 09.00–17.30 Mon–Sat, noon–16.00 Sun
✉ Post office 4 Wentworth St, IV51 9EJ; ☎01478 612533; w portreepostoffice.co.uk; ☉ 09.00–17.30 Mon–Sat

WHAT TO SEE AND DO A stroll along the harbour presents the prettiest views of Portree. If you have been travelling around the islands for some time, the main thing to do here is to enjoy civilisation: eat some fish and chips, stock up on supplies and visit the tourist information centre to help plan your next adventures.

The Braes Rightfully most famous for the Battle of the Braes (page 56), the Braes Peninsula is a peaceful backwater, great for cyclists, wildlife watching and walks.

Camas a' Mhòr Bheòil and An Àird The long curve of **Camas A' Mhòr Bheòil** is one of Skye's best beaches; it has some stone and rocks, but the far end is sandy. Possibly more special than the beach itself is the view across the water to the slopes and points of Ben Tianavaig further north. For those seeking relaxation, the beach might be enough; redshank feed along the northeast shoreline and sheep graze quietly on the grass.

Those with a little more energy could explore the whale-tail-shaped **An Àird Peninsula** (beyond the northwestern end of the beach). At the northern point of the peninsula is Dunan an Aisilidh, a ruinous, galleried dun that has some similar features to a broch and probably dates from the Iron Age. From this strategic point, you have a spectacular view across the Narrows of Raasay, the stretch of water

> ## THE LUMP
>
> 'The Lump' is a small peninsula south of Portree Harbour, also known as the Meall, Sròn a' Mhill and the Sugar Lump. The coast path, which runs between the Portree Free Church of Scotland and the hospital, gives ever-changing panoramic views. From the north of the Lump you can look down over Portree Harbour, with an attractive row of houses up on the hill and fishing boats anchored below. A hum of chugging boat engines, seagulls and squawking rooks accompanies you as you follow the coast path until, rounding a corner, everything goes quiet and the bustle of the town is long forgotten; there are tall, twisted trees, some monkey puzzles and a wonderful view out to Ben Tianavaig.
>
> In the centre of the Lump is a green lawn, which makes a pleasant place for a picnic, and the small Apothecary's Tower. Built in 1829, the tower was originally used to inform passing ships that medical assistance was available, in addition to serving as a dispensary. Climbing to the top gives a splendid view over Portree and, on a clear day, you can just see the Old Man of Storr.

between An Àird and Inverarish, and infinitely further north through the channel. Look out for the seals that live on Raasay's west coast and maybe even porpoises or dolphins on calm days. In the southeast part of the whale tail are a small series of wonderful caves, bridges, archways and sea stacks. Be very careful all the way along this coastline as drops can appear suddenly. It is a very special place and you are more than likely to have it to yourself.

A grassy path down to Camas a' Mhòr Bheòil and An Àird starts just past the post box in the township of Gedintailor (✛ 57°20'17"N 6°06'50'W). To reach this spot, travel south from Camastianavaig on the B883 until you reach a left turn for an even more minor road marked towards 'Gedintailor, Balmeanach, Peinachorrain'. If you have a car, it's best to find somewhere to park near this turning and walk the remaining 500yds as there is no parking near the start of the path.

UIG AND THE TROTTERNISH PENINSULA

Trotternish has Skye's most iconic landscapes and there are many unexpected beautiful places (although, alas, the Old Man of Storr is somewhat a victim of its glowing reputation). With endless hiking opportunities, towering cliffs, fossilised dinosaur footprints, abandoned villages and secret archaeology, you could spend weeks in Trotternish and barely scratch the surface. Uig, on the west coast, is the peninsula's busiest settlement, despite only having a couple of hundred residents, and has ferry links to the Outer Hebrides.

It is important to note that there is hardly any phone signal anywhere on Trotternish, making some amount of forward planning, in addition to this book, an OS map (Explorer 408: *Skye – Trotternish & The Storr*) and/or a GPS device, essential.

GETTING AROUND
By bus Compared with other rural areas of Skye, Trotternish is relatively well served with buses, but you should still check timetables closely to avoid getting stuck. The peninsula is served by Citylink and Stagecoach services (page 28).

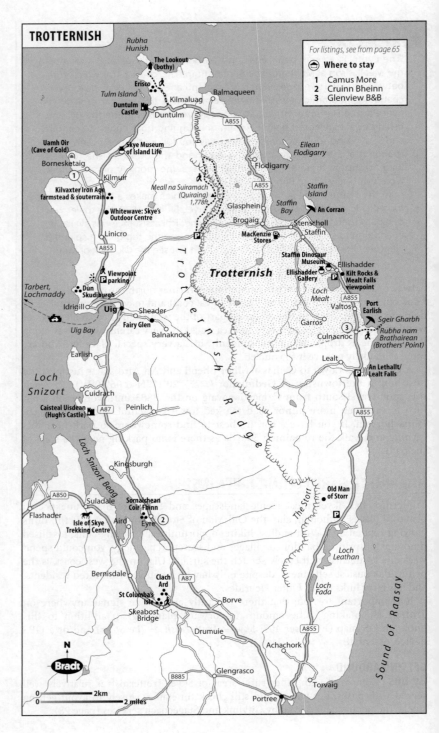

TROTTERNISH

Rubha Hunish

The Lookout (bothy)

Erisco

Tulm Island

Duntulm Castle

Kilmaluag

Balmaqueen

Duntulm

For listings, see from page 65

Where to stay
1   Camus More
2   Cruinn Bheinn
3   Glenview B&B

Uamh Oir (Cave of Gold)

Bornesketaig

Skye Museum of Island Life

Flodigarry

Eilean Flodigarry

Kilmuir

Kilvaxter Iron Age farmstead & souterrain

Meall na Suiramach (Quiraing)
▲ 1,778ft

Glasphein

Brogaig

Staffin Bay

Staffin Island

An Corran

Whitewave: Skye's Outdoor Centre

Linicro

A855

Trotternish

MacKenzie Stores

Stenscholl

Staffin

Staffin Dinosaur Museum

Ellishadder Gallery

Ellishadder

Kilt Rocks & Mealt Falls viewpoint

Viewpoint parking

Dùn Skudiburgh

Tarbert, Lochmaddy

Idrigill

Trotternish Ridge

Uig

Sheader

Loch Mealt

Valtos

A855

Port Earlish

Fairy Glen

Balnaknock

Uig Bay

Garros

Sgeir Gharbh

3

Rubha nam Brathairean (Brothers' Point)

Earlish

Culnacnoc

Loch Snizort

Cuidrach

Caisteal Uisdean (Hugh's Castle)

Peinlich

A87

Lealt

An Lethallt / Lealt Falls

A855

Kingsburgh

A850

Suladale

Flashader

Sornaichean Coir' Fhinn

Aird

2

Eyre

Isle of Skye Trekking Centre

Old Man of Storr

The Storr

Loch Leathan

Bernisdale

Clach Ard

A87

Loch Fada

St Columba's Isle

Borve

Skeabost Bridge

Sound of Raasay

Drumuie

A855

Achachork

Bradt

N

Glengrasco

B885

Torvaig

Portree

0   2km
0   2 miles

64

After meeting on a walking holiday on Arran and going on to complete a life-changing year-long 4,000 mile walk across Europe, Helen and Paul Webster decided to move to Skye. Their work running holiday chalets brought them into contact with many visitors to the island, who often asked for walk recommendations. With the aim of providing comprehensive information about walking routes, as well as a cost-effective place for smaller accommodation providers to advertise, Helen and Paul decided to set up Walkhighlands (w walkhighlands.co.uk) in 2006.

A decade on, Walkhighlands now attracts over 25,000 daily visitors and covers thousands of walks across Scotland. It is remarkably well researched and accurate, with route descriptions and marked maps covering everything from easy strolls to real mountaineering, while remaining free to use.

I asked Helen if she had any advice for people who are only just starting to get into hiking. Her response was: 'Start small, check the weather, take snacks and waterproofs and let the adventure begin – there's a lifetime of walking out there but be warned it can get addictive!'

Cycling, walking and hitchhiking With such dramatic scenery, it's a shame to rush through Trotternish. From strenuous hikes to easy footpaths, there are infinite walking opportunities and, for many people, exploring on foot is the most rewarding way to enjoy the landscape. Though the stretch of road between Portree and the Old Man of Storr can be busy, cyclists who do not mind the odd hill will love the northern half of Trotternish. With the Skye Bridge as an open gateway, hitchhiking is arguably a little less safe than on the smaller islands, but crime is still very uncommon and hitchhiking is very easy.

WHERE TO STAY *Map, page 73, unless otherwise stated*
While occasional B&Bs are dotted along Trotternish's ring road, the bulk of the peninsula's accommodation is found in Uig which, for a small port town, has a great range of options. With so much to explore, Trotternish is a perfect place to book a self-catering cottage; extensive options are listed on w walkhighlands.co.uk/skye/cottages_trotternish.shtml.

🏠 **The Ferry Inn** (4 rooms) Uig IV51 9XP; ☎ 01470 542300; w theferryinnskye.com. Stylish, luxury accommodation above the restaurant & bar in a 19th-century building. 'Bay view' rooms are slightly smaller than rear-facing 'woodland view' rooms. Family business; 2-night min stay. **££££**

🏠 **Uig Hotel** (18 rooms) Uig IV51 9YE; ☎ 01470 542205; w uig-hotel-skye.com; ⊕ Feb–Dec; ♿. Good 3-star hotel, up the hill to the south of town. Comfortable rooms, some with baths, nicely finished. Split between main hotel & lodge, but staff & quality are the same. Lodge is £15 cheaper a night, but rooms are sea-facing, bigger & newer; it's a 30yd walk from the hotel, but parking is directly in front. **££££**

🏠 **Cruinn Bheinn** [map, opposite] (3 rooms) 4 Eyre, Kensaleyre IV51 9XB; ☎ 01470 532459; w cruinnbheinn.co.uk; ⊕ Mar–end Oct. In a quiet location, this small B&B has comfortable rooms looking across Loch Snizort. There's also a luxury self-catering chalet (sleeps 2; £840/week) with large windows making the most of the glorious views. Less than 15mins' drive from Portree. **£££**

🏠 **Glenview B&B** [map, opposite] (3 rooms) Culnacnoc IV51 9JH; ☎ 01470 562248; w glenviewskye.co.uk. Across the road from Brothers' Point (page 68), professional chef Simon & his wife Kirsty run this characterful B&B. With the sort of shabby-chic décor boutique hotels aim for but often miss, rooms are spacious with home-baked cookies on arrival. Optional, very reasonably priced early morning meditation or Hatha yoga offered, plus fully catered restorative yoga & yarn retreats, & natural dyeing & knitting workshops. **£££**

🏠 **Woodbine B&B** (5 rooms) On the A855, Uig IV51 9XP; 📞 01470 542243; **w** woodbineskye. co.uk. Friendly B&B in traditional, whitewashed stone croft house. Guest lounge with wood burner. Good value. Min 2-night stay. **£££**

✳ 🏠 **Dun Flodigarry Hostel** (30 beds) Flodigarry IV51 9XB; 📞 01470 552212; **w** flodigarry-hostel.scot; ♿. Family run since 1992, this is the best sort of old-school hostel. The large building is spectacularly situated on cliffs above the ocean. Very spacious, well-equipped kitchen & staff with decades of experience; they offer hiking advice & have wall maps marked-up with walks in the area. Campers can use the kitchen & there's communal seating inside. **£**

🏠 **The Cowshed Boutique Bunkhouse** (34 beds & 8 pods) Near Uig IV51 9YD; **m** 07917 536820; **w** skyecowshed.co.uk; ♿. New luxury bunkhouse with good facilities & great views across Uig Bay. Bunks have privacy curtains. Pods sleep 3 adults or 2 adults & 2 children & are furnished with bedding, tiny kitchens & en suite. It's a 35min walk or few minutes' drive south of Uig ferry port on the main road. **£**

⛺ **Camus More** [map, page 64] Kilmuir IV51 9YS; 📞 01470 552312. Beautiful, peaceful camping with very basic facilities (no shower). **£**

⛺ **Uig Campsite** Uig IV51 9XU; 📞 01470 542714; **w** uig-camping-skye.co.uk. Basic but friendly campsite for both tents & motorhomes. Quiet, but conveniently located next to the ferry terminal. Pet friendly. **£**

🍴 **WHERE TO EAT AND DRINK** *Map, page 73, unless otherwise stated*

As with accommodation, the majority of Trotternish's eating establishments are in Uig. While most of Skye seems to shut down in winter, the presence of the ferry port allows many places in Uig to stay open.

🍴 **The Ferry Inn** (page 65) ⏰ 18.00–20.30 Tue–Sat (might change in winter). Elegantly presented food made from local ingredients. Tasteful, modern interior with distressed wood & grey/blue colour scheme. Book in advance. **£££**

🍴 **Uig Hotel** (page 65) ⏰ Feb–Dec 07.30–09.30, noon–15.00 & 18.00–20.30 daily; ♿. Busy restaurant catering for all. Favourites include venison with a sweet sauce, haggis with Talisker sauce; & vegetarian walnut loaf. Book ahead. **££**

🍴 **The Galley Seafood & Café** Carnbeag, Earlish IV51 9XL; **m** 07485 133316; ⏰ noon–20.00 Tue–Sat; ♿. Fresh seafood, fish & chips, burgers, etc. Good portions & cheaper than anywhere in Uig for evening meals. **£**

☕ **Columba 1400 Café** Staffin IV51 9JY; 📞 01478 611407; **w** columba1400.com/locations/ cafe-a-shop; ⏰ summer 10.00–20.00 Mon–Sat, winter 10.30–15.30 Mon–Fri; closed 3 weeks at Christmas. Modern, bright & spacious café with views across to the Quiraing. Very welcoming with extensive & affordable menu. Columba 1400 is an award-winning social enterprise & charity, providing leadership training for young people; the café raises funds. Good cause, good food & great view. **£**

☕ **Ella's Café** The Sheiling, Uig IV51 9XX; 📞 01470 542797; 🇫 TheSheiling; ⏰ 10.00–16.00 Tue–Sat. Good home-baked cakes, lunches, bread & soup. Same building & business as the Sheiling craft & antique shop (see below). **£**

SHOPPING
Arts and crafts

✳ **Ellishadder Gallery** [map, page 64] 4 Ellishadder, Culnacnoc IV51 9JE; 📞 01470 562734; **w** ellishaddergallery.co.uk; ⏰ Apr–Oct noon–16.30 Mon–Thu. Beautiful woven throws & scarves in 'Skye colours'. Prices reflect long & involved process of weaving intricate colours & patterns on

a traditional loom. Also serves fair-trade/organic coffee, cake & soup (£).

The Sheiling [map, page 73] Uig IV51 9XX; 📞 01470 542797; 🇫; ⏰ 10.00–16.00 Tue–Sat. Craft & antique shop with collectable Scottish books.

Shilasdair Yarn [map, page 64] Glenview B&B (page 65); **w** shilasdair-yarns.com; ⏰ noon–

17.00 Mon–Fri, noon–15.00 Sun. British wool yarns dyed naturally using plants from Skye.

❋ **Trotternish Gallery** Kilmaluag, by Duntulm, IV51 9UQ; 📞 01470 552302; ⏰ variable, when sign is displayed outside. Not far from Skye's most northerly point, in a small house decorated with colourful buoys, is Bill & Susie Lawrence's house, with the gallery doubling as Bill's studio & their living room during the evenings. Susie is a photographer, but Bill's intricately detailed landscapes, wooden boats & traditional houses in pen & coloured pencil take up most of the wall space.

Uig Pottery [map, page 73] The Pier, IV51 9XX; 📞 01470 542421; ⏰ Oct–Apr 09.00–17.00 Mon–Sat, May–Sep 09.00–18.00 Mon–Sat, 11.00–16.00 Sun. Large shop with working pottery inside.

Food shops *Map, page 73*
Isle of Skye Brewing Co (Leann an Eilein) The Pier, Uig IV51 9XP; 📞 01470 542477; w skyeale. com; ⏰ 10.00–18.00 Mon–Fri, 10.00–16.00 Sat, noon–16.00 Sun; ♿. Award-winning craft-ale brewery. Range includes everything from a 7% Cuillin Beast ale to more refreshing IPA, golden ale & lager.

Rankins Uig IV51 9XP; 📞 01470 542213; w rankins-skye.co.uk; ⏰ 08.30–18.30 Mon–Sat; ♿. Well-stocked, independently owned licensed grocer. ATM.

Staffin Stores Stenscholl, Staffin IV51 9JS; 📞 01470 562354; ⏰ 09.00–18.00 Mon–Sat; ♿. Relatively large & well-stocked community-owned grocery store. Laundry service.

Uig Filling Station & Shop Ferry port, Uig IV51 9XX; 📞 01470 542774; ⏰ 08.00–20.00 Mon–Sat, 10.30–17.00 Sun; ♿. Quite expensive, but has essentials including alcohol.

SPORTS AND ACTIVITIES
Skye Cruises The Pier, Uig IV51 9XX; m 07469 720621; w skyecruises.com. 3hr cruises exploring Loch Snizort in a 1940s fishing boat, carrying up to 12 passengers.

SkyeXplorer Boat Trips The Pier, Uig IV51 9XX; m 07803 564896; w puffinsandwhales.co.uk. Trips around protected Ascrib Islands & Waternish Peninsula with chance to see minke whales & sea eagles, as well as puffins & seals. Best May–Jul.

Staffin Gym Above Staffin Community Hall, IV51

9JS; w staffin-trust.co.uk/leisure; ⏰ 06.00–22.00 daily. Small but well equipped with bikes, rowing machines, treadmills, weights, etc. Community owned. Day/week £5/10.

Whitewave: Skye's Outdoor Centre [map, page 64] Linicro, Kilmuir IV51 9YN; 📞 01470 542414; w white-wave.co.uk. Kayaking, canoeing, climbing & abseiling, mountain boarding, archery & guided walks for families, groups & individuals.

OTHER PRACTICALITIES
Fuel MacKenzie Stores, Stenscholl, Staffin IV51 9JS (⏰ 09.00–18.00 Mon–Sat, 11.00–14.00 Sun); Uig Filling Station & Shop (see above)

✉ **Post** [map, page 64] Brogaig IV51 9JY 📞 01470 562209; ⏰ 09.00–noon Mon–Sat); Rankins (see above; ⏰ 09.00–13.00 & 14.00–17.30 Mon–Fri, 09.00–13.00 Sat)

WHAT TO SEE AND DO
The east coast of the Trotternish Peninsula Travelling north from Portree on the A855, the landscape quickly becomes mountainous and **the Storr**, the range of mountains behind the Old Man of Storr, soon comes into view. Around 4 miles north of Portree, you pass the lovely lochs of Fada and Leathan, before reaching the car park for the **Old Man of Storr**. The uphill walk to reach this famous rock pinnacle is just under 3 miles return, with an elevation gain of 935ft. Although the route starts (from the car park) on a substantial track, it diminishes into an anarchy of trodden paths, muddy in places and not always particularly clear; sturdy boots and a bottle of water are recommended, along with appropriate clothing for the weather. In high season it is best to arrive early or late to enjoy your visit without the crowds that throng here for most of the day.

As much as I would like to tell you the Storr is an over-hyped destination, it really isn't the case; the 'Old Man' (a somewhat miraculous pointed rock stack) and the whole surrounding mountain range are incredible. Given just the right amount of mist, clouds shift slightly to reveal different crags, and a dampening silence descends over the area. It is tempting to walk between the cliffs and stacks of rock, but remember that this whole area has been formed by landslides and falling rocks are a distinct possibility.

Further north is **Lealt Falls** (An Lethallt). A popular stop along the road, there is a large car park here with a wooden platform (♿) in place to give you a great view over the waterfall and canyon. At the bottom of the cliffs, on the shore, are the remains of a 19th-century diatomite works. Skye diatomite is a silica-rich sediment formed by microscopic algae and was of interest for its potential use in the production of dynamite during the 1880s. The iron-roofed construction on the south of the river is a disused salmon fishing station.

🧍 *Rubha nam Brathairean (Brothers' Point)*

Distance: 2 miles; time: 2 hours; start/end: Culnacnoc; OS Explorer map: 408 Skye – Trotternish & The Storr

Taking in ruined buildings, a rocky shore at Port Earlish and the spectacular headland of Brothers' Point, this is not a particularly strenuous walk, though it would be challenging for someone with a fear of heights. The quiet bay at Port Earlish is worth visiting even if you do not want to complete the whole route.

If you have a car, park it some 150yds north of Glenview B&B (in Culnacnoc), where there is a small car park (⊕ 57°35'05.4"N 006°09'27.7"W). The walk starts opposite the Glenview: pass Brothers' Point Cottages and look out for a wooden sign directing you right, down to the shore. On the left, you will come to Taigh Ruaraidh Dhomhnaill a' Chuirn, the atmospheric ruin of a farmstead at Port Earlish, which has been unoccupied since the late 19th century.

Footprints of sauropods and theropods, older cousins of the T Rex, have been found on the shoreline on the tidal area of Sgeir Gharbh, between Port Earlish and Brothers' Point itself; to get here, turn right when you get down to the shore at Port Earlish and follow the coast. For children, it is a glorious place for rock pooling and there are plenty of indentations that could be dinosaur footprints and might well be, but I must admit that I was not able to positively identify them myself. (Spend some time looking at pictures online first and visit the Dinosaur Museum in Staffin for more information; see opposite.) This is a wonderful, rocky bay with inquisitive common seals and a few hazards to be aware of: large waves crashing on the rocks may come up further than you expect and, once you get higher on to the grassy area between the bay and Brothers' Point, there are steep drops down to the rocks below.

Walk around the shore, keeping the sea on your left, until you come to a couple of ruined buildings and can see a way to safely ascend the slope to a broad, grassy platform. From here there is a narrow path beside a steep drop, on the middle ground between the cliffs above and below it. Once you reach the base of the headland, where the twisted form of Brothers' Point stretches out directly in front of you, it is quite obvious that you must follow the small and dubious path, keeping on the left-hand side of the ridge in order to get out to the promontory. This is easier than it looks at the beginning and, once you have climbed up to the highest point, halfway along the peninsula, you will see a wide grassy area leading out to the point itself. From here you can see the Old Man of Storr and Kilt Rocks on a clear day. Look out for circular holes, the remains of an obvious quern quarry

(✣ 57°35'12.8" N 6°08'16.8" W) in the rocks below around 55yds southeast of the point. Return along the same route.

Northern Trotternish

At **Kilt Rocks and Mealt Falls** is a large car park and a viewing point over the towering cliffs (♿). With dramatic basalt columns, named for their resemblance to the pleats of a kilt, and a narrow waterfall plummeting 196ft down to the sea, this quick stop is a favourite with photographers. Take some time to scan the sea for dolphins, porpoises and other marine mammals.

Nearby is the **Staffin Dinosaur Museum** (Ellishadder; w staffindinosaurmuseum. com; ◷ Easter–Oct 10.00–16.00 Mon–Fri; adult/child £2/1), a small museum in a traditional cottage with an amazing collection of dinosaur fossils and information. This is also the best place to ask for advice about finding footprints in the area.

Although it is well known that there are **dinosaur footprints** on **An Corran beach** near Staffin, this fact does not make them any easier to find (roughly ✣ 57°38'13.8"N 6°12'17.4"W). There is an interpretation board at the car park here, but it is worth studying the photo to see what you are looking for, as the map is quite inaccurate. While I was scouring the ground, I was lucky enough to meet a local woman who showed me two ornithopod footprints. To find them, head down the ramp that runs from the car park to the beach; they are about 5yds east (towards the sea) from the lowest boulder on the ramp. The footprints have three toes, each around the same size as a human foot, and are positioned as if the creature was walking towards the sea. They are set into rock, which looks like the fossilised ripples of a sand bed; this rock is covered with green algae, which might make them difficult to distinguish; at times the tide brings up sand, making them impossible to see. Depending on the conditions, an adventurous person in a sturdy wheelchair could potentially access this site.

Marginally further north, **Brogaig** and **Glasphein** – two close hamlets with around 50 white houses between them – are nestled at the base of the mighty **Meall na Suiramach** (1,778ft); the eastern slopes of this mountain descend into the landslides known as the **Quiraing**.

Quiraing loop

Distance: 4 miles, or 6½ miles with extension; time: 3 hours, or 4 hours with extension; start/end: Viewpoint car park at the summit of the minor road between Staffin and Uig; OS Explorer map: 408 Skye – Trotternish & The Storr

The Quiraing, pronounced 'kirrang', is another of Skye's hotspots, and though the car park has recently been extended, it can still be difficult to find a spot. There are more mountain rescue call-outs in this area than in the substantially more dangerous Black Cuillins, so it is not somewhere that should be underestimated. Strong winds are amplified over the plains and up the slopes; the path is a little unclear at times and takes you close to the edge, so check the wind forecast (page 27) first before deciding to set out.

Take the path, opposite the car park, signposted towards 'Flodigarry via Quiraing' for 100yds before following the smaller, steeper path to your left that heads up Maoladh Mòr. After around 400yds the ascent becomes more gentle and the path begins to contour around the hill, with excellent views of Staffin Bay and Staffin Island. Cross over the stile and take the faint path to your right, which begins to climb a grassy slope. Stay on the path closest to the edge; as you get to the top of the hill, small cutaways at the tops of the crags give you amazing views of the spires and rock formations of the Quiraing below. The intermittent path passes by a small cairn on the right; from here it is possible to make a straightforward detour to the trig point at the peak of Meall na Suiramach by turning left.

From the peak, the cliff path winds along the edge for a few hundred yards more before descending with views into the valleys and little lochs; you'll see the imposing rock-walled, flat-topped summit of Leac nan Fionn to the east and the next plateau – Sron Vourlinn – to the northeast. As the boggy path heads downhill and begins to plateau out, you can see small villages near the northernmost point of Skye. On your left are the cliffs of Sgùrr Mòr. Eventually you will reach a stile on the right that crosses a wire fence; climb over the stile and then head down the steep, eroded path to the bottom of the valley. The route then heads south–southeast below the cliffs.

Follow the path as it meanders through the hillocks and rocks at the base of the cliffs on your right; you will come to a cairn and a junction off to your left that you should ignore. Soon you will catch a glimpse of Loch Cleap in the distance. Crossing a stile, you begin to get into the rocky pinnacles that the Quiraing is famous for. Crags begin to appear in the cliffs, which open out to reveal the Needle rock stack up above you. Pass between the cliffs and the Prison, a large rock structure good for rock climbing, listening out for the echo of your footsteps. The path then descends through a boulder field and, keeping right at the junction, starts to climb steadily. Continuing to the car park is fairly straightforward from here, just continuing along the path, but care should be taken to find sure footing and hand placement in a number of the gulleys, which are sometimes wet, with loose rocks.

The remote far north The peaceful crofting land in the far north of Trotternish, between Flodigarry and Uig, is a breath of fresh air after the busier roads further south. There are many ruined buildings, some abandoned since the Clearances, as well as rusty barns and current, traditional homes with whitewashed walls and slate roofs.

🚶 The Lookout over Rubha Hunish and Erisco ☀

Distance: 3 miles; time: 2 hours; start/end: Kilmaluag; OS Explorer map: 408 Skye – Trotternish & The Storr

This route leads to and from a former coastguard lookout with spectacular views over the most northerly point of Skye – Rubha Hunish – where, on a calm day, you have a decent chance of seeing marine mammals. The return leg visits the abandoned settlement of Erisco. It is not particularly challenging, but it does cross boggy ground.

Leave the main road at the Kilmaluag phone box, in-between the tiny townships of Kilmaluag and Duntulm. The number 57 bus stops here, and there is a car park 50yds down the track, just before first the cattle grid.

Cross the cattle grid and follow a sign pointing left that says 'Rubha Hunish 2.5km', taking this path northwest along the higher ground above a shallow valley on your left. Out to the west is Duntulm Castle and small, grassy Tulm Island not far offshore. As you continue you will notice the ruined settlement of Erisco down in the valley to your left.

After just over a mile, on an intermittent, but relatively easy-to-follow path, you should go through a kissing gate (✦ 57°41'41.6"N 006°20'26.1"W); go through this. Continue towards the channel between two low hills and after around

500yds you will see a small trail leading off to the right; take this up the hill and head north to the Lookout (⊕ 57°42'05"N 6°20'41"W), a small building with big windows.

Inside the Lookout are binoculars and identification charts for whales and dolphins, along with star constellations and an information board about Dave Brown, a wilderness lover, who the Lookout is dedicated to. This building is now a Mountain Association bothy where you are welcome to sleep, but as it is well known among hikers you are unlikely to have it to yourself. There is obviously no rubbish collection here, so as always, please take everything away with you and leave the bothy clean.

After you have absorbed the spectacular view over Rubha Hunish, scanned the ocean for dolphins and maybe eaten your sandwiches, return to the kissing gate the way that you came.

From the kissing gate you can make the short walk down to Erisco (⊕ 57°41'35"N 6°20'27"W) where eight ruined but well-preserved cottars' houses are placed along the line of a township enclosure wall. These houses were built by people who had been evicted from elsewhere by Lord MacDonald to make room for sheep; it is known as an 'improvements' settlement and is the best example of one on Skye. After the Crofters' Act of 1886 the inhabitants moved away again, hopefully to better and bigger land. Around the same area are quite a few earlier and more damaged houses with lazy-bed cultivations. These are obviously from an earlier settlement in the same spot, though not much is known about them.

From Erisco, find a slight path that leads 300yds southeast back up to the original track you began on and follow it back to the car park.

The west coast of Trotternish

The oldest parts of **Duntulm Castle** (◷ open access) were built in the 14th and 15th centuries; what's left of it sits in a dramatic clifftop position on the west coast, not far from where the ring road starts to head south. This area saw many years of feuding between the MacDonalds (of Sleat) and the MacLeods until it settled as the seat of MacDonalds in the 17th century. In 1732 Sir Alexander MacDonald was looking for something a bit more comfortable and robbed the stones from Duntulm to build his new residence Monkstadt House, 6 miles further south. There is a place to park at the corner of the road and the castle ruins are a short walk away on a grassy path. Be sure to look down at the sea as an otter lives along this coastline and you might even see porpoises or dolphins. There is also a **cairn to Flora MacDonald** (page 56) and a great view out to small, lumpy **Tulm Island** and of the coastline to the north.

UAMH OIR – CAVE OF GOLD

Uamh Oir (⊕ 57°39'36"N 6°24'36"W), meaning Cave of Gold in Gaelic, is a very special place on the northwest coast. Towering basalt columns rise from the sea, similar to those that form Fingal's Cave on Staffa (see box, page 185), but much less frequently visited. Seabirds use the cliffs to nest and gannets, shags, gulls and guillemots fish in the surrounding waters.

A short walk along the coast from Bornesketaig can be navigated with OS Explorer map 408 (*Skye – Trotternish & The Storr*) and is described by Walkhighlands (w walkhighlands.co.uk/skye/caveofgold.shtml). Take extra care on the steep, muddy path down the grassy slope to the cave.

Heading further south on the A855, do not miss the **Skye Museum of Island Life** (Kilmuir; w skyemuseum.co.uk; ⊕ Easter–Sep 09.30–17.00 Mon–Sat; adult/child £3/0.50), which aims to demonstrate how crofters lived and worked in the area. A number of traditional thatched houses are arranged to show a different element of crofting life from around the end of the 18th century. The Croft House, the largest of the group, is set out to represent a home with a kitchen and old-fashioned box bed in the bedroom. There is also a barn, full of agricultural objects; the Weaver's Cottage, depicting a workshop with loom and spinning wheels; a blacksmith's workshop; and the Ceileigh House, which contains old documents and photos of Skye.

Kilvaxter Iron-Age farmstead and souterrain (⊕ 57°38'26.4"N 6°22'35.1"W; ⊕ open access; donation requested; &) This 2,000-year-old grass-covered roundhouse and underground tunnel is a great example of a souterrain, and is one that you are actually able to go inside, although you might need wellies and waterproofs.

Uig and around
Spread around Uig Bay, this small port town has a lot going on, including ferries to the Outer Hebrides (page 56). It is a good place to stock up on supplies, have a pint or get some fish and chips. Note that extra care should be taken on the stretch of road that leads in from the north, being narrow with sharp hairpin bends.

Uig Wood
A band of broad-leaved trees follows Uig Bay 600yds southeast from the village hall; Uig Wood comprises over 17ha of native woodland around the town, which can be explored on indicated walking paths. The mature woodland provides a valuable habitat for butterflies and interesting lichens; listen out for the distinctive songs of chiffchaffs and other small woodland birds.

From the centre of Uig, another path starts just west of Woodside Farm and leads upstream along the banks of the tumbling River Rha towards **Rha Falls**. Also part of Uig Wood, the trees in the steep-sided ravine are more slender and it is only a couple of hundred yards to the double cascade of Rha Falls.

Uig Tower
On the hill south of the town, overlooking the bay, is the folly Uig Tower. This short stone tower was built around 1860 for Major William Fraser who was the owner of Kilmuir Estate. His house, Uig Lodge, was washed away in the great flood of 1877 just after he had organised Skye's last clearances. Visible from both the bay and the road, it is best observed from a distance as bulls are kept in the surrounding field.

Fairy Glen
In the hills east of Uig, between Sheader and Balnaknock, the **Fairy Glen** has become one of the busiest tourist honeypots on Skye. The highlight of this landscape of small hillocks is the rocky protrusion called **Ewan's Tower**; climbing the few metres to the top gives you a good view over the area. The turning to reach the glen is just south of Uig Hotel. Note, however, that due to the site's overwhelming popularity the single-track road to it gets very congested and parking is extremely limited – there's only enough space for a few cars to park safely, and a real possibility of getting your car stuck in a muddy bank when you try to turn around. Walking or cycling the 1½ miles from Uig is likely to be less stressful (and quicker!), as is visiting in early morning or evening, when the crowds are fewer.

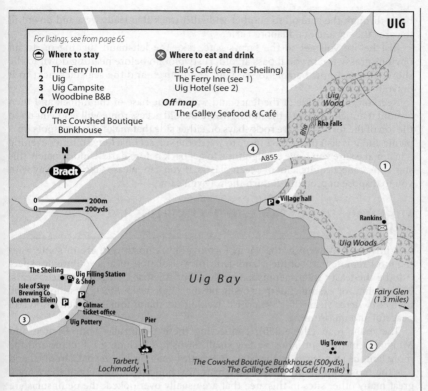

Caisteal Uisdean (Hugh's Castle) This ruined square tower stands guard over the entrance to Loch Snizort Beag. Probably dating from the early 17th century, the ground-floor walls are solid, without any openings apart from some narrow holes in deep embrasures. The castle is best known for its association with Uisdean MacGhilleasbuig Chlerich, the nephew of Donald Gorm of Sleat who, having failed in his plot to murder his uncle and become chief, fled to the Outer Hebrides where he was captured. He died in the dungeon at Duntulm.

The castle is near the few buildings that make up South Cuidrach, just over a mile's walk south of the township of Cuidrach. If you have a car, park it near Cuidrach: either in the disused quarry and walk to the junction where a green sign points left towards 'South Cuidrach 1.5m', or in the small parking place there if there is room.

Dùn Skudiburgh
Distance: 3 miles; time: 2 hours; start/end: Viewpoint car park between Totescore and Uig; OS Explorer map: 408 Skye – Trotternish & The Storr

This is an easy return walk to visit Dùn Skudiburgh, a complex fortification, of which the oldest parts are thought to be prehistoric.

If you have a car, park it at the indicated viewpoint parking (⊕ 57°36'07.8"N 6°22'40.5"W) on the corner of the A855, about 600yds south after the sign for 'Totescore' or 2 miles north of Uig, with the postbox and bus stop.

Walk 200yds south along the road from the car park to find a track going off to the right, towards a large green barn. Follow the track and take the left fork at the barn, through the gate on to another wide dirt track that leads west and downhill towards the sea and Scuddaborg Farm.

Just before you get to the farm's gate, take the left-hand turning on to an obvious grassy track; you'll pass an old, rusty plough before heading down to the shore. You will now be able to see Dùn Skudiburgh and the sea stack next to it on your right.

Keep on the sea side of the fence and walk to the base of the hillock and then around it anticlockwise to the north, where the old access route will lead you up to the top of the fort. There are rocky bays on either side that make glorious spots for a picnic and it is also the perfect place to watch the sun set on a long summer evening – just make sure you leave enough time to get back before dark! Unfortunately this shoreline collects quite a lot of ocean plastic. If you can, please take a bit away with you to dispose of properly. Return the way you came.

EDINBANE, DUNVEGAN AND THE DUIRINISH AND WATERNISH PENINSULAS

Duirinish and Waternish, the wings forming Skye's northwest, are in some ways the most remote parts of the island. Duirinish's isolation means you might expect it to be the least visited peninsula on Skye, but this has changed in recent years. Neist Point, for example, despite being off the single-track B884, gets more traffic than elsewhere. Meanwhile Waternish, lacking any major tourist attractions, is still peaceful and unassuming.

The main road (the A850), connecting these peninsulas with Portree and Minginish in the south, hosts a few small townships including Edinbane and the more famous Dunvegan. In the latter, the castle – ancestral home of Clan MacLeod – is the most famous and impressive historical building on Skye, but there are a great many other sites in this area that are usually overlooked; the peninsulas are dotted with Iron-Age brochs and ruined medieval churches, with carved grave slabs and turbulent histories.

As half the coastline and interior are totally uninhabited, there are infinite opportunities for hiking. Dramatically positioned lighthouses and steep seabird cliffs can be found on the coastal extremities, while sea lochs provide more gentle waters to the interior.

GETTING AROUND This large area of Skye is served by only a few roads, leaving big areas that are inaccessible to vehicles. While the A850 has two lanes, the Duirinish and Waternish peninsulas have only single-track roads, some of which have pot-holes and blind summits or corners.

By bus Stagecoach (page 57) run a service between Portree and Edinbane, Dunvegan and Glendale (Duirinish).

WHERE TO STAY There's lots of accommodation options at the top end of the market, but this side of the island is distinctly lacking in cheaper options.

Greshornish House [54 C3] (10 rooms) Greshornish IV51 9PN; 01470 582266; w greshornishhouse.com. Grand old manor house set in 30 acres, with a cannon in the grounds. Once owned by Kenneth MacLeod, who founded Edinbane (page 78) in the 19th century. Full-sized snooker table & lawn games. Rooms all different in size, shape & decoration, but generally large. Master rooms are enormous & regal. Price reduced massively in winter. **£££££**

🏠 **The House Over-By** [54 B4] (6 rooms) Colbost IV55 8ZT; 📞 01470 511258; **w** threechimneys.co.uk; ♿. The communal areas have dramatic details, including an intricate, boldly coloured stained-glass doorway, & enormous, expressive seascapes on the wall. Huge windows allow you to have b/fast or evening drinks overlooking Loch Dunvegan. Dressing gowns, well-stocked minibar, coffee machine, fresh fruit, home-baking, fresh milk, mineral water & everything else you might expect from super-luxury accommodation – all reflected in the price. 2 rooms have sea views. Run by the same people as The Three Chimneys (see below), which is next door. **£££££**

🏠 **Edinbane Inn** [54 C3] (6 rooms) Edinbane IV51 9PW; 📞 01470 582414; **w** edinbaneinn. co.uk; ⏱ Feb–Dec. Tasteful, modern interior with touches of tartan. All newly refurbished in muted colour scheme of grey, blue & whites. Above a lively restaurant & bar. **££££**

🏠 **Hillstone** [54 B4] (3 rooms) Colbost IV55 8ZT; 📞 01470 511434; **w** hillstonelodge.com. Architect-designed modern building with huge windows overlooking Loch Dunvegan. Meticulously decorated with Skye Weavers' tweed & luxurious finishings. Drinks licence. Previous winner of the Taste Award for 'Best B&B on Skye'. Adults only. Min 2-night stay. **££££**

🏠 **Ronan House** [54 C3] (3 rooms) 21 Upper Edinbane, Edinbane IV51 9PR; 📞 01470 582449; **w** ronanhouse.co.uk. A friendly B&B run by locals Ronnie & Anne, with fantastic views across the valley & small village of Edinbane. You would really need a car or bicycle to stay here as it is quite far off the A850. **£££**

⛺ **Kinloch Camping** [54 B4] Dunvegan IV55 8WQ; 📞 01470 521531; **w** kinloch-campsite.co.uk; ⏱ mid-Mar–mid-Oct; reception: 09.00–11.00 & 14.30–19.00. Well-run campsite in great location at head of Loch Dunvegan. Free Wi-Fi & phone charging, plus tide-tables & wildlife sightings displayed. **£**

⛺ **Skye Camping & Caravanning Club Site** [54 C3] Edinbane IV51 9PS; **w** campingandcaravanningclub.co.uk; ⏱ Apr–Sep. Great spot on the banks of Loch Greshornish. Tents, motorhomes & caravans. Inexpensive yurt (sleeps 2 adults & 2 children) & pods (also sleeping 2 adults & 2 children) have no furnishings at all, but pods are right by the water. Both min 2-night stay. **£**

Weekly rental

🏠 **On the Croft** [54 C3] Nuig Hse, Upper Edinbane IV51 9PR; 📞 01470 582221; **w** edinbane-self-catering.co.uk. 2 cottages, Tigh Dubh (sleeps 4; ♿), a cosy converted blackhouse, & Merman Cottage (sleeps 4), a traditional stone house, are situated on a magical 12-acre croft. A peaceful, green location & in many ways like stepping back in time. Handmade wooden furniture, Edinbane Pottery & Skyeskyns throws inside. Helen also offers Shiatsu therapeutic massage or Reiki sessions in a bespoke pod on site (**w** stepsonthecroft.co.uk). £800/week.

3

🍴 **WHERE TO EAT AND DRINK** With the Inner Hebrides' only Michelin star and a number of other celebrated restaurants, foodies are truly spoilt for choice on this part of the island.

🍴 **Loch Bay** [54 B3] Stein IV55 8GA; 📞 01470 592235; **w** lochbay-restaurant.co.uk; ⏱ Mar–mid-Dec 17.30–20.45 Tue & Sat, 18.15–20.45 Wed–Fri, mid-Mar–Oct also 12.15–13.00 Wed–Fri. Michelin-starred restaurant in a traditional cottage in this charming harbour village, serving contemporary Scottish food with classic French influences. Choose the seafood tasting menu (eve only). **£££**

🍴 **Greshornish House** [54 C3] (see opposite) ⏱ noon–16.30 (afternoon tea) & 18.30–20.30. This historic manor house in a remote location serves a market menu, changing each day. Pretty restaurant with fairy lights for evening meals. Afternoon tea, served in a grand dining room or sunny conservatory, needs to be booked 24hrs ahead. **££**

🍴 **The Three Chimneys** [54 B4] Colbost IV55 8ZT; 📞 01470 511258; **w** threechimneys.co.uk; ⏱ lunch: Apr–Oct noon–13.45 daily, dinner: mid-Jan–mid-Dec 18.30–21.15 daily. Traditional whitewashed building with slate roof & expected number of chimneys. Iconic, top-end restaurant. Choose tasting menu or à la carte. Delicately balanced flavours, high-quality local ingredients, seasonal produce. **£££**

✕ Edinbane Inn [54 C3] (page 75) ⊕ Feb–Dec noon–14.00 & 17.00–21.00 daily. Busy bar & restaurant specialising in local seafood, including Skye mussels & squid. Homemade pies. Book ahead for restaurant. ££

⟱ Blas [54 B4] Dunvegan IV55 8WA; ☎01470 521841; w blas-skye.co.uk; ⊕ Apr–Oct 11.00–19.00 Mon–Fri, 09.00–19.00 Sat. Coffee, lunch & takeaways. Haddock & chips, cullen skink, soup & children's options. Homemade jam & chutney also on sale. £–££

⟱ Café Lephin [54 A4] Glendale IV55 8WJ; ☎01470 511465; w cafelephin.co.uk; ⊕ Mar–Oct around 11.00–17.00 Mon–Sat. Tea & coffee, light lunches, home-baking & local ale. £

ENTERTAINMENT AND NIGHTLIFE

Dark Sky w visit-waternish.co.uk/dark-skies-waternish. Waternish has been recognised as an exceptional place for stargazing; on a clear night, when the moon is not too bright, you can see the Milky Way & a number of other astronomical features that are often obscured by light pollution elsewhere.

Edinbane Inn [54 C3] (page 75) Hosts traditional Scottish music from 21.00 to 23.00 on Tue & Fri & a cèilidh 14.30–16.35 every Sun.

SHOPPING
Arts and crafts

Edinbane Pottery Edinbane IV51 9PW; ☎01470 582234; w edinbane-pottery.co.uk; ⊕ 09.00–18.00 daily. Working pottery selling thick crockery in lovely blues & terracotta shades. Dishwasher & microwave safe.

Gilleasbuig Ferguson Rare Books Tigh na Mara, Skeabost Bridge IV51 9NP; ☎01470 532808; w gilleasbuig.co.uk. Owner is a local history enthusiast & has been collecting rare Scottish books for 15 years.

Hebridean Alpaca Company 1 Lochside, Dunvegan IV55 8WB; ☎01470 52577; w hebridean-alpacas.co.uk; ⊕ Mar–Dec 11.00–16.00 Tue–Sat; ♿. Wool from their own alpacas, with photos of alpaca faces on labels. Clothes, scarves, hats, gloves & alpaca bedding. In addition to owning 18 alpacas they also import fair-trade wool.

Ian Williams Lan Mara, Skeabost Bridge IV51 9NP; ☎01470 5322401; ⊕ 11.00–16.00 Tue–Fri. Bright ceramics, paintings & visual poetry.

Raven Press Gallery Colbost IV55 8ZS; ☎01470 511748; ⊕ Easter–Oct 10.00–17.30 Tue–Sat. Incredibly detailed low-grain boxwood prints & other local artwork.

Sam Peare Textiles Loch View, Edinbane IV51 9PW; ☎01470 582247; w samanthapeare. co.uk; ⨎. Recycled vintage materials combined with embroidery into accessories & homewares inspired by the natural world. Check Facebook for opening times.

Skye Makers Gallery Dunvegan IV55 8WB; ☎01470 521666; w skyemakers.com; ⨎; ⊕ Feb–Dec 11.00–17.00 Tue–Sat. Changing exhibitions from local artists. Don't miss the downstairs gallery. They also organise workshops.

Skyeskyns, Yurt Tea & Coffee [54 B3] 17 Lochbay, Waternish IV55 8GD; ☎01470 592237; w skyeskyns.co.uk; ⊕ Apr–Oct 09.00–18.00 daily, Nov–Mar 09.30–17.30; ♿. Free guided tour (page 78; note no tours in final 45mins of opening). Showroom & shop with sheepskins, clothing & weaving. Proper coffee & homemade cake in on-site Yurt café £.

Skye Weavers [54 A4] 18 Fasach, Glendale IV55 8WP; ☎01470 511201; w skyeweavers. co.uk; ⊕ Apr–Oct 10.00–18.00 Tue–Sat. Bicycle-powered loom. Shop with woven accessories & soft furnishings.

Food shops

Fasgadh Stores Dunvegan IV55 8WA; ☎01470 521432; ⨎; ⊕ 09.00–19.00 Mon–Sat, 11.00–17.30 Sun; ♿. Basic grocery shop.

Fruit & Nut Place Dunvegan IV55 8WA; ⨎; ⊕ 10.30–18.00 Mon–Sat. Doesn't look like much from the outside, but this corrugated shed is packed with a great selection of loose, often local fruit & veg, plus eco-cleaning products, vegan ingredients & magazines.

Geary Crofts Produce Geary, Waternish IV55 8GQ. Eggs, cheese, baking & vegetables when available.

Glendale Croft Produce Milovaig IV55 8WR; ☎01470 511354; ⨎. Honesty box stall with seasonal produce & free-range eggs. Vegetables & salad picked to order when available.

Glendale Shop & Post Office 2 Lephin, Glendale IV55 8WJ; 01470 511266; w glendaleshop.co.uk; 10.00–18.00 Mon–Sat. Little shop with basic groceries.

Orbost Farm [54 B4] Orbost Farm, Dunvegan IV55 8ZB; 01470 521828. Lamb, mutton, pork, beef, wild venison, sausages & burgers. Phone ahead to check availability.

Outdoor gear

The Highland Ordnance Company Unit 4, Lochside, Dunvegan IV55 8WB; 01470 521535; Feb–Dec 10.30–15.30 Wed–Sat, longer hours in summer. Mr Kinnemond-Miller has been running this shop for 20 years, selling fishing gear, camping gas, binoculars, walking boots & socks. Good range of OS maps & some local guidebooks, but the 'ordnance' in the name actually refers to cannons – weapons are also for sale.

SPORTS AND ACTIVITIES

Divers Eye Stein IV55 8GD; 01470 592219; w divers-eye.co.uk. Various trips including wildlife watching, fishing, one-way drop-off to Waternish Point (hike back) & landing on uninhabited Isay Island where there is an abandoned settlement & huge numbers of birds.

Isle of Skye Trekking Centre [map, page 64] Croft 2, Suladale IV51 9PA; 01470 582419; w theisleofskyetrekkingcentre.co.uk. Family-friendly pony trekking across open moorland & through the hills. 1hr £30 pp.

OTHER PRACTICALITIES This remote corner of Skye is lacking in some of the amenities you might expect. For non-emergency medical necessities, you will have to head back to Portree.

Fuel Atholl Filling Station, Dunvegan IV55 8WA; 08.00–20.00 Mon–Sat, 10.00–17.00 Sun

Post Dunvegan IV55 8WA 01470 521201; 09.00–17.00 Mon–Tue & Thu–Fri, 09.00–13.00

Wed, 09.00–12.30 Sat); Edinbane, Community Hall, Old Post Office Row, IV51 9PW (13.00–15.00 Tue); Glendale Shop & Post Office (see above)

WHAT TO SEE AND DO For those coming from Portree, the A850, which runs west through the sleepy settlement of Skeabost Bridge, is the usual starting point for journeys into the Waternish and Duirinish peninsulas; aside from a couple of interesting shops (see opposite) and an excellent walk (see below), there's little to detain you here, and most visitors continue straight through to Edinbane or Dunvegan.

St Columba's Isle and Clach Ard

Distance: 1¼ miles; time: 1 hour; start/end: Prabost Junction (on the A850); OS Explorer map: 410 Skye – Portree & Bracadale

Steeped in the past and legends as far back as the Picts, this easy, short walk is a must for anyone interested in history or archaeology.

Heading west on the A850 from the direction of Portree, there is a small turning to the right marked to Peinmore, Tote and Prabost, which crosses a cattle grid. The number 56 bus also stops here (ask for Tote). Take the first left almost immediately after the cattle grid and follow the road until you reach Skeabost Bridge, which crosses the River Snizort. Just before is a small footpath to the right, which will take you to the small bridge across to St Columba's Isle (57°27'12"N 6°18'21"W).

On this small islet, at the point where the river joins the loch, is an ancient burial site and the late medieval foundations of Snizort Parish Church. It is thought to have served as a cathedral church of the Bishops of the Isles, with an even older building having once served the same purpose on this site. The Chapel or 'Teampall' of St Columba is further west, shrouded by a tree, but more complete; this building is thought to be from around the 11th to 13th centuries. According to folk history, 28 Nicolson chiefs are buried here; a 16th-century carved knight slab is the most impressive grave, but it's worth exploring the whole island to find others marked with a skull and crossbones.

To continue to the carved Pictish stone, Clach Ard (⊕ 57°27'30.5"N 6°18'05.5"W), return to the bridge the way you came, and then walk about 100yds east until you see an unmarked turning to the left.

Follow this road for about 270yds before taking a turning to the right, which will take you into the back of Peinmore; the road ends at a T-junction where you will find Clach Ard. Erected in its present position in 1880, having previously been used as a door jamb in a cottage at Tote, this 7th-century Pictish symbol stone is one of only a couple found on Skye and generally one of very few archaeological remnants of the Picts. The symbols have been identified as a crescent, V-rod and disc.

To return, head southeast (to your right if you are looking at Clach Ard) along the road and walk for about 400yds until you reach another T-junction. Here, turn right again and walk south for around 500yds to reach the starting point.

Edinbane and the Waternish Peninsula
The A850 now bypasses **Edinbane**, [54 C3] the biggest settlement along the first stretch of the road, though it is so small that it is easy to enter and leave without ever realising you've arrived. This was not always the case: in the 19th century, having made his fortune in India, Kenneth MacLeod of Greshornish and Gesto (a rival of the MacLeods of Dunvegan) founded Edinbane as a pioneering, self-sufficient model settlement with an inn, mill, school and a hospital, the first on Skye. However, as Portree grew during the 20th century and transport links improved, Edinbane's significance dwindled.

Around 4 miles further along the A850 is the turning for the **Waternish Peninsula** and, on the left a little further on, a car park for the **Fairy Bridge** (⊕ 57°28'12"N 6°32'30"W). This modest, flat-topped arch bridge is part of one of many traditions relating to the so-called Fairy Flag (page 81) at Dunvegan. In this tale, a chief of Clan MacLeod married a fairy, but she was forced to leave him after 20 years to return to fairyland; as she left across the Fairy Bridge she gave him the enchanted Fairy Flag as a parting gift.

Stein and around
[54 B3] Stein is Waternish's biggest village, but that isn't saying much. Three small and picturesque rows of white cottages stand overlooking Loch Bay and Beinn Bhreac across the water; a couple of majestic old boats rest by a small jetty and free-roaming chickens peck around the verges of the car park. Note that this is one of only a couple of places to park on Waternish.

Just north of Stein is **Skyeskyns** (page 76; ♿), where you can take a free guided tour of the tannery. Visitors are shown how sheep skins are fleshed on a traditional wooden beam before being paddled in a salty pickle and transferred to a tanning bath; later the leather is oiled, stretched, dried, buffed, trimmed, combed and ironed.

Dùn Hallin
[54 B3] A well-preserved Iron-Age broch, Dùn Hallin (⊕ 57°32'25"N 6°35'11"W) has magnificent views across to Isay Island and Duirinish. While many of Scotland's brochs are now little more than piles of rubble, Dùn Hallin is a perfect circle: 11 rows of large stone blocks have survived the last two millennia, giving us some indication of how the complete, taller structure must have once been

LADY GRANGE

In 1732, Rachel Chiesley (known as Lady Grange) was kidnapped by her MP husband, Lord Grange. His brother, John Erskine, had led the failed Jacobite rebellion of 1715 and Lord Grange himself was sympathetic to the Jacobite cause. After their marriage broke down due to his affairs, Lord Grange feared his wife would expose him. He took her to the Outer Hebrides and claimed that she had died; in fact, she had been left on St Kilda. Somehow managing to communicate with a cousin, she was moved again by Lord Grange – to Skye – before a chance of rescue and spent the final three years of her life on the island under the 'care' of Norman 22nd chief of Clan MacLeod. Here she was kept on Waternish Peninsula, usually in a local house, but possibly, under suspicion of her managing to send out another cry for help, for some time in a cave on Idrigil Point as well. She died in 1745 and her gravestone can be found at Trumpan Church; however, as it wasn't erected until 140 years after her death it is unlikely to mark the exact spot of her burial.

Far from being a damsel in distress, Rachel Chiesley appears to have been a fiery, determined and unpredictable character. She is portrayed intricately in Margaret Macaulay's book *The Prisoner of St Kilda: The True Story of the Unfortunate Lady Grange*.

assembled. It's possible for readers of this guide to park at Waternish Free Church in Hallin between Monday and Saturday in order to visit the broch, but please only do so if there are two or fewer cars in the car park already. A track (starting at ⊕ 57°32'23"N 6°35'58"W) runs to the right-hand side of the church (roughly east), past a telephone box and over a cattle grid; after about half a mile you should be able to see the broch standing on the hill.

Trumpan Church [54 B2] The main road up Waternish ends at Trumpan where the ruin of **Trumpan Church** stands quietly looking across to North Uist. The site of a 1578 massacre, it is a haunting place to visit. The MacDonalds set fire to Trumpan Church in 1578 as part of an ongoing feud (see box, page 119): it was full of Clan MacLeod worshippers at the time. According to folk history, one girl escaped and ran to Dunvegan Castle (she must have been very fit as it is 11 miles) and the heroic MacLeods hastened to Ardmore Bay with their charmed Fairy Flag (page 81) to destroy the invading force. This became known as the Battle of the Spoiling of the Dyke as the bodies were buried in a ditch. Trumpan Church is still roofless and missing large parts of its wall, with one arched doorway remaining. There are some late medieval carved slabs around the graveyard, the remains of a font and several interesting graves. A few yards southwest from the church is **Clach Deuchainn**. This is a prehistoric standing stone, also known as the Priest's or Heaven Stone. According to tradition, if an accused person can find the hole in it with their finger while blindfolded, they are innocent.

Waternish Point
Distance: 8½ miles; time: 3–5 hours; start/end: Trumpan car park; OS Explorer map: 407 Skye – Dunvegan/Dun Bheagan
The route to Waternish Point is a long coastal walk with incredible views, sprinkled with archaeology and with great wildlife-watching opportunities.

Walk back along the road from the car park, for around 500yds to where the road takes a sharp corner.

On your left here at the corner is a gate leading to a track that runs alongside a stone wall. Listen out for the croaking sound of corncrakes in summer as they thrive here. You can follow this track all the way to the end, but after around 2 miles be sure to look out for **Dùn Borrafiach** (✪ 57°34'43"N 6°37'35"W), a well-preserved Iron-Age broch that is around 400yds east of the path on your right-hand side; it is one of the best examples on Skye and well worth a detour.

Closer to the end of the track you will pass another broch, **Dùn Gearymore** (✪ 57°35'21"N 6°37'33"W); this is more severely robbed of stones, probably to build the more recent buildings around it, but retains enough detail that you can make out the gallery between its double walls.

Soon afterwards, the small, white **Waternish Lighthouse** that stands on **Waternish Point** comes into view and you can bear left off the track as it veers to the right near two posts, following a very faint path towards the gap in a dry-stone wall. Follow the coast along the clifftops to reach the lighthouse. Keep an eye out for sea eagles and great skuas in particular, but there are many seabirds here, plus a decent chance of spotting minke whales if the sea is calm.

It is possible to continue along the coastline here, though it becomes much more challenging and would require your own assessment. It's much easier to return the way you came.

Dunvegan

Dunvegan [54 B4] The village of Dunvegan is most famous for its castle, which bears the same name. The roofless, ruined parish church of **St Mary's**, 400yds east of the village centre, dates from the 18th century. Although St Clement's Church in Rodel on Harris was the main burial ground for the MacLeod chiefs, some are also buried here, in addition to many generations of MacCrimmons, who were hereditary pipers to Clan MacLeod. The most interesting late medieval carved grave slabs here are those near the spiked obelisk, with another example near the entry to the church.

Giant MacAskill Museum (41 Kilmuir Rd, Dunvegan; ☎ 01470 521296; w dunveganmuseums.co.uk/GiantMacAskill.html; ⊕ Easter–Oct 09.30–18.00 daily; adult/concession/child £2/1.50/free) Set in a traditional thatched cottage, this museum is dedicated to the eponymous Angus MacAskill (1825–63) who, at 7ft 8in (2.36m) still remains the tallest Scotsman to have ever lived. MacAskill was renowned for outrageous feats of strength; the small museum presents some of his achievements and includes a model of the man himself and replicas of his bed, table and a chair. Possibly most amazing is the size of his socks.

Dunvegan Castle (¾ mile north of Dunvegan village; ☎ 01470 521206; w dunvegancastle.com; ⊕ Apr–mid-Oct 10.00–17.30 Mon–Fri; adult/concession/child/family £14/11/9/34) This grand, largely 19th-century castle is built around the remains of a much older one, with elements from as early as the 13th century; the site itself is thought to have been fortified since prehistoric times. A naturally defensive position, above a wall of rock overlooking Loch Dunvegan, the present structure began with a curtain wall enclosing the promontory, parts of which can still be seen. It was originally accessed through the sea gate, which remained the only entrance until 1748 and is still an imposing sight today. The site was owned by Clan MacLeod for 750 years; the family's motto 'Hold Fast' certainly seems to have been successful with Dunvegan Castle.

DÙN FIADHAIRT

This peninsula takes its name from the Iron-Age broch in its centre, where you can still identify some of the intricacies of the construction, including the chambers between walls, steps and lintels. In the southeast you have unrivalled views across the water to Dunvegan Castle and the common seal colony living around the islets in between. In the west, the distinctive MacLeod's Tables on Duirinish Peninsula are visible on a clear day, and to the east, eagles can often be seen flying above the forest by Loch Suardal.

If you have a car, park just before the A863 crosses over the dam on Loch Suardal, 2 miles north of Dunvegan, being careful not to obstruct the gate. It's best to take the OS Explorer map (*407 Skye – Dunvegan/Dun Bheagan*) to help you to easily find your way on to Dùn Fiadhairt Peninsula.

In many ways more interesting than the castle itself are its contents, many of which have associated folk tales or history, including heirlooms such as Sir Rory Mor's drinking horn and the Fairy Flag, a tattered piece of silk, which is thought to have originally come from Asia and is associated with several myths and legends. Another interesting collection relates to the Jacobite rebellion, with a lock of Bonnie Prince Charlie's hair and objects belonging to Flora MacDonald (page 56) including her stays, a type of fully boned bodice worn as underwear.

Coral Beach [54 B3] The road north from Dunvegan leads, after about 4 miles, to the busy car park for one of Skye's most attractive stretches of sand, **Coral Beach**. From here it's a 1-mile walk to the beach; the route starts (and is signposted) from the western side of the car park and is easy to follow. The beach is formed from dead pieces of maerl, a coralline red algae, which dries out to be white and makes a striking sight in juxtaposition with the seaweedy black rocks along the route.

Duirinish Duirinish, dominated by MacLeods in all senses, is distinctive for the flat-topped mountains of Healabhal Mhòr and Healabhal Bheag, known as MacLeod's Tables. A folk story tells that when the chief wanted to impress a visitor he took them to dine on Healabhal Mor. For keen hikers there is a route and map on Walkhighlands (w walkhighlands.co.uk/skye/macleodstables.shtml).

Beyond the places listed below, further exploring in Duirinish should be done with the aid of an OS map and compass; the south is an uninhabited wilderness that only the most intrepid are most likely to explore.

Neist Point [54 A4] Neist Point must be one of the most photographed spots on Skye and is definitely the most famous lighthouse in the Inner Hebrides. In summer months drivers should expect to do plenty of reversing on the scenic but tiny single-track side road that leads here. The lighthouse itself is nothing more special than countless others in the region, but its westerly position, at the end of a steeply undulating path, gives the impression of a building at the edge of the world. If possible, visit in the shoulder seasons to avoid the worst of the crowds as, even in the evenings, the car park gets busy with campervans (whose drivers must be much braver than me).

Dùn Beag [54 C4] Though outside the Duirinish Peninsula, the Iron-Age broch of Dùn Beag (⊕ 57°21'37"N 6°25'33"W) can be easily visited en route to or from Minginish. Just 300yds away from the A863, on the eastern side of the road, this

excavated broch is one of the finest examples of its kind in the region. Originally from the late 1st millennium BC, it also shows signs of re-use in the early medieval period. The gallery, cell and stairway can still be seen between the inner and outer dry-stone walls.

MINGINISH AND THE CUILLIN HILLS

The mighty Cuillins, visible on the horizon from as far south as Mull and by far the most impressive mountain range in this region, dominate the landscape of Minginish Peninsula. Any serious hiking into the Cuillins will require research and preparation beyond the scope of this book, but for most people it will be enough just to be in their presence. Accessed down long, winding stretches of single-track road, Minginish also has a couple of Skye's finest sandy beaches and endless lengths of dramatic coastline. While most residents are employed in modern occupations, crofting is still an integral part of society here; the majority of people live in the few small settlements that run along the south coast of Loch Harport.

GETTING AROUND   A lack of public transport means that Minginish is difficult to access without a car or bicycle. Roads are single track and winding, so journey times can take longer than anticipated.

By bus   A MacDonald (page 57) run between Portree and Fiskavaig once a day from Monday to Saturday.

By taxi   Carbost Cars (m 07342 006644; w carbostcars.business.site) also offers island tours and airport transfers, in addition to regular taxi services.

 WHERE TO STAY   Minginish is the best place on Skye to find budget accommodation, which helps make it a great destination for hikers and people who love the outdoors. While Glenbrittle is positioned among the Cuillins, staying somewhere along the road that leads out to Portnalong maintains a good balance between a dramatic backdrop and some of the comforts of civilisation.

Sligachan Hotel   [55 D5] (22 rooms) Sligachan IV47 8SW; 01478 650204; w sligachan.co.uk; **Bunkhouse** (20 beds) & **Self catering** (3 properties) 01478 650458; w sligachanselfcatering.com; **Caravan Park & Camping** m 07786 435294; Apr–Oct. Though these pose as separate businesses, they are all owned by the same family & within walking distance of each other. The setting would be idyllic if it wasn't on the edge of a busy road; the Cuillins make a spectacular backdrop & there's a river tumbling down into Loch Sligachan. The whole place is understandably busy with hikers & holidaymakers as it is the perfect spot from which to start exploring the Cuillins. Hotel **££££**; self-catering £1,800/week; bunkhouse & camping **£**

Taigh Ailean Hotel   [55 C5] (5 rooms) Portnalong IV47 8SL; 01478 640271;

w taighailean.scot. Owners Johnny & Katie, originally from England, are a welcoming couple, involved with the local community. All rooms are clean & comfortably furnished. Comfortable guest lounge with open fire, books & games. Min 2-night stay. Dogs welcome. **£££**

The Old Inn Lodge & Waterfront Bunkhouse   [55 C5] (5 rooms & 24 beds in bunkhouse) Carbost IV47 8SR; 01478 640205; w theoldinnskye.co.uk; . Lodge has pleasant en-suite private rooms on B&B basis. Simple bunkhouse with great views across the loch & good kitchen facilities. **£–£££**

Croft Bunkhouse   [55 C5] (bunkhouse sleeps 14, self catering sleeps 16) Portnalong IV47 8SL; m 07834 827524; w skyehostels. com. A variety of friendly hostel accommodation: bunkhouse, self-contained family units, twin rooms & heated wooden wigwams. Situated on peaceful croft beside Loch Harport. **£**

🏠 **Glenbrittle YHA** [55 C6] (25 beds) Glenbrittle IV47 8TA; 📞01478 640278; **w** hostellingscotland.org.uk/hostels/glenbrittle; 🕐 Apr–Sep. Basic hostel, great base for walking. Kitchen, USB charging points, bike shed, drying room, laundry, limited shop & alcohol sold. No Wi-Fi. Call ahead out of high season. **£**

⛺ **Glenbrittle Camping** [55 C6] Glenbrittle IV55 8WF; 📞01478 640404; **w** dunvegancastle.com/glenbrittle/campsite; 🕐 Apr–Sep; ♿.

WHERE TO EAT AND DRINK

✖ **The Old Inn** [55 C5] (see opposite) Carbost IV47 8SR; 📞01478 640205; **w** theoldinnskye.co.uk; 🕐 Easter–Oct 07.45–09.30 & noon–21.00 daily, Nov–Easter 07.45–09.30, noon–15.00 & 17.00–21.00 daily; ♿. Old-fashioned pub with friendly staff serving decent food (inc b/fast); open fire in winter. Favourite with locals. Dog friendly. Traditional live music from 21.00 Thu & Fri all year round. **££**

✖ **Taigh Ailean Hotel** [55 C5] (see opposite) 🕐 Apr–Oct 18.00–21.00 daily, Nov–Mar 18.00–21.00 Sat & Sun. Hearty Scottish food with an emphasis on local produce. Unusual additions such as vegan haggis. Casual bar upstairs with pool table & restaurant downstairs (also relaxed).

SHOPPING
Arts and crafts
Cath Waters Gallery & Shop [55 C5] Allt Mòr, Carbostbeg, Carbost IV47 8SH; **w** cathwaters.scot; 🕐 10.00–16.00 Mon–Sat (flexible). Digital collage, Scottish landscape & textures. Artwork along with cushions, mugs, etc. Cath used to be a biologist, but found a successful change of direction during maternity leave.
On The Croft 7 Fernilea, Carbost IV47 8SJ; 🕐 10.00–17.00 daily; ♿. Woollen jumpers, ponchos & wool. Following a long history of Minginish weaving, Sally learnt how to spin as a way of using the wool shorn off her 10 Jacob's sheep. Also hand dyed. Husband Ray hand-turns wood.

ACTIVITIES
Sea Skye Marine 📱 07789 914144; **w** seaskye.com. Trips out to Neist Point, Loch Bracadale & MacLeod's Maidens: the last being 210ft sea stacks,

Spectacularly placed campsite right on the beach & surrounded by the Cuillins. **£**

Weekly rental
🏠 **Heatherbell** [55 C5] (sleeps 6) Carbost IV47 8SU; 📞01478 640324; **w** isle-of-skye-holiday-cottages.co.uk. Le Creuset pots & pans, heavenly showers & huge brown leather sofas, this is luxurious self-catering. There's an incredible view across Loch Harport & the Cuillins & the house has absolutely everything you need, including an excellent range of Skye- & Hebridean-themed books, some of which are reasonably academic. £1,145/week.

Scottish gins & whiskies, own real ale 'Gillean'. Building has a slightly confusing layout & resident long-haired sausage dog. **££**

☕ **Caora Dhubh Coffee Company** [55 C5] Carbost IV47 8SR; **w** www.caoradhubh.com; 🕐 10.00–17.00 daily; ♿. A small takeaway café, Caora Dhubh is one of only 2 coffee shops on Skye featured in the *Scottish Independent Coffee Guide*. Artisan craft roasters from Scotland & a small selection of tasty baked goods. The Janszoon V2.0 Blend 'shows the milk who's boss'. **£**

☕ **Glenbrittle Camping** [55 C5] (see above) 🕐 Apr–Sep 08.00–20.00 daily. Cakes & a specific blend of coffee, which they visit the growers to choose. **£**

Food shops
The Oyster Shed Carbost IV47 8SE; 📱 07746 935348; **w** theoysterman.co.uk; 🕐 11.00–17.00 Mon–Sat. Not exactly a farm shop as advertised, but does sell a wider range of groceries & seafood than anywhere else in Carbost. ATM.
Sconser Scallops Sconser IV48 8TD; 📞01478 650304; **w** sconserscallops.co.uk. Fresh scallops. Call to order 24hrs in advance.
The Stop Shop Carbost IV47 8SR; 🕐 09.00–17.45 Mon–Fri, 09.00–21.00 Sat & Sun. Very limited groceries; only bare essentials.

home to many seabirds. Also whole-day Harris Distillery & Shiant Isles puffin tour. All great for wildlife.

OTHER PRACTICALITIES

⊞ Medical Carbost Medical Practice, Carbost IV47 8SR; ☎ 01478 640202

⊠ Post Carbost IV47 8SR (🕒 08.30–12.30 Mon–Fri); Sconser Lodge Hotel, Sconser IV48 8TD (🕒 10.00–noon Mon)

WHAT TO SEE AND DO If Minginish has a hub, it is undoubtedly **Carbost** [55 C5]. A loosely arranged string of pretty, white buildings, the small village is nestled on the bank of Loch Harport, surrounded by mountainous scenery in all directions.

Talisker Distillery (Carbost IV47 8SR; ☎ 01478 614308; w malts.com; 🕒 Mar–Oct 09.30–17.00 Mon–Sat, 10.00–17.00 Sun, Nov–Feb 10.00–16.30 Mon–Sat, 10.30–16.30 Sun; tours & tastings £10–45; ♿) Founded in the early 19th century, Skye's oldest distillery hosts various tours where you can learn about the traditional whisky-making process and take a look at their enormous copper pot stills, traditional worm tub and casks. Tastings include an option with locally handmade chocolates.

Talisker Bay A long minor road leads from Carbost to Talisker Bay, a spectacular beach. To get there, it's a 1-mile walk from the end of the road; you can park at the side of the road before the sign that says 'Talisker House, Private Road, No Cars' sign. Follow the arrow that points 'to the beach', along the track to the left. Keep to the right, on the lower ground, when you reach the fork in the track (after a cattle grid). You'll pass Talisker House and shortly afterwards the wonderful rocky and sandy beach, with a slender waterfall on the right-hand side and a towering rock stack on the left; it makes a delightful spot for a picnic.

Fairy Pools and Glenbrittle The main reason most people drive down towards Glenbrittle is to visit the **Fairy Pools** [55 C6] (£5 parking). Unfortunately, as beautiful as they once were, their accessibility has now got the better of them. The attraction here is the carved rock pools, formed over many years by the course of the river, but the fluorescent colours you are likely to see on Instagram are edited. I'm including them because not to would be too obvious an omission, but the paths have now been trampled and eroded by thousands of feet and the banks have turned into a mud pit; there are plenty more magical places to discover on Skye. If your curiosity gets the better of you, please keep to paths and bear in mind that the money from the parking charge is used for conservation by the Outdoor Access Trust. Personally, I'd recommend you keep going down the road to visit Glenbrittle instead, where there is a wide, grey sandy beach at the head of Loch Brittle, and a large campsite.

Rubh' an Dunain [55 C7] The coast path leading southwest from Glenbrittle ends at Rubh' an Dunain, a headland of great archaeological importance. Around Loch na h-Airde, which nearly separates the final lump of land from Skye, there is an incredible example of a **Neolithic chambered cairn** to the north (⊕ 57°09'50"N 6°18'46"W); a **potential Viking port** (⊕ 57°09'40"N 6°18'33"W; page 53), an **Iron-Age promontory fort** (⊕ 57°09'38"N 6°18'31"W) and a small **ruined settlement**, which was still home to the MacAskills of Rubh' an Dunain in the 1860s, to the south.

It would be best to use a map (OS Explorer 411 *Skye – Cuillin Hills*) to explore here, or you can use the route described on Walkhighlands (w walkhighlands. co.uk/skye/rubhandunain.shtml).

Coire Lagan

Distance: 6 miles; time: 4 hours; start/end: Glenbrittle campsite; OS Explorer map: 411 Skye – Cuillin Hills

Taking you right up into the Black Cuillins, this hike has an ascent of 1,935ft, with an element of challenge and spectacular views, though it keeps to a relatively simple and not particularly dangerous route. It is suitable for those who are quite fit and have some hiking experience. Though there is an excellent path for the majority of the walk, the final stages require some clambering; you will need to use your hands at certain points, but only for balance rather than to pull up your own weight. Make sure to check the weather forecast before you set out, and that are you are appropriately equipped for a moderate walk (page 34). This description only applies to late spring, summer and early autumn conditions, when winter hiking equipment should not be needed.

A solidly built stone path begins from behind the Glenbrittle campsite toilet block. Take the path west uphill ignoring the coast path that leads off to the right. Assuming visibility is good, you should be able to guess the location of the corrie from fairly early on in the walk; it is directly below the spikiest summits in view, Sgurr Mhic Choinnich.

Ignore a second turning and keep to the left fork heading directly up the hill. Look out for red deer on your way up, and on a clear day you should be able to see Rùm and Canna. Keep on the most obvious path until you reach two large cairns.

From here the path gets smaller and splits at times until you reach an area of solid rock and slight waterfalls. Earlier in the season, when water levels are higher, you should stay to the left of the main stream and take some time finding the easiest route up. You will have to use your hands to help you.

Shortly after the trickiest part, you find yourself in the bowl of Coire Lagan as a small but beautiful loch comes into sight. The Munros Sgùrr Dearg, Sgùrr Mhic Choinnich and Sgùrr Alasdair surround you from right to left.

Once you've had your fill of the view, descend carefully to the double cairns. From here there's an optional detour of just over a mile: take the turning to the right, which leads you past Loch an Fhir-Bhallaich and close to a slender but towering waterfall. The path is quite easy to follow and eventually leads you down to the road at Glenbrittle. Follow the road back around to the car park. Alternatively, you can retrace your steps down the path.

BROADFORD AND ELGOL

Down-to-earth Broadford may not be the prettiest place on Skye, but it's is a busy little town with a thriving community and a good range of amenities and places to eat. By contrast, Elgol is a stunning village with unbeatable views across Loch Scavaig to the Cuillins, though it has very few amenities.

GETTING AROUND Broadford is easily accessible on a number of **bus routes** (page 57) and Elgol is served by a Stagecoach service (page 28), but you will have to plan your trip carefully around the times. If you are **driving** down to Elgol, be sure to allow plenty of time as it is a popular place to take boat trips from and even the large car park often doesn't have enough space for the number of visitors.

WHERE TO STAY *Map, page 90, unless otherwise stated*

🏠 **Coruisk House** [55 E7] (4 rooms, 2 suites) Elgol IV49 9BL; 📞 01471 866330; w coruiskhouse. com. Simple but elegantly decorated accommodation with a minimal colour scheme.

Occasional antiques hint at the building's 300-year history: an original bath in the Upper Steadings suite or a carefully placed antique chair in a bedroom. Accommodation, like the food, is quiet & intimate. Prosecco is provided on arrival with a recommendation, in good weather, to take it down to the beach for sunset. Evenings are peaceful. Excellent b/fasts including a delicious homemade granola. **££££**

🏠 **Suilven B&B** [55 E7] (1 room, 1 pod) Elgol IV49 9BL; ☎01471 866379; w elgolbedandbreakfast.wordpress.com. See ad, page 95. Run by part-time nurses Donald & Eileen, both originally from the Hebrides. Dbl has unattached private bathroom. Also a cosy wooden pod with own small bathroom & kitchenette. Views of Eigg & Rùm from pod & b/fast room. Brand-new bistro opening soon. **£££**

✳ 🏠 **Otter Lodge** (6 rooms) Harrapool, Broadford IV49 9AQ; ☎01471 822954; w otterlodgeskye.co.uk. See ad, page 95. Owned & run by outdoor enthusiasts Vanessa & Martin, this relaxed B&B is a perfect choice for hikers, kayakers or climbers who want something more spacious & comfortable than a hostel. Martin used to run the bakery in Bowmore on Islay & bakes sourdough bread for b/fast. Bedrooms are spacious with views out towards to sea or the wildflower meadow behind. Most have shared bathrooms. Practical guest lounge with fridge, microwave, fair-trade coffee & plenty of OS maps. Large drying room for kit. **££**

🏠 **Broadford Backpackers** (40 beds) High Rd, Broadford IV49 9AA; ☎01471 820333; w broadfordbackpackers.blogspot.com. Bit of an odd place, as it shares the building with a funeral director. Colourful rooms & décor, if a bit dark in corridors. Small lounge with sofas & DVD player. Generally a little run down but the cheapest option in Broadford. Some private rooms. **£**

🏠 **Skye Basecamp** (36 beds) Lime Park, Broadford IV49 9AE; ☎01471 820044; w skyebasecamp.co.uk; ♿ call ahead. Pleasant dorm rooms with good facilities including large kitchen, communal lounge, pool table, drying room for kit & laundry. **£**

⚑ **Camping Skye** Pairc nan Craobh, Broadford IV49 9DF; ☎01471 550420; w campingskye. com; 🕐 mid-Mar–early Nov & Christmas; ♿. This excellent not-for-profit, community-owned campsite has an unpromising location, with an unappealing entry opposite a builders' merchant on the northern outskirts of Broadford. Once on the site, however, it is quiet & secluded from the rest of town with a green forest backdrop & extensive grounds. The reception (🕐 16.00–21.00) is staffed by knowledgeable locals who can advise motorhome & caravan drivers on which roads might be suitable for them to drive. New & comprehensive facilities; free Wi-Fi. Call to check availability. **£**

✗ **WHERE TO EAT AND DRINK** *Map, page 90, unless otherwise stated*

✗ **Coruisk House** [55 E7] (page 85) 🕐 Mar–Oct 19.00–21.00. Carefully crafted dishes made with local, seasonal produce. Langoustines, lobsters & squat lobsters are creel-caught nearby; rope-grown mussels from Sleat; hand-dived scallops from off Sconser; & wild venison from MacLeod's Tables. They grow their own edible flowers & are starting to grow salad. Wine list compiled after the owners visited vineyards in France & Italy. Reservations required. **£££**

✗ **The Claymore** Broadford IV49 9AQ; ☎01471 822333; 🇫; 🕐 May–Oct 16.00–21.00. Relaxed, family restaurant specialising in seafood. **££–£££**

✳ ✗ **Café Sia** Ford Rd, Broadford IV49 9AB; ☎01471 822616; w cafesia.co.uk; 🕐 summer: restaurant 09.30– 21.30 (takeaway from 08.00) daily, winter: 10.00–20.30 daily; Jan closed 2–3 weeks. Wood-fired pizzas, mouth-watering courgette fries, real fruit smoothies, haggis/vegetarian haggis & melted cheese on toasted ciabatta, vegan cheese & gluten-free options. Sit-in or takeaway (from Siaway, round the corner). Gets very busy; evening bookings recommended. **£–££**

🍴 **Deli Gasta** The Old Mill, Harrapool, Broadford IV49 9AQ; ☎01471 822646; w deligasta. co.uk; 🕐 08.30–17.00 daily. Fresh salad, baked goods & deli sandwiches, plus proper coffee. Sit inside or takeaway. **£**

🍴 **Elgol Shop** [55 D7] Elgol IV49 9BL; ☎01471 866329; 🇫; 🕐 summer: 10.00–17.00 Mon–Sat, winter: 11.00–15.00. A small blue trailer serving coffee, soup, seafood, ice cream & home-baking. **£**

SHOPPING
Arts and crafts
The Handspinner Having Fun [map, page 90] Old Pier Rd, Broadford IV49 9AE; 📞01471 822876; w handspinnerhavingfun.com; ⊕ 09.30–17.30 Mon–Sat. Shop selling yarn & hand-knitted garments. Also runs workshops.

Ragtag [map, page 90] Unit 3 Pairc nan Craobh, Broadford IV49 9AP; 📞01471 822043; w ragtagskye. org; 📘 Rag Tag n Textile; ⊕ 11.00–15.00 Mon–Fri. Secondhand shop, handmade upcycled gifts, knitted accessories & toys. Also hosts affordable creative workshops & courses open to all. Local social enterprise focusing on mental health & environment.

Food shops
Co-op [map, page 90] Main St, Broadford IV49 9AE; 📞01471 822649; ⊕ 07.00–22.00 daily; ♿. Large grocery store with bakery. Fuel & banking facilities.

Mrs Mack's Farmshop 12 Torrin, IV49 9BA; m 07881 664009; 📘; ⊕ Feb–Dec 10.00–14.00 Tue–Sat. Tiny cabin well off the road, selling own beef (Highland & shorthorn) & small selection of local goods. Also coffee, filled rolls, fresh sandwiches, homemade cakes & ice cream. Run by Mrs Mack, the wife of the farmer. Outdoor seating with rural views.

ACTIVITIES
Misty Isle Boat Trip Elgol IV49 9BL; 📞01471 866288; w mistyisleboattrips.co.uk. Trips out to Loch Coruisk, a magical place surrounded by the Cuillins (one-way option for hikers). Also excursions out to the Small Isles & wildlife-watching trips with puffins (May–Jul) & seals. Possibility of seeing dolphins, basking sharks & minke whale.

Skye Guides (page 58) Mountaineering.

OTHER PRACTICALITIES
✚ **Hospital** Dr MacKinnon Memorial Hospital, High Rd, Broadford IV49 9AA; 📞01471 822491
Library Ford Rd, Broadford IV49 9AB; 📞01349 781230; w highlifehighland.com/libraries/broadford-library; ⊕ 10.30–14.00 & 15.00–17.00 Tue–Fri

✚ **Medical centre** Broadford Medical Centre, High Rd, Broadford IV49 9AA; 📞01471 822460
✚ **Pharmacy** Ford Rd, Broadford IV49 9AB; 📞01471 822235
✉ **Post office** Ford Rd, Broadford IV49 9AB; 📞01471 822201; ⊕ 08.00–18.00 Mon–Sat, 09.00–17.00 Sun

WHAT TO SEE AND DO While **Broadford** makes a good base for exploring further afield, there is little to detain you in the town itself.

Around Broadford About 1 mile east of Broadford, **Waterloo Beach** is a peaceful stretch of sand and seaweed with views out to the tiny uninhabited island of Pabay and the mainland beyond. To get there, follow a side road marked to Waterloo from just east of Broadford.

An easy, waymarked 8-mile walk (♿) starts near the filling station in the centre of Broadford and follows the old **marble railway line**, which until 1912 carried marble from the mines to Broadford Pier. It gives good views of the surrounding hills without climbing any elevation. The route is described on Walkhighlands with a map (w walkhighlands.co.uk/skye/marble-line.shtml); it can be extended significantly to visit the coastal villages of **Suisnish** (⊕ 57°10'20"N 5°59'14"W) and **Boreraig** (⊕ 57°10'35"N 5°56'27"W), to the south, which were both cleared in 1853. The extended route will also take you past several waterfalls and give you stunning views over Loch Slapin and to Blà Bheinn. Navigating is simple with a good map and compass, or you can follow the route suggested by Walkhighlands (w walkhighlands.co.uk/skye/boreraigsuisnish.shtml).

Elgol and around [55 E7] The few loosely sprinkled houses that make up Elgol cling to green fields above the cliffs around Port Na Cullaidh. With a spectacular

Prince Charlie's Cave is actually one of 13 such-named caves in Scotland, according to Tony Oldham's book *The New Caves of Scotland*; the legend goes that Bonnie Prince Charlie spent his last night here before escaping to Mallaig on the mainland. Situated on the coast south of Elgol, it would certainly have been a remote spot to reach overland in those days.

The coast path, which starts as gravel before being reduced to mud and glass, leaves from the upper of Elgol's twin car parks near the pier and heads southwest. Follow the path south around the clifftops for about 1½ miles until you reach Port an Luig Mhòir: a wide, rocky and pebbly beach with an easy route down to it. From here, to reach the cave, you need to turn right and walk west around the small, protruding headland made of wide, flat rocks. There are several caves and tunnels in this area, but Prince Charlie's Cave (✪ 57°08′06″N 6°06′21″W) is around 200yds from the small headland. About 10ft above the level of the beach, in a dark crack, with some boulders lodged in the base of the entrance and a patch of grass growing on the left, it is not particularly obvious from ground level and requires a short scramble, using your hands, to get inside. The space is deeper than it first appears. You will need a good torch.

view across Loch Scavaig to the Cuillins and the small island of Soay, there's no doubt that this is an extremely picturesque corner of Skye. Most people come and go in one day, simply arriving and leaving for a boat trip straight away, but there is plenty more to explore on foot.

Dùn Grugaig The ruins of the prehistoric fort Dùn Grugaig (✪ 57°08′07″N 6°04′30″W), are thought to date from the 7th or 6th centuries BC. Hidden from view by trees, the ruins can be found towards the southern end of Glasnakille. If you have a car, park it opposite the khaki green barn and walk 10yds further south down the road before taking a turning to the left, just before the corner of the fence. A faint, thin dirt path then leads downhill through the trees. Before long, you will reach a grassy promontory and the remains of the fort. Be very careful of the cliffs here.

SLEAT, KYLEAKIN AND THE SOUTHEAST

Sleat Peninsula in the far south and Skye's southeastern elbow are the only entry points from the mainland. While those travelling over the bridge will arrive in the village of Kyleakin, the majority of those coming over on a ferry will arrive in Armadale on Sleat. Often overlooked, Sleat has some beautiful scenery and peaceful beaches. There are no fewer than four substantial castle ruins in the area and several splendidly positioned lighthouses. This is a unique and picturesque part of Skye to visit, easily overlooked on the charge further north.

GETTING AROUND While Sleat's only bus routes run along the main A851 road from Armadale, and there are not many pathways for exploring on foot, this is a perfect peninsula to discover by bicycle.

By bus Stagecoach (page 28) runs services from Armadale to Broadford, Portree and Kyle of Lochalsh.

Car hire and taxis

🚗 **Drive Skye** Armadale; 📞01471 844361; w driveskye.com

🚗 **James' Taxi & Tours** Sleat; m 07894 442209; w skye-bus-tours.com

Bike hire

🚲 **South Skye Cycles** (page 57) Can deliver to Armadale, Broadford, Kyle of Lochalsh, or anywhere in-between; enquire for deliveries further afield.

WHERE TO STAY *Map, page 90*

🏠 **Kinloch Lodge** (19 rooms) Kinloch IV43 8QY; 📞01471 833333; w kinloch-lodge.co.uk. A 17th-century building in a beautiful lochside location; manicured lawns & grove of trees. Ornate antique furnishings, comfortable chairs & open fire in shared spaces. Large, luxuriously decorated bedrooms with great views. Optional spa packages. **£££££**

🏠 **Thistles B&B** (2 rooms) 34 Camuscross, Isleornsay IV43 8QS; 📞01471 833280; w thistlesonskye.co.uk; ⊕ Easter–Oct. Large, luxury rooms with French doors & Juliet balconies looking over the Sound of Sleat. Tastefully decorated with personal touches, Skye Skins rugs & tweed furnishings. Guests are greeted with a small bottle of local whisky. **£££££**

🏠 **The Inn @ Àird a Bhàsair** (10 rooms) Ardvasar IV45 8RS; 📞01471 844223; w the-inn-at-aird-a-bhasair.com. Sea or woodland views. Friendly staff, clean & comfortable. **££££**

🏠 **White Heather Hotel** (7 rooms) The Harbour, Kyleakin IV41 8PL; 📞01599 534577; w whiteheatherhotel.co.uk; ⊕ Apr–Oct. A large B&B rather than a hotel. Decoration is a bit dated, but good facilities & views across harbour to Castle Maol. Free to use washer/dryer, small fridge & freezer, plus small guest study with computer. **£££**

SPAR CAVE

The walk to Spar Cave can only be done at low tide (page 27). Entering into the upper parts of the cave involves a scramble up some easily gripped but very steep rocks, so take care. You should bring at least one strong torch per person and be very aware of the incoming tide.

From the T-junction as you enter Glasnakille, head right and then take a left through the gate into a field, walking next to some ruins on your left. Follow the faint path that leads towards the sea and down a slope. At the bottom of the slope there is a path to your left, which you should follow for 50yds before taking the path to your right. After 100yds you will come to a steep path that takes you through a crevice down to the shoreline. Walk out towards the sea and clamber over the rocks, following the coastline with the sea on your right. Pass one inlet and then continue until you get to a larger gorge with vertical rock walls, which leads into the cave. The route up the gorge towards the cave is tidal and it is slippery to clamber over the rocks and seaweed.

There is a small dry-stone wall at the entrance to the cave and two possible tunnels: choose the one on the left and follow the passage as it gradually begins to open out. After about 12yds, the walls and floor become covered by white calcium carbonate (spar) and a steep section leads up to a plateau. Standing in this part of the cave, you are surrounded by glistening, cascading formations known as flowstone; water flows down the steeper sections forming clear pools of water at your feet. Popular with visitors since Victorian times, it's an eerie, otherworldly place. Even without the incoming tide, there is a distinct feeling that you should not stay too long.

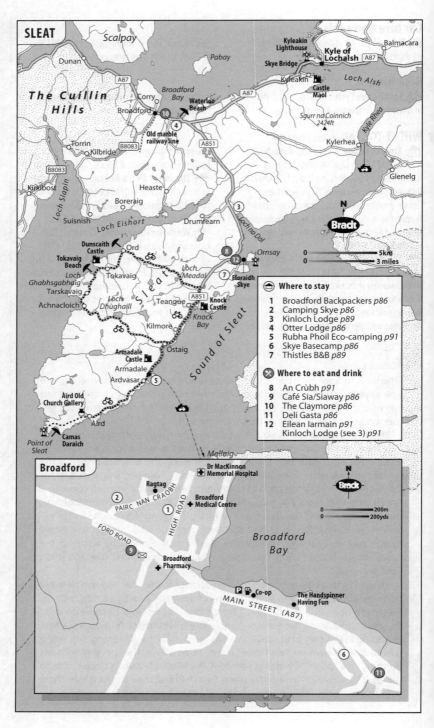

SLEAT

Scalpay

Dunan

Pabay

The Cuillin Hills

A87

Corry

Broadford Bay

Broadford **10**

Waterloo Beach

4

Old marble railway line

Torrin

Kilbride

B8083

A851

Heaste

Kirkibost

Boreraig

Loch Eishort

B8083

Suisnish

Drumfearn

Loch Slapin

Dunscaith Castle

Ord

3

Loch na Dal

8

Ornsay

12

Tokavaig Beach

7 **Eloraidh Skye**

Loch Ghabhsgabhaig

Tokavaig

S l e a t

Loch Meadal

Tarskavaig

Loch Dhughaill

Teangue

A851

Achnacloich

Kilmore

Knock Castle

Knock Bay

Armadale Castle

Ostaig

Armadale

Ardvasar

5

Sound of Sleat

Aird Old Church Gallery

Aird

Point of Sleat

Camas Daraich

Mallaig

Kyleakin Lighthouse

Skye Bridge

Kyle of Lochalsh

Balmacara

A87

Kyleakin

Loch Alsh

Castle Maol

Sgurr na Coinnich 2424ft ▲

Kylerhea

Kyle Rhea

Glenelg

N

Bradt

| 0 | | 5km |
| 0 | | 3 miles |

🛏 Where to stay
1 Broadford Backpackers *p86*
2 Camping Skye *p86*
3 Kinloch Lodge *p89*
4 Otter Lodge *p86*
5 Rubha Phoil Eco-camping *p91*
6 Skye Basecamp *p86*
7 Thistles B&B *p89*

✖ Where to eat and drink
8 An Crùbh *p91*
9 Café Sia/Siaway *p86*
10 The Claymore *p86*
11 Deli Gasta *p86*
12 Eilean Iarmain *p91*
    Kinloch Lodge (see 3) *p91*

Broadford

Dr MacKinnon Memorial Hospital ✚

Ragtag ●

2 PAIRC NAN CRAOBH

1

HIGH ROAD

Broadford Medical Centre ✚

FORD ROAD

9 ✉

Broadford Pharmacy ✚

Broadford Bay

N

Bradt

| 0 | | 200m |
| 0 | | 200yds |

🅿 🛒 Co-op

The Handspinner Having Fun

MAIN STREET (A87)

6

11

🏠 **Homeleigh B&B** (3 rooms) Ardvasar IV45 8RU; ☎ 01471 844752; w homeleigh-skye.co.uk. Comfortable, well-run B&B, with sea views from all rooms. £££

🏠 **Skye Backpackers** (53 beds) Kyleakin IV41 8PH; ☎ 01599 534510; w skyebackpackers. com. Colourful, cheap & cheerful with quite a lot of beds for the size of the kitchen. Wellie rental available. £

🏕 **Rubha Phoil Eco-camping** (12 pitches) Armadale Pier, Ardvasar; m 07393 830403; w earth-ways.co.uk. Basic, small-scale, environmentally friendly tent-only campsite on a quiet peninsula with choice of forest or sea-view pitches. Run by a nature-based community that aims to inspire people to live from the land using permaculture, enhance the ecosystem & reduce human impact. Surrounding wildlife includes seals, otters & an abundance of birds. Compost toilets, hot showers & no electricity. Slow travellers staying 2-nights min who travel without flying preferred. No drones, dogs, hen or stag parties. £

Weekly rental

☀ 🏠 **Shore Cottage** (sleeps 5–9) Ord, Sleat; ☎ 01360 622680 (no Sun calls); w cottageguide. co.uk/shorecottage. Characterful extended croft house with wonderful games room & large bay window overlooking the loch to the Cuillins beyond. Beautiful, peaceful location. Great for 1 large family or 2 smaller ones. £825/week.

WHERE TO EAT AND DRINK *Map, opposite*

🍴 **Hotel Eilean Iarmain** IV43 8QR; ☎ 01471 833332; w eileaniarmain.co.uk; ⏰ noon–14.30 & 18.00–20.45 daily. Delicate fine dining & heartier bar meals in a beautiful location looking out over Sound of Sleat & Knoydart. The feeling of a traditional country house. £££

🍴 **Kinloch Lodge** (page 89) ⏰ 12.30–16.30 & 18.30–21.00 daily. An institution. Acclaimed Scottish food by renowned Brazilian-born chef Marcello Tully; lunch, afternoon tea & dinner. Held a Michelin Star for a long time. Cooking workshops often held. £££

🍴 **The Inn @ Àird a Bhàsair** (page 89) ⏰ noon–15.00 & 17.00–21.00 daily. Friendly staff, & choice of whiskies from local distillery. Small pub to one side is a favourite with locals. Pool room behind with 2 tables. Also does takeaway. ££

🍴 **Skye Bridge Seafoods** The Old Filling Station, Kyleakin IV41 8PQ; m 07766 529907; f; ⏰ 10.00–20.00 daily. Fish & chip shop in small white cabin just outside Kyleakin; run by friendly local Arnie. Tasty, & you can be assured the fish is fresh & less oily than some other Skye offerings. No indoor seating. £

☕ **An Crùbh** Duisdale Beag, Sleat IV43 8QU; ☎ 01471 833417; w ancrubh.com; ⏰ summer: 10.00–16.30 daily; takeaway: 16.30–19.30 Fri–Sat, winter: 10.00–16.30 Thu–Sun; ♿. 'The hub' in Gaelic. Community enterprise in modern building of glass, wood & stone, in an isolated spot. Café is a light, open space with big windows to see the hills. Good coffee, cakes, soup & mains such as burgers. Also hosts exhibitions, concerts, cèilidhs & yoga sessions. £–££

ENTERTAINMENT AND NIGHTLIFE Seall (w seall.co.uk) has up-to-date listings for concerts, cèilidhs, performances and other events around Sleat.

SHOPPING
Arts and crafts

Àird Old Church Gallery Àird of Sleat, Ardvasar IV45 8RN; ☎ 01471 844362; w airdoldchurchgallery.org. Atmospheric watercolour landscapes by Peter McDermott & contemporary jewellery by Heather McDermott.

The Blue Studio Tarskavaig, Sleat IV46 8SA; ☎ 01471 855368; w macartorg.wordpress.com; ⏰ summer: 10.00–18.00 daily, winter: call first.

Donald MacKenzie's playful musical, figurative & landscape paintings.

Floraidh Skye Isleornsay, Sleat IV43 8QR; ☎ 01471 833347; w floraidhskye.co.uk; ⏰ 10.00–17.00 Tue–Fri, 10.00–16.00 Sat. Wool, silk, tweed & cashmere clothing & accessories.

Gallery An Talla Dearg Hotel Eilean Iarmain, IV43 8QR; ☎ 01471 833332; w eileaniarmain. co.uk/an-talla-dearg-gallery; ⏰ 10.00–18.00 Mon–Fri, 11.00–16.00 Sat & Sun. Art gallery where local artists exhibit work in exchange for helping to run the gallery.

Food shops

An Crùbh (page 91) Speciality & local foods including fruit, vegetables & fresh bread. Also gifts & alcohol.

Armadale Stores Armadale IV45 8RS; 01471 844249; w sleat.org.uk/sleatcommunitytradingltd. asp; summer 08.30–17.30 Mon–Fri, 08.30–15.30 Sat, winter 09.30–17.30 Mon–Tue & Thu–Fri, 09.30–13.30 Wed & Sat. Small,

community-owned shop with a selection of groceries, chocolate & alcohol. Fuel, too.

Pràban na Linne Eilean Iarmain; w gaelicwhisky.com; summer 10.00–17.00 Mon–Sat, 11.00–16.00 Sun, winter 10.00-17.00 Mon–Fri. This small shop produces 3 Gaelic whiskies & 1 gin (Uisge Lusach) & offers tastings.

Skye Bridge Seafoods (page 91) Fresh locally sourced fish & shellfish for sale. Van is travelling around the south of the island. Call or check Facebook for details.

SPORTS AND ACTIVITIES

South Skye Cycles (page 57) Cycling tours to Knoydart & other places. Can be adapted to theme of your choice: geographical, environmental, cultural, historical, etc. Also bike hire & repairs.

South Skye Sea Kayak w southskyeseakayak. co.uk. See ad, 2nd colour section. A peaceful & exciting way to reach remote stretches of coastline. Good for wildlife spotting. Suitable for beginners. Half day/full day £60/90 pp.

OTHER PRACTICALITIES

✚ **Medical** Sleat Medical Practice, Kilmore IV44 8RF (01471 844283)

✉ **Post offices** An Crùbh (page 91); Armadale Stores (see above; summer 08.30–17.30 Mon–

Tue & Thu–Fri, 08.30–13.30 Wed & Sat, winter 09.30–17.30 Mon–Tue & Thu–Fri, 09.30–13.30 Wed & Sat); Cameron, Kyleakin IV41 8PL (10.00–13.30 Tue & Thu)

WHAT TO SEE AND DO

Kyleakin Coming over on the Skye Bridge, the first settlement on the island is Kyleakin. There isn't too much to detain you here, but the picturesque **Kyleakin Lighthouse**, designed by the Stevenson family who were responsible for constructing nearly all of Scotland's lighthouses between the late 18th and the mid 20th centuries, is visible across the water on the small island of Eilean Ban. In the east, **Castle Maol** (57°16'23"N 5°43'14"W) is an atmospheric-looking ruin that was a 15th-century MacKinnon stronghold. You can visit at low tide, when the exposed shoreline means that you can walk around the point anticlockwise and find your way up on the far side; a high-tide land route is possible, but much more difficult due to thick undergrowth.

Sleat On Sleat, the pretty village of **Isleornsay** sits just across from the tidal island of **Isle Ornsay** and another Stevenson creation, **Isle Ornsay Lighthouse**, which is confusingly built on the nearby islet of **Eilean Sionnach**.

Teangue In the village of Teangue, you can join a tour of **Torabhaig whisky distillery** (01471 833447; w torabhaig.com; 10.00–17.00 Mon–Fri, 10.00–16.00 Sat & Sun; ; tours £10). Up and running since 2017, this is a small, traditional distillery, and Skye's second. Tours take 45 minutes and conclude in a tutored tasting of their Mossburn Island Blend, as Torabhaig itself is not ready yet. A couple of hundred yards away is the ruin of **Knock Castle**, built by the MacLeods only to be captured by the MacDonalds; it was passed between the two clans several times before settling as a stronghold of the latter. There are stories of a Green Lady or Gruagach who is said to haunt the castle.

Armadale Castle (✆01471 844305; w armadalecastle.com; ⊕ 09.30–17.30 daily (reduced in winter); adult/child/family £8.75/7.20/25; ♿) is said to be the ancestral home of Clan MacDonald. It has extensive gardens with huge, mature trees, perfect for picnics and long afternoons of exploring. The castle, strictly speaking an early 19th-century mansion house, is a ruin that you can only observe from the outside. There is also a well-organised museum, predictably quite heavy on MacDonald-specific history, but including other highlights such as a Gaelic poetry trail, a 100-year-old 18ft skiff and full-scale replicas of Clan MacDonald West Highland grave slabs, which you are encouraged to touch.

A loop around Sleat

Distance: 22 miles, or 31 miles including extension to the Point of Sleat; time: 2–3 hours, but best as a full day; start/end: Ardvasar; OS Explorer map: 412 Skye – Sleat/Sleite

When I asked Andy from South Skye Cycles (see opposite) if he thought it was a good idea for me to describe this route as one to do on bikes, he told me I would be 'uncovering Skye's best-kept cycling secret'. He also suggested that cyclists should go prepared with food and drink; be especially careful to look where they're going as the road surface can be rough with blind summits; and take the route clockwise for a wind-assisted ride.

Cycle north from Ardvasar as far as **Ostaig** where there is a post box on the corner and a turning to the left marked to Achnacloich (5 miles), Tarskavaig (6 miles) and Tokavaig (8 miles). Take this road and cycle west, initially through some broad-leaved trees and farmed fields on either side.

Climbing up into the hills, the Cuillins will begin to unfold in front of you as the landscape becomes wilder and rockier. Pause on the banks of **Loch Dhùghaill** to take in the view as the landscape becomes rough with heather, and look out for wading birds.

Descending through the woods, you will shortly be at **Achnacloich**, where there is a shingle bay in front of the white house at Gillean.

Following the road to the north, you will shortly come to **Tarskavaig**, where the tiny Communities Hall sometimes hosts a pop-up café during July and August. Take your time to look out west towards Rùm and Canna. Just after the hall, you can take a turning left down into the village and visit **The Blue Studio** (page 91), or continue on higher ground past **Loch Ghabhsgabhaig** on your left, towards Tokavaig.

Passing two pebbly beaches, you will come to a track leading off to the left marked 'Footpath to Castle'. Leaving your bike off the side of the road, walk down this track to find the remains of **Dunscaith Castle**. Also known as the Fortress of Shadows, the site is named after Sgàthaich, a warrior maiden who, according to tradition, made an earlier fort here her home. Sgàthaich is said to have only trained young warriors who were already brave enough to break through the defences of the fortress. According to folk history, this is where she trained the Irish folk hero Cu Chulainn. The current castle was built around the 13th century and passed between clans MacDonald, MacLeod and MacAskill, before being captured by King James I of Scotland and finally abandoned in the 18th century. It is certainly a ruin, but an impressive one with a striking archway and broken bridge. The pebbly beach just behind it, with views across some tiny islets towards Ben Meabost and the Black Cuillins behind, makes a splendid, sheltered spot to stop for a picnic.

Back on the road, you will bump over lumpy ground before eventually reaching the small sandy bay at **Ord**. This is one of Skye's loveliest beaches; with similar views to those from Elgol, but only a fraction of the visitors. When you have had your fill, continue along the road east and return through birch trees, moorland and past little **Loch Meadal** before reaching the main A851 road.

Take a right at the T-junction with the A851 to return to Armadale, looking out for **Knock Castle** (page 92) which will appear across **Knock Bay** on your left. Passing **Teangue** and **Kilmore**, you will eventually get back to the start.

Those with even more energy should continue down from Ardvasar towards the **Point of Sleat** where there is a small lighthouse. This headland has spectacular views out to Eigg, Rùm and the Ardnamurchan Peninsula, as well as good chances of seeing marine mammals and seabirds such as gannets. On the return trip, do not miss the opportunity to detour down to **Camas Daraich**, undoubtedly one of the finest beaches on Skye.

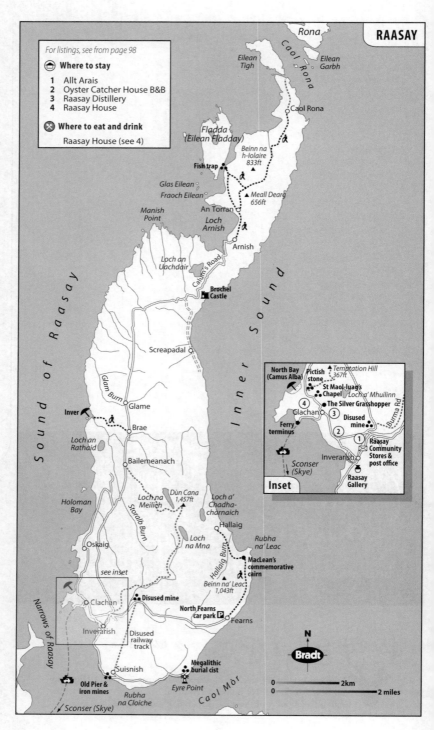

Rona

Caol Rona

Eilean Tigh

Eilean Garbh

Caol Rona

Eilean Fladday
Fladda (Eilean Fladday)

Beinn na h-Iolaire 833ft ▲

Fish trap ●

Glas Eilean
Fraoch Eilean

▲ *Meall Dearg 656ft*

An Torran ●

Manish Point

Loch Arnish

Arnish ●

Loch an Uachdair

Calum's Road

Brochel Castle ■

Sound of Raasay

Inner Sound

Screapadal ○

Glam Burn

Glame ○

Inver ↗

Brae ○

Loch an Rathaid

Bailemeanach ○

Holoman Bay

▲ *Dùn Cana 1,457ft*

Loch na Meilich

Storab Burn

Loch a' Chadha-charnaich

Hallaig

Loch na Mna

Rubha na' Leac

● **MacLean's commemorative cairn**

Oskaig ○

see inset

▲ *Beinn na' Leac 1,043ft*

Clachan ○ **Disused mine** ●

Hallaig Burn

Inverarish ○

Disused railway track

North Fearns car park P

Fearns ○

Narrows of Raasay

Suisnish ○

⚓ **Old Pier & iron mines**

Megalithic burial cist ●

Eyre Point

Rubha na Cloiche

⚓ *Sconser (Skye)*

Caol Mòr

N

Bradt

0 ——— 2km
0 ——— 2 miles

Inset box:

For listings, see from page 98

⊝ **Where to stay**

1 Allt Arais
2 Oyster Catcher House B&B
3 Raasay Distillery
4 Raasay House

✖ **Where to eat and drink**

Raasay House (see 4)

Inset map:

North Bay (Camus Alba) ⚓

▲ *Temptation Hill 367ft*

Pictish stone ●

St Maol-luag's Chapel ●

Loch a' Mhuilinn

(4) **The Silver Grasshopper** ●

Clachan ○ (3)

Disused mine ●

Ferry terminus ●

Burma Rd

⚓

(2)

(1)

Raasay Community Stores & post office ⊠

Inverarish ○

Sconser (Skye)

Raasay Gallery ⚓

Inset

⚓ → *Sconser (Skye)*

4

Raasay (Ratharsair)

With turquoise waters that lap into quiet, sheltered coves, plus rocky hills, woodland paths and remarkably fluffy white sheep, Raasay is a breath of fresh air. Measuring just 14 miles long and 4 miles wide, the island is dwarfed by its bigger, busier neighbour Skye and, with regular ferries travelling between the two, is often thought of as an extension of the larger island. This is, of course, a huge injustice – though it might look small in comparison, there is much more to do and see on Raasay than can be accomplished in a couple of days.

The island's highlights include flat-topped Dùn Cana in the centre of the island; a hike to the top gives spectacular views over Raasay, across to Skye and as far as Applecross on the mainland. The north of the island is wild and uninhabited, providing ample opportunity for adventurers to explore, including the beautiful tidal island of Fladda, once home to a whole community, and a whole host of other fascinating abandoned places including the ruins of pre-Clearance villages and the oppressive, industrial remains of the mining industry.

Much of Raasay's land is run by Forestry and Land Scotland (Inverness; ✆ 0300 067 6100; w forestry.gov.uk/scotland), which has created intermittent ugly scars on the southern landscape where trees have had to be felled. To their credit, however, Forestry and Land Scotland (formerly the Forestery Commission) has long provided jobs and supported the island's economy, in addition to – and particularly of interest for visitors – maintaining excellent walking paths and producing the best free tourist map of the island.

HISTORY

The history of Raasay is intricately linked with that of the MacLeods, who used both Raasay and Rona, the smaller island to the north, for pirating activities from the 16th century. After supporting Bonnie Prince Charlie in the 1745 rebellion (page 56), the MacLeods went into hiding on the island, which resulted in Raasay House (home to the MacLeod Chief of Raasay) and many other homes being burnt down by government troops.

In the 19th century, like many landowners at the time, John MacLeod found himself in debt and finally sold Raasay in 1843 to a George Rainy. After this, life for the island's ordinary inhabitants became increasingly difficult. In a rather bizarre and unusual move, Rainy banned marriages and, echoing the Clearances elsewhere, began to evict villages in order to replace people with sheep. As well as abroad, many people were forced to move to Rona. By the 1860s, hundreds of people had been forced off the island – to nearby Rona and abroad.

In 1912 William Baird bought the island with the intention of opening an iron mine. He built a small railway, pier, kilns and the two rows of cottages now known as Inverarish Terrace for the workers. Operations had barely begun before World

War I broke out, and many of those who would have worked in the mine had to go away to fight. However, the war effort required iron ore and thus in 1916 William Baird signed an agreement to run the mine on behalf of the military. Later that year, the northern part of Inverarish was turned into a prisoner of war camp.

In 1922 the island was bought by the government and the responsibility of managing it was given to the Forestry Commission, providing much-needed employment for islanders. Despite this, the population of Raasay has more or less steadily declined over the following decades, and is currently around only 160 people.

GETTING THERE AND AWAY

BY FERRY CalMac (✆ 08000 665000 or, from outside the UK, +44 1475 650397; w calmac.co.uk) runs year-round services from Sconser on Skye to Clachan on Raasay; the port is on the southern edge of the village. This vehicle and foot passenger ferry takes around 25 minutes, with ferries running between two and ten times a day. Tickets cannot be booked in advance; arrive at least 15 minutes in advance. Single fares cost £6.50 for a vehicle and £2 for passengers.

BY SMALL BOAT Raasay House (see opposite) can arrange pickup/drop-off in Sconser or Portree on Skye (adult/child £20/10 plus £60 standing charge; £120/150 min booking applies).

GETTING AROUND

As it's often thought of as little more than an extension of Skye, in actuality Raasay can seem bigger than you might expect. From the ferry terminal in the south to Arnish in the north is just over 10 miles of driving, but the single-track road is slow and winding. With plenty of time and decent weather, a combination of walking and cycling is the perfect way to enjoy the island at a leisurely pace.

BIKE HIRE
武 **Raasay House** (see opposite) Hires out bikes (half/whole day £15/25) & e-bikes (half/whole day £30/45).

 WHERE TO STAY, EAT AND DRINK *Map, page 96*

Accommodation options on the island are generally centred around the two small townships of Clachan and Inverarish, which are so close together that it is difficult to extract one from the other. Despite being limited in number, accommodation here is of excellent quality, offering everything from dorm rooms to luxury suites. Note, however, that there is no campsite on the island.

Raasay Distillery (6 rooms) Borodale Hse, Clachan IV40 8PB; \ 01478 470178; w raasaydistillery.com; ゟ. The most exclusive & upmarket accommodation option on Raasay, part of the brand-new, attractive & modern distillery building (page 101). The 2 'luxury' rooms have sea views, but all are of a very high standard. Honesty box bar. **£££££**

✻ **Raasay House** (21 rooms) Clachan IV40 8PB; \ 01478 660300; w raasay-house.co.uk; ⏲ Feb–Nov; ゟ. An enormous sandstone building that's almost 300 years old, situated just 300m from the ferry port. Overlooking its own attractive grounds, with splendid views of the Narrows of Raasay & the Cuillins on Skye. Always the island's focal point, Raasay House has successfully transitioned from the exclusive home of Clan MacLeod to the community-owned extravaganza it is now. It describes itself as a 'unique island experience' & this is where the vast majority of activity on Raasay happens. Accommodation ranges from dorm bunk beds (from £15) to deluxe super-king rooms with a sea view (over £250). As well as being the only place to eat on the island, they also organise all manner of activities & rent out bikes. Staff are outstandingly happy & helpful, & there's a historic library for guests to use, with comfortable sofas, wood burner, ancient books & other objects that give an impression of how it would have once been (there's also board games & children's books). Games room upstairs with pool table, table tennis & table football, while interesting projects with local artists aim to inject some more character into the relatively new interior. Fast Wi-Fi. Dog friendly.

The restaurant (⏲ Feb–Nov 11.00–16.00 & 17.30–20.00 daily; ££) is open to non-residents. Expect local & seasonal ingredients from the walled garden at the back of the house, plus Wild Raasay Venison, Raasay Crofters' Association langoustine & fish from Skye. Particularly excellent mussels & great vegetarian/vegan menu. Lunch is simpler with soup, toasted flatbreads, haddock & chips or scampi. **£–£££££**

✻ **Oyster Catcher House B&B** (4 rooms) The Avenue, Inverarish IV40 8PA; \ 01478 660277; w oystercatcherhousebandb.co.uk. Elizabeth, originally a geography teacher from the mainland, & her husband Darryl run this immaculate B&B. There is a large separate guest living/dining room with comfortable sofas, reclining armchairs & a sea view. Daily home-baking, with an extensive range of cakes, plus homemade jams & a fridge for guest use. Photos, maps & information about the best things to see on the island; information that's not easy to come by. Elizabeth can also tell you where seals, eagles & otters live, & share the tide table. Packed lunches can be arranged in advance & Darryl offers to cook simple, hearty dinners in the few winter months when Raasay House is closed. **££–£££**

Allt Arais (3 rooms) 7 Mill Park, Inverarish IV40 8PA; \ 01478 660237; w allt-arais.co.uk. Owner Anda is originally from the Outer Hebrides & speaks Gaelic. Spacious en-suite bedrooms & comfortable guest sitting room with impressive, modern wood burner. Excellent b/fast. Evening meals available when Raasay House closed in winter. **££**

SHOPPING AND GALLERIES

Raasay's few shops and galleries are clustered in the south of the island (along with the majority of its population).

Raasay Community Stores 29/30 Inverarish Tce, IV40 8NS; \ 01478 660203; ◼; ⏲ 09.00–17.30 Mon–Sat. Good range of groceries including fruit & vegetables, Raasay Crofters' Association venison & Raasay Dexter beef. Local guidebooks & maps.

Raasay Gallery Ferryview, West Suisnish IV40 8NX; \ 01478 660241; w raasaygallery.co.uk; ⏲ Apr–Oct 11.00–17.30 Mon–Fri, Nov–Mar 11.00–16.00 Mon–Fri (though note hours can be flexible). Purpose-built gallery exhibiting striking oil paintings in bold colours by owner Gordon J

Cheape: portraits, abstracts & landscapes. Also a couple of other local artists.

The Silver Grasshopper The Old Telephone Exchange, Clachan IV40 8PB; ☎01478 660265; **w** thesilvergrasshopper.com; ☺ summer 13.00–17.00 Mon–Sat, winter variable. This tiny white building with slate roof sells elegant jewellery, handmade on Raasay.

OTHER PRACTICALITIES

Fuel The nearest fuel stations are in Portree & Broadford on Skye, so make sure you fill up before you arrive.

✚ Medical The lack of full-time medical care on Raasay is a controversial issue. Portree Medical Centre (☎01478 612013) visits Raasay regularly & offers some services.

✉ **Post office** ☺ 09.30–noon Mon–Sat

WHAT TO SEE AND DO

AROUND CLACHAN AND INVERARISH Two eroded stone mermaids greet everyone who arrives on the island by the Skye ferry; bought by the final MacLeod of Raasay, they were reportedly partly to blame for his bankruptcy in the mid 19th century. The ferry terminal sits in Churchton Bay on the southern edge of Clachan – made up of a scattering of buildings – and from here the village spreads into Inverarish, the island's main settlement, which is around a mile further east.

Around 300yds from the ferry terminal sits Raasay House (page 99); a path leads around its right-hand side to **St Maol-luag's Chapel**. The crumbling remains of this 13th-century church rest on what is thought to have been an earlier religious site from around the 6th century; according to folk history, St Moluag (c510–592) founded the site himself. The surrounding graveyard is a silent and slightly eerie place, sheltered by tall trees. The chapel shows its age through centuries of lichens, well-established moss cushions and a fascinating array of ferns; it has a well-preserved arched window in the east gable and an arched tomb recess on the inner south wall. Slightly to the south is the memorial chapel, which was built much more recently in 1839. The main interest here is a small carved face that peers out from above the east window and is thought to have been saved from an earlier building.

OUTDOOR ACTIVITIES AT RAASAY HOUSE

An outdoor activity centre long before it started offering hotel accommodation, Raasay House (page 99) has been running for 30 years. Boat trips into Raasay Sound are the main event outside high season, but during the summer they have a whole programme of activities, including numerous RIB boat trips, all with the chance of seeing seals, seabirds, dolphins, sea eagles and natural rock formations, with an optional landing on Rona (£30–72 pp). They also offer sailing on a traditional Hebridean fishing boat, coasteering, sea and loch kayaking, rock climbing on the cliffs near Brochel Castle and Calum's Crag, abseiling and archery, among other things (£20–50 pp, min size group bookings apply).

Note that many activities have a lower age limit for children, can be weather-dependent and require a certain amount of practical clothing. Check their website (**w** raasay-house.co.uk) for the most up-to-date schedule and call them (☎01478 660300) for more details.

Heading northwest from here, the road passes a rather mysterious and well-preserved **Pictish stone**, standing opposite the pebbly **North Bay (Camus Alba)**. Believed to have been carved around the latter half of the 7th century, the stone has three well-defined carvings, which are a good example of the mixture between early Christian and Pictish culture at the time. The early Christian cross of arcs and chi-rho scroll are at the top; below them are two distinctive Pictish symbols: a sideways tuning-fork symbol halfway down and, at the bottom, a crescent and V-rod. It's notable for being one of only a few Pictish stones discovered in west Scotland (over 200 have been found in eastern Scotland). To the left of the stone is a path marked with red waymarkers, which leads to the top of **Temptation Hill**, with splendid views both across Raasay and out to Skye. Heading back downhill, blue markers lead off to the right at the south end of the small Loch a' Mhuilinn; follow them to reach the distillery (see below). It's worth picking up the free leaflet from Forestry and Land Scotland (page 97), who maintain these marked paths, which has a detailed colour map of this area.

Raasay Distillery
(Borodale Hse, Inverarish; ☏ 01478 470178; w raasaydistillery. com) Although Raasay's whisky is not yet mature, you can still tour the distillery (on the main road between Clachan and Inverarish) and taste their 'While We Wait' single malt, which is supposed to give a representation of the finished product. A daily distillery and cask warehouse tour is scheduled daily at noon (adult/child £10/5); there is also a regular distillery tour (adult/child £10/5), and a whisky and chocolate tasting (adult/child £15/£5) that includes handmade Highland chocolates. It's well worth joining the tour that includes a warehouse visit: the towering rows of wooden casks are an impressive sight in themselves, but it's the rich oaky smell of maturing whisky that leaves a lasting impression.

The distillery hosts a great calendar of events, including live music and art exhibitions; check their website for up-to-date information.

TO THE NORTH OF THE ISLAND
Suisnish Old Pier and the iron-mining industry
By far the most imposing and impressive remains of Raasay's iron-mining history are found down at Suisnish, 1 mile south of Inverarish. Giant funnel-like ore hoppers, abandoned buildings, the concrete pier (built 1913–14) and a huge anchor are reminiscent of brutalist architecture and dominate the scene, but there is also a pebbly beach here that is a good place to spot seals.

Eyre Point
Following the road east from Suisnish takes you towards Eyre Point, where there is a small, white **lighthouse**; around 80yds north are the remains of a cairn and a **Megalithic burial cist** (⊕ 57°20'04"N 6°01'19"W). If you are travelling by car, park it at the end of the road (do this at the sign saying 'end of public road') and follow the main track between two fenced fields. Shortly after passing a ruined building in the field on your left, you will see the large stones of the burial chamber protruding high out of the ground some 22yds north of the track. When I visited Raasay I was unfortunately put off trying to get any closer owing to broken gates and ewes with new lambs, but this might be easier to do at another time of the year. Eyre Point is also one of the best places on Raasay to see otters; go early morning for the best chance.

Dùn Cana
The most spectacular views on Raasay can be enjoyed by climbing the island's highest peak, Dùn Cana (1,457ft; also called Dùn Caan). This flat-

topped peak, which can be seen clearly from Skye, has views across the Narrows of Raasay to the whole of Skye's east coast, as well as to the Cuillins and across the Inner Sound to Applecross and the mainland. There are waymarked routes from Bailemeanach (2 miles) and the Burma Road (just under 3 miles), plus a circular route from Inverarish that is nearly 10 miles long; Walkhighlands describe this last option in detail with a map (w walkhighlands.co.uk/skye/duncaan.shtml).

Brochel Castle With a commanding view across the Inner Sound to Applecross on the mainland, Brochel Castle is a construction of mysterious origins, thought to date from the late 15th or early 16th century. Using a clever combination of strategic positioning and natural rock, combined with masonry, intricate brickwork and lime mortar, the castle is around 49ft high with a commanding position over the northeast coastline. This strategic vantage point was used by the MaCleods to control their wider territory. As the castle remains unrestored, precarious and missing much of the original structure (including its tallest tower), it is dangerous to get too close, but nonetheless the remains still make an imposing sight on the shore.

Calum's Road Heading north from Brochel Castle, the 'main' road becomes Calum's Road. Calum and Charles MacLeod initially constructed a track from Torran to Fladda, further north, between 1949 and 1952, funded by the local council. Residents of the island's far north campaigned for many years for further funding and assistance to connect their homes with the rest of Raasay; eventually the Department of Agriculture's engineering department carried out some initial rock blasting work. However, Calum – also a lighthouse keeper on Rona, not to mention postman, crofter, writer and local historian – ultimately decided to build the road himself. Between the 1960s and 70s, armed with Thomas Aitken's 60-year-old book *Road Making & Maintenance: A Practical Treatise for Engineers, Surveyors and Others*, he almost single-handedly built the 1¾-mile stretch of road between Arnish and Crochel Castle with little more than hand tools. Work on the road, which has steep climbs and descents, traversing boggy moorland and between rocky cliffs and sheer drops, must have been unimaginably hard. Once he had finally finished, the road was surfaced by the local council, but there was nobody left living in the north except Calum and his wife. It makes for a poignant drive or cycle, especially after reading *Calum's Road*, a well-researched book on the subject by Roger Hutchinson.

🏃 HALLAIG
Distance: 4 miles; time: 2–3 hours; start/end: North Fearns car park; OS Explorer map: 409 Raasay, Rona & Scalpay

Famous as the eponymous village in Sorley MacLean's 1954 poem, Hallaig was Raasay's largest settlement prior to the Clearances. The village was evicted in 1854 by George Rainy (page 97) who had recently purchased the island; reading Sorley MacLean's poem among the abandoned buildings is a haunting experience.

The road out towards Fearns is dotted with abandoned buildings and, even with just a little knowledge of the area's history, it's hard not to begin to feel a sense of the lost communities before you even reach the beginning of the walk.

From North Fearns car park an obvious track follows higher ground, heading initially northeast and then north along the coastline and beneath the cliffs of Beinn na' Leac, with the sea on your right. The views across to the mountains on the mainland make the first part of the walk well worth doing and you have one of the best chances of seeing eagles on Raasay.

After about 1½ miles, the route passes a commemorative cairn with MacLean's original Gaelic poem and its English translation engraved on to metal plates.

Shortly afterwards, the way begins to get rougher as it passes through some birch woods; you will have to negotiate a route below the ravines in Hallaig Burn before heading uphill towards the remains of over 40 roofless buildings in various states of ruin, with low stone walls that have begun to grow grass on top (✪ 57°22'20"N 6°00'30"W). To return, retrace your steps.

BRAE TO INVER BEACH

Distance: 2 miles; time: 1–2 hours; start: Brae; end: Inver; OS Explorer map: 409 Raasay, Rona & Scalpay

To reach the starting point, head north of Inverarish for about 4 miles; you'll find a small parking place next to a high fence and metal gate on the left-hand side of the road. The scant remains of the deserted settlement of Brae are beyond the fence and you'll see a small wooden signpost marked 'Inver 1.5km'.

Pass through the gate and continue past the ruined houses on your left. Head downhill towards a wooded area and a lower fence with a metal gate; do not go through the gate but instead bear left and follow a small, often muddy path down through the trees. From this point on the path is narrow but easy to follow.

Most of the route goes alongside what starts as a tumbling stream, but is soon joined by others to become a bigger river that flows into rapids down through a naturally carved rocky canyon. The path weaves through magical birch woods with a carpet of moss and lichens growing from the tree branches, before opening out on to a stretch of heather moorland with a beautiful view towards the Skye Cuillins. Heading back into woodland, there are stepping stones over a small adjoining stream, followed by a ruined building on your right.

Finally, the path leads you out of the trees on to a pebbly beach, divided by the river mouth, where you can picnic while admiring the view out to Skye. Retrace your steps to return to the starting point.

TO FLADDA AT LOW TIDE

Distance: 5 miles; time: 1–2 hours; start/end: Arnish; OS Explorer map: 409 Raasay, Rona & Scalpay

The north of Raasay is mostly uninhabited and, with the weather often changing quickly, it would be unwise to attempt much walking in the area without being well prepared for a day hike (page 34). For this walk you will need to check tide times in advance (page 27).

One hundred years ago the island of Fladda (Eilean Fladday) hosted a whole community; the population, lacking amenities or even a bridge to connect them to Raasay at high tide, has now dispersed. Only three houses remain and these are not lived in continually throughout the year.

Coming by car, park at Arnish and take the path to the left of the few houses there, which leads along Raasay's west coast. As you wander through twisted birch woods, look out for interesting mushrooms and toadstools in autumn, before the view opens out over the beautiful Sound of Raasay and the tiny islets of Fraoch Eilean and Glas Eilean. Fladda is up ahead; at low tide the beach that connects the island to Raasay shows signs of an old, squared fish trap on the shore.

Assuming you have checked the tide times in advance, it is easy if a little slippery on the seaweed to cross the beach over to Fladda. Do not underestimate this smaller island's size, however; though only around 2 miles long, unless you've come out at the very start of low tide you might struggle to make your way around it in time for the returning tide. That said, it is worth taking the time to look out to sea from the island's west coast as you might catch a glimpse of seals, porpoises or dolphins. With enough time before high tide, it's possible to walk northwest through the old village, which is mostly ruined buildings, towards Loch Mòr, a small lake in the centre of the island.

Back on Raasay, you can return to Arnish the same way you came or take an alternative route southwest, which leads uphill, inland towards the hill, Meall Dearg. This option leads you up into uninhabited hills and eventually to a junction where you can choose to go right, back to Arnish, or left and north in the direction of Rona.

5

The Small Isles

Frequently overlooked, the Small Isles archipelago is made up of Eigg, Rùm, Muck, Canna and Sanday and sits to the south of Skye. Joined by a bridge, Canna and Sanday are generally referred to as a single entity, with 'Canna' often used to describe both islands.

The islands' populations do not relate to their size. Rùm, the biggest at just over 40 square miles, has only around 30 inhabitants, while Canna (just over 5 square miles) is home to around 20 people, which means it cannot currently sustain a school; smaller Muck, a mere 2.2 square miles has around 46 people. Eigg's population of 110 is a little over those of Rùm, Canna and Muck combined – unsurprisingly, the island has the most regular ferry connections and receives the most visitors. Note that cars are forbidden on all of the islands (unless you have a disabled blue badge), ferry times are irregular and often cancelled due to bad weather, and mobile phone reception is almost non-existent – in many ways, the Small Isles feel like the final frontier. While travelling around the islands in a hurry is tricky and inconvenient, visitors who can spend more time here, particularly those who love the outdoors and wildlife or are looking for true peace and quiet, will find ample reward. Birdwatching is a particular highlight, with each island offering something particularly special for twitchers: Rùm and Eigg are both good places to spot birds of prey such as hen harriers and golden and sea eagles, while Rùm is also visited by enormous numbers of Manx shearwaters (see box, page 114); Canna has fantastic seabird colonies including puffins (page 122) and Muck has an abundance of ground-nesting birds.

Distinct in appearance, Eigg, Canna and Muck have some similarity in their volcanic formation (page 4). For those of us who aren't geologists, perhaps the most exciting result of this is the basalt columns, similar to the more famous examples at Fingal's Cave on Staffa (see box, page 185) and the Giant's Causeway in Northern Ireland, which are found on all three islands and at their most impressive on Canna (page 127). Rùm is a conspicuous addition to the group, with a landscape distinct from the other Small Isles – made up primarily of Torridonian sandstone, gabbro, peridotite and granite, which have resulted in a wet heathland, the island is mostly infertile for cultivation and as a result has never been heavily populated.

HISTORY

The Small Isles have a rich and varied archaeological landscape. In the 1980s, evidence of Mesolithic nomad activity on Rùm was thought to be the oldest sign of settlement in Scotland, but this title has now been lost after more recent discoveries elsewhere. There have been findings of 9,000-year-old bloodstone arrow heads on the island as well as Neolithic axe heads (Eigg) and thumbnail scrapers (Muck).

The islands' Bronze-Age inhabitants left over 30 round cairns across the archipelago and large numbers of hut circles (page 267) on Canna and Eigg. There are numerous forts (or duns) dating from the Iron Age (around 800BC to AD100): six on Eigg, four on Canna, three on Rùm and one on Muck (page 131).

Canna and Eigg were both important Christian sites in the early medieval period. The township of A' Chill (which no longer exists thanks to the Clearances; page 15) on Canna is thought to have been the site of a chapel founded by Columba in the late 6th century; Saint Donnán, another priest who attempted to introduce Christianity to the Picts, is the patron saint of Eigg where he was martyred.

Although Norse place names are common, they are more topographical than relating to settlements; some artefacts have been found, mostly on Eigg, including a boat that was uncovered as the sand washed away at Laig Bay, and a sword at Kildonnan.

Unsurprisingly, the more modern history of the Small Isles is as brutal as anywhere in Scotland. In later clan times, the Small Isles were passed between owners including the Clanranald, the MacLeans of Coll and the Earls of Argyll. Situated away from the mainland, the relationships between landowners and ordinary people were particularly unbalanced here, with the lairds rarely living on the islands and deciding the islanders' fates remotely. The 1780s and 90s saw waves of emigration due to high rents and overcrowding; as the kelp industry was thriving at this time, landlords disapproved of the exodus and took measures to ensure the population did not decline. The Clanranalds, for example, built crofting townships

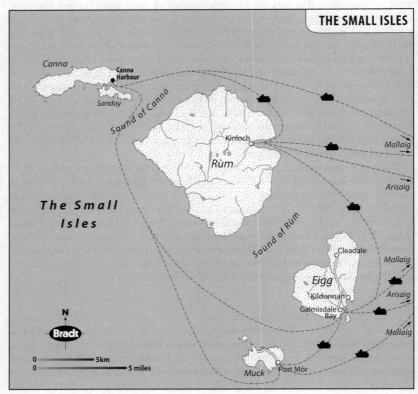

RÙM, RUM OR RHUM?

Throughout this guide we've opted to use the Scottish Gaelic spelling to refer to the island of Rùm; both this spelling and the Anglicised version – Rum – are widely used. Rhum was a Victorian variation invented by George Bullough (page 112) to save him the embarrassment of being called the 'Laird of Rum'. Although you might come across this spelling in old books, it's no longer used or considered correct.

to accommodate more workers. The economic and social situation changed entirely when the kelp market collapsed at the end of the Napoleonic Wars in 1815 and the Clearances began.

From 1826 to 1828 nearly the whole population of Rùm was forced to emigrate to make way for more profitable sheep. On 11 July 1826 alone, 300 people left the island on two ships bound for Nova Scotia. This was a traumatic event by all accounts, with a shepherd reporting: 'The wild cries of the men and the heart-breaking wails of the women and children filled the air between the mountainous shores.' Somewhat ironically, Lachlan MacLean (who was renting the island) then realised that he needed someone to look after his 8,000 sheep and had to subsequently collect some other poor souls who had been cleared from Mull and Skye. Only a decade later, the mutton market collapsed and Rùm became a largely uninhabited sporting estate, where wealthy people from mainland Great Britain came to shoot deer. Around the same time the MacLeans evicted around half the population of Muck and 150 people sailed on the *St Lawrence* from Tobermory to Cape Breton in Canada. The remaining inhabitants were allowed to build houses in the village above Port Mòr and tried to sustain themselves by fishing, but by 1835 they had all left the island. In 1851 all the inhabitants of Canna were moved to Sanday in what became known as the Great Clearance. A' Chill, inhabited for hundreds of years, was cleared and flattened to the extent that now there is nothing left of it to be seen.

Since the Clearances, the Small Isles have struggled to establish permanent populations, but recent years have seen a shift in power towards residents. The entirety of Eigg was bought out by the community in 1997, since when the population has been steadily increasing, and Kinloch, Rùm's only village, was bought by the community in 2010. The rest of Rùm is owned by Scottish Natural Heritage and managed as a nature reserve. Canna is now owned by the National Trust for Scotland and Muck seems to be thriving under its current private ownership.

GETTING THERE AND AWAY

BY FERRY **CalMac** (✆ 08000 665000 or, from outside the UK, +44 1475 650397; w calmac.co.uk) runs services from Mallaig on the mainland (page 264) to all four of the Small Isles most days of the week during summer, usually stopping at more than one of the islands on each journey. You cannot take your car without special permission, which is usually only granted to residents, people with disabilities or those working on the islands. Blue disability badge holders can arrange for a vehicle permit by calling in advance: Eigg/Muck ✆ 01349 781083; Rùm ✆ 01687 462404; Canna ✆ 01687 462563. Foot passengers are not required to book in advance.

Eigg has the most frequent crossings, with six weekly (1hr 15mins); the other islands have five crossings a week (Rùm 2hrs 20mins; Muck 1hr 40mins to 2hrs; Canna 2hrs 30mins to 3hrs 40mins). Winter services are reduced to around three weekly sailings. Ferries can be cancelled due to weather at any time, but it happens more frequently between September and March.

Inter-island travel Depending on how the timetable is arranged, you can usually travel in either direction between Rùm and Canna (2–4 weekly; 1hr); Eigg and Canna (2 weekly; 2hrs 10mins); Muck and Canna (weekly; 1hr 35mins); Eigg and Rùm (weekly; 1hr); and Eigg and Muck (1–2 weekly; 50mins). Note that it's not possible to travel between Rùm and Muck without landing somewhere else first.

BY SMALL BOAT Arisaig Marine (✆ 0168 450224; w arisaig.co.uk) runs services from the end of April till September on the MV *Sheerwater*, a small passenger boat, between Arisaig and Eigg (daily; adult/child 11–16 years/child 1–10 years £18/14/10), Muck (5 weekly; adult/child 11–16 years/child 1–10 years £20/14/10) and Rùm (twice weekly; adult/child 11–16 years/child 1–10 years £25/14/10). You are advised to book in advance. These trips, which focus on wildlife watching, usually only offer between 2 hours and 5 hours ashore, but single fares might be available on request. There is a good chance of seeing marine mammals such as seals and maybe minke whales, porpoises or common dolphin, as well as basking sharks and seabirds.

MOORINGS AND ANCHORAGES Visit Small Isles (w visitsmallisles.com/si/travel-tools/for-yachtsmen) provides useful information about anchorages on Muck and Eigg.

Canna Moorings for £10/night. Pay in the honesty box at Canna Community Shop (page 125).
Rùm Moorings for £10/night in Loch Scresort, a short distance from the CalMac pier. Payment can be made at the Rum Bunkhouse (page 110), the Isle of Rum Shop & Post Office (cash only; page 111), or online at w rumbunkhouse.com/moorings-payments.

OTHER PRACTICALITIES

MEDICAL There is no resident doctor on any of the islands, but Eigg does have the Small Isles Medical Practice (✆ 01687 482427; ⊕ 09.00–noon Mon–Fri) in Grianan, which is also a dispensary. Eigg is visited by a doctor once a week, while Rùm, Muck and Canna are all visited once every other week (weather depending). It is therefore usually more convenient to travel to Mallaig (page 265) for non-emergency medical services or a pharmacy. In an emergency, follow the usual procedure of calling ✆ 999 or 112; coastguards or island-based 'first responders' will initially assist with any emergency care. If necessary, an evacuation can be carried out via ferry, air ambulance, lifeboat, coastguard helicopter or private charter, depending on the circumstances. More information can be found on w visitsmallisles.com/si/about/local-and-emergency-services.

EVENTS

MAY
Isle of Canna 10K w theisleofcanna.com/isle-of-canna-10k. New trail run.

JULY
Fèis Eige Family event on Eigg with music, dance & celebrations of Gaelic heritage.
Small Isles Games Hosted by a different island each year. Look out for community notices.

The Howlin' Fling w lostmap.com. Eigg's hugely
popular contemporary music festival.
Muck Raft Race Muck; ■ isleofmuck

RÙM

The island of Rùm, with a diameter of around 8 miles, is the largest of the Small
Isles. Unique among the Inner Hebrides, it appears as a cluster of mountains rising
directly out of the sea. The highest point is Askival (2,664ft); the mountains are
in fact the eroded roots of an ancient volcano that would have once stood around
6,560ft high. The island's entire small population lives in its sole settlement, the
village of Kinloch on the east coast, while the rest of the island is a nature reserve,
making it a particularly special place for hikers and birdwatchers. Along with the
Manx shearwaters, of which 200,000 arrive each spring, the island also provides
the perfect habitat for red-throated divers, golden plovers, white-tailed sea eagles
(there are two breeding pairs) and its three pairs of golden eagles. Look out for
white-tailed eagles gliding over the bay, whereas golden eagles are often up above
ridges. In late summer, you might be lucky enough to see basking sharks.

GETTING AROUND Visitors are not allowed to bring cars on to the island, but Blue
disability badge holders can arrange for a vehicle permit by calling in advance.
Rùm is otherwise best explored under your own steam, either on foot or by bike.
Kinloch, the island's only village, is just a 10-minute walk from the ferry terminal,
on the island's east coast.

Bike hire
🚲 **Rum Crafts** PH43 4RR; ☎ 01687 462744;
e fliss@isleofrum.com. Sturdy, well-maintained
mountain bikes & helmets. £15/day.

WHERE TO STAY *Map, page 110*
While Rùm does not have a hotel or any particularly high-end offerings, the
island's accommodation options all provide good value for money. Excluding the
two bothies, all places to stay are found in Kinloch. Note that Fliss, who runs both
Ivy Cottage and Bramble Bothy, comes to the ferry terminal to collect her guests'
luggage (and the guests themselves if needed). Otherwise, baggage transfer to the
bunkhouse/campsite is available on arrival (£1 pp); look out for Dave the pier
master, who is usually wearing a high-vis jacket.

🏠 **Bramble Bothy** (sleeps 2) Kinloch PH43
4RR; ☎ 01687 462744; w ivycottageisleofrum.
co.uk. Small, but perfectly formed, this sustainably
built shepherd's hut is off-grid without sacrificing
either aesthetics or comfort. Fully fitted with
proper bedding, armchairs, an amazing modern
compost loo, wood burner, fridge, hob & sink.
Right on the shore of the loch. **£££**
🏠 **Ivy Cottage Guest House** (2
rooms) Kinloch PH43 4RR; ☎ 01687 462744;
w ivycottageisleofrum.co.uk. Having

moved to Rùm to work for Scottish Natural
Heritage, owner Fliss has lived on the island for 20
years & is a great source of local information. The
rooms (1 family & 1 dbl) & the conservatory dining
room have fantastic views over Loch Scresort.
Rooms are spacious, but have sloped ceilings; both
are en suite. Dinner, B&B offered. **£££**
🏠 **Harbour BBQ Bothy** (sleeps 4–6) Kinloch
PH43 4RR; ☎ 01687 460328. Basic accommodation in
a heptagonal wooden cabin with reindeer-hide rugs,
BBQ grill & chimney in the centre. Solar lighting. **£**

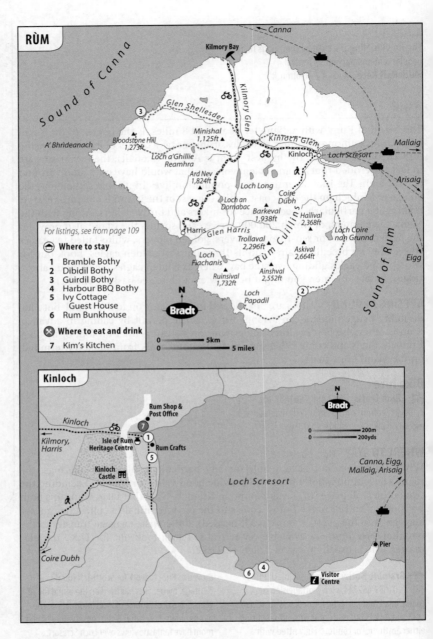

Kilmory Bay

Sound of Canna

Canna

A' Bhrideanach

Glen Shellesder

Bloodstone Hill
1,273ft

Minishal
1,125ft

Kilmory Glen

Kinloch Glen

Loch a'Ghillie
Reamhra

Mallaig

Kinloch ○ Loch Scresort

Ard Nev
1,824ft

Arisaig

Loch Long

Loch an
Dornabac

Coire
Dubh

Eigg

Barkeval
1,938ft

Hallival
2,368ft

Loch Coire
nan Grunnd

Harris

Glen Harris

Trollaval
2,296ft

Rùm Cuillins

Askival
2,664ft

Sound of Rum

Loch
Fiachanis

Ruinsival
1,732ft

Ainshval
2,552ft

Loch
Papadil

For listings, see from page 109

Where to stay

1 Bramble Bothy
2 Dibidil Bothy
3 Guirdil Bothy
4 Harbour BBQ Bothy
5 Ivy Cottage
    Guest House
6 Rum Bunkhouse

Where to eat and drink

7 Kim's Kitchen

Bradt

N

0 _____ 5km
0 _____ 5 miles

Kinloch

Bradt

N

Kinloch

**Rum Shop &
Post Office**

7

**Kilmory,
Harris**

**Isle of Rum
Heritage Centre**

1

● **Rum Crafts**

5

**Kinloch
Castle**

Loch Scresort

0 _____ 200m
0 _____ 200yds

*Canna, Eigg,
Mallaig, Arisaig*

Coire Dubh

6 4

**Visitor
Centre**

● **Pier**

Rum Bunkhouse (20 beds, 2 cabins & campsite) Kinloch PH43 4RR; ☎ 01687 460318; w rumbunkhouse.com; ♿. Community owned & a credit to the Isle of Rùm Community Trust. The bunkhouse is modern & well equipped, with large communal areas, wood-burning stove & a whole wall of windows giving panoramic views of the shoreline. You can eat your meals in a bird hide with a decent chance of seeing otters. Campsite is beautifully situated on the water's edge with basic facilities including toilets, showers (£1.50/5mins), water taps & a small

3-sided shelter. Cabins are pod-type structures sleeping 1–4 people & simply have mattresses inside. Welcoming manager Jed first came to Rùm as a geology student around 5 years ago. Atmosphere is generally relaxed & guests are an interesting congregation of Hebrides & hiking enthusiasts. Good Wi-Fi. Charging points in communal areas not bedrooms. Fantastic, warm drying room for kit. Dogs allowed in cabins, but not bunkhouse. **£**

⋀ The Mountain Bothy Association w mountainbothies.org.uk. Operates 2 bothies on Rùm: Guirdil (northwest Rùm) & Dibidil (southeast Rùm). These are free to use, but be sure to adhere to the rules (explained online) & to leave the place clean & tidy.

WHERE TO EAT AND DRINK   *Map, opposite*

✗ Kim's Kitchen Village Hall, Kinloch PH43 4RR; ☎ 01687 498247; **f** isleofrumteashop; ⊕ Apr & May 10.00–16.00 Mon, Wed & Fri, noon–15.00 Tue & Thu, May–Oct 10.00–16.00 Mon–Fri, 10.00–15.00 Sat; dinner also available some evenings, but check & book ahead. Homemade soup, filled baguettes, coffee, cakes & 3-course evening meals (£25 pp), with fish & chips on Fri. Note that opening hours are subject to change. **£–££**

SHOPPING

Rum Crafts Kinloch PH43 4RR; **f**; ⊕ summer daily. Local crafts, including bloodstone necklaces, crochet accessories, soap, marmalade & fudge.
Shop & Post Office Kinloch PH43 4RR; ☎ 01687 460328; e rumshop@email.com; ⊕ variable. Basic groceries & post office. Also sells alcohol & is popular local hang-out spot in evenings.
Tattie House Crafts Kinloch PH43 4RR; **f**; ⊕ daily. Handmade greeting cards, knitting & local artwork.

SPORTS AND ACTIVITIES

Fishing Those interested in fishing should contact the island's ranger (e ranger@isleofrum.com) and pick up an information leaflet from the Village Hall; this explains where fishing is allowed and has an attached catch report form that must be returned to the Village Hall (⊕ open access) or the Scottish Natural Heritage Office (PA43 4RR; ⊕ 09.00–17.00 Mon–Fri). Between 1 March and 15 October, loch fishing is only allowed in Loch Papadil, Loch Coire nan Grunnd, Loch Dornabac, Loch Fiachanis, Loch a' Ghillie Reamhra and Loch Long, due to nesting red-throated divers and greenshank. Loch Fiachanis is particularly recommended for catching brown trout early in the year. Coastal fishing is unrestricted, and sea trout, mackerel and flatfish can be caught at sea.

Wildlife activities Each summer, the Rùm Community Ranger puts on an incredible schedule of wildlife-spotting sessions, guided walks, boat trips and evening talks (check w isleofrum.com/isleofrumevents.php for dates & schedule; adult/child £5–10/2.50–5). The 'Rum Pelagic Experience' boat trip is a wildlife-watching excursion that goes to Soay in order to coincide with the post delivery; one of Soay's two residents then has to row out to meet the boat.

OTHER PRACTICALITIES

⊟ Internet Wi-Fi & a computer with internet access is available in the Village Hall (£1/30mins).
Phone Mobile phone reception is very limited on the island, but there is a payphone by Rum Crafts.
Toilets Public toilets can be found in the campsite & Village Hall, & there is a compost toilet at the ferry terminal.

WHAT TO SEE AND DO Approaching **Kinloch** on the ferry, you'd be forgiven for wondering where the village is; a couple of houses peer out from behind tall trees, but they're strung out around the bay. Though there are a few more buildings hidden from view, the settlement is little more than that. That said, Rùm is surprisingly well set up to receive visitors. The 10-minute walk along the coast from the ferry to Kinloch is well signposted and passes various buildings along the way.

The small, free **Visitor Centre** is a good introduction to Rùm's natural heritage and walks. It is usually unstaffed and you are welcome to visit at any time; there's good information, games and a couple of useful amenities inside as well as a **children's playground** behind. After this, you will quickly reach the Harbour BBQ Bothy and campsite (page 109), before eventually coming to the unmistakable **Kinloch Castle** on your left.

Apart from Kinloch, the rest of the island is wilderness. With only two proper tracks, one to Kilmory and one to Harris, and a few unmarked walking trails, further exploration requires outdoor gear, energy and supplies. The mountainous interior and rugged coastline make for endless hiking possibilities for those who are prepared.

Kinloch Castle (PH43 4RR; ☎ 0131 314 4181 (SNH Reserve Office); e kinlochcastle@nature.scot; w isleofrum.com/thingstodo.php; ☉ Apr–Oct 1

45min tour daily Mon–Sat; adult/child £9/4.50) Between 1897 and 1900, George Bullough employed 300 people to build this ludicrously extravagant hunting lodge. A huge, square-based red sandstone construction, the castle-like building has various towers and a colonnaded veranda, which once had a glass roof, around three-quarters of its exterior.

Although the building itself is not particularly old by Scottish standards, a tour is well worth doing just to see the contents. Entering the Great Hall, visitors are greeted by the glassy stares of many mounted stag heads, enormous Japanese sculptures and various moth-eaten animal skins, including that of a lion.

Despite its deteriorating state, the somewhat obscene level of post-Victorian eccentricity is immediately obvious; highlights include one of only three orchestrions in the world – an instrument machine that is supposed to sound like a whole orchestra playing at once; a beautiful series of Rùm landscapes by George Gordon Byron Cooper; a huge 3D model of Rùm; and a rather disturbing number of stuffed animals, including hummingbirds that were brought over to live (and die) in the castle's hot houses, a capercaillie, and half a tarpon fish that must have been twice as long as a human is tall when it was alive.

At the time of writing, the castle's future is unclear: it is still owned by Scottish Natural Heritage, but it will most likely be taken over by the Kinloch Castle Friends Association (w kinlochcastlefriends.org) who hope to restore it. The castle can only be visited on one of the daily tours, which last around 45 minutes and are timed to coincide with ferry times; exact times are displayed on the castle door.

Isle of Rum Heritage Centre (PH43 4RR; ✆ 01687 460340; w isleofrumheritagecentre.co.uk; ⊕ late-Apr–Oct 13.00–16.00 Mon–Fri) Just past Ivy Cottage Guest House is a small red building hidden in the trees. This is the old dairy, which local enthusiast Sylvia now runs as a small history/archaeology centre detailing some of Rùm's past, from 8,500 years ago to the most recent Clearances.

Walks and cycle routes
The routes to the abandoned coastal settlements of Kilmory and Harris are Rùm's only 'roads' and, while they can also be walked, it is much faster and more instantly gratifying to cycle (page 109). **Wildlife watching** is very accessible on Rùm; exploring beyond Kinloch will improve your chances of seeing species such as golden eagles as well as lots of red deer.

Hike up to Coire Dubh
Distance: 3 miles; time: 2 hours; start/end: Kinloch Castle; OS Explorer map: 397 Rùm, Eigg, Muck, Canna & Sanday
This is a relatively easy hike with an elevation gain of 920ft. Within an hour you are into the wilderness, with great views of the surrounding mountains and down over the coast around Kinloch.

The path leaves from beside the stream that runs just to the south of Kinloch Castle; it's on the left-hand side if you are looking at the castle from the front.

Walk past the castle and then bear away from it to the left, walking between two huts to find the start of the path. The route runs southwest, with the burn (Allt Slugan a' Choilich) never far from its left-hand side, through evergreen trees, passing crystal-clear pools and an impressive canyon, all the way up to Coire Dubh (✪ 56°59'53"N 6°18'07"W). After about a mile, take a moment to admire the Manx shearwater sundial, a fitting memorial to biologist Wilf Nelson who died falling from Bloodstone Hill on the west coast in the 1980s.

Coire Dubh is a gentle bowl in the landscape where several small mountain streams meet, surrounded by Barkeval and Hallival mountains with an open view back down over Kinloch, Loch Scresort and the range of An Mullach Mór behind. It is a good place to look out for golden eagles and red deer.

From here you can return along the same path.

Cycle to Kilmory Bay
Distance: 9 miles; time: 3 hours; start/end: Kinloch; OS Explorer map: 397 Rùm, Eigg, Muck, Canna & Sanday
Begin at the crossroads just north of Kinloch Castle, just before the bridge that heads towards the shop; take the marked track directly inland and head in this direction for around 2 miles. The track is extremely bumpy and rocky for the first section, but soon levels out to a predominantly smooth dirt track. This route takes you through Kinloch Glen and woodland, then across moorland, along the base of Barkeval hill, until you come to a fork near the base of Minishal. At the time of writing, the sign at this junction had deteriorated and was illegible; you need to take the right fork to go towards Kilmory (left goes to Harris; page 114) and head north into Kilmory Glen. Soon you will see a notice explaining that you are entering the 'Isle of Rùm Red Deer Project' (see box, page 115) and hopefully come across some of the deer themselves.

After about 2 miles, the track reaches Kilmory Bay, a sheltered sweep of sandy beach. There are a couple of glorious sandy beaches and some interesting sea stacks

Every summer, Rùm becomes home to around a third of the world's entire population of Manx shearwaters. An attractive bird with a white front and black back, they have a curved end to their beak and are just over 30cm long. Manx shearwaters can be seen on Rùm from March until September, but their numbers only become really spectacular in June and July. Breeding around the peaks of Askival (2,664ft), Hallival (2,368ft) and Trollaval (2,296ft), their breeding grounds are not easy to access, something that is made even more complicated by the fact that they only return at night.

The most adventurous and dedicated of birdwatchers can hike up to Coire Dubh (page 113) in the early evening and head over to the northeast face of Hallival before dark. Once here, sit down (be careful not to cover a burrow as you do so), turn off your torch and wait for the birds to return; be sure to sit still as they swoop down, squawking and cackling noisily, to their burrows. Trollaval, a peak to the southwest, got its name from Norse settlers, who heard the shearwaters' noises from the mountain and thought they came from trolls. Even if you can't make the hike, you should still be able to hear the birds in the evening and look out for them fishing off the coast during the day.

Scottish Natural Heritage (w nature.scot; SNH Reserve Office ☎ 0131 314 4181) usually run a guided trip at the end of July. If you decide to go alone, you should check current advice with the Reserve Office first, take a good torch with plenty of battery life, warm and waterproof clothes, and preferably a GPS device to help with the return trip. The darkness doesn't last long in summer, so another option is to wait on the mountain until it's light enough to see properly. Flasks of hot drinks are a must.

and caves on the west side of Kilmory Bay. Look out for sea eagles, otters and larger marine mammals as well as birds such as curlews and eider duck.

Just above the mouth of the river is the old settlement of Kilmory and its churchyard. This village was inhabited before the Clearances and is thought to have been a religious site from at least the 7th or 8th centuries. To make the most of Kilmory Bay, bring supplies and make this into a longer day trip.

🚲 Cycle to Harris

Distance: 16 miles; time: 5 hours; start/end: Kinloch; OS Explorer map: 397 Rùm, Eigg, Muck, Canna & Sanday

This is a longer cycle ride that includes quite a steep hill. Starting from the crossroads between Kinloch shop and castle, take the inland route until you reach a fork. Choose the left-hand track and continue in this direction on the biggest and most obvious route, passing some small waterfalls and a dam as well as the turning to Bloodstone Hill and Loch a' Ghillie Reamhra leading off to the right, which you should ignore.

Continuing on the same track you will cycle past Ard Nev on your right and the summits of Hallival, Askival, Ainshval and Ruinsival a little further away, walling you in on the left. Of the little lochs that appear in the foreground, Loch an Dornabac is the biggest, with a mountainous backdrop as you begin to descend.

Passing the bulbous volcanic extrusion of An Dornac on the left, the conspicuous columns of Bullough Mausoleum and black, rocky Harris Bay will soon come into view in the distance. The path curves around to the right and lazy beds (page 267) are still visible in fields, showing that this area was once cultivated. Harris was home to a small township before the Clearances and you can still see the low stone wall ruins of their houses on the higher ground around the bay.

The mausoleum, inspired by ancient Greece, is a fittingly ostentatious tribute to the Bulloughs, commissioned by the same Sir George Bullough as Kinloch Castle (page 112) around 1900. Some 80yds northwest and faintly visible from the mausoleum is a partially buried mosaic that marks the original family vault, destroyed on George's instruction after it was likened to a gentlemen's lavatory. Harris Bay itself is a small cove fringed by black rocks; a perfect place to sit quietly and look out for otters, white-tailed eagles or larger marine mammals. It's worth allowing a whole day for the trip to make the most of Harris Bay and its surrounds.

INTRODUCED ANIMALS AND THE ISLE OF RUM RED DEER PROJECT

All of the largest animals on Rùm have historically been introduced or reintroduced. The island is supposed have the oldest **Highland pony** stud in the world and the long-haired **goats** are descendants of those brought over for wig making before the Clearances. In 1975, Rùm was the first place in Scotland for **sea eagles** to be reintroduced after they had become extinct in the UK during the 20th century; this turned out to be quite a successful project as there are now estimated to be around 130 pairs spread across the west Highlands' coast and islands.

Red deer are native to the UK and considered by many to be the most majestic and iconic of Scotland's animals. Their history on Rùm is complex. In 1580, during a survey of the area, James VI noted that Rùm had a good population of deer; by 1787, they were extinct on the island, only to be reintroduced for sport by the 2nd Marquis of Salisbury in 1845. At that time the deer were an important economic asset to landowners, as Rùm was used as a hunting retreat.

While some deer stalking still takes place on the island, the population around Kilmory and Mullach Mòr has been protected and studied by the Isle of Rum Red Deer Project (w rumdeer.biology.ed.ac.uk) since 1972. The Kilmory study area is the easiest place on the island to see red deer. Noticeable by their collars, the studied deer are less nervous of people and unlikely to run away as you walk past them; nevertheless it is important not to approach them directly and to keep dogs under control.

The studied red deer population have helped inform our understanding of red deer and ungulate populations in general; among many less worrying discoveries, the deer have been shown to be affected by climate change, with all their seasonal behaviours getting earlier over the years.

Perhaps the biggest benefit of the project to casual visitors is that these deer are much more tame than those in wild parts elsewhere in Scotland. If you are calm and quiet they are unlikely to run away from you as you walk or cycle past but, as with any large animal you are unsure of, do not attempt to approach them. Be especially careful during calving season (May–June) when, like sheep or cows, mothers will get distressed if you disturb them; and during the rut (September–November) when stags are at their most aggressive and can be dangerous to humans.

The Small Isles RÙM

5

115

EIGG (EIGE)

The second largest of the Small Isles and by far the most populous, dramatically beautiful Eigg is community owned and runs on sustainable energy. The mighty An Sgùrr (1,293ft), left over from a volcanic eruption 58 million years ago, dominates the skyline: looking north from Galmisdale Bay, on the southeastern coast, it is a huge steep-sided lump of rock rising far above its surroundings, but looking at Eigg from further south it appears as a long, humped ridge – the spine of a sleeping lizard. The island's coastline is mostly rocky, with high cliffs and a couple of wide sandy beaches. Hiking is less intensive than on Rùm, but nonetheless the views can be spectacular.

In 1695, Martin Martin wrote that 'natives dare not call this isle by its ordinary name of Egg when they are at sea, but island Nim-ban-More' (the isle of big women). We aren't given any further explanation, but stories and references to mythical women circulate the island in the forms of place names and folk tales. It is perhaps the richest of the Small Isles for archaeological sites, many of which are accessible by an undemanding bike ride.

GETTING AROUND Cars are only allowed on the island for residents or for Blue Badge holders, but as its road network is the best in the Small Isles it is particularly convenient for exploring on two wheels.

Bike hire

✱ ᦜᦜ **Eigg Adventures** PH42 4RL; w eiggadventures.co.uk. Well-maintained, quality mountain bikes with helmets, friendly service & good local information. Also offers kayak hire & guided walks. £15/day.

Taxi

🚗 **Charlie's Taxis** ☎ 01687 482404

 WHERE TO STAY *Map, opposite*
Eigg has excellent accommodation options, ranging from luxury bed and breakfast to simple camping. Self-catering listings can be found on w isleofeigg.org/accommodation. There are toilets and shower (£2) at the pier.

🏠 **Kildonan House** (3 rooms) Kildonan PH42 4RL; ☎ 01687 482446; w kildonanhouseeigg.co.uk. Lovely 18th-century farmhouse filled with character in secluded location. No en suites, but the dbl room has a shower & 2 twins each have a small wash basin. The dbl is quite grand with

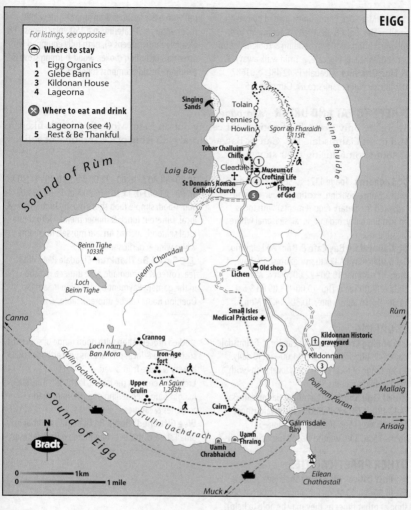

For listings, see opposite

Where to stay
1 Eigg Organics
2 Glebe Barn
3 Kildonan House
4 Lageorna

Where to eat and drink
Lageorna (see 4)
5 Rest & Be Thankful

wonderful views over the mountainous mainland, while the twins are smaller with slanted roofs. Marie is a local & provides an excellent welcome to Eigg. Loads of books & a wood-burning stove in the communal sitting room. At the lower end of this price range. **£££**

Lageorna (2 rooms) Cleadale PH42 4RL; ☎ 01687 460081; w lageorna.com. Stunning views over Laig Bay & the Rùm Cuillins. High-quality B&B accommodation with luxurious finishings. Both rooms have great sea views from large windows & are spacious enough to sit & relax in bad weather. No TVs, but good Wi-Fi connection. Having lived on Eigg for the last 40 years, owner Sue is a wealth

of information. Good green credentials. 3-course dinner (**££**) & packed lunches (**£**) available. **£££**

✴ **Glebe Barn** (22 beds) PH42 4RL; ☎ 01687 315099; w glebebarn.co.uk. This spacious bunkhouse, 1 mile from the pier, has the comfortable feeling of a large family house. There is plenty of space in the bedrooms, a large communal area for sitting & dining, & sofas in a big conservatory with incredible views over to the mainland. There are local-interest books & maps. Tamsin, who runs the bunkhouse, has lived on Eigg all her life; she can give good tips on walks & the island. **£**

Ⲗ **Eigg Camping Pods** (3 pods) Galmisdale Bay PA42 4RL; ☎ 01687 347007; w eiggcampingpods.

com; ⊕ Mar–Oct. Community-owned pods with small heater, light & electricity, sleeping up to 4. You must bring your own bedding & cooking kit (or eat at Galmisdale Bay café, a 1min walk away). **£**
Å Eigg Organics Cleadale PA42 4RL; 📞01687 482480; w eiggorganics.co.uk. Camping (£5 pp) with basic facilities & an amazing view, plus rudimentary self-catering in a 15ft yurt (sleeps 3) & Cleadale Bothy (sleeps 4), both fully equipped with essentials including cooker, wood-burning stove & bedding. Outside compost toilets. **£**

✕ WHERE TO EAT AND DRINK *Map, page 117*

There are only a couple of options for eating out on Eigg. Most visitors are likely to end up in Galmisdale Bay Café & Bar, a central gathering place and hive of activity, at some point during their stay.

✕ Lagéorna (page 117) ⊕ some evenings, with advance booking. Exciting 3-course menu (adapted for dietary requirements) with focus on sustainability: organic, local, seasonal where possible. **££**
✕ Galmisdale Bay Café & Bar An Laimhrig, Galmisdale Bay PA42 4RL; w galmisdale-bay. com; ⊕ summer 10.00–22.00 Mon & Wed, 10.00–17.00 Tue & Thu, 10.00–23.00 Fri & Sat, 11.30–16.30 Sun, winter 10.30–14.30 Mon,

10.30–14.30 & 16.00–22.00 Wed, 10.30–14.30 & 16.00–23.00 Fri, 11.30–16.30 Sat, 13.00–23.00 Sun. Good, simple food that's mostly homemade & local. Different lunch & dinner menus. Affordable local seafood, such as Arisaig mussels in creamy white wine & garlic sauce. **£–££**
▭ Rest & Be Thankful Cleadale PA42 4RL. Tea, coffee & homemade cake under a gazebo in the garden. Payment by donation in jam jar. Opening hours can be unpredictable. **£**

SHOPPING

Isle of Eigg Craft Shop An Laimhrig, Galmisdale Bay PA42 4RL; ⊕ May–Sep 11.00–16.30 daily. A nice range of local crafts, plus local maps with marked hiking routes.
Isle of Eigg Shop An Laimhrig, Galmisdale Bay PA42 4RL; 📞01687 482432; w isleofeiggshop. com; ⊕ May–Sep 10.00–17.00 Mon–Sat, noon–16.30 Sun, winter: closed Tue & Sun. Well-

stocked grocery shop with good range of specialist, sustainable & local products as well as basics. Also bakery & loose fruit & veg.
Lichen Centre of the island, PA42 4RL. Tiny shop in light blue shed selling organic, handmade toiletries & candles.
Wee Gift Shed Rest & Be Thankful (see above). Small shed with clever handmade gifts & felting.

OTHER PRACTICALITIES

✉ **Post Office** Isle of Eigg Shop (see above); ⊕ 10.00–14.00 Mon–Tue, noon–14.00 Sat (ask in shop at other times as they may be able to help).

SPORTS AND ACTIVITIES

Eigg Adventures (page 116) Sit-on-top kayak hire: sgl/dbl £20/40 for 2hrs around the Galmisdale Bay area. Bike hire, sailing, archery & walking tours also available, plus a ladies running retreat (around £395/3 nights) & a weekly running club.

WHAT TO SEE AND DO
The south

Kildonnan Historic Graveyard Situated about 3 miles (by road) from Galmisdale Bay, **Kildonnan Historic Graveyard** appears to have been used for burials from prehistoric times through to the modern day and is also thought to be the site of Saint Donnán of Eigg's monastery, founded in the 7th century. Donnán, a contemporary of Columba, is said to have been martyred on Eigg in 617, though the circumstances are unclear. The best legend goes

THE PEOPLE WHO GOT IN THE WAY

In 1577 around 400 people were massacred in a cave called Uamh Fhraing on the south coast of Eigg. This is part of a grisly running storyline of feuding and revenge between the clan chiefs of the MacDonalds of Clanranald and the MacLeods of Dunvegan on Skye.

It begins on Eilean Castell, the small island opposite Galmisdale Bay where the ferry comes into Eigg. A group of women, tending to the cattle there, were abused by passing MacLeod men who were on their way back to Skye from Glasgow. These men were killed by the women's male friends from Eigg, who were an extension of the MacDonald clan; as a result, the MacLeods came back to the island to avenge the deaths. Seeing the MacLeods coming, the inhabitants of Eigg hid in Uamh Fhraing. (If there were really 400 of them then it must have been extremely squashed!) After a while, growing impatient, they sent out a scout. The story goes that the scout was caught and his footprints 'in fresh snow' were followed back to the cave. The MacLeods built a huge fire, blocking the small entrance to the cave, and smoked all the hiding islanders to death.

In retaliation, the MacDonalds sailed to Dunvegan and burnt a church full of worshippers alive at Trumpan (page 79). This string of atrocities is one of the most easy-to-follow examples of how dangerous life could be as an ordinary person living in the times of clan warfare. Chiefs had an ultimate power over the lives and deaths of their extended clansmen and communities living on small islands and remote peninsulas were totally at the mercy of their whims.

that the Pictish queen sent her warrior women to kill Donnán and his monks. After beheading them, the women saw bright lights above the dead and heard enchanting voices. Entranced, they followed the lights up towards An Sgùrr and were led into Loch nam Ban Mora (Loch of the Great Women) where they drowned.

There is nothing to see of Donnán's monastery today, but there is a ruined church here, built by the 16th-century MacDonald chiefs of Clanranald and which has several interesting carvings. Outside the church there is an elaborate cross shaft dating from the late 14th century in the distinctive type of design associated with the Iona school of sculpture, similar to those on Islay and Oronsay. Inside the church is a stone slab with a double symmetrical cross inside a circle that is thought to be from the 8th or 9th century, a small carving mounted on the wall called Sheela-na-gig (goddess), which is probably pre-Christian, and a number of early grave slabs. A number of carved crosses from Kildonnan can now be found in St Donnán's Roman Catholic Church (page 121). The site overlooks the 19th-century house at Kildonnan Farm, Eilean Chathastail (the island off Galmisdale Bay) and out towards the mountainous mainland.

Uamh Fhraing and Upper Grulin

Distance: 5½ miles; time: 3½–6 hours; start/end: Galmisdale Bay; OS Explorer map: 397 Rùm, Eigg, Muck, Canna & Sanday

This walk takes in two poignant historical sites including the cave of Uamh Fhraing and an abandoned village, as well as glorious coastal scenery, with An Sgùrr dominating the landscape inland.

To reach the cave from Galmisdale Bay, walk along the road that climbs up the hill, passing the camping pods on your right, and continue around half a mile through mature sycamore trees. Ignore the turning on the right towards the Community Hall and instead look for a gatepost (⚘ 56°52'41.2"N 6°08'22"W) on your left marked with a small yellow arrow and a pink circle. Go through this gateway on to a substantial track for a short time until you see an obvious turning to the left that heads south. Follow this track until you see a faint path indicated by a pink circle; take this new path.

The path dwindles into a sheep track as it veers to the west, but is quite simple to follow all the way down to steep steps over a tiny river, with the entrance to Uamh Fhraing (⚘ 56°52'25.1"N 6°08'43.9"W) in the cliffs on your left.

Commonly referred to as the **Massacre Cave** (see box, page 119), Uamh Fhraing has been a dark tourist attraction since the 19th century when there were still decomposed bodies in there. Eventually the population of Eigg became so embarrassed by this that they carried out proper Christian burials. There are no bones to see now, and the cave is relatively easy to access. You will need a torch if you want to go inside and doing so is very much 'at your own risk' as loose rocks occasionally fall from the roof.

From the cave you can decide which way to go: clamber over the rocks 500m further west to the **Uamh Chrabhaichd** (Cathedral Cave) at low tide; head back the way you came to Galmisdale Bay; continue your walk on to the abandoned village of Upper Grulin (as described below); or even head up to An Sgùrr (see below).

To go to Upper Grulin or An Sgùrr, head back up the hill to the main track. The direct route turns left up the hill Cnoc Leathan, just before you reach the red house; you can then cut across the fields to head north. Keep on the left-hand side of the trees towards the iconic grey- and red-roofed house in the shadow of An Sgùrr, which makes a very striking scene. In the early 19th century this building was a Tacksman's house, improved by the profits of the kelp industry, but it has also been a post office, inn, shooting lodge, factor's house and the proprietor's residence.

Head around to the right-hand side of the house and turn left on to the track. Around 100m further is a cairn and a small sheep track off to the right, which leads to An Sgùrr, but to reach Upper Grulin continue along the original track, passing wind turbines on your left. After around 1½ miles you come to a cluster of ruins and one restored building, which mark the remains of **Upper Grulin** (⚘ 56°52'45"N 6°10'44"W), Grulin Uachdrach in Gaelic (seen as such on some maps).

Grulin means 'stony place' and is associated with a mythical battle between the giants Daedalus and Biannual, with the peculiar boulders scattered around the area thought to have been left as a sign of their struggle. Cleared in 1853, this is the best example of an abandoned village in the Small Isles, with traces of at least 42 ruined buildings, some above and some below the track, in various stages of disintegration, which span several generations of inhabitants through the 18th and mid 19th centuries. All are roofless save one traditional white bothy, which is in the process of renovation, and some others have walls complete to shoulder height. There is also an **Iron-Age dun** (⚘ 56°52'44"N 6°10'48"W) on the southwest edge of the township, but it is difficult to identify among the ruins of more recent buildings.

Retrace your steps to return to Galmisdale Bay; alternatively, you can head up An Sgùrr by following the directions below: this will add another 3 miles and 885ft of elevation to your walk.

🚶 An Sgùrr

Distance: 5 miles; time: 3–4½ hours; start/end: Galmisdale Bay; OS Explorer map: 397 Rùm, Eigg, Muck, Canna & Sanday

An Sgùrr is Eigg's iconic, rocky peak and the island's most popular hike. The panoramic views from the top are spectacular and there is a great feeling of accomplishment from reaching the top of what looks to be an impossible climb from below. This walk reaches a summit of 1,289ft, but the route is actually quite simple, with no need to use your hands on the ascent.

From Galmisdale Bay, walk northwest along the road uphill keeping the camping pods on your right and continue around half a mile through the woodland. Ignore the turning on the right towards the Community Hall and instead go through the gateway (✪ 56°52'41.2"N 6°08'22"W) on your left that's marked with a small yellow arrow and a pink circle.

Follow this track through the field, aiming towards a single stone house (✪ 6°52'44"N 6°08'53.8"W). Just after passing behind the house, turn left on to the next track and follow it for just over 100yds until you see a small path on your left-hand side, marked by a stone cairn.

This rough and quite easily lost path leads to the base of the towering rock, before heading around and behind it on the right-hand side, north of the rocky cliffs. The climb still looks unfathomable at this point, with the path running along the northern edge of An Sgùrr for just under half a mile. A way becomes apparent as the path cuts up into the side of the hill, through a small crevice in the rock (✪ 56°53'06.7"N 6°10'24.5"W).

Once up on the saddle, take some time to look south, down to the ruins of Upper Grulin (see opposite) below and across to the northwest to the crannog in Loch nam Ban Mora (Loch of the Great Women; there is a strange folk association that it was once home to some abnormally big women).

Having soaked up the views, turn to the left and make your way around the scant remains of an **Iron-Age fort** (✪ 56°53'04"N 6°10'09"W) and along the southern edge of the summit towards the trig point in the east. There are fantastic views out to Rùm, Muck and Ardnamurchan, with the Skye Cuillins behind the northern part of Eigg on a clear day.

Once you've had your fill of the views, return the same way.

The north If you are able, the best way to reach the north end of Eigg is on a bicycle (page 116). Once you have conquered the hills after leaving Kildonnan or Galmisdale Bay, the central stretch is gently undulating with very little traffic. This is a good place to look out for hen harriers who prey on small birds and rodents on the open moorland. Few people live in this part of the island, but there is the small Lichen shop (page 118) and a small natural history visitor centre and museum inside the **old shop** (🕐 24/7; free). Continuing towards **Cleadale** you have the option of two lovely beaches: the broad, sandy **Laig Bay** or, further north, the smaller and more secluded **Singing Sands**. The pretty, white, St Donnán's Roman Catholic Church sits near the northern end of Laig Bay. Apart from during Sunday services, you are welcome to enter the church and have a look at the carved crosses saved from Kildonnan; some are fragments, but there is a wonderfully detailed 9th-century cross in Pictish style.

Sgorr an Fharaidh
Distance: 3½ miles; time: 3 hours; start/end: just south of Lageorna; OS Explorer map: 397 Rùm, Eigg, Muck, Canna & Sanday

Like the more famous An Sgùrr (see opposite), this is a climb that looks totally impossible from the bottom but which turns into a relatively easy hike once you

5

know the route. Sgorr an Fharaidh is a dramatic, rocky ridge that sits on the east side of the island's main road.

The route begins just south of Lageorna B&B; walk under the washing line and follow a sheep trail up to a wooden stile. You are aiming for the gully between two points; the one on the right being particularly sharp. The path heads up through a fern and bluebell grotto, the latter in flower around May, towards a stone wall that appears to block the gully, but actually has steps to help you climb up over it.

You will come to a grassy glade with ferns and heather around it and a tiny waterfall in front. Turn right here, climbing up a path and around the severe-looking rocks in front. You then come to a stile in the fence that leads on to a path bearing around to the left; this then takes you north along the edge of the cliffs, which is now on your left. Thankfully the path does not come close to the edge (it's a steep drop!), though you generally follow it all the way along the top. From here you have a bird's-eye view down over Cleadale and the beaches, and out towards the Rùm Cuillins. This tends to be a good place to spot the island's golden eagles.

Follow the path past the **Finger of God**, a conspicuous and mostly detached pinnacle of rock, and around the cliff's natural curve, which allows for different angles of the view at each point. Eventually you will pass a few small lochs and then come to a trig point and a fence on the left. Stay on the east side of the fence until you reach a small metal gate.

From here, a path (⊕ 56°56'13.1"N 6°08'38.8"W) leads down to the east in the direction of Singing Sands before you climb up on to the final crown of rock. It would be a shame to miss the panoramic view from this final, small summit; afterwards, return to the path leading downhill. It is a narrow sheep trail, but easy to follow down a series of many hairpin bends to the bottom.

Soon after there's a path to your right that leads southeast towards the few buildings near the bottom of the cliffs that make up Tolain. Look out for light purple Hebridean orchids growing among the grass in spring and summer.

Skirt around the buildings at Tolain to get back on to the 'main road' and head south towards Cleadale. In between Tolain and the farmhouse at Howlin are the turf-covered remains of the settlement of **Five Pennies**. The name refers to 'pennylands', part of a system of valuing land according to fertility, which probably came from the Norse and was taken on by subsequent powers in Scotland. Like Upper Grulin, the history here is complex, with many generations of habitation. The earliest reference is in a charter from 1498, but most of what we can see is much later than that, including some small houses, which would have been lived in by the poorest members of the community, known as 'cottars' at the time as a reference to their small cottages.

Continue on to Cleadale where, opposite Eigg Organics, is **Tobar Challuim Chille**, a holy well dedicated to St Columba, and slightly further south, on the left-hand side of the road, the **Museum of Crofting Life** (⊕ 24/7; donation requested). This is a traditional cottage left largely as it was abandoned, with small collections of other objects such as fishing gear and cobbler's tools.

Following this, you pass the war memorial on your right and are soon back at the start of the walk.

CANNA (CANAIGH) AND SANDAY (SANDAIGH)

Arguably the most remote of all the Inner Hebrides, Canna and Sanday feel like a reward for those who take the time to travel there. Joined by a bridge, the two islands share a community and are most often referred to as a single entity, Canna. Unspoilt and impossibly beautiful, Canna is structured like a tiered wedding cake with bands of basalt columns separating plateaus where the sheep and cows graze. These lush, green fields run down to the coastline, where there are towering sea stacks and secluded coves.

At low tide it is possible to walk across the sand between the two islands, but there has been some form of connecting bridge since the late 19th century. Canna is the larger of the two islands and currently houses more of the population, although this has not always been the case.

Peace, wildlife and scenery are many people's reasons for coming to the Hebrides and it's hard to find anywhere better than Canna for these things. The lime-based basalt columns form many of Canna's towering cliffs and rocky protrusions. Healthy white cheviot and unusually tall, brown zwartble sheep graze on remarkably green grass along with two types of cow: Aberdeen Angus and the visitors' favourite, Highland cattle. Excluding rabbits, of which there are plenty, wild land mammal species are limited. There are, however, otters and several colonies of grey seals. Between June and September, enormous basking sharks can sometimes be seen from the shore and the very luckiest of people might spot porpoise, dolphin and even occasionally killer whale. More (seasonally) reliable are the seabirds, particularly puffins, kittiwakes, shags, guillemots and razorbills, all of which nest on the islands. There is also a nesting pair of golden eagles and a pair of sea eagles, as well as peregrine, long-eared owls and numerous other species.

WHERE TO STAY   *Map, page 124*

Canna has a small handful of accommodation options, all of which have wonderful sea views. Toilets for public use can be found at the pier, community shop and at The Square, which also has showers (£1). Note that groceries are available at the community shop (page 125) but are expensive, so it's advisable to bring supplies across with you.

Tighard Guest House (3 rooms) PH44 4RS; \01687 462474; w tighard.com. Spacious rooms in an Edwardian house, positioned up on a hill with spectacular views & a lovely garden. Only 1 room has an en suite, though the other 2 have private bathrooms. **£££**

Canna Bunkhouse (8 beds) PH44 4RS; \01687 462477; w cannacampsite.com. This traditional whitewashed stone cottage with lime-green door & window frames sits prettily on the hillside under a crown of basalt columns. It is simple & old-fashioned inside, but has everything you need &, at £15 pp, it must be the cheapest bunkhouse in the whole region. The view out over farmland to the harbour, Sanday & Rùm beyond is unbeatable. **£**

Canna Camping, Caravans & Pods (3 pods, 2 caravans) PH44 4RS; \01687 462477; w cannacampsite.com. The campsite & pods are above the village in an isolated spot with beautiful views. Pods (sleep 4/5) are simple with only mattresses inside; you can hire bedding packs for your stay. Toilets are on site, but you have to walk 10mins to the farm for a shower. The 2 caravans (sleep 4–6) are more central, just on the edge of the extremely quiet 'main road', next to the farm & overlooking the harbour (choose West Caravan for the best view). The caravans are pretty dated, but clean & comfortable with small bathrooms, kitchens & electric mattress warmers. Manager Isebail, who also runs the bunkhouse (see left) & works on the farm, has lived on Canna all her life. **£**

Weekly rental

Burnbank (sleeps 4) Sanday PH44 4RS; \01687 462829. Traditional crofting cottage that feels even further away from it all with 2 twin rooms, Wi-Fi & telephone. £450/week.

WHERE TO EAT AND DRINK   *Map, page 124*

Canna Café West Bothy PH44 4RS; \01687 482488; w cafecanna.co.uk; ⏰ May–Sep 11.00– late Wed–Mon. High-quality local ingredients including foraged seaweed, lobster, crab,

CANNA & SANDAY

For listings, see from page 123

Where to stay
1 Burnbank
2 Canna Bunkhouse
3 Canna Camping, Caravans & Pods
4 Tighard Guest House

Where to eat and drink
5 Canna Café

Sound of Canna

Rum, Mallaig

Muck, Eigg

Dùn Beag
Dùn Mòr

Coroghon Castle
Almàn
Black Sand Beach

Canna Community
Shop
Canna House
Rhu Church
St Edward's Church

Compass Hill 458ft

A'Chill (Keill)
The Square
St Columba's Chapel & old mill stone

Canna Harbour

Sanday

Eilean a' Bhàird

Eilean Ghreannabric

Suileabhaig

Carn a' Ghaill 689ft

Traigh Bhàn

Talabric 93ft

Benn Tighe 590ft

Háslam

Na Fiaclan

Ged na h-àighne Duibhe

Canna

King of Norway's Grave

Souterrains

Rubha Langanais
Camas Thairbearnais

Tarbert Bay

Tarbert

Sgorr Nam Ban-naomha

Rubha Sgorr nan Ban-naomha

Standing stone
Conagéaraidh
Garrisdale
Leob on Fhionnaidh

Sliabh Meadhonach 488ft

An Steidh

Garrisdale Point
Dùn Channa
Dùn Teadh
Sròn Ruail 323ft

Sliabh Meadhonach 439ft

N

Bradt

0   1km
0   1 mile

langoustine, venison from Rùm, cheese from Mull & rabbit. Lunches include soup, paninis & rabbit sausage rolls. Evening meals are more exciting & complex. Booking ahead advised. £ (lunch), ££ (dinner)

SHOPPING

Canna Community Shop PH44 4RS; ⏲ 24/7 with honesty box; ♿. A good range of souvenirs including affordable knitted hats, homemade 'Canna Kitchen' jams & chutney, books & artist prints. Groceries are limited & quite expensive. Free drinking water, plus tea- & coffee-making facility (£1). Free Wi-Fi & option to pay on PayPal if you don't have cash.

OTHER PRACTICALITIES

Phone There is basically no mobile phone reception anywhere on Canna but there is a phone box next to the post office.
✉ **Post Office** PH44 4RS; ⏲ summer 10.00–16.00 Mon–Sat. Located in a green shed next to a telephone box, close to The Square. Worth supporting if you can.
Waste/beach cleaning There are big containers at the pier for refuse & recycling. Beach cleaning is actively encouraged.

WHAT TO SEE AND DO

Canna Harbour With sailing boats bobbing on the water and views across to Sanday, and backed by two churches (and a third across the water), Canna Harbour must be one of the most picturesque in Scotland, and a wander around it is an inevitable part of any visit.

The harbour's first landmark is the rounded, brown-stone **Rhu Church**, built in the early 20th century as a memorial to the previous owner of the island, Robert Thom, and aptly known as the Rocket for its cylindrical, pointed spire. Following the road north and then west around the harbour, you'll first pass the shop and Canna Café, before seeing a gate leading to **Canna House**. Canna's obvious 'Big House' was built around 1863 by Donald Macneill and was later home to Canna's last private owners, the historian and folklore scholar John Lorne Campbell and his wife Margaret. The house is currently closed to the public, but visitors are welcome to explore the gardens (free).

A further 550yds past here is the small, white Change House, built in the late 18th century and still inhabited today; here you'll also find the island's phone box and post office. Another 220yds west will take you to the **old mill stone** and **St Columba's Chapel**; the latter had a short interlude as the post office before being returned to a religious building.

The Square At the heart of Canna Farm, The Square is usually a hive of activity, busy with working dogs, sheep, cows and the people looking after them. It also hosts a small museum (⏲ open access) in the Old Dairy with a lot of interesting information and artefacts. Opposite the farm is **Eilean a'Bhàird** (Island of the Bard), named after Alasdair mac Mhaighstir Alasdair, a poet who served as factor of the island in the 18th century; he supposedly composed his greatest song while sheltering on the island under an upturned boat.

Sanday At just 0.71 square miles, Sanday is only a sixth of the size of Canna, with much of the western end of the island designated as crofting land. Even if you only have time for a flying visit, the beautiful sandy beach, **Traigh Bhàn**, makes a trip across the bridge worthwhile. The beach is hidden behind the sand dunes and rocks just a couple of hundred metres to the west of the bridge. In spring, the hill behind the beach is colourful with wildflowers.

The east side of Sanday is accessed by the coastal road, to your left after you cross the bridge, which runs as far as **St Edward's Church**. This Roman Catholic church was built in 1890, after the Clearances on Canna, when there was a much larger Catholic community on Sanday. It was also used by visiting fishermen from Barra and Eriskay, but has always had problems with damp and has now fallen into disrepair.

Heading southeast along the stone wall from the church will take you to the southern coast. This is the quiet end of the island and a wonderful place to see seals among the skerries and wading birds, such as lapwings with their slow irregular flight and wailing call. Rùm dominates the views from here.

From here, follow the coast anticlockwise until you reach the spectacular grassy, flat-topped sea stacks of **Dùn Mor** and **Dùn Beag**. From the end of April to July there are puffins nesting here, but other seabirds such as guillemots, fulmars, kittiwakes, razorbills and shags can also be seen.

Following the coastline north and then west, you'll pass the small lighthouse and then a couple of secluded coves. Don't forget to look out to sea, as there are good chances of seeing basking sharks during the summer months.

𝕏 A' Chill

Distance: ¾ mile; time: 30 mins; start/end: just west of St Columba's Chapel, east of Canna Farm; OS Explorer map: 397 Rùm, Eigg, Muck, Canna & Sanday

Just west of St Columba's Chapel, a gate marked with an orange arrow indicates the beginning of a path that leads to the site of the pre-Clearance village A' Chill (Keill). Leading through a mixture of conifers and broad-leaved trees, the path is lined with wild garlic and bluebells flowering in May.

Although there is nothing to see of A' Chill, it once had 32 houses. All the houses were flattened after residents were evicted in 1851 to make way for sheep, and all that is left in the area now is a graveyard. An impressive **8th- or 9th-century cross** remains here, depicting the Adoration of the Magi, where the 'three kings' gave baby Jesus gifts, and various animals. About 60yds west is the **Punishment Stone**, an ancient form of corporal punishment where the offender's thumb is said to have been jammed into the small hole.

100yds further south from the Punishment Stone is the **graveyard**, which itself has some interesting carved slabs.

To return to the harbour head towards the sea; as you come to a stone wall, bear right through a gate marked with an arrow. Keep heading in the same direction until you reach the main road.

𝕏 Black Sand Beach and Compass Hill

Distance: 2½ miles; time: 2 hours; start/end: Canna Community Shop; OS Explorer map: 397 Rùm, Eigg, Muck, Canna & Sanday

This easy but rewarding walk takes you through magical woodland and open fields to a pristine sandy beach.

Take the path that starts to the right (east) of Canna Community Shop, which leads past some sheds before beginning to climb through the woodland. Here are broad-leaved sycamores, hawthorn and cherry, the beginnings of a beautiful mature patch of woodland that has been planted for shelter from the wind. Follow the path past a polytunnel, with a high wall on your left; this is the boundary to Canna House gardens (page 125).

When you reach a pink buoy rope swing there should be a sign with four arrows. Choose the direction that leads towards 'Upper Wood Path to Corigan'; this is the higher of two thin paths leading off to the right.

Wade through the wild garlic, an unmistakable smell even if you can't identify it on sight, and enjoy the **woodland**, purple with bluebells and speckled with yellow primroses in spring. The view soon opens out over an abandoned barn and, further west, two of the islands' three churches.

When you reach a gate on your right, head through it and cross a field towards the barn. Noticing the old water pump on your left, head through the gate down to the **beach** and, if the weather is accommodating, take some time to enjoy a picnic or paddle here.

Across the streaked sand to your left, at the far east of the bay, is the ruin of **Coroghon Castle**, standing on top of sheer basalt cliffs, over 65ft high. The small stone structure consists of two rooms that incorporate the natural rock as partial walls. It is thought to have been a prison, used in the 17th century for the unbalanced Donald MacDonald of Clanranald to hold his wife, Marion MacLeod, hostage.

Once you've had your fill of exploring or paddling, head back through the gate near the barn, where you can choose whether to retrace your steps to the harbour or walk up Compass Hill.

To climb **Compass Hill**, look for another gate much higher and off the right (northeast). Follow the faint, grassy track that leads towards this gate and go through it. Turn right and follow grassy tracks, past a radio mast to the east and the more gently sloped side of Compass Hill. Once you have enjoyed the view at the top, you can either head back to the barn and find the track that leads west back to the village, or continue around the coast to the north, where there is a string of spectacular, if precarious, viewpoints. Take great care if you go to look at the viewpoints as gusts of wind can come up unexpectedly.

Souterrains, the King of Norway's Grave and Canna's western coastline

Distance: 13 miles (with several options to turn back sooner); time: 8–10 hours (for the full route) start/end: Canna Farm; OS Explorer map: 397 Rum, Eigg, Muck, canna & Sanday

This long walk visits seven archaeological sites around some of the most spectacular coastal scenery in the Inner Hebrides. While some of the route follows tracks or route indicators, other parts cross rough ground where some navigation is required. The western half of Canna is uninhabited, but you are likely to come across some very free-range sheep and cows.

Following the southern coastal road west from Canna Farm, with the sea on your left, you can follow the occasional orange arrows that mark the route as far as the souterrains (page 128).

After passing the majority of the houses, take the right turning through a metal gate, marked towards Tarbert and the campsite.

Passing the campsite on your right, and walking below the huge crowns of basalt columns, notice the biggest rocky promontory sticking out into the sea with a small island off its point; the dangerous rocks around this island are called **Na Fiaclan** or 'the teeth' (✪ 57°02'59"N 6°32'18"W).

Some 550yds further towards Tarbert is a steep-sided sea channel called **Geò na h-Ighne Duibhe** ('the chasm of the black-haired girl'), named after someone who fell into it and drowned. If you're walking along this coastline in the summer months, scan the ocean for basking sharks, which are seen fairly regularly.

Shortly after the channel, the track climbs inland towards a gate followed by a sharp corner, which leads downhill towards a beautiful beach and Tarbet's one building. At the corner, look for the small, orange arrow pointing right (✪ 57°03'35"N 6°32'57"W) and leave the main track here to follow a less distinct path next to a dyke, going roughly north for around 660yds.

After crossing through a hole in an old dry-stone wall, keeping to the left of a small lumpy hill and going over a couple of rudimentary wooden bridges, the faint path splits and another arrow indicates a right-hand turn.

Choose the path following the middle ground, around the side of another small hill, and you should find the entry to the **souterrains** (⊕ 57°03'52.5" N 6°32'50.4"W) around 220yds after the last wooden bridge. Set in a lumpy, green, grassy area, characteristic of prehistoric human activity, the souterrains appear as two holes, with some exposed stonework and, on the northern one, a lintel supporting the roof. Look out for golden and sea eagles, of which there is one pair of each on the islands, as well as peregrines and other, smaller birds.

There aren't any further orange arrows to follow from here, but you can find the King of Norway's Grave by continuing northwest for around 330yds into a steep-sided channel that leads towards the sea. Following grassy sheep tracks, head around the left-hand side of a dry-stone wall and you should come down to a flat, grassy promontory, **Rubha Langanais**, with incredible views of the cliffs and coastline in both directions.

The King of Norway's Grave is about 220yds from here at the base of the hill, on the west of the promontory. Regularly placed stones in the vague shape of a boat indicate what has traditionally been thought to be a Viking ship burial; the other explanation is a **kelp kiln**, which initially seems less exciting until you really think about what that life must have involved. Campbell reported that any interference with the King of Norway's Grave was thought to bring a thunderstorm. There is a similar example of a kelp kiln on Tiree (page 153).

Take some time to enjoy the area. Shags nest on the basalt cliffs at the end of the point and in summer there are decent chances of seeing basking shark, porpoise or dolphin. On clear days, Skye's Cuillin Hills can be seen to the northeast, with the Outer Hebrides' Uists further west, but it still feels like the edge of the world.

From Rubha Langanais you can return the way you came, making the return walk about 6 miles in total from the village, or continue further by climbing the hill behind the King of Norway's Grave and hiking southwest until you reach the low, shallow part of Canna, which bisects the island into two oval lumps.

From here, keep to the east of the wall that runs all the way across the island, walk south beside it until you reach the original, substantial track at Tarbert and a gate going through to the west (⊕ 57°03'31"N 6°33'12"W). If you like, you can go down to the lovely sandy beach here or continue walking around the southwest coast, through a gate and along increasingly dramatic clifftops. Most of the time there is a vague path on this southern route, making it much easier than tramping along the northwest.

Slightly less than a mile after the gate, down below you at the base of the cliffs, is a grassy promontory with some obvious circular ruins (viewed from ⊕ 57°02'48'N 6°34'17"W). Named **Rubha Sgorr nan Ban-naomha**, which translates to something along the lines of 'the grassy slope headland of the holy women', this unlikely spot is thought to have been an early Christian establishment of Celtic origins. With no easy access from the sea and at the base of a 295ft cliff, its location is quite remarkable and unique in the Hebrides.

If you have walked all of this in one day, you are already at around 5 miles with 3 miles left to walk back to the village, so there is no shame in turning back now. Those with plenty more energy can continue along the coastline, keeping to the clifftops as you head west. The scenery on this stretch is breathtaking, reminiscent of the Faroe Islands – you're certainly unlikely to see similar to this in the entire region.

Reaching the far west, on the coastline below the trig point (⊕ 57°02'49"N 6°36'16"W) is another unlikely ruin. Set on a flat-topped sea stack, inaccessible without rock climbing, are the scant remains of the Iron-Age fort of **Dùn Channa**. Unlike at Rubha Sgorr nan Ban-naomha, it is hard to make out traces of the buildings here, but on careful inspection, you can see the remains of a stone wall, half covered with grass.

If you have walked this route as a whole, you have now walked about 8 miles. Continuing and making the full circle is tempting, but be aware that the ground is quite a lot rougher on the northern coastline, so the easiest route is to head back the way you came.

If you decide to make the full circle, continue to follow the clifftops. There is another fort, **Dùn Teadh** (⊕ 57°03'16"N 6°36'17"W), down by the sea in the northwest, which you can also admire from a distance. The remains of this structure are noticeable by an almost straight wall cutting across the neck of a broad, grassy headland. Compared to Dùn Channa or Rubha Sgorr nan Ban-naomha, it's easier to imagine how Dùn Teadh was accessed along the wide, grassy skirt at the bottom of the cliffs.

A little further northeast you can make out a **standing stone** and then, on a grassy area between two beaches, the severely ruined but easy-to-distinguish remains of a settlement at **Conagearaidh**, which you can also view from above. There is a colony of seals around here, whose howls you might hear drifting across the bay.

Inland around 300m from the cliff above Conagearaidh, is the ruined township of **Garrisdale** (⊕ 57°03'17"N 6°35'34"W), which was once one of the four farms into which Canna was divided. It was cleared in the 19th century.

In fact, there is so much archaeology in this area that you are constantly passing it. John Hunter's book *The Small Isles* (page 270) or careful study of Canmore (**w** canmore.org.uk) will help you to identify and interpret some of it.

MUCK (MUC)

One of the smallest islands featured in this book, Muck is only 2½ miles from east to west as the crow flies; following the road from the south to the north, it only takes half an hour to walk across the island. However, its craggy coastline of stretching skerries makes walking around it a great deal longer; something most people couldn't expect to complete in one day. Inland is green and notably fertile, having been used as a farm for many centuries, which it mostly still is. Residents are particularly welcoming and happy to tell visitors about the island. Almost a quarter of the 46 inhabitants are children and the island supports a thriving primary school.

Muck's rocky coastline is a haven for wildlife, with huge colonies of both grey and common seals living close to the shore, making the island one of the easiest places to see them in the Inner Hebrides. In spring, game birds such as red grouse, snipe and pheasant fly out as you walk and nesting herons are surprisingly abundant; at any time of year you are likely to see them standing peacefully in small coves around the island.

WHERE TO STAY *Map, page 130*

For such a tiny island, Muck has a lot of good accommodation options. For more information and further self-catering options, visit **w** isleofmuck.com.

🏠 **Gallanach Lodge** (8 rooms) Gallanach PH41 2RP; 📞 01687 462365; **w** gallanachlodge. co.uk; ♿. Welcoming accommodation with a grand sitting/dining room with comfortable leather sofas, a wood-burning stove & panoramic views over the bay. Solid wooden beds made on Rùm. Shared bathrooms. **£££**

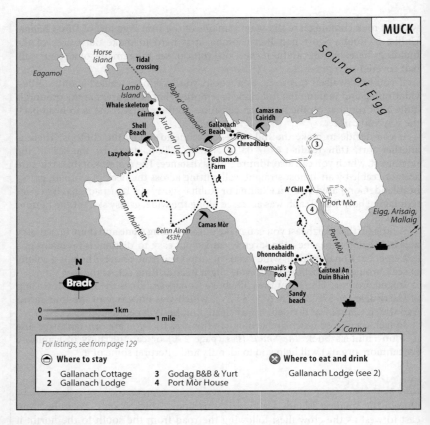

For listings, see from page 129

Where to stay
1 Gallanach Cottage
2 Gallanach Lodge
3 Godag B&B & Yurt
4 Port Mòr House

Where to eat and drink
Gallanach Lodge (see 2)

Port Mòr House (6 rooms) Port Mòr PH41 2RP; 01687 460001; w isleofmuckguesthouse. co.uk. Homely, family-friendly accommodation with spacious rooms: 2 family rooms, 3 twins & 1 dbl share 4 bathrooms. The 3-course dinner (included in the price) makes use of local produce. DBB **£££**

Godag B&B (2 rooms, 1 yurt) Between Port Mòr & Gallanach PH41 2RP; 01687 460264; w muckyurt.wordpress.com; ⊕ Apr–Sep. Kelly & Lewis, a friendly young couple with children, run this simple B&B in a secluded location in the east of Muck. Evening meals can be provided & are filling & homely. They also have a yurt (sleeps 5) in a wonderful location in its own field on a secluded stretch of shoreline looking out to Eigg & Rùm; compost toilet nearby & shower

available in community hall (see opposite). Rooms **££**, yurt **£**

Bunkhouse (4 rooms) Port Mòr PH41 2RP; m 07833 195654; e bunkhouse@isleofmuck. com. New, purpose-built wooden building with 3 bunk rooms & 1 dbl. Well equipped with oven, washing machine, baby seat & travel cot. Sea view from communal rooms. Exclusive use available. £20 pp; extra charges for towels (£3) & bedding (£5). **£**

Weekly rental

Gallanach Cottage (sleeps 7) Gallanach PH41 2RP; 01687 462362; e info@isleofmuck. com. Cosy, simple traditional cottage with spacious bedrooms, garden & amazing sea views. £480/ week.

WHERE TO EAT AND DRINK *Map, above*
Gallanach Lodge (page 129) Quality food in a grand dining room with a wonderful view.

Choice of local shellfish or lamb, & can cater for requirements; £25 for 3 courses & coffee.

Non-residents welcome if not fully booked, but must call ahead. ££

📺 **The Craft Shop & Tea Room** Port Mòr PH41 2RP; m 07908 956822; ⏰ summer 11.00–16.00 Fri–Wed. Home-baking, sandwiches & soup, as well as shellfish meals. Evening meals can be arranged in advance. Also a large selection of local crafts including knitted garments. £

SHOPPING AND OTHER PRACTICALITIES Muck does not have a grocery shop, so it is vital to stock up before you arrive.

Community Hall Port Mòr PH41 2RP; ☎ 01687 462365; e lodge@isleofmuck.com. A relatively large black building next to the school. Facilities include sports hall, Wi-Fi, toilets & showers, paid for in honesty box. Small heritage centre & games room upstairs.

Green Shed Port Mòr PH41 2RP; ⏰ 24/7. Honesty box shop with a good range of local crafts.
🌐 **Internet** Free Wi-Fi in small pebbledash building next to port.

WHAT TO SEE AND DO Even if you are only on Muck for a short time it is worth walking across the island to Gallanach, which has the island's best sandy beach. Exploring the island further, Beinn Airein is Muck's highest hill and gives the best views across the Small Isles; familiarising yourself with the distinctive silhouettes of Rùm, Eigg and the mainland will ensure that you never get lost while walking on Muck. There is plenty of uninhabited land to tramp around and you are welcome to do so but, as always, be considerate of the working farm and take care not to disturb livestock (see box, page 47).

Port Mòr Muck's capital Port Mòr, where the ferry arrives, is an eclectic mix of well-spaced buildings, mostly on the east of a natural harbour. Following the road, with the harbour on your left, you will pass through the centre of the village, with the large black community hall and school just a little further up the hill on your right.

Leaving Port Mòr, the main road travels northwest towards Gallanach Beach. Just after passing a road on the left you'll see a burial ground and, slightly further north, the rubble remains of a township called **A' Chill** (the old village or Sean Bhaile; ⊕ 56°50'11"N 6°13'53"W) consisting of at least 48 buildings from different periods. Abandoned by the mid 19th century, it is the best surviving example of an old settlement on Muck. There were two early Christian crosses in the burial ground, one of which can now be seen in the Community Hall. There is also a rounded stone memorial dedicated to two islanders and a student who drowned near Horse Island while trying to shoot stags.

Caisteal An Duin Bhain and the Mermaid's Pool
Distance: 3 miles; time: 1–2 hours; start/end: Port Mòr; OS Explorer map: 397 Rùm, Eigg, Muck, Canna & Sanday

Caisteal An Duin Bhain (⊕ 56°49'39"N 6°13'39"W), a large, prehistoric fort, is on the opposite side of Port Mòr Harbour to the ferry terminal. Start at the junction near A' Chill and take the road to the left; follow this south for roughly 110yds until you reach a fork, where you should choose the track on the right.

Just after the stone house with swings outside, you will come to a sharp corner, where you should leave the track to continue in the same direction south. Walk around half a mile over higher ground until you reach the fort. It is an obvious round lump, covered in grass on top, but with some visible remains of the walls above the natural rock. Climbing on top is not difficult and proves to be an excellent viewpoint across the sea to Ardnamurchan.

From here, continue around the coast for around 660yds, with the sea on your left until you reach a ruined farmstead (✥ 56°49'40.7"N 6°13'55.5"W) and vague remains of a slipway at **Leabaidh Dhonnchaidh**, as well as a restored building.

Some 220yds further south from the restored building is the **Mermaid's Pool** and a series of deep rock pools that are only exposed at low tide; at low tide, a walk a little further around the coast will lead you to a tiny, beautiful, **sandy beach**.

To return to Port Mòr, simply retrace your steps.

Port Mòr to Gallanach From Port Mòr it takes around half an hour to reach the north coast on foot. If you turn off right at a sharp corner to the left (just past a barn) and follow the grassy track down to the gate in a dry-stone wall, you will come to the little beach of **Camas na Cairidh**. Here, a dragon spine tail of rocks divides sand from a rocky beach and acts as a natural pier so you can walk out into the sea when the tide is right. This stretch of coast is frequented by otters and a good place to sit quietly and look out to sea for large mammals and birds.

A quarter of a mile further west is the old **Port Chreadhain** (✥ 56°50'32"N 6°14'53"W), which consists of two slipways and a quay used up until the 19th century; part of a large common seal colony rest on the rocks here, so be careful not to startle them. A little further is **Gallanach Beach**, by far Muck's most glorious stretch of sand. At low tide, you can see the remains of an old, rocky **fish trap** in the sand directly below the farm. There are flocks of oystercatchers and a variety of interesting things in the area such as an anchor and various old farm implements.

Northwest from Gallanach The headland of **Àird nan Uan** can be reached by taking a gated turning to the left just after Gallanach Farm and then turning right and walking north after about 100yds. There are two cairns here from the Neolithic or Bronze Age, the more northern of which has also been used as the MacEwen family grave.

Near the end of the headland, on the Gallanach side, you can climb down to the shore, where there is a whale skeleton. The piece of land to the north, which nearly gets cut off at high tide, is **Lamb Island**. From here it is just about possible to walk out to the larger **Horse Island** on a low spring tide. It's advisable to check your tide calculations with a local in advance, and to wear tough-soled water shoes and take sticks as the crossing requires negotiating seaweed-covered rocks. Hundreds of birds nest on Horse Island, with the cliffs at the north end supporting a small population of difficult-to-spot puffins. Allow yourself at least half an hour to get back across to Lamb Island.

Following the coastline from Àird nan Uan, with the sea on your right, will bring you to a restored croft house with a turf roof. Around 220yds further on is **Shell Beach**, a secluded little cove whose name is explained on closer inspection.

⋏ Beinn Airein and Camas Mòr
Distance: 3 miles; time: 2 hours; start/end: Gallanach; OS Explorer map: 397 Rùm, Eigg, Muck, Canna & Sanday
This walk covers terrain that can be boggy, with an ascent and descent of 453ft. To reach Shell Beach from Gallanach, take the small gate on the left just after the farm buildings and walk directly west across the base of Àird nan Uan Peninsula.

From Shell Beach head inland, passing through a dry-stone wall and continuing for a couple of hundred yards. Notice the regular ridges in the ground that create a striped pattern; these are lazy beds (page 267).

From here, a track leads around an old wall (⊕ 56°50'17.5"N 6°16'02.7"W); follow it for about 300yds before bearing off left and heading into the valley, Gleann Mhairtean keeping the stone cliffs on your left.

From the valley you can climb up Beinn Airein (453ft) by first climbing up to the saddle with Beinn Airein on your right and then choosing one of the small paths that climbs up to the top (⊕ 56°49'52"N 6°15'32"W).

Heading out to the summit, near the edge of the cliffs overlooking the coast, there are wonderful views out to Ardnamurchan, Mull and Coll. You can see the beach Camas Mòr (Big Bay) below on the left. There is a route down to the bay through the steep fields below: pass through a metal gate and then head down towards the bay, keeping on the right of the fence posts.

Camas Mòr is a designated area of Special Scientific Interest due to its incredible array of fossils that date from between 60 million and 3 billion years ago, particularly gryphaea, a type of oyster known as 'devil's toenails', which are obvious even to the casual observer.

To return to Gallanach Farm and the main road from the bay, head directly north (inland) around the left-hand side of the trees and out to the back of the farm. Aim for the far left of the farm buildings, on the left-hand side of a fence that climbs a small hillock, and you will shortly reach the gate (⊕ 56°50'24"N 6°15'22"W) back on to the main road.

INNER HEBRIDES ONLINE

For additional online content, articles, photos and more on the Inner Hebrides, why not visit w bradtguides.com/innerhebrides?

6

Coll (Cola) and Tiree (Tiriodh)

Jutting out into the Atlantic, with nothing to protect them from thousands of miles of wind and swell, Coll and Tiree are the most westerly and, by that measure, the most remote islands in the archipelago. With sweeping stretches of fine sand and secluded coves of coloured pebbles, spectacular beaches can be found on both islands. The machair here (crushed shells blown ashore to form a calcium-rich base) supports a unique ecosystem of delicate plants, insects and birds. Coll and Tiree are well known for their croaking corncrakes, but in springtime the sky is a cacophony of whooping lapwings, honking geese and the melodies of hundreds of tiny songbirds.

Geologically, both islands are made from ancient crystalline rocks, some of the oldest in Europe; formed during the Lewisian period, they underwent a lengthy and complicated process of folding and high temperature metamorphism deep within the Earth's crust. Particularly on Coll, but also on Tiree, this process has left veins of black and sparkling pink and grey quartz. The marginally warmer waters of the Gulf Stream provide good feeding grounds for gigantic basking sharks and marine mammals – and even the occasional coconut from the other side of the Atlantic. In winter, the islands' isolated positions make them incredible places for stargazing.

Like most siblings, Coll and Tiree are bound together by circumstance; they have as many distinguishing features as the qualities they share. Although there are only 2 miles of sea separating them and both islands are low lying (at 462ft Ben Hynish on Tiree is the highest hill between them), their landscapes are visibly different. Central Tiree is a vast, flat plain with its only hills in the corners; in contrast, Coll is made up of lumpy hillocks – rock erupts from the heather inland and coastal sand dunes form miniature landscapes that rival Skye's Fairy Glen (page 72) without a hint of the accompanying Instagram fanatics. Despite both islands being a similar size geographically, Tiree's population of over 700 people is the fourth largest in the Inner Hebrides and several times bigger than Coll's 170. Particularly well known for its watersports, Tiree also gets many more visitors.

HISTORY

Despite their seemingly remote locations, Coll and Tiree have been inhabited since prehistoric times, with remnants left from every era. Peculiar Megalithic cup-markings on Tiree's Ringing Stone and sporadically placed Bronze-Age monoliths give us little insight into the people, but there are many fortresses from the Iron Age, including a couple of brochs; the excavated Dùn Mòr on Tiree is a splendid example.

Columba, usually associated with Iona and much celebrated for his role in having brought Christianity to Scotland, founded a daughter monastery, Magh Luinge, on Tiree, though it is uncertain where. His feelings on the island are unclear, as he is reported to have banished Iona's unwanted demons to Tiree, as well as sending

ARCHITECTURE ON COLL AND TIREE

Of the houses built on Coll and Tiree in the 19th and 20th centuries, there is an interesting distinction in architectural style. On Tiree the main dwelling type was the Hebridean blackhouse, with double walls and a streamlined, hipped roof that did not overhang the walls. On Coll, single walls and overhanging roofs were the norm. This is thought to be a result of either the slightly more sheltered conditions on Coll or maybe just a difference in the landowner's ideas. There is now a mixture of buildings on both islands, but Tiree still has a much higher density of blackhouses than any other Inner Hebridean island.

monks there for penance. Around this time, under Dál Riata in the 6th century, Coll was controlled by the Cenél Loairn family whose descendants would later resurface under the name MacLean and, if all the claimed connections are to be trusted, popped up again to buy Breachacha Castle in 1965.

The Norse followed at the end of the 8th century, leaving several forts on Coll and many place names across both islands; Tiree's capital Scarinish, for example, derives from a translation of 'cormorant point' – a name that rings true to this day.

The 12th to 17th centuries – the reign of Somerled and his descendants the 'Lords of the Isles', and then subsequent clan rulers – was a turbulent period for both islands, with residents held hostage to the whims of feuding leaders who sought revenge and power. Tiree passed from the MacDougalls to the MacDonalds and finally to the MacLeans, who eventually went bankrupt and sold the island to the Campbells in 1674. The Campbells, Dukes of Argyll, still own the majority of Tiree to this day. A branch of Clan MacLean were granted Coll by Alexander of Islay, Lord of the Isles from 1423 to 1449, and managed to hold on to the island for nearly 500 years.

By 1800, Coll had around 1,000 inhabitants, while the population of Tiree, swelled by the landscape's remarkable fertility, built up to almost 4,500 in the 1830s. Money from the kelp industry and the relative efficiency of growing potatoes supported ever-growing numbers until potato blight and the crashing kelp market led to a starving, destitute population on Coll in the 1830s and a similar fate befell Tiree following the potato famine of 1846. Large numbers from both islands emigrated by choice, and the Clearances here were not as savage as in some parts of the highlands and islands – though the stories about them are nuanced, including that of an 1886 rebellion on Tiree that led to two warships being anchored and the conflict finishing with a sports day where the local team famously beat the marines.

Tiree has a proud history as a pivotal RAF base during World War II and remnants of this time are easy to spot as you travel around the island. Crossapol (on Tiree) was also the site of an Italian prisoner of war camp, but apparently the men were often free to walk around the island as they pleased.

Today, Tiree has the strongest Scottish Gaelic presence in the Inner Hebrides – around a third of the population are still able to speak the language, whereas the figure on Coll, and across Argyll generally, is closer to 4%. Tiree also has a higher concentration of crofting land; contrastingly, most of the land on Coll is now privately owned, following the death of the last laird in 2012.

GETTING THERE AND AWAY

Note that campervans, caravans and those camping with a car are not allowed to arrive on Tiree without first booking a pitch (page 145).

6

No matter how tired you might feel from the previous stages of your journey, falling asleep on the ferry to Coll and Tiree would be a mistake. Remember to take your coat on board whatever the weather, so you can sit out on deck and scan the ocean for wildlife. Calm seas improve your chances of spotting harbour porpoises, common and bottle-nosed dolphins, minke whales and basking sharks. On the other hand, rough weather and strong winds are a good time to search the skies for seabirds; during summer there are large numbers of gannets, razorbills, guillemots, kittiwakes, shags, fulmars and Manx shearwaters, and there's a slim possibility of seeing puffins.

Leaving Oban, look back to McCaig's Tower, the impressive, round folly that dominates Oban's skyline, and the ruins of Dunoile Castle before the ship passes between tiny Maiden Island on the starboard side and Kerrera's obelisk to the port side (appropriately, a memorial to David Hutcheson, one of the founders of the ferry company that later became Caledonian MacBrayne or CalMac).

Shortly afterwards, you will pass between Lismore Lighthouse, one of the most spectacular in the region, and Duart Castle on Mull, narrowly avoiding the notorious Lady's Rock. This is the entry point into the Sound of Mull. For the next 25 miles you will travel between the east coast of Mull and the wild, mainland Morvern Peninsula. Taking occasional glances at one of the wonderful nautical route maps to be found in the ferry's corridors, you should be able to identify the ruined castle on Ardtornish Point (Morvern side) followed by the colourful houses of Tobermory's harbour opposite the mouth of Loch Sunart, which divides Morvern from the Ardnamurchan Peninsula on its northern bank. A little later, the imposing Mingary Castle, now encasing a luxury hotel, stands overlooking the Sound of Mull's northern entry, with Glengorm Castle, an impressive 19th-century country house on the other side, southwest.

The ferry sails onwards into open water. On a clear day, the dramatic outline of Rùm appears behind Ardnamurchan Lighthouse and, with the low shape of Coll growing larger to the west, you might be able to spot the tiny Treshnish Isles to the south. Those going on to Tiree will pass by this string of unique islands quite closely; getting the best possible view of the Dutchman's Cap (see box, page 185) without going on a special boat trip.

By ferry CalMac (✆ 08000 665000 or, from outside the UK, +44 1475 650397; w calmac.co.uk; ♿) runs daily from Oban to Coll in around 2 hours 40 minutes, or it's 4 hours to Tiree (Coll: cars/foot passengers £48/9.30; Tiree: cars/foot passengers £58.55/16). The journey between Coll and Tiree on the same ferry takes 55 minutes (cars/foot passengers £16/3.55). Once a week in summer a ferry also goes from Coll and Tiree to Castlebay on Barra (marked with 'A' on the same timetable; cars/foot passengers £48/9.30), which takes 2 hours 45 minutes. Note that crossings are cancelled on a fairly regular basis during winter and rough weather.

Ferries arrive in Arinagour on Coll (half a mile south of the village) and Scarinish on Tiree (half a mile northeast of the main village); on Coll, the Coll Hotel (page 139) and Kip Poulson (✆ 01879 230479), can provide pre-arranged pickup (for a fee).

top	The seabird cliffs on Colonsay are teeming with thousands of razorbills, shags, guillemots, gulls and fulmars (KF) page 212
above left	Known locally as 'tystie', black guillemots nest on exposed coastal cliff faces (G/S) page 10
above right	On Coll, Tiree, Iona and Islay, listen out for the rare corncrake's distinctive 'crex crex' call from April into the summer (E/S) page 11
below left	Spectacular white-tailed eagles soar over coastal waters, especially around Mull (MM/S) page 10
below middle	Shags stand proudly on coastal rocks and nest among cliffs across the islands (MF) page 10
below right	Look out for short-eared owls in moorland glens across the archipelago (MC/S) page 10

above   Grey seals are a common sight along the islands' coastlines (MF) page 9

left   One quarter of the world's whale and dolphin species visit Inner Hebridean waters; pictured here a common dolphin (RD/S) page 9

middle left   Otters are relatively common, but elusive (MF) page 8

below   The waters here are one of the best places in the world to see basking sharks (MP/S) page 10

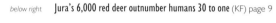

above	Boxing mountain hares in their winter coats (WF/iS) page 9
below left	Originally introduced to the Inner Hebrides, goats now roam the islands in feral herds (KS/S) page 115
bottom left	Elusive pine martins live on Skye, Seil and Mull (MM/S) page 9
below right	Jura's 6,000 red deer outnumber humans 30 to one (KF) page 9

above   The old Tor Mòr quarry and beach on Mull (KF) page 178

left   Thrift (also known as sea pink) along the coast of Islay (KF)

below left   Sheltered bays are perfect for kayaking (IBM/S) page 33

below   Tiree is world famous for its watersports (NH/DT) page 147

bottom   The incredible basalt columns around Staffa's Fingal's Cave have inspired centuries of art and music (EA/S) page 185

above   The Needle is an iconic sight along Skye's Quiraing landslide (AW/iS) page 69

below left   The Paps of Jura dominate the island's landscape (KF) page 243

below right   The majority of Rùm is a mountainous wilderness, but adventurous hikers can spend the night in bothies such as Dibidil in the remote southeast (4/S) page 111

above   Medieval fortress Duart Castle hosts an excellent museum (Sp/S) page 172

left   Tiree has the Inner Hebrides' highest concentration of traditional blackhouses (KF) page 20

below   The prehistoric Bodach and Cailleach standing stones on Gigha are thought to represent a man and woman (KF) page 257

above   In the 18th and 19th centuries, the Slate Islands were at the centre of the Scottish slate mining industry; here the weathered slates cover the beach in Cullipool, Luing (KF) page 204

below left   Ruined houses that once formed part of the township Upper Grulin on Eigg, cleared in 1853 (KF) page 120

bottom left   Dùn Hallin, an Iron Age broch on Skye's Waternish peninsula (KF) page 78

below right   The Picts left little more than carvings to remind us of their existence; pictured: Clach Ard on Skye (KF) page 78

MOORINGS

Coll Caledonian Maritime Assets Ltd, Arinagour PA34 4DB; ✆ 01475 749920; w cmassets.co.uk

Tiree Gott Bay Moorings, PA77 6UH; ✆ 01879 220074; w isleoftiree.com/gott-bay-moorings

BY AIR Coll Airport is located in the southwest of Coll; Hebridean Air (w hebrideanair.co.uk) fly here from Oban. There is no public transport, but both the Coll Hotel (page 139) and Kip Poulson (see opposite) can provide pickups when possible (arrange in advance).

Tiree Airport is in the centre of the island and served by flights from Glasgow with Loganair (w loganair.co.uk) and from Oban with Hebridean Air (page 259). Pickup can be arranged with the Ring 'n' Ride bus service (book up to a week in advance; page 145) or John Kennedy Taxis (✆ 01879 220419). Car hire is also available (page 145).

COLL

Coll, the more northerly of the two islands, is often described by visitors and residents alike as 'what the Hebrides used to be like'. Far from almost everything except Tiree, the island has a close-knit community, with several inhabitants happily insisting that 'you have to be mad' to live there. Visiting in sunny spring, when the machair is sprinkled in rare carpet flowers and turquoise water laps at two dozen spotless, fine sandy beaches, you begin to wonder if they are trying to foster that impression in order to keep the island a secret. Life is centred around the main village, **Arinagour**, a planned settlement built around 1800 in the hope of establishing a new linen industry, where strings of small, white cottages look out across a quiet single-track road to their harbourfront gardens; a row of whitewashed, round trawler weights forms a picturesque notice not to drive on the grass and everybody seems to have at least one boat waiting for their sunny days off. Arinagour boasts a couple of shops, two excellent places to eat and all of the island's amenities.

Low lying but lumpy inland, Samuel Johnson's description from 1773 still applies today:

> Col is not properly rocky; it is rather one continued rock, of a surface much diversified with protuberances, and covered with a thin layer of earth, which is often broken, and discovers the stone. Such a soil is not for plants that strike deep roots; and perhaps in the whole island nothing has yet grown to the height of a table.

There are still very few trees, but farming continues and flocks of sheep and herds of cattle, including free-roaming bulls, inhabit most corners of the island.

GETTING AROUND There is no public transport on the island but hitchhiking makes a decent option and most locals will happily give you a lift – just bear in mind that some areas receive very little traffic so you could be waiting a while.

It is important to note that the northeast corner of Coll is called the 'East End' by locals; the southwest is known as the 'West End' and thus your bearings might get slightly skewed.

By bike At roughly 13 miles long and 3 miles wide, Coll is the perfect size for cycling.

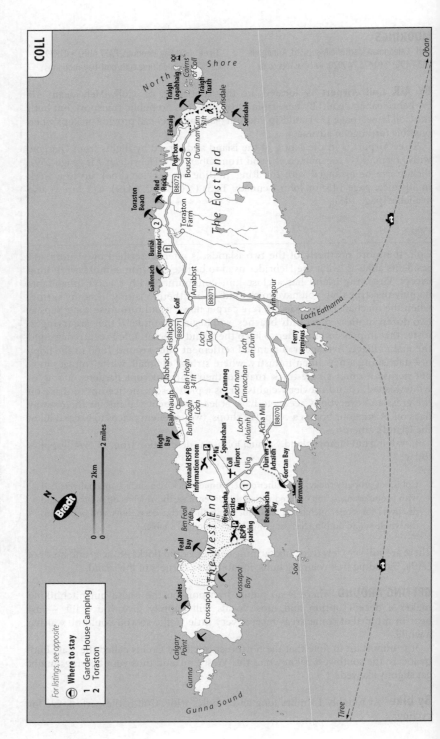

For listings, see opposite

Where to stay
1 Garden House Camping
2 Toraston

COLL

N

Bradt

0   2km

0   2 miles

North Shore

Cairns of Coll

Tràigh Logabhaig

Tràigh Tuath

Sorisdale

Eileraig

Druim nan Carm Rift

Post box

Bousd

B8072

The East End

Red Rocks

Toraston Beach

Toraston Farm

Burial ground

Gallenach

Arnabst

Golf

B8071

Grishipoll

Clabhach

Arinagour

Loch Eatharna

Ferry terminus

Ballyhaugh

Ben Hogh 341ft

Ballyhough Loch

Loch Cliad

Loch an Duin

Crannog

Loch nan Cinneachan

Hogh Bay

Totronald RSPB information room

Na Sgeulachan

Coll Airport

Uig

A'Cha Mill

Loch Anlaimh

B8070

Dùn an Achaidh

Gortan Bay

Harmonie

Feall Bay

Ben Feall 66ft

Breachacha castles

RSPB parking

Breachacha Bay

Caoles

The West End

Calgary Point

Crossapol

Crossapol Bay

Gunna

Gunna Sound

Soa

Tiree

Oban

COLL and TIREE Coll

Bike hire

An Acarsaid Arinagour Arinagour PA78 6SY; ☎01879 230329; e info@anacarsaid; ⏰ summer 09.00–13.00 Mon–Sat, winter 09.00–12.30 Mon–Sat. Road bikes £20/day inc helmet.

By car All Coll's roads are single track. It can be difficult to know where to park as, away from Arinagour, the only indicated, official parking places are the two in the RSPB reserve (Totronald and at the end of the road towards Crossapol Beach) in the southwest. As always, avoid blocking gateways or passing places.

WHERE TO STAY *Map, opposite*

Coll's accommodation options are limited, but excellent in each price range.

The Coll Hotel (6 rooms) Arinagour PA78 6SZ; ☎01879 230334; w collhotel.com. An inn since 1802, but newly refurbished, bright & modern, this busy hotel is a credit to Coll. 4 rooms have views over the bay. Family room has original & ridiculously deep bath. New accommodation for people with mobility problems is planned. Contact the hotel about wild camping (£) in the grounds behind the hotel. There's access to a shower if you buy dinner in the hotel. **££££**

Tigh na Mara Guest House (7 rooms) Arinagour PA78 6SY; ☎01879 230354; w tnmcoll.com. Friendly & welcoming owner Paula has won just about every award available to an affordable B&B: straight 5s on Tripadvisor, '4 Star Guesthouse' & 'Taste Our Best' for using local products from Visit Scotland; the list goes on. She has spent years compiling local information, which is provided in folders for guests. Fiercely family friendly. Local b/fast specials include seasonal scallops. Home-baking & complimentary whisky in guest lounge. Packed lunches on request (in advance). Paula also runs The Wee House (sleeps 3) next door, a small self-catering cottage (£375/week). **£££**

Coll Bunkhouse (16 beds & 2 spots for motorhomes) Arinagour PA78 6SY; ☎01879 230217; w collbunkhouse.com; ♿. New, purpose-built building run by An Cridhe community centre & local charity Development Coll. Modern, well-equipped kitchen & lounge. Laundry. Dogs allowed. **£**

Garden House Camping Between Breachacha & Uig PA78 6TB; ☎01879 230374; e collcampsite@hotmail.com; ⏰ Apr–end Sep. Set in an 18th-century walled garden, ¼ of which is set aside for campers. Once part of Breachacha Castle & referred to by Johnson & Boswell in 1773. Mature trees on one side attract plentiful songbirds & corncrakes croak in surrounding RSPB reserve at night. Short walk to Breachacha Bay. Basic facilities. No dogs. No Wi-Fi. Note that the turning is easily missed (56°35'49.3"N 6°36'46.5"W). **£**

Toraston Beach & dunes on the northwest coast, PA78 6TE; m 07554 095464, 07748 647818. Wild camping is permitted at this isolated spot with no facilities. Call Heather & Tom for permission. Free.

WHERE TO EAT AND DRINK *Map, opposite*

Coll's options for eating out are even more limited than its accommodation, but also high quality.

The Gannet Restaurant The Coll Hotel (see above); ⏰ food: noon–14.00 & 18.00–20.30 daily; bar: 11.00–22.00/midnight. Good food with quality ingredients: locally caught lobster, crab, langoustines, squat lobster & dived scallops; baking & ice cream made on site; seasonal vegetables. Attractive, newly decorated restaurant with wooden furnishings, brown leather & exposed stonework. Bar overlooking harbour. Garden seating. **££**

Island Café Shore St, Arinagour PA78 6SY; ☎01879 230262; w theislandcafe.business.site; ⏰ Apr–Sep 11.00–14.00 & 17.30–20.00 Wed–Sat, noon–18.00 Sun, Oct closed, Nov–Mar 11.00–14.00 & 17.00–20.00 Fri & Sat, noon–18.00 Sun. Not just a café, but also a restaurant serving tasty, hearty meals as well as baguettes & all-day fry-ups. Good range for vegetarians/vegans. Friendly family business in low-key, colourful setting. **£–££**

SHOPPING

An Acarsaid Arinagour (page 139) Gift shop with Katie Morag children's books (set on Coll) & wool, rugs, knitted jumpers, etc, from own Hebridean sheep. Take the left after Island Café.

Island Stores Arinagour PA78 6SY; ☏01879 230484; ⊕ summer 10.00–12.30 Mon & Tue, 10.00–17.30 Wed, 10.00–13.00 Thu & Fri, 10.00–16.00 Sat, winter hrs reduced. Basic food supplies. Possible to call in advance to pre-order before arrival.

✳ **Lighthouse Gallery** Arinagour PA78 6SY; ☏01879 230479; w kippoulson.com; ⊕ open access. This shed hosts a tiny gallery selling beautiful watercolours. To get here, follow the road & signs up the hill past the post office for around 500yds; it's well worth the walk.

T.E.S.Co Arinagour PA78 6SY; ☏01879 230262; ⊕ Apr–Sep 10.00–13.00 Mon–Fri, 10.00–17.00 Sat, winter hrs reduced. A brilliant little shop selling organic, ethical & unusual food, alcohol, toiletries & cleaning products.

SPORTS AND ACTIVITIES Summer, particularly July and August, is the best time to see basking sharks; while boat trips offer better chances, they can also be seen off the coast, so don't forget to look out for fins and tails poking out of the water while you're at the beach.

Boat trips

Basking Shark Scotland m 07975 723140; w baskingsharkscotland.co.uk; ⊕ summer. Low-impact small-group tours guided by marine biologist; 1 weekly departure from Coll Ferry Port. £195 pp (discounts for children).

Golf

Coll Golf Course Cliad Farm, PA78 6TE; ⊕ Jun–end Aug. Ask in the Coll Hotel (page 139). Day: adult/child/family £10/3/20; week: adult/child/family £15/5/30.

OTHER PRACTICALITIES Coll's excellent community centre **An Cridhe** (Arinagour PA78 6SY; ☏ 01879 230000; w ancridhe.com; ⊕ 09.00–21.00 daily; ♿) has a gym, toilets, showers, paid internet, tea and coffee. Check their noticeboard for events.

Fuel Coll Fuel, Arinagour PA78 6SY; ☏01897 230388; ⊕ summer 10.00–noon Mon & Sat, 16.00–18.00 Wed; winter hrs reduced.

✚ **Medical** Coll Medical Practice, Arinagour PA78 6SY; ☏01879 230326; ⊕ 09.30–10.30 Mon, Wed & Fri, 17.00–18.15 Tue & Thu

✉ **Post office** An Acarsaid, Arinagour PA78 6SY; ☏01879 230329; ⊕ summer 09.00–13.00 Mon–Sat, winter 09.00–12.30 Mon–Sat

EVENTS Check w visitcoll.co.uk for yearly dates and information.

March and October

Coll & the Cosmos w collbunkhouse.com/dark-skies-coll-cosmos. A w/end-long course in astronomy to celebrate Coll's special dark skies (adult/teen £90/75).

May

Coll Bird Festival w collbunkhouse.com/coll-bird-festival. A long w/end with guided walks, talks, a boat trip, meals & a cèilidh.

July

Isle of Coll Fishing Competition Arinagour; f. One of the competition rules is that locals must bring a visitor along with them in their boat. Organisation is a little haphazard, so either ask someone in advance (in person or on the Facebook page) or just turn up on the day & see if anyone can fit you in.

August

Coll Half Marathon w collhalfmarathon.org.uk. Running races including half marathon, 10k, 5k & children's 1k.

WHAT TO SEE AND DO Coll's main attractions are its beaches, birds and basking sharks. There's plenty on the island to explore, but rushing around to try and see everything would be severely missing the point. The island's main village, Arinagour, is pretty but very small, so it's likely you'll spend most of your time exploring the rest of the island.

The north coast
Beautiful, secluded, sandy beaches are strung along the north coast of Coll for over 6 miles between the North Shore and Gallenach.

Beaches between Sorisdale and Eileraig
Distance: 2½ miles; time: 2 hours; start: Sorisdale; end: Eileraig; OS Explorer map: 372 Coll and Tiree

This walk starts at Sorisdale, once a thriving community and still a working croft, which has a pleasant beach, but it's well worth pressing on north around the coast to the wild North Shore. It finishes in Eileraig, but there isn't much in the way of paths and you can walk as much or as little of the coastline as you like before rejoining the road, which is never more than a mile away.

At **Sorisdale**, parking is permitted in an unlikely spot to the left of the sign that reads 'keep clear turning only' but take care not to block the exit or gate. Look for the wooden sign next to a gate that directs you towards 'the bay 150m' and 'North Shore 650m'; follow this footpath for 160yds to the coast. The beach at Sorisdale, once a thriving community, is pleasant but is nothing compared with the wild North Shore.

Keep the sea on your right and walk north for around a mile along the coast; the route passes a small bay lined with colourful pebbles and on clear days you should be able to make out the curious outline of Eigg and mountainous Rùm on the northern horizon. Descend through the dunes to **North Shore**: try to follow paths where you can to avoid harming the fragile habitat, and look out for orchids among the marram grass.

The scattering of tiny islands laid out before you are known as the **Cairns of Coll** and were bought in 2014 by the author Alexander McCall Smith for £300,000, in an attempt to preserve them. He intends to do 'absolutely nothing' with them and donate them back to the Isle of Coll as a nature reserve when he dies. They are home to a large colonies of common and grey seals, which you might see bobbing inquisitively in the water around North Shore or basking on rocks.

The first of the North Shore beaches you reach is **Tràigh Tuath**, followed by smaller **Tràigh Logabhaig** around 500yds to the west.

At the far western side of Tràigh Logabhaig you can climb up to **Druin nan Carn** (151ft) for a better view over the coast, before descending towards the small pebble and sand bay at **Eileraig**, where a long-ruined farmstead overlooks the coast.

Continuing further from here requires cutting inland and negotiating around fences, so it makes a sensible point to head to the road and form a circular walk back to Sorisdale.

From Bousd to Hogh Bay
Fantastic beaches are the East End's main attraction, but take a moment to notice a couple of historical sites and other points of interest. On the **post box** (✛ 56°40'57.8"N 6°29'12.1"W) at Bousd, 'GR' indicates a date between 1910 and 1936, the reign of King George V. A mile west of Bousd, **Red Rocks** (**Tràigh Thorastain**) is a beautiful sandy beach with tidal islands opposite Cloiche Farm and only about 100yds off the road. Though it isn't wheelchair

accessible, it might be a good option for people who can't walk great distances due to its proximity to the road. The **burial ground** beside the road at Torastan has some interesting grave slabs that might be from the 17th or 18th centuries and the sand dunes west from here are among the most impressive on the island. These sandy hillocks are similar in appearance to Skye's Fairy Glen, but you are infinitely more likely to have them to yourself.

Further southwest, the T-junction at **Arnabost** is marked by many colourful buoys hanging on the fence. Continuing to the road end at **Ballyhaugh**, you can park a car carefully in the reserved spaces on the sides of the road before the cattle grid and gate of the Hebridean Centre in order to do the walk in the box below.

Hogh Bay, backed by dunes, might win the prize of the most spectacular beach on Coll. There are rip currents here, making it an inadvisable place to swim, but the waves can be perfect for experienced surfers. It can be reached from Ballyhaugh or by following the track north from the RSPB car park at Totronald.

The southwest There are a couple of hidden beaches and archaeological sites that can be found along the south coast and by following the airport road from

CLIMBING BEN HOGH

At 347ft, Ben Hogh is Coll's highest hill; the short climb affords a spectacular view across the Inner Hebrides.

Starting at Ballyhaugh, walk through the gate marked to 'Hogh Bay', but then bear left around the lake towards a second gate, a good place to see barnacle, Greenland white-fronted and greylag geese, as well as tufted ducks and other species.

Head along the southeast bank of the lake on an intermittent path that sticks to higher, dry ground. Cross two broken dry-stone walls and walk about 100yds past the east end of the lake before heading uphill to the saddle between three vague peaks. The peak to the southeast is a few feet higher, but the ground is very boggy in-between them so, unless you are really intent on reaching the top, it is better to head up left just before you reach the highest part of the saddle and find a small stile (⊕ 56°37'43.5"N 6°35'55.2"W) over the fence there. From the OS marker, on a good day, you can see as far as Jura and the Treshnish Isles, including the distinctive Dutchman's Cap or Bac Mòr, a wide, flat rim around a single round lump, to the south; the Outer Hebrides northwest; and Rùm directly north. Some 50yds north is the **Rocking Stone** a boulder left by a glacier or thrown by a giant depending on who you ask. It is balanced on three stones; I did not try rocking it and would not advise it either.

From the top, find a sensible route down towards a large rock in a dry-stone wall (⊕ 56°37'51.7"N 6°35'57.9"W), 200yds northwest of the Rocking Stone, where the wall can be crossed without damaging it. Head in the general direction of two blackhouses on the other side of the road, but take the diversion to a small ruined settlement that is still relatively intact with some windows and doors. From here, bearing slightly right and going over the hill, you will see the collection of houses that form Clabhach and a couple of gates to the road. Turning left on the road, it is less than a mile back to your starting point of Ballyhaugh.

There are also an unusually high number of ancient **crannogs** (page 266) in Coll's interior, but you will need to navigate to them across boggy ground. For enthusiasts, the following are particularly worth the effort of visiting: **Dùn Anlaimh** (⊕ 56°37'08"N 6°35'06"W) in **Loch nan Cinneachan** with the remains of a causeway that, according to tradition, was later defended by a Norse chief; one (⊕ 56°36'34"N 6°35'01"W) in **Loch Anlaimh** slightly further south; the remains of two crannogs (⊕ 56°38'17"N 6°33'22"W) in **Loch Cliad**; and another one (⊕ 56°37'44"N 6°32'49"W) in **Loch An Duin**.

Arinagour, although not all have sensible parking nearby. Arriving by bike (page 137) will give you easier access to the crannogs in particular, otherwise you can drive to the RSPB parking and explore the West End from there.

Just after Acha Mill, just south of the B8070, is a ridge of pink and white quartz. This once provided a natural defensive position for the Norse fort **Dùn an Achaidh** (⊕ 56°35'53"N 6°35'27"W), of which a few courses of stone wall remain.

Another mile west along the road, there is walking access to **Gortan Bay**; a lovely sandy beach with the remains of a shipwreck. You can just about find somewhere to park off the road without blocking the passing place or gate, opposite a large wooden shed and pretty white house with a slate roof and small glass conservatory on the front. Follow the track beyond this gate for just under a mile to its end, where you need to bear slightly left to get to the beach. The *Harmonie*, a wooden barque from Norway, was stranded in the bay in 1890, an accident which, thankfully, nine out of her ten crew survived. The shipwreck (⊕ 56°35'12.3"N 6°36'03.8"W), only accessible at low tide, is a gnarled spine of planks and metal, slimy with green seaweed and providing solid anchorage for a limp forest of bladderwrack. Take off your shoes and socks as the sand can be soft and waterlogged here when the tide has just receded.

Breachacha Bay and its castles Wide, sandy Breachacha Bay, home to many ringed plovers, is dominated by three enormous (privately owned) buildings: the imposing grey fortress close to the shore, a likely home for a Disney villain, is the reconstructed **(Old) Breachacha Castle**; behind it, if looking from the beach, is the ostentatious mansion house known as **(New) Breachacha Castle**; and the third, a flamboyantly crenellated construction, lower than the others on the shoreline further south, is still a working farm.

Totronald The two standing stones at Totronald are known as **Na Sgeulachan** (Teller of Tales) (⊕ 56°36'35.3"N 6°37'09.6"W). James Boswell, writing about his Hebridean explorations in 1773, recounts a traditional practical joke associated with these 'triangular flagstones':

Of latter times they are used for putting a trick on any stranger who is passing that way. He is desired to lie down behind the easternmost one (or westernmost, according to the route he is on) and told that he will hear everything that is said by the company, who stand at the other stone; and while he is lying in patient attention, the company get off and leave him; and when he at last gets up, he finds himself all alone.

The **RSPB information room** at Totronald gives some good information about the birds and wildlife living in the area and allows you to record your sightings, along with checking those of others. There is a special corncrake-viewing platform here, plus an official car park (but no toilet facilities). Along with Balranald in North Uist, Coll is one of the best places to see corncrakes in the UK. They are still notoriously difficult to spot, but their 'crex-crex' croaks come from all directions in summer and particularly towards the end of April and beginning of May. From spring to September, the RSPB reserve is filled with all manner of birds including swooping lapwings, redshanks and burbling snipe with their elongated beaks. Winter is dominated by honking Greenland white-fronted, barnacle and greylag geese, but you might see hen harriers, merlins or tiny, fat snow buntings.

The West End The West End of Coll is wild, surrounded by fine sandy beaches and only possible to explore on foot after parking at the RSPB car park at the road end, slightly east of Crossapol and Feall Bay. An 8-mile walking route to remote **Calgary Point** is described by Walkhighlands (w walkhighlands.co.uk/islands/calgary-point.shtml).

Feall A track from the RSPB car park leads about a mile northwest to Ben Feall. At only 216ft, this hill manages to give a commanding view out to Rùm in the north, the Treshnish Isles in front of the Ross of Mull and Ben More (page 169) to the southeast, and even the Paps of Jura in the far distance; Tiree barely rises above Gunna, the uninhabited island beyond Coll's West End. There is a strange arrangement of large stones here thought to be an ancient burial cist (✪ 56°35'54.9"N 6°39'10.5"W) and a more obvious memorial seat dedicated to the last Laird of Coll, who died in 2012.

The smaller hill just to the southwest of Ben Feall was once the site of a fort; there is little to see of it now, but its strategic position affords a spectacular view over sandy Feall Bay. Heading down to the beach, listen out for seals singing mournfully on the rocks. There is rubbish disposal for beach plastic at the RSPB car park if you feel like doing a good deed.

TIREE

Known to some in Gaelic as 'Tìr bàrr fo thuinn' (the land below the waves), Tiree is remarkably difficult to distinguish from a distance. Only nearly upon arrival do you begin to see the expanse of carefully placed, unassuming houses spreading into the distance on patchwork green croft land. Walking along the miles of spotless sand or taking a dip in the crystal-clear waters that surround it is enough for most holidaymakers, though the island is also famous for its watersports. Whether you take the plunge or not, there is nowhere quite comparable in the Inner Hebrides.

GETTING AROUND At 12 miles long and 3 miles wide, with attractions and settlements spread evenly across the island, Tiree is too big for most people to get around on foot, but with some unusually good alternatives on offer you do not necessarily need to bring a vehicle.

By car Tiree has a good range of indicated car parks. It is important not to drive on the machair or sand dunes as this destroys the unique and fragile habitat that makes Tiree so special.

Car hire

🚗 **Maclennan Motors** Scarinish PA77 6UH; 📞 01879 220555; e info@maclennanmotors.com; 🅕. Book in advance; drop-off & collection from airport available for £10 extra.

By bike
As most of the island is very flat, cycling can be an excellent option, but strong winds might make you appreciate the extra power injection from an e-bike.

Bike hire

🚲 **Tiree Fitness** Tir a Chladaich, Sandaig PA77 6XQ; m 07867 304640; w tireefitness.co.uk/bike-hire. Fitness enthusiasts Will & Becky offer high-quality bike hire. Mountain bikes & hybrids (day/additional days/week £15/10/65), e-bikes (day/additional day/week £25/20/120), kids' bikes, tag-alongs & child seats available. They also do bike servicing, repair, spares & sales. Book in advance & collect from Sandaig or they can deliver to your accommodation, the pier or airport.

On-demand bus

🚌 **Ring 'n' Ride** 📞 01879 220419; w argyll-bute.gov.uk/tiree-ring-n-ride; 🕐 07.00–18.00 Mon–Sat (Tue till 22.00 in summer); ♿. This amazing on-demand bus service is available anywhere on Tiree. Journeys can be booked up to 1 week in advance & up to 1hr before (if available). There is space for 1 person in a wheelchair.

Off-road wheelchairs

Tiree Trust The Island Centre, Crossapol PA77 6UP; 📞 01879 220074; w isleoftiree.com; ♿. 2 different types of wheelchair for using on beach & grass. Free to borrow, phone ahead.

WHERE TO STAY *Map, page 146*

In addition to the accommodations below, there is a huge amount of self-catering options on Tiree – they are great for longer stays, but you must book well in advance. Some properties are traditional blackhouses or croft houses and can even be right on the beachfront; w isleoftiree.com/accommodation provides uncommonly comprehensive listings with photos. Note that campervans, caravans and motorhomes are not allowed on Tiree without first booking a pitch. For campers (see below), **drinking water**, **toilets** and **chemical waste disposal** are available opposite An Iodhlann Museum in Scarinish, while there is a **shower** at Pier Laundry. Self-service **Pier Laundry** (Pier, Scarinish PA77 6UH; 📞 01879 220440; w pierlaundry.co.uk; 🕐 24/7) and Fiona Malcolm's **Linen Hire** (📞 01879 220045; e ifitiree@gmail.com) are also available on the island.

❋ 🏠 **Rockvale Guesthouse** (5 rooms) 35 Balephetrish, PA77 6UY; 📞 01879 220675; w rockvaletiree.co.uk; ♿. This high-quality B&B is exceptional value. En-suite bedrooms are quiet & comfortable, bed linen is Egyptian cotton, there is a guest lounge with book exchange & good information on walks/Tiree in general. Above & beyond all of this, however, is the b/fast, which includes a delicious homemade granola & an extensive range of choices such as: Kintyre Kipper; fruit smoothies; poached eggs on potato scones with fried mushrooms, spinach & pesto; as well as full Scottish or vegetarian b/fasts. Peaceful location surrounded by green fields & a short walk from Balephetrish Bay. Dogs accepted by prior arrangement. Drying space for wetsuits, bikes, etc. 2-night min stay. **£££**

🏠 **Millhouse Hostel** (sleeps 16) Cornaigmore PA77 6XA; 📞 01879 220802; w tireemillhouse.co.uk. Interesting location near historical mill. Light, spacious dorm rooms (£25 pp) & small private rooms sleeping 1–3 people, with basic communal facilities. Free washing machine for clothes. A few pounds more than other hostels in the region, probably due to Tiree's watersports crowd. **£**

⛺ **Balinoe Campsite** Near Balinoe & Heylipol PA77 6TZ; m 07712 159205; w tireecampsite.

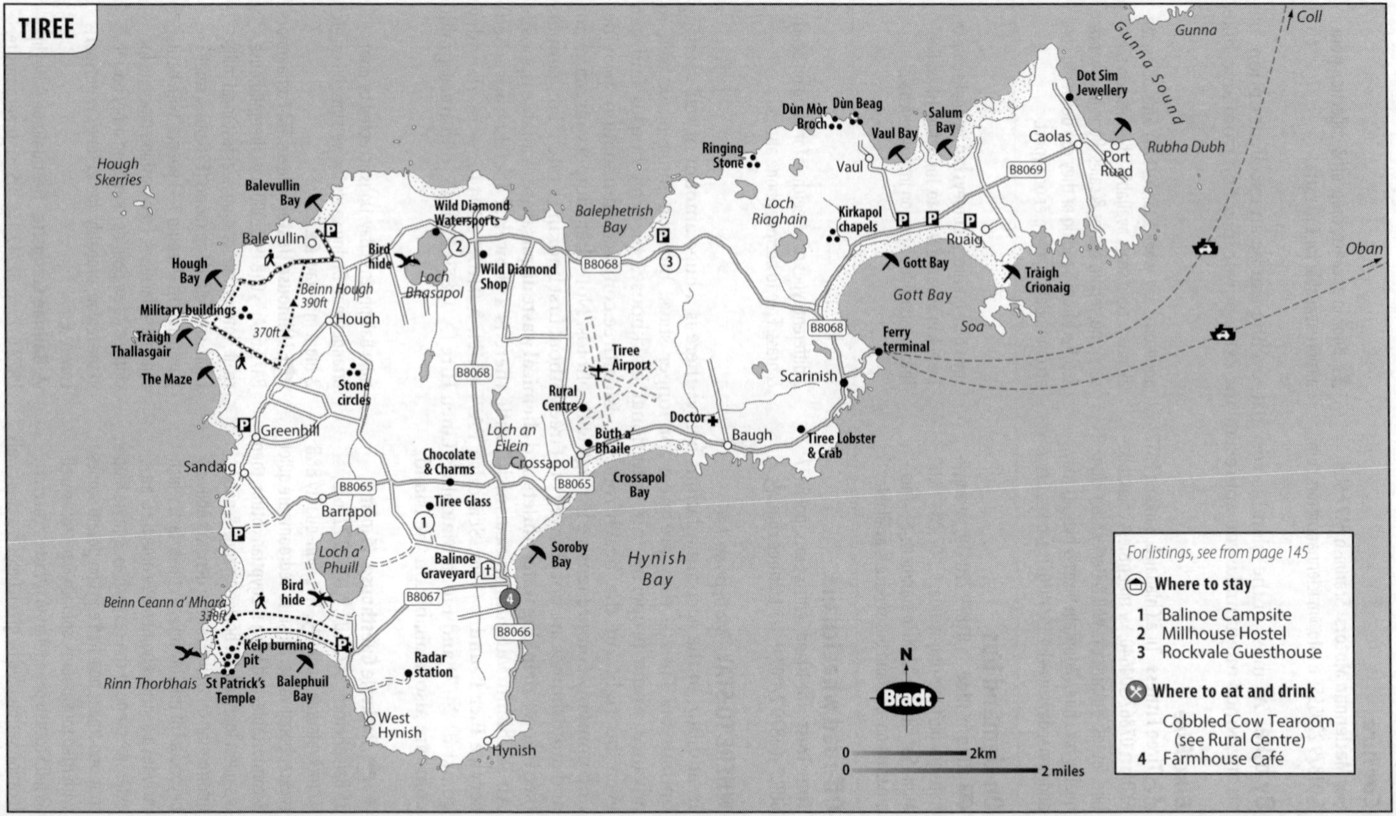
TIREE
Coll
Oban
Gunna
Gunna Sound
Rubha Dubh
Dot Sim Jewellery
Caolas
Port Ruad
B8069
Dùn Mòr Broch
Dùn Beag
Vaul Bay
Salum Bay
Vaul
Ringing Stone
Loch Riaghain
Kirkapol chapels
Ruaig
Gott Bay
Tràigh Crionaig
Soa
Ferry terminal
B8068
Scarinish
Tiree Lobster & Crab
Baugh
Doctor
Hough Skerries
Balevullin Bay
Balevullin
Wild Diamond Watersports
Bird hide
Loch Bhasapol
Wild Diamond Shop
Balephetrish Bay
Hough Bay
Beinn Hough 390ft
Hough
Military buildings
370ft
Tràigh Thallasgair
The Maze
Stone circles
Tiree Airport
Rural Centre
Buth a' Bhaile
Loch an Eilein
Crossapol
Crossapol Bay
Greenhill
Sandaig
Chocolate & Charms
Tiree Glass
B8065
Barrapol
Loch a' Phuill
Balinoe Graveyard
Soroby Bay
Hynish Bay
Beinn Ceann a' Mhara 338ft
Bird hide
B8067
B8066
Kelp burning pit
Rinn Thorbhais
St Patrick's Temple
Balephuil Bay
Radar station
West Hynish
Hynish
N
Bradt
0 2km
0 2 miles
For listings, see from page 145
Where to stay
1 Balinoe Campsite
2 Millhouse Hostel
3 Rockvale Guesthouse
Where to eat and drink
Cobbled Cow Tearoom (see Rural Centre)
4 Farmhouse Café

co.uk; ⊕ Apr–Oct. Lovely, old-fashioned campsite surrounded by working croft land. Inside seating & kitchen for campers in modernised World War II Nissen hut. Barn for storage of bikes, watersports equipment, etc. 2 cute & very basic pods & 1 bothy (sleeps 3 or 4 squashed) have mattress & electricity, but you'll need to bring your own bedding. Bookings via website only. £

⋏ **Croft Camping** ☎01879 220074; w isleoftiree.com/croft-camping. This scheme was set up to protect Tiree's delicate machair habitats & contribute something towards the traditional crofting communities that are the mainstay of island life. A series of around 10 participating crofts are spread around the island, with a livestock-free piece of land set aside in each for up to 3 camping pitches. £

WHERE TO EAT AND DRINK *Map, opposite*

Opening times on Tiree seem to be particularly sporadic and there is not a huge variety of options, so it is best to plan ahead if you want to eat out.

✖ **Ceabhar Restaurant** Sandaig PA77 6XQ; ☎01879 220684; w ceabhar-restaurant-and-bun-dubh-brewery.business.site; ⊕ Apr–Oct 19.00–21.00 Wed–Sat. This is the best place to eat on Tiree, but extremely popular & difficult to get a table without reserving well in advance. Ever-changing menu with local produce 'if not Tiree, then Scottish'. Always meat, fish & vegetarian/vegan options. ££

✖ **Cobbled Cow Tearoom** The Rural Centre, Crossapol PA77 6UP; ☎01879 220096; ⊕ 10.00–16.00 Tue, 10.00–15.30 Wed & Thu, 10.00–19.30 Fri & Sat, 14.00–18.30 Sun; ♿. Light lunches & hearty evening meals. Sun carvery. Takeaway sometimes available. £–££

⊑ **Farmhouse Café** Balemartine PA77 6UA; ☎01879 220107; ▓; ⊕ Apr–Oct; ♿. With chickens queueing at the front door & a sunny conservatory overlooking farmland with Highland cows & ponies. Good coffee, cakes & light lunches. Small shop attached sells own highland beef as well as Tiree-made candles, fudge, wood turning, T-shirts, etc. £

⊑ **Yellow Hare** Pier, Scarinish PA77 6TN; ☎01879 220440; w yellowhare.co.uk; ⊕ Apr–Aug 10.00–16.00 daily (sometimes later/earlier); ♿. Good coffee & home baking, plus a tasteful gift shop. £

SHOPPING
Arts and crafts
Chocolate & Charms Tràigh a Chiobair, Heylipol PA77 6TY; ☎01879 220037; ▓ chocolatescharms; ⊕ Mar–Jun & Sep–Dec 13.00–17.00, Jul & Aug 11.00–17.00 Mon–Sat. Jeweller Becky runs this excellent little shop/café. Her jewellery is lovely & very affordable, taking inspiration from the natural colours & shapes of Tiree including using moulds from shells found on the beach. Delicious chocolate made on Tiree by her friend Jo. Also sells local-interest books. Café sells homemade cakes.

Dot Sim Jewellery Greasamull, Miodar Rd, Caolis PA77 6TS; m 07906 002896; w dotdotsim. com; ⊕ Apr–Oct noon–17.00 daily (flexible). Elegant high-end jewellery.

Tiree Glass Ceosabh, Balinoe PA77 6TZ; ☎01879 220627; w tireeglass.co.uk; ⊕ Apr–Oct

10.00–17.00 Tue–Fri. Recycled, kiln-form glass creations.

Food shops
Bùth a' Bhaile Crossapol PA77 6UP; ☎01879 220581; ▓; ⊕ 08.00–18.00 Mon–Sat, Apr–Oct also noon–17.00 Sun; ♿. Large, friendly, independent shop selling groceries, baked goods, alcohol, newspapers, secondhand books & just about everything else.

Co-op Scarinish PA77 6UH; ☎01879 220326; ⊕ 07.00–22.00 daily. Small supermarket.

Tiree Lobster & Crab Failte, Heanish PA77 6UL; m 07765 422831; ▓; ⊕ 09.00–18.00 daily. Refrigerated vending machine selling fresh, local seafood. Must be seen to be believed. Accepts card payments.

SPORTS AND ACTIVITIES
Watersports Tiree's conditions for wind- and kitesurfing are among the best in the world making it Scotland's most famous watersports location. Tiree born

and bred, William Maclean established Wild Diamond (w wilddiamond.co.uk) 22 years ago, when the sports first started to take off; he and his professional staff offer lessons, courses and equipment hire for abilities ranging from 'beginner to super-hero level' for windsurfing, bodyboarding, kitesurfing, surfing, kayaking and stand-up-paddleboarding. For kit visit their shop (Cornaig PA77 6XA; m 07712 159205; ☉ Jul & Aug 10.00–17.00 Sat–Thu, 10.00–18.00 Fri, noon– 17.00 Sun Apr–Jun, Sep & Oct 09.00–11.00 Mon–Sat 09.00–11.00, Nov–Mar on request).

Boat trips

Tiree Sea Tours m 07765 422831; w tireeseatours.co.uk. Boat trips to Skerryvore Lighthouse, the Treshnish Isles to see puffins, & Staffa, Iona & Coll for lunch, as well as wildlife-watching trips. You have a good chance of seeing marine mammals & basking sharks during the summer months. £30–£55 pp.

Other sports and activities

Tiree Trekking (m 07833 031764; w tireetrekking.com; ½ hr/hr £20/38 pp) offer pony trekking along Balinoe Beach. You could join **Tiree Polar Bears** (🇫), an informal wild swimming group; or **borrow a telescope** (Tiree Trust; ☎01879 220074; deposit £20) as Balevullin is an official Dark Skies stargazing site (w www. darkskydiscovery.org.uk). **Tiree Fitness** (Tir a Chladaich, Sandaig PA77 6AQ; m 07867 304640; w tireefitness.co.uk) host trail running & training camps, fitness sessions & a small gym.

OTHER PRACTICALITIES

$ Bank Royal Bank of Scotland, Scarinish PA77 6UH; ☉ 10.00–12.30 & 13.30–16.00 Mon, Tue & Fri. UK RBS & NatWest customers can withdraw cash inside bank. Foreign bank customers might be able to get a cash advance with debit/credit card & photo ID. No ATM.

Fuel MacLennan Motors, Pierhead, Scarinish PA77 6UH; ☉ 09.00–17.00 Mon–Fri, 09.00–13.00 Sat

🖳 Internet Rural Centre, Crossapol PA77 6UP; ☎01879 220677; ☉ 10.00–18.00 Mon–Sat

✚ Medical Baugh Surgery, Baugh PA77 6UN; ☎01879 220323; ☉ reception: 09.00–noon & 13.30–18.00 Mon–Fri; walk-in appointments: 09.00–11.00 Sat

✉ Post office Scarinish PA77 6UH; ☉ 09.00– 17.30 Mon–Wed & Fri, 09.00–13.00 Thu, 09.00–12.30 Sat

EVENTS

May

Tiree 10K & Half Marathon w tireefitness. co.uk/events/tiree-10k. Hugely successful running races that started in 2006. Entry opens in Sep & fills up immediately.

July

Fèis Thiriodh w feis-thiriodh.com. Festival of music, language & culture.

Tiree Agricultural Show w tireeshow.co.uk. Highland dancing, farm animal showing, after-show cèilidh.

Tiree Music Festival w tireemusicfestival.co.uk. Camping music festival with 2,000 tickets; always sold out.

September

Tiree Ultramarathon w tireefitness.co.uk/ tiree-ultramarathon. A spectacular 35-mile run around the whole island. Entry opens in Sep & fills up immediately.

October

Tiree Wave Classic w tireewaveclassic.co.uk. The longest-running professional windsurfing event in the world, founded in 1986. Fleets ranging from Juniors to World Cup Professional Windsurfers.

WHAT TO SEE AND DO

Scarinish and around Distinctive white-walled blackhouses with Tiree's characteristic tarred black roofs, along with the sandy beach and skeletal remains of the large schooner *Mary Stewart* make Scarinish Harbour both picturesque and interesting. The *Mary Stewart*'s final sailing was in 1937, after which she was left to rest on the beach for some time before eventually being blown up for firewood.

In a red corrugated metal building, at the west end of Scarinish, **An Iodhlann Museum** (PA77 6UH; ✆ 01879 220793; w aniodhlann.org.uk; ⊕ Jul & Aug 11.00–17.00 Mon–Fri; Sep–Jun 09.00–13.00 Mon, Wed & Thu; donations welcome; ♿) is Tiree's small, but excellent heritage centre. Information is well presented, interesting and easy to understand. There is not a huge amount in the way of physical exhibits, but highlights include Tiree-related military remnants like a homemade cigarette lighter made in the 1930s using parts of a brass grease gun, a Neolithic or Bronze-Age saddle quern, and a full female outfit from the 1800s. A genealogy service is also available (£5/hr).

An Turas, winner of 'Scottish Building of the Year' in 2003 is a Marmite attraction. A long, partially roofless modern structure, built by two young architects and a group of artists who aimed to celebrate Tiree's natural and architectural heritage, it has also been referred to as an 'elongated bus shelter'. The small structure is just on the left of CalMac's office at the ferry terminal, so you can decide for yourself.

The east The vast, smooth expanse of **Gott Bay** (Tràigh Mhòr) stretches 2 miles east from Scarinish. Patterned sand slips into turquoise water, the intensity of blue increasing incrementally with the depth of the water. Sunny days glimmer on ripples further out or, in high seas, the horizon is broken by white horses. When you can see it, the horizon is lined by the Treshnish Isles with Ben More behind. To the west of the beach is Mallachaig, 'the cursed rock', which was condemned never to grow seaweed after Columba tried to tie his boat there and it got washed away. For drivers, there are several marked car parks at the eastern end of the beach. On the shore near the settlement of Ruaig is **Naomhaig** (✛ 56°31'23" N 6°46'25"W), 'the blessed one', another rock that Columba managed to secure his boat to – successfully this time, meaning it was allowed to continue hosting seaweed. In this direction you will also find the **tidal island of Soa**. A visit just before low tide (page 27) might allow you to walk across. Surrounded by water and sand, this horseshoe of grass and rocky shoreline supports flocks of birds – Arctic terns soar above black-headed gulls, swooping lapwings, dunlin and passing families of shelduck – during nesting season the raucous chorus will remind you to tread carefully and stay on the grassy track where possible to avoid accidentally stepping on eggs. Do not linger too long as the tide rises quickly across the flat sand that separates Soa from 'mainland' Tiree. Just past the headland at Ruaig, Gott Bay turns into **Tràigh Crionaig**. Depending on the wind, this can be a more sheltered sandy beach, with rows of rocks and seaweed leading out into the sea and the few buildings off to one side.

At the far eastern end of the island is **Port Ruad**. The landowner has specified a spot for parking with a sign. From here, head down a grassy track which veers downhill to the left and you will pass a few picturesque whitewashed blackhouses with black felted roofs. The beach (✛ 56°32'33"N 6°44'01"W) is a beautiful and secluded bay, with views across Gunna Sound to Coll; look out for basking sharks. At low tide, the stretch of barnacle-encrusted rock on the southern edge has fascinating rock pools. Some are deep enough for kelp to grow in, whereas others are shallow and coated pale pink; a perfect place for children and interested adults to discover sea anemones, small blennies, crabs, sea urchins and maybe even starfish.

Occupying the summit of a rocky knoll, only 5 minutes' walk from the hamlet of Vaul, are the exceptionally well-preserved remains of an Iron-Age broch and its outworks. Thought to be around 2,000 years old, the characteristic round building was partly excavated in the late 1800s, before the remainder of the soil was removed to achieve its current state in the 1960s. During the broch's habitable existence, its walls are thought to have been about 26ft high and it would have been used as a stronghold. Though the remaining wall is only around 6ft high, much of the building's original features can be gleaned from its remains. The central space is over 29ft in diameter and enclosed within a characteristic double dry-stone wall and gallery construction, which adds another 14ft of width in all directions. Shards of pottery found during excavation imply it was built by an invading force, but there were also bronze and silver rings, rotary querns, glass ring beads, tools, and weaving and metalwork tools, among other things. A later addition was a 'disarticulated skeleton', buried after an apparently violent death, potentially relating to the Vikings.

Some 500yds east of the broch, just past a miniature blackhouse, is a second grass-covered fort, **Dùn Beag**. Thought to be an oval dun rather than another broch, this one is also worth a visit.

There are more sandy beaches around the northeast, though they are generally better left for exploring on foot or by bicycle, as finding places to park is difficult.

Kirkapol chapels These two ruined chapels of religious and historical importance can be found behind Tiree Lodge Hotel on Gott Bay. The Norse origins of the name 'Kirkapol' – with 'kirk' meaning church – imply the religious significance of this settlement pre-dates both chapels. The nearer of the two ruined buildings, set within its own walled graveyard, is a 14th-century parish church. In front of the church's largest entry archway, there are a set of horizontal grave slabs, one of which, currently severely overgrown, has what is thought to be the oldest representation of a claymore in Scotland. In a similar design, but smaller and set on a hill overlooking the area, is the ruin of an older 13th-century chapel. There is a good interpretation board at the entrance, which might help you identify several small Latin crosses that have been incised into rocks around the area; these are also thought to imply an earlier origin of Christian worship. More examples can be found at St Patrick's Temple in the southwest (page 153).

The north coast

Ringing Stone From the east end of Balephetrish Bay, a long stretch of yellow-grey sand in the centre of the island's north coast, you can walk 1½ miles along the coast to the Ringing Stone (⊕ 56°32'09.3"N 6°50'16.1"W). This large and obvious boulder was brought to this spot by the last Ice Age, 10,000 years ago. The circular cup markings are thought to be Megalithic in origin, and a small interpretation sign nearby suggests a theory behind them; you may as well guess your own interpretation as evidence from this time period is totally inconclusive. Local folklore has it that the rock was thrown over from Mull by a giant and that Tiree will sink into the Atlantic if it is ever removed. If you hit it with another stone, it emits a strange ringing tone, hence the name.

This stretch of coastline is home to Arctic terns, sanderlings, ringed plovers, oystercatchers, eider and many other species.

Loch Bhasapol The bird hide at Loch Bhasapol affords good chances of seeing ducks such as pochards as well as sedge warblers, reed buntings and the hen harriers coming to eat them, among the reeds and still water. To reach it, take the turning towards Kilmoluaig, just after you pass Wild Diamond Windsurfing School, and park off the road in front of the ruins of a cottage. The bird hide is 100yds southeast; there are some ID charts and benches inside. According to folk history, the 'Battle of the Sheaves' might have been fought between Loch Bhasapol and Cornaigmore Beach: the islanders apparently drove off an invading force of Vikings using bundles of plants as weapons.

Balevullin In the northwest corner of the island are the sprinkling of traditional houses, farm buildings and wandering livestock that make up **Balevullin** and, at the end of the road, stunning **Balevullin Bay**. This attractive sandy beach, busy in summer, is a favourite with surfers.

Hough Bay, Beinn Hough and the remains of a World War II RAF station

Distance: 5 miles; time: 3 hours; start/end: Balevullin Bay car park; OS Explorer map: 372 Coll & Tiree

This meandering walk takes in open farmland, sand dunes and a long stretch of beach, before climbing 390ft Beinn Hough; potentially a little muddy underfoot, it is otherwise relatively unchallenging.

From Balevullin Bay car park, follow the single-track road back through the village; the thatched cottage with red doors on your right is one of the finest examples of a traditional blackhouse in all of the Inner Hebrides.

At the T-junction, turn right and follow the tarmacked track up the hill, past an ugly concrete building on your left, the first and least interesting of the World War II remnants en route. This track will lead you all the way down to Hough Bay, but there are several intriguing **military buildings** along the way ($\oplus$ 56°30'42.9"N 6°58'37"W). More recently some of these buildings have been used as sheep barns. The floor is unsafe, so just peer inside from the doorway.

Heading west, towards the sea, you will eventually come to the lengthy stretch of sand and colourful pebbles that forms Hough Bay. There are grey seal colonies on the rocks far offshore; you might see one bobbing in the water, but also listen for their plaintive howling drifting across the bay. On a clear day you can see the Outer Hebrides from here.

As you follow the sheep tracks through the dunes, look out for orchids, which flower from May into the summer, and notice the small, yellow, slipper-like flowers: bird's-foot trefoil (*Lotus corniculatus*), sometimes known as 'eggs and bacon', which also bloom in warmer months. Modestly pretty, these flowers are a good source of food for the caterpillars of several butterflies and moths, which you should also look out for around your feet.

Reaching the end of Hough Bay, you should meet a track running up towards the hill, Beinn Hough.

If you are not in a rush, take some time to explore the area before taking it. Only 200yds south, invisible from the end of Hough Bay, are a couple of small, sheltered pebbly beaches called **Tràigh Thallasgair**. These are home to eider duck and curlew and make a pleasant place to stop for a picnic.

Take the track towards Beinn Hough. In spring, your walk along this track will be accompanied by noisy oystercatchers, lapwings and geese as you pass more military remains towards the base of the hill.

Beginning to climb the hill on a small path, you will soon reach a broken tarmac road, which will take you uphill, off to the left and around a hairpin bend before reaching a mast. Look out for dark purple marsh orchids here. The loud humming at the mast informs you that it is still in use, so keep a sensible distance and find the small sheep trail leading off to the left, just before you reach the fence.

You can follow this path up to the top, where there is a 360° view of the whole of Tiree, patchwork croft land and unassuming houses scattered across the central plains and, on a clear day, Skye to the north and the Outer Hebrides northwest. Beside the trig point is another ruined RAF building; though the concrete is undeniably ugly, the stunning views through broken windows give these buildings an uncertain appeal, similar to that of Brutalist architecture.

Follow the intermittent and broken series of small concrete steps and posts down to a small lower military building before heading slightly left towards the lowest part of a saddle in the hill and down towards the north coast on a grassy path.

From here, aim for the rusty gate posts of a long-lost gate and continue north for about 200yds more until you reach the same track you began the walk on. Turn right on to this track and head back into Balevullin village.

The west Travelling south from Balevullin, the main road forks at the few houses that make up Hough. If you take the left fork, southeast, and continue for about half a mile you will notice a blue sign on your right marking 'stone circles'. Do not expect Stonehenge or even the atmospheric circle at Lochbuie on Mull (page 172), as all but one of the stones across these two massive circles have either fallen over or been robbed. Despite the unspectacular positioning and surrounding sheep dung, the space seems to hold a heavy silence and, since the stones are thought to date from the Neolithic or Bronze Age, we should perhaps not be too critical of the damage they have endured over the several thousand years since their positioning.

The Maze The Maze (Tràigh Thodhrasdail/Ghrianal on the OS map), a long sandy bay, backed by dunes and interrupted only by occasional beautifully smooth, sculpted, stripy rocks, might just be the most spectacular beach on Tiree. On calm days, tiny ringed plovers pace up and down at the edge of each lapping wave, picking out titbits to eat. There is parking at Greenhill, 200yds away, although the sandy track down to Greenhill was quite severely eroded at the time of my visit and not easy to negotiate in a small car.

Loch a' Phuill In the southwest of Tiree there is a **bird hide** overlooking Loch a' Phuill. In early autumn this is an excellent place to watch dunlins, more ringed plovers and redshank, along with black-tailed godwits, greenshanks and whimbrels. Other birds such as gulls and kittiwakes visit to wash in the fresh water and speedy swallows swoop up midges in the summer. There is parking at Balephuil Bay.

🧍 Balephuil Bay, St Patrick's Temple and Kenavara seabird cliffs

Distance: 3 miles; time: 2 hours; start/end: Balephuil Bay; OS Explorer map: 372 Coll & Tiree
This varied circular walk visits a spectacular beach, several archaeological sites and cliffs that are home to large populations of seabirds. The route covers sand and grassy paths, climbing to a grand height of 338ft.

Balephuil Bay, another of Tiree's lovely sandy beaches, is slightly dominated by the 'golf ball' radar station to the east; a useful navigation tool from almost anywhere on the island. With the sea on your left, walk west along the beach until you reach its end and follow the low grassy tracks along the shore. There is an obvious **kelp burning pit** or kiln (⊕ 55°27'21.3"N 6°58'10.7"W), rare evidence of an industry that was once the backbone of the Tiree's economy.

Follow this grassy track until it leads you up through the yellow irises to **St Patrick's Temple** (⊕ 56°27'12.7"N 6°58'19.6"W). All that remains standing of this medieval chapel is part of the east gable end, but there are two cross-incised stones and the grass-covered remains of several other buildings, possibly huts, on platforms in the vicinity. There is no evidence that St Patrick ever visited Tiree.

The path begins to climb around the coast from here and soon brings you to some spectacular seabird cliffs, where swooping fulmars guard their nesting sites in the cliffs below during the summer months.

Follow sheep tracks to the southwest corner, where the fence starts. There is nothing but the Atlantic Ocean between this point and America. Take the time to search for Skerryvore Lighthouse (see below) on the southwest horizon.

Keep the fence between yourself and the sea on your left and follow it north until you reach a large cairn with a wooden cross embedded. Head down into the saddle and up to the higher peak of **Beinn Ceann a' Mhara**.

From here you can follow the fence down towards the ruins of a sheep pen, before heading towards the giant 'golf ball' on small paths through the machair and strange sand-dune hillocks. Eventually you will reach a fence and have to skirt around it via the beach before getting back to the car park.

The far south

The southernmost peninsula of Tiree ends in two unconnected roads. Common seals can often be seen basking on rocks from the end of the road at **West Hynish**, but visiting **Hynish** (on the eastern coast) is particularly interesting. Hynish was the base for building the magnificent Skerryvore Lighthouse and was later used as the shore station, housing the lighthouse keepers and their families. What is left now is a strange assortment of buildings, with a round signal tower used between 1844 and 1937 to provide semaphore communication with the lighthouse. Other points of interest at Hynish include the pier and harbour, now filled with sand, and two excellent exhibitions put on by the Hebridean Trust (w hebrideantrust.org): **The Story of Skerryvore Lighthouse** (Morton Boyd Hall, Hynish; ⊕ May–Sep open access; £3 suggested donation; ⅙) and **The Treshnish Isles** (Old Cowsheds, Hynish; ⊕ May–Sep open access; £3 suggested donation; ⅙).

The central south coast

At the junction of the roads to Hynish and Balephuil is **Balinoe Graveyard**, also known as Soroby. It is thought, without any proof I'm aware of, that this is the site of a monastery founded by Columba and presided over by St Baithane, his cousin. There is nothing to see of a monastery, but the graveyard was used by the MacLean chiefs between 1390 and 1680 and the strange and rather squat **Maclean's Cross** (⊕ 56°28'12.2"N 6°53'57.2"W) may be of interest. Carved into a Latin cross on one side and Celtic on the other, it is conspicuous in the graveyard and thought to be early medieval.

Heading north, the road passes **Loch an Eilein** and **Island House**, a private residence, which stands on the remains of the island's only castle. A MacLean garrison tried to hold this castle after their bankrupt chief sold Tiree to the 8th Earl of Argyll, Archibald Campbell, in 1674. Campbell successfully besieged the castle on at least one occasion around the years 1678–9 and by the time John

Fraser was minister on Tiree (1678–97) he described the castle as 'ane ruinous tour surrounded with ane trintch of stone and earth'. The stone walls here were built during the potato famine around 1846 by the starving, but able-bodied, proportion of the population in exchange for famine relief aid.

The road to the airport will also lead you to the **Rural Centre** (PA77 6UP; w isleoftiree.com/places/rural-centre; ⊕ 09.00–18.00 Mon–Sat; free), which has some interesting information about crofting on Tiree throughout the year, and the Cobbled Cow Tearoom (page 147).

Crossapol Bay (Tràigh Bhagh) is a beautiful sandy bay alongside the road that returns to Scarinish. There was an Italian prisoner of war camp here during World War II and you can still see the remains of various military buildings along this stretch of road.

7

Mull (Muile) and Iona (Ì Chaluim Chille)

Wild and mountainous, Mull is synonymous with its soaring eagles; with thriving populations of both white-tailed and golden species, you have better chances of seeing them here than anywhere else in the UK. Golden eagles are particularly at home around lofty peaks; at 3,169ft, Beinn Mhòr (meaning 'large mountain') is Mull's highest, and also its only Munro. Despite the climb, on a clear day the effort to reward ratio is probably the most favourable of all the Inner Hebridean hikes, providing a viewpoint over the whole region: you can see the Skye Cuillins in the north, Jura's Paps in the south and just about everything in-between. Curiously, Mull is not known for its beautiful beaches, although the island's stretches of sand are also superlative, if mostly hidden away at the end of boggy romps or delicate cliff paths.

Mull is deceptively large and, with a population hovering somewhere under 3,000 (over a third of which live in the capital Tobermory), is totally uninhabited for large swathes of its south and west coastline. The majority of the interior is also inaccessible by road and, outside of its few main townships, the honesty box shop is still going strong. With fertile land and an abundance of seafood, some of Mull's most surprising delights can be found in tiny farm shops and producers' markets.

Although Mull is a large island, it is not as 'developed' as you might imagine. Shops and restaurants close earlier than you might expect, there are very few ATMs, and many small places will only accept cash. Pre-booking accommodation is essential, especially in summer.

Off the far west of the Ross of Mull, the tiny island of Iona is well known for its association with the 6th-century monk St Columba and his role in spreading Christianity into Scotland. Though half the islands in the Inner Hebrides claim to have some association with the saint, the evidence on Iona is indisputable. This idyllic speck of land is where he grew his monastic community, building a much earlier incarnation of Iona Abbey, which for centuries was the dominant religious and sometimes even political institution in the region. Top of the list for both pilgrims and history enthusiasts, Iona Abbey is popular with day visitors, but those who stay a little longer, taking the time to discover the island's secluded coves and flower meadows, will be rewarded with the peace and tranquillity that we can only assume attracted Columba to settle there in the first place.

MULL

HISTORY Continually inhabited since the last Ice Age, there is evidence of Mesolithic people living in coastal caves on Mull and, later, Neolithic farmers.

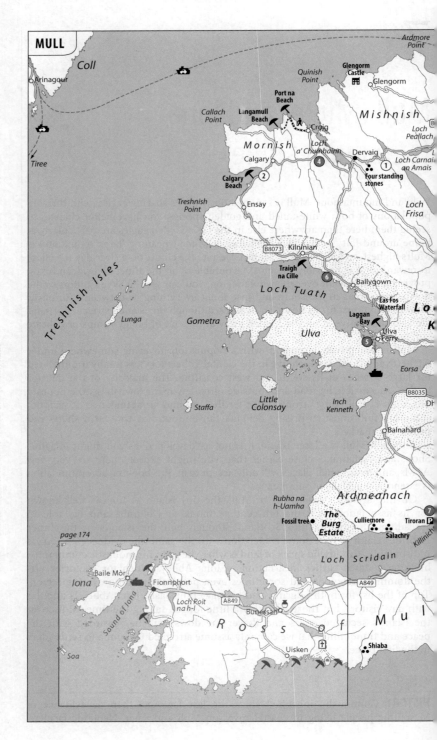

Coll

Arinagour

Ardmore Point

Tiree

Callach Point

Mornish

Calgary

Quinish Point

Glengorm Castle

Glengorm

Mishnish

Loch Peallach

B

Port na Beach

Langamull Beach

Croig

Loch a' Chumhainn

Dervaig

(1)

Loch Carnai an Amais

(4)

Four standing stones

(2)

Calgary Beach

L

Treshnish Point

Ensay

Kilninian

B8073

Loch Frisa

Traigh na Cille

(6)

Ballygown

Loch Tuath

Lo K

Eas Fos Waterfall

Treshnish Isles

Lunga

Gometra

Ulva

Laggan Bay

(5)

Ulva Ferry

Eorsa

Staffa

Little Colonsay

Inch Kenneth

B8035

Dh

Balnahard

Rubha na h-Uamha

Ardmeanach

(7) P

Fossil tree

The Burg Estate

Culliemore

Salachry

Tiroran

Killinich

page 174

Iona

Baile Mòr

Fionnphort

Soa

Sound of Iona

Loch Pòit na h-I

A849

Bunessan

Loch Scridain

A849

Mu l

Ross of Mull

Uisken

Shiaba

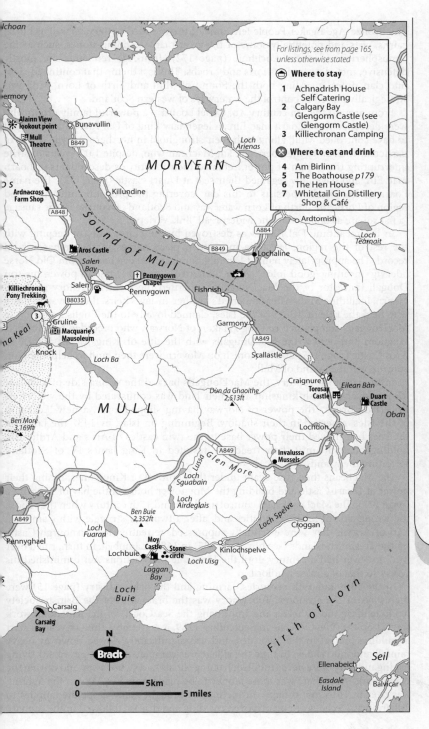

For listings, see from page 165, unless otherwise stated

🛏 **Where to stay**
1 Achnadrish House Self Catering
2 Calgary Bay Glengorm Castle (see Glengorm Castle)
3 Killiechronan Camping

✕ **Where to eat and drink**
4 Am Birlinn
5 The Boathouse *p179*
6 The Hen House
7 Whitetail Gin Distillery Shop & Café

Ichoan

ermory

Alainn View lookout point
Mull Theatre
○ Bunavullin

MORVERN

○ Killundine

Loch Arienas

B849

Ardnacross Farm Shop

A848

Sound of Mull

○ Ardtornish

A884

Loch Tearnait

Aros Castle
Salen Bay
Salen ○
Killiechronan Pony Trekking
B8035
Gruline ○
3
Macquarie's Mausoleum
Knock ○

na Keal

3

† Pennygown Chapel
Pennygown

○ Lochaline

○ Fishnish

Loch Ba

Garmony ○

A849

○ Scallastle

Craignure ○
Torosay Castle
Eilean Bàn
Duart Castle
Oban

Dùn da Ghaoithe 2,513ft ▲

MULL

Ben More 3,169ft ▲

Lochdon ○

A849

Lussa
Glen More

Invalussa Mussels ●

Loch Sguabain
Loch Airdeglais

Loch Spelve

Ben Buie 2,352ft ▲

Loch Fuaran

A849

Pennyghael ○

Croggan ○

Moy Castle
Stone circle
Lochbuie ●
Laggan Bay

○ Kinlochspelve
Loch Uisg

Loch Buie

Firth of Lorn

○ Carsaig
Carsaig Bay

N
Bradt

0 ———— 5km
0 ———— 5 miles

Ellenabeich

Easdale Island

Seil

Balvicar

The Bronze-Age Beaker People left some of their corded pottery, as well as burial cairns, cists and potentially some of the great many standing stones, such as the atmospheric circle near Lochbuie (page 172). Iron-Age remnants are mostly defensive, including various forts and brochs. This is a theme that continued right into clan times; guarding both the Sound of Mull and Firth of Lorn, Mull was strategically placed to control the waterways of western Scotland.

From around the 5th century AD, Cenél Loairn – a powerful family group who were descendants of Loarn mac Eirc, a legendary king of Dál Riata – are thought to have controlled Mull, along with their stronghold in northern Argyll. This is of particular interest to members of Clan MacLean who, despite 1,000 years of strife interrupting their reign of power, retained their identity as descendants of Loarn mac Eirc and have now regained their seat at Duart Castle (page 172). The name Loarn or Loairn also persists to this day, covering the predominantly mainland region of Lorne, the Firth of Lorn waterway and Scotland's favourite Lorne sausage (a flat square as opposed to the widespread 'link' variety).

In the meantime Dál Riata was destroyed by the Norse who, in keeping with the rest of the region, left little more than place names in the archaeological record. The appropriately named Dervaig, for example, originates from Old Norse ('dervig' meaning 'good inlet'). After Somerled's (page 14) rise to power, his son Dougall (ancestor of the MacDougalls) inherited the former territory of Cenél Loairn, including Mull. After Somerled's brother-in-law's heirs, the Crovan dynasty who held the title of 'Kings of the Isles', claimed loyalty to the English crown, the MacDougalls complained to King Haakon of Norway, who preceded to split their kingdom and bestow the MacDougalls with the title of 'Kings of the Hebrides'. Aros Castle (page 167) and Ardtonish on Movern were then built to help maintain control over the Sound of Mull.

In the late 13th century, the MacDougalls backed the wrong side of a violent dispute over Scottish kingship and their land was confiscated by the victorious Rovert de Bruys. The power of Norway having slipped away, a new 'Lordship of the Isles' emerged in their shadow. Beginning on Islay, by 1437 the Lords of the Isles had moved their power base to the twin castles of Aros and Ardtonish, holding on to it until their treachery resulted in King James IV of Scotland forfeiting their lands.

The MacLeans then rose again under the approval of King James, basing their power at Duart Castle and building the Moy tower house at the bay of Loch Buie (page 172). The MacLeans held control until the mid 17th century when they chose the wrong side of religious politics and, after a two-year struggle with Campbell, Earl of Argyll, they were eventually suppressed, retreating to Cairnburgh Castle on the Treshnish Islands (see box, page 185) in 1680. Campbell, in turn, ruled over Mull for over half a century until the Heritable Jurisdictions Act diminished his power to that of a mere landlord.

In the 18th and 19th centuries, farming and the kelp industry (page 15) were mainstays of the economy. Tobermory was the brainchild of the British Society for Extending the Fisheries and Improving the Sea Coasts of the Kingdom: work started on the 'New Village' in September 1789, a regrettable time of year to start a building project in the Hebrides, and was significantly slowed down by heavy rainfall and mud slides. In time the village was completed, but hopes of a thriving fishing industry were never fulfilled; herring shoals had swum away and during the Napoleonic Wars there was more money to be made from kelp. When the fighting was over in 1815, the collapse of the market brought many desperate families to Tobermory. Decades of poverty, overcrowding and disease followed in the capital.

Just as things seemed to be improving on Mull, the potato blight around 1845 brought famine and forced many families to seek better fortunes elsewhere. The Clearances were as complicated here as anywhere in the Highlands, with some tenants receiving a voluntary 'assisted passage' abroad and others being forcibly removed. Often people simply couldn't afford to pay for an onward journey and were evicted into extreme poverty and survival in an urban environment that they did not know. Francis Clark's evictions on the nearby island of Ulva were particularly notorious, with a population decline from 500 to 150 over the course of a decade. A story in Tobermory's Mull Museum recounts how one bed-ridden woman had the thatch removed from her roof, excluding a small portion just over her bed. The population of Mull declined from 10,000 to 3,000; meanwhile, the Campbells could still afford to build turreted manor houses such as Torosay 'Castle', completed in 1858. By the turn of the 20th century, Mull was home to more sheep than people.

Tobermory became a naval base in World War II with Commodore Sir Gilbert Stephenson, known as 'The Tobermory Terror', given the task of setting up a training station there. In 1964, the construction of a new pier in Craignure allowed regular motor vehicle transport to Mull for the first time which, along with improving mainland access for inhabitants of the island, enabled the growth of the island's tourist industry. While the more traditional industries of agriculture, fishing and forestry continue, tourism provides seasonal income for much of Mull's population throughout the summer months.

GETTING THERE AND AWAY

By ferry The vast majority of people reach Mull by ferry. **CalMac** (✆ 08000 665000 or, from outside the UK, +44 1475 650397; w calmac.co.uk) runs three services to Mull.

From **Oban** (page 259) to Craignure takes around 50 minutes, sailing as often as ten times a day in summer or as little as three times a day in winter (cars/foot passengers £13.75/3.70). Vehicles must be booked in advance.

Less common routes run between **Tobermory** and **Kilchoan** on the mainland Ardnamurchan Peninsula (35mins, up to 7 times daily in summer & infrequently Mon–Fri in winter; cars/foot passengers £8.90/2.80); and **Fishnish** on the east coast of Mull to **Lochaline** on mainland Morvern (18mins; max of 14 daily in summer; min 4 daily in winter; cars/foot passengers £7.35/2.50). Tickets for vehicles cannot be booked in advance on these two routes.

Moorings

Tobermory Harbour pontoon and moorings ✆ 01688 302876; m 07917 832497; w tobermoryharbour.co.uk. Toilets, showers & laundry.

Ulva Ferry Pontoon m 07557 378953; w ulvaferrypontoon.co.uk. Berthing for up to 52ft vessels. Pricing structure dependant on size of boat & length of stay.

GETTING AROUND

Holidaying on Mull without a car is perfectly feasible if you stay close to the main road between Tobermory, Craignure and Fionnphort. To reach some of the island's more remote locations, however, you will most likely want your own wheels, or have plenty of time and patience for hitchhiking.

By bike Mull is undeniably hilly, but the scenic western coastal route is a proper expedition for fit cyclists. The long track out to Burg Estate (page 169) and the forestry trails in north Mull are good for less serious cyclists or those who are keen to avoid cars.

Bike hire

🚲 **Cycle Mull** Eas Brae, Beadoun, Tobermory PA75 6QA; 📞 01688 302923; w cyclemull.co.uk. Both e-bikes & mountain bikes to hire.

By bus Bus travel is quite feasible on Mull, but you'll need to check times and stops online or in a bus stop before travelling. Many services do not run on Sundays and are drastically reduced in winter.

🚌 **West Coast Motors** 📞 01586 552319; w westcoastmotors.co.uk; ♿) currently run:

95/495: Craignure–Salen–Tobermory
96/496: Craignure–Bunessan–Fionnphort
494: Tobermory–Dervaig–Calgary

🚌 **Ulva Ferry Community Transport** (m 07775 531301; w ufct.co.uk; ♿) run a minibus service from Calgary via Ulva Ferry to Salen from Fri to Sun on request. The minibus or their electric car can also be booked for other journeys when available.

Driving Excluding the A roads, which run up the island's east coast and along the south, the majority of driving on Mull is remarkably slow and tricky; even the A roads are mostly single track and on others you will have to negotiate around few passing places, hairpin bends and surprise, monstrous pot-holes. Driving times should not be underestimated; it can easily take 3 hours to get from Calgary to Fionnphort if there are many cars coming the other way.

TOURIST INFORMATION AND TOURS For **tourist information**, visit the Craignure iCentre (The Pier, PA65 6AY; 📞 01680 812377; w visitscotland.com; ⊕ Jul & Aug 09.00–18.15 Mon, 08.15–18.15 Tue–Sat, 10.00–18.15 Sun, Sep–Jun 09.00–17.00 Mon, 08.30–17.00 Tue–Sat, 10.00–17.00 Sun; ♿). Many island tours are also wildlife orientated, where local knowledge really comes into play.

Enjoy Mull Salen PA72 6JF; 📞 01680 300162; w enjoymull.co.uk. Group minibus tours focusing on history, geology & wildlife, or private hires. Pickup available from Tobermory, Craignure & Fishnish.
Mull Magic Tobermory PA75 6QP; 📞 01688 301213; w mullmagic.com. Guided walks ranging from easy to challenging, covering different areas of Mull & Iona.
Mull Wildlife Tours Craignure PA65 6AY; 📞 01680 812440; w mullwildlifetours.co.uk. Wildlife- & nature-orientated day tours with a max of 4 guests, starting in Craignure. Very reasonably priced.
Nature Scotland Tobermory PA75 6NR; m 07743 956380; w naturescotland.com. A range of tours including small-group, nature-orientated day tours with short walks; conservation & research expeditions; & more serious hikes into Mull's mountainous wilderness regions. Tours usually start from Tobermory.

EVENTS

April
Mull Music Festival Tobermory; m 07765 244396; 📘. Small, free music festival.

May
Mull Sevens w mullrugby.co.uk

June
The Mull Sportive w mullsportive.co.uk. 43/87-mile cycling race courses around Mull.

June/July
Round Mull Race w obansailingclub.org. Sailing competition.

July
Highland Games Erray Park, Tobermory; 📘. Traditional Highland dancing, tossing the caber & hammer throwing as well as piping & track events.

July/August

Mull Half Marathon, 10k & Junior Races Tobermory; **w** mullrunners.com

August

Bunessan Show Bunessan; ⓕ. Lively agricultural show, which regularly hosts performances from the Mull & Iona Pipe Band.

September

Mendelssohn on Mull Festival **w** soundwavesscio.org.uk/mendelssohn-on-mull-festival

Mull Fiddler's Rally Aros Hall, Tobermory; look out for notices in shops. Fiddlers (violin players) from all over Scotland gather together for 1 evening.

October

Mull Rally **w** mullrally.org. Closed-road car rally.

December

Tobermory fireworks Locals & visitors gather on the harbourfront to watch a public display around midnight to celebrate Hogmanay.

TOBERMORY A decade ago this colourful fishing port town was mostly known to a certain generation and their parents as the setting of the BBC children's TV programme *Balamory*. My first visit in 2004 was accompanied by a constant background hum of the cheery theme tune; the show finished in 2005 and although it's still possible to find related souvenirs, sanity seems to have returned to the town. Less pricey than Skye's Portree (page 58) and with quite a bit more going on than Islay's Bowmore (page 221), Tobermory is my personal favourite of the islands' capitals and makes a good base for both solo travellers and those without their own transport. Although the colourful houses appear to have a hint of irony in a downpour, there are a good range of short indoor activities to entertain children and adults alike.

Where to stay *Map, page 162*

Tobermory is a lively place to stay with plenty of good accommodation options.

🏠 **Tobermory Hotel** (15 rooms) 53 Main St, PA75 6NT; ☎ 01688 302091; **w** thetobermoryhotel. com; ♿. Stretches across several recently refurbished, historic fishermen's cottages. Cosy, well-managed hotel with a bar & restaurant (page 162). **££££**

🏠 **Fairways Lodge** (4 rooms) Erray Rd, PA75 6PS; ☎ 01688 302001; **w** fairways-lodge.co.uk. Andrew has been running this spotless B&B for 9 years. It is in an elevated position, a little way out of the main town & perfect for golfers as it is right next to an excellent 9-hole course (page 163). Lovely balcony with amazing views over Calve Island. **£££**

🏠 **Lonan B&B** (3 rooms) Off Western Rd, PA75 6RA; ☎ 01688 302082; ⊕ Easter–Oct. Welcoming local lady Jean runs this homely B&B in a peaceful residential area, a short walk away from Tobermory

Harbour. Round, sunny conservatory for guests to relax in. Full Scottish b/fast. Good value. **££**

🏠 **Tobermory Youth Hostel** (27 beds) Main St, PA75 6NU; ☎ 01688 302481; **w** hostellingscotland.org.uk/hostels/tobermory; ⊕ end Mar–Sep. Light pink building run by Hostelling Scotland. Moderately sized kitchen & common room. Choice of private & shared rooms. **£**

🏕 **Tobermory Campsite & Caravan Holidays** Dervaig Rd, PA75 6QF; ☎ 01688 302615; **w** tobermory-campsite.co.uk; ⊕ Nov–early Feb or on request in winter. Friendly, green campsite 1⅓ miles out of Tobermory (about 30mins' walk). Also inexpensive shepherd's huts. Must bring own bedding, but has kettle, toaster, microwave & fridge. Motorhomes must book ahead. Free Wi-Fi. **£**

Where to eat and drink *Map, page 162*

Right on the harbour's edge, Tobermory is an excellent place to try some seafood. Eating establishments are proud to source their ingredients locally.

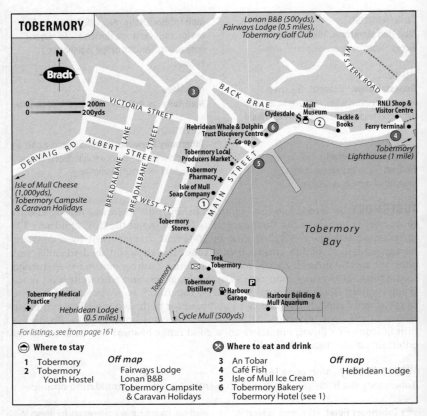

TOBERMORY

N

Bradt

Lonan B&B (500yds),
Fairways Lodge (0.5 miles),
Tobermory Golf Club

WESTERN ROAD

BACK BRAE

VICTORIA STREET

0   200m
0   200yds

3

Clydesdale

Mull
Museum

Tackle &
Books

RNLI Shop &
Visitor Centre

2

Ferry terminal

DERVAIG RD

ALBERT STREET

BREADALBANE LANE

BREADALBANE STREET

WEST ST

Hebridean Whale & Dolphin
Trust Discovery Centre

6

Co-op

Tobermory Local
Producers Market

Tobermory
Pharmacy

Isle of Mull
Soap Company

1

MAIN STREET

5

4

Tobermory
Lighthouse (1 mile)

Isle of Mull Cheese
(1,000yds),
Tobermory Campsite
& Caravan Holidays

Tobermory
Stores

Tobermory Bay

Trek
Tobermory

Tobermory

Tobermory
Distillery

P

Harbour
Garage

Harbour Building &
Mull Aquarium

Tobermory Medical
Practice

Hebridean Lodge
(0.5 miles)

Cycle Mull (500yds)

For listings, see from page 161

Where to stay

1   Tobermory
2   Tobermory
     Youth Hostel

Off map
Fairways Lodge
Lonan B&B
Tobermory Campsite
& Caravan Holidays

Where to eat and drink

3   An Tobar
4   Café Fish
5   Isle of Mull Ice Cream
6   Tobermory Bakery
     Tobermory Hotel (see 1)

Off map
Hebridean Lodge

Hebridean Lodge 1 Baliscate, PA75 6QA; 01688 301207; w hebrideanlodge.co.uk; 18.30–20.30 Mon–Fri. High-quality food with a strong focus on local produce; menu dependent on season & that day's catch. Reservations only. £££

Tobermory Hotel (page 161) 17.00–21.15 daily. Cosy with exposed stone walls in restaurant & open fire when it's cold enough to light it. Bar is more relaxed. ££–£££

Café Fish The Pier, PA75 6NU; 01688 301253; w thecafefish.com; Mar–Oct 11.00–15.00 & 17.30–10.00 daily. Good, reliable, local seafood. ££

An Tobar Argyll Tce, PA75 6QB; 01688 302211; w comar.co.uk; 11.00–15.00 Tue–Sat; . Set in an old church overlooking the harbour;

it is a steep climb up there, but worth it for inexpensive vegetarian food. £

Isle of Mull Ice Cream Main St, PA75 6NT; w isleofmullicecream.co.uk; Apr–Oct 11.00–18.00 daily (flexible). Little pink building on the seafront. Ice cream made on site from local milk. Bench behind possibly has the best view of any eatery in Tobermory. £

Tobermory Bakery 26 Main St, PA75 6NU; 01688 302225; ; summer 08.45–16.00 Mon–Sat, 10.00–15.00 Sun, winter 08.45–15.00 Mon–Sat. Light blue building on harbourfront. Big cups of proper coffee, home-baked cakes, soup, filled rolls & pastries. Excellent vegan sausage rolls. Table service or takeaway. Also bread, exciting flavours of jam & small deli with local produce: venison, highland beef, cheese, etc. £

Entertainment

An Tobar (see above). Exhibition centre that hosts art exhibitions, concerts & events.

Shopping

Nearly all Tobermory's shops are located on Main Street in the colourful buildings overlooking the harbour. While there are not many options for clothes shopping, there are a good variety of small independent shops selling both essentials and gifts.

Food shops

Co-op 33 Main St, PA75 6NT; 01688 302004; 10.00–19.00 Mon–Sat, 12.30–22.00 Sun. Small supermarket with bakery.

Isle of Mull Cheese Sgriob-ruadh Farm, PA75 6QD; 01688 302627; w isleofmullcheese.co.uk; 09.00–17.00 daily. Beautiful farm (the only dairy farm on the island) selling excellent cheese, with farm shop & café attached.

Tobermory Local Producers Market Aros Hall, PA75 6NU; noon–14.00 Mon. All the best of local produce: scallops, seasonal vegetables, honey, venison, bread, pies…

Tobermory Stores 60 Main St; f; summer Apr–Oct 08.00–20.00 Mon–Sat, 09.00–15.00 Sun, winter 09.00–17.00 Mon–Sat, 09.00–15.00 Sun. Meat from Glengorm, Isle of Mull Cheese, takeaway coffee & other local products.

General supplies

HWDT 28 Main St, PA75 6NU; 01688 302816; w hwdt.org; Apr & May 09.00–17.00 Mon–Fri, Jun 09.00–17.00 daily, Oct 09.00–17.00 Mon–Fri, Nov–Mar flexible. Zero-waste laundry liquid & other products. Take your own bottles to refill.

Isle of Mull Soap Company 50 Main St, PA75 6NT; w isleofmullsoap.scot; Nov–Dec & Feb–Mar 10.00–16.00 Mon–Sat, Apr–Oct 09.00–22.00 Mon–Sat, 10.00–16.00 Sun. Handmade soap & eco-toiletries such as bamboo toothbrushes.

Tackle & Books 7 Main St, PA75 6NU; 01688 302336; w tackleandbooks.co.uk; 09.30–13.00 & 14.00–17.30 Mon–Sat. Bookshop selling guidebooks, stationery & art supplies. Also fishing tackle.

Trek Tobermory Main St, PA75 6NR; Apr–Oct 09.00–21.00 daily, Nov–Mar 10.00–16.00 daily. Reasonably priced outdoor gear & friendly service.

Sports and activities

Fishing

Tackle & Books (see above). This is the best place to get information & a map about fishing on Mull. They also issue permits for Loch Torr, Loch Frisa, Loch Sguabain, the Glen Lochs, River Aros, River Bellart, River Lussa, Mishnish Lochs & Aros Loch. Organises no experience necessary, keep what you catch Sea Angling Trips with group sizes of 5–12 (2/3/4hrs £22/32/42).

Golf

Tobermory Golf Club Erray Rd, PA75 6PS; 01688 302387; w tobermorygolfclub.com. 9-hole course overlooking Tobermory Bay.

Wildlife and boat trips

Sealife Surveys 01688 302916; w sealifesurveys.com. Long-standing wildlife-watching boat trips with the hope of finding seals & maybe even minke whales, basking sharks, dolphins, harbour porpoise & white-tailed eagles. Work alongside HWDT (see above) & the aquarium (page 164). £20–90 pp, depending on length of trip.

Other practicalities

$ Bank Clydesdale Bank; 20 Main St, PA75 6NU; 08457 826818; 09.15–16.45 Mon–Tue & Thu–Fri, 09.45–16.45 Wed

Fuel/mechanic Harbour Garage, Ledaig car park, PA75 6NR; 01688 302103; summer 08.00–18.00 Mon–Fri, 08.00–18.00 Sat, 09.00–17.00 Sun, winter 08.00–18.00 Mon–Fri, 08.00–16.00 Sat, 10.00–13.00 Sun

Medical Tobermory Medical Practice, Rockfield Rd, PA75 6PN; 01688 302013

Pharmacy Tobermory Pharmacy, 46 Main St, PA75 6NT; 01688 302431; f; 09.00–17.00 Mon–Tue & Thu–Fri, 09.00–13.00 Wed & Sat

Post office Tobermory Post Office, Hus Gate, Ledaig, PA75 6NR; 09.00–17.30 Mon–Tue & Thu–Fri, 09.00–13.00 Wed, 09.00–12.30 Sat

What to see and do Tobermory has a whole string of fantastic little attractions, with more diversions for children than most small Scottish towns. Mull's cultural and natural heritage is presented in a varied and engaging manner, with something for visitors of all ages and a whole range of interests.

Mull Aquarium (Ledaig, PA75 6NR; ☏ 01688 302876; w mullaquarium.co.uk; ⊕ Easter–Oct 09.30–17.00 daily; adult/concession/child £5.50/4.50/4) Keeping animals for a maximum of four weeks, this little gem is Europe's first 'catch and release' aquarium. Local fishermen and children bring in interesting species, and staff at the aquarium use them to educate visitors. Octopus, probably the most exciting marine guest, are only kept for two weeks and released before they learn how to escape their tanks. Popular touch-pool demonstrations are hosted hourly in summer months, where visitors have a chance to hold species such as starfish, squirting scallops, hermit crabs and urchins.

Tobermory Distillery (Ledaig, PA75 6NR; ☏ 01688 302647; w tobermorydistillery. com; ⊕ Apr, May, Sep & Oct 10.00–17.00 daily, Jun–Aug 10.00–18.00 daily, Nov–Mar 10.00–16.00 Mon–Sat, noon–16.00 Sun) Originally established as Ledaig Distillery in 1798, Tobermory is Mull's only distillery and one of the oldest in Scotland. It produces two contrasting single malts: the non-peated Tobermory and the heavily peated; plus a new Hebridean gin. Tours range from £12.50 per person for a 45-minute tour, including a dram of 12-year-old single malt, to a £35 per person experience where you can try three whiskies straight from the casks and learn about how the casks affect the maturation process.

Hebridean Whale & Dolphin Trust Discovery Centre (28 Main St, PA75 6NQ; ☏ 01688 302816; w hwdt.org; ⊕ Apr & May 09.00–17.00 Mon–Fri, Jun 09.00–17.00 daily, Oct 09.00–17.00 Mon–Fri, Nov–Mar flexible) This modern exhibition centre has an inspiring and informative film playing, touch-screen information about species and distribution, and a couple of whale bones. Check in advance for scheduled talks and activities.

Mull Museum (Columba Bldgs, Main St, PA75 6NY; ☏ 01688 301100; w mullmuseum.org.uk; ⊕ Apr–Oct 10.00–16.00 Mon–Sat (other times, library & archives by arrangement); free or £5/year membership for library/archives) An endearingly old-fashioned museum crammed with invaluable, well-researched information and interesting exhibits, including delicate jewellery thought to have been lost by medieval pilgrims on their way to or from Iona. It's worth visiting towards the beginning of your time on the island if you're a history or archaeology enthusiast; as well as providing vital background information, it can help you locate and interpret the most interesting archaeological sites on the island.

RNLI Shop and Visitor Centre (Ferry port, PA75 6NU; free) A small exhibition about the Royal National Lifeboat Institution with a little information and history, as well as fun outfits for children to try on.

Tobermory Lighthouse The lighthouse path is marked just past the RNLI centre on the left-hand side of the pier. This 2-mile return walk is easily followed along the coast, running through mature, broad-leaved woodland, with bluebells in May and the scent of wild garlic. Eventually the view opens up across to Ardnamurchan with fishing boats bobbing in the Sound. Look out for cetaceans, which are regularly seen on this stretch of water. You will soon reach the lighthouse, which you cannot go inside. Keep a close eye on small children and dogs as there are steep drops in places.

NORTHERN AND CENTRAL MULL Covering a large proportion of the landmass and a tiny proportion of inhabitants, northern and central Mull are fantastic for wildlife, discovering unknown archaeological sites and generally exploring the wilderness.

Getting around The only public transport serving this part of Mull is a request service run by Ulva Ferry Community Transport (page 160).

Where to stay *Map, page 156*
Townships are few and far between in this wild part of Mull and accommodation options are sporadically placed. Booking in advance is essential in summer and many places close between October and April. Further self-catering options are listed at w visitmullandiona.co.uk/listing-type/self-catering.

🏠 **Glengorm Castle** (5 rooms) 5 miles northwest of Tobermory PA75 6QE; 📞01688 302321; w glengormcastle.co.uk. Built in 1860, Glengorm Castle is an imposing, turreted manor house that offers B&B & a range of self-catering properties on the estate (page 167). Complimentary whisky in the library next to a huge fire, & large sitting rooms with sea views. Tower rooms have original baths. **££££**

🏠 **Lip na Cloiche** (2 rooms) Ballygown, near Ulva Ferry PA73 6LU; 📞01688 500257; w lipnacloiche.co.uk; ⏰ mid-Mar–Oct. Traditional cottage with friendly owner Lucy who also runs beautiful open garden. Decoration is the most creative sort of eccentric with collections of china horses & floral touches. Carefully sourced b/fast with homemade bread, local bacon & own eggs. **££**

🏠 **Tigh-na-Mara** (4 rooms) Dervaig PA75 6QW; 📞01688 400278; w mullbandb.co.uk; ⏰ May–Oct. Local resident Catherine provides a warm welcome to the small village of Dervaig. Bedrooms & guest living room overlook the grassy loch shoreline, frequented by otters. 2 rooms en suite, 2 rooms shared bathroom, but will never be asked to share with strangers as Catherine does not like to fill all her rooms at once. B/fast includes own free-range eggs. **££**

🏠 **Dervaig Bunkrooms** (6 beds) Dervaig Village Hall, PA75 6QN; m 07435 656420; w dervaigbunkrooms.co.uk; ♿. Modern bunkhouse with 4- & 2-bed rooms, available as private or shared. **£**

🏕 **Killiechronan Camping** Killiechronan Estate, PA72 5JU; 📞01680 300403; ⏰ Mar–Oct. Very basic camping in lovely spot on the shore of Loch Na Keal. Sinks & toilets at farm. **£**

🏕 **Pennygown Holiday Park** Glenforsa, Aros PA72 6JN; m 07799 711125; w pennygownholidaypark.com; ♿. Camping on the banks of the Sound of Mull with lovely view of Morvern; also next to the A849, which makes it a little less peaceful. **£**

🏕 **Calgary Bay** w calgarybay.co.uk/info.htm. To the south of Calgary Bay is a space allocated for small campervans & tents. Public-access toilets. Free, donations welcome.

Weekly rental
🏠 **Achnadrish House Self Catering** (sleeps 2/6) Dervaig PA75 6QF; 📞01688 400388; w achnadrish.co.uk. A 200-year-old shooting lodge divided into 3 parts (the owners' house, the White Cabin & the Wing) with pigs & chickens. Ideal location for walking, cycling & wildlife. White Cabin/Wing £750/350.

Where to eat and drink *Map, page 156*
✗ **Am Birlinn** Penmore Mill, Dervaig PA75 6QS; 📞01688 400619; w ambirlinn.com; ⏰ noon–14.30 & 17.00–21.00 Wed–Sun; ♿. Beautifully presented, high-quality local food

in an impressive modern wooden building. **££**

✗ **The Bellachroy** Dervaig PA75 6QW; 📞01688 400314; w thebellachroy.co.uk; ⏰ summer

12.30–14.30 & 18.00–20.30 daily, winter hrs reduced. Homemade Scottish dishes & local seafood in the 'Oldest Inn on Mull'. ££

☐ **Calgary Art in Nature** Calgary PA75 6QQ; ☎01688 400256; w calgary.co.uk; ☼ Easter–Oct 10.00–17.00 daily. Coffee, b/fast rolls, home-baked cakes & lunches in attractive café with outside eating area. Also small selection of local meat & cheese. £

☐ **Glengorm Coffee Shop** Glengorm Castle, PA75 6QE; ☼ end Mar–Oct 10.00–17.00 daily. Fresh cakes & seasonal produce from estate including beef, venison & lamb. Salad grown in walled garden. £

✴ ☐ **The Hen House** Fanmore, Ulva Ferry PA73 6LX; ☎01688 500238; ⓕ; ☼ Mar–Oct flexible, Nov–Apr possibly w/ends. Small wooden shed with picnic tables outside & incredible view of Ulva. Delicious quiche. Tries to avoid single-use plastic with wooden forks, paper plates & discount for own cup. £

☐ **Whitetail Gin Distillery Shop & Café** Tiroran PA69 6ES; ☎01681 705163; w whitetailgin.com; ☼ 11.00–17.00 Sun–Fri. Small gin distillery, farm shop & café. New Whitetail Gin is for sale in the shop; it is 47% & uses local botanicals such as winter savoury, heather, pine needles & kelp. £

Entertainment

🎭 **Mull Theatre** Druimfin PA75 6QB; ☎01688 302211; w comar.co.uk; ♿. 100-seat theatre hosting both local dramatic performances & visiting plays from further afield. In partnership with An Tobar (page 162).

Shopping

Ardnacross Farm Shop Aros PA72 6JS; w ardnacross.com/farm-shop; ☼ flexible. Lamb, beef & venison straight from the farm.

Dervaig Post Office & Stores Dervaig PA75 6QJ; ☎01688 400208; w dervaigshop.co.uk; ☼ 09.00–18.00 Mon–Sat, noon–14.00 Sun; ♿. Incredibly large & well-stocked grocery shop considering location. Fresh fruit & veg, meat & dairy, coffee machine, alcohol & snacks.

Dervaig Producers' Market Dervaig Village Hall; w dervaigvillagehall.co.uk/whats-on. Check website for dates.

Salen Spar, Malcolm Elliot Post Office & Stores Ltd Salen PA72 6JB; ☎01680 300472; ☼ 08.00–20.00 Mon–Sat, 10.00–17.00 Sun. Relatively large grocery shop, also sells local-interest books.

Sports and activities

Killiechronan Pony Trekking Killiechronan Estate (near Gruline), PA72 6JU; w mullponytrekking.webs.com. Riding over hills or along the beach.

Mull Charters Ulva Ferry PA73 6LY; ☎01680 300444; w mullcharters.com. Flexible wildlife-watching, photography or fishing trips in boats carrying up to 12 people. Good chance of seeing eagles.

Turus Mara Ulva Ferry PA73 6LY; ☎01688 400242; w turusmara.com. Boat trips out to the Treshnish Isles & Staffa from Ulva Ferry. Puffins May–Jul & other great wildlife opportunities.

Other practicalities

Fuel MacDonald's Filling Station, Salen PA72 6JF; ☼ 07.30–18.00 Mon–Sat, 10.00–17.00 Sun, closed Christmas & New Year.

✚ **Medical** Salen Medical Practice, Ardmor Rd, Salen PA72 6JL; ☎01680 300327

✉ **Post offices** Dervaig Post Office & Stores (see above); Salen Spar (see above); Ulva Ferry, Laggan Ulva Farm, PA73 6LT (☼ 09.00–13.00 Mon–Fri)

What to see and do

The central east coast The ruins of **Pennygown Chapel** stand just to the east of the A849 in central Mull, with views across the Sound of Mull to Movern. Thought to be from the 13th century, the site is shrouded in myth; people used to leave small requests for the fairies until one day a chancer left a small stick and asked for it to be turned into a ship's mast; the fairies responded by moving out, never to be heard of since. Look out for the figures of a man and woman carved in relief on two 17th-century grave slabs. Inside the chapel is the intricately carved base of a 16th-century cross.

Heading north from the small village of Salen, also the easiest place to cut across to the west coast, there are a couple of gently rotting old boats on the muddy shore; the skerries and islets around **Salen Bay** are frequented by common seals. On the other side of the bay is **Aros Castle** (⊕ 56°32'01"N 5°57'54"W); already in ruins by Martin Martin's visit in 1695, it was initially built by Clan MacDougall who held it for a while before losing it to the MacDonalds; they later lost it to the MacLeans. If you have a car, take the turning towards 'Aros Mains' and park in the small indicated car park; you can explore on foot from there.

Closer to Tobermory, the woodland **Alainn View lookout point** (♿) looks out over a majestic waterfall in the Aros River. Those without mobility issues can also walk down the steep path to a second waterfall; it leaves from just to the left of the viewpoint and is marked with red sticks. From the shore, just 10yds from the second waterfall, is a lovely view across to Tobermory Harbour; if you turn left, you can walk into Tobermory (1 mile); right will take you towards an old pier.

The far north A windy road leads out to **Glengorm Castle** (guided walks: w glengormwildlife.co.uk), an extensive 19th-century manor house now run as a B&B (page 165). Although the interior is reserved for guests, the surrounding estate is a rewarding area to visit. Now quiet and secluded, Glengorm had an unpleasant beginning; James Forsyth, who bought the estate in 1850, removed around 70 tenants over the following few years before he built his new 'castle'. There's a story that he asked an old woman what his new residence should be called, not understanding that her suggestion, 'Glengorm' (meaning 'the blue glen'), referred to the smoke from the burning roofs of the houses of those he evicted. The current owners are much more hospitable and there is a café (see opposite) and visitor centre, plus guided walks by a wildlife ranger, focusing on history, geology or wildlife, including weekly headland watches with the hope of seeing porpoises, dolphins or whales. Visitors are welcome to park in the car park near the café and explore the estate on foot; there are several interesting archaeological sites to be found. Keep an eye out for the five mating pairs of hen harriers.

Two secluded sandy beaches in the far north

Distance: 4 miles return or 2 miles for just Port na Beach; time: 2 hours; start/end: Croig; OS Explorer map: 374 Isle of Mull North & Tobermory

Calgary (page 168) has a well-deserved a reputation as Mull's finest beach, but Port na Beach and Langamull are two hidden gems with only a fraction of its visitors. The route out to them is easy-going, initially following tracks that become grassy or sandy in places; the section between Port na Beach and Langamull crosses open fields and gentle coastline.

From the B8073, take the turning for Croig and park in a small place opposite the harbour and sea wall (⊕ 56° 36' 19"N 6° 14' 05"W). You can walk out to the tiny island beyond the sea wall for an interesting perspective, before walking along the track marked 'Croig Farm'; it's just over a mile north to beautiful **Port na Beach** (⊕ 56° 36'43"N 6°15'16"W). This idyllic pocket of sand is only beaten in peacefulness by **Langamull Beach**, a further mile southwest across grassy, unpathed coastline. Higher ground gives you a view out to Rùm and Coll and you might see seals bobbing in the sea. At Langamull, green grass runs down to the sea, where sheep graze quietly on small islands and the water is tropically turquoise. To return, retrace your steps to Croig.

Towards Dervaig The road to Dervaig from Tobermory (the B8073) passes some peaceful lochs before heading down a couple of sets of sharp hairpin bends. The second set of hairpins are surrounded by clusters of standing stones; there is a small car park at the top of the hill, and another smaller place to park at the sharp corner below. Just southwest of the graveyard at this second parking place, you will notice a quite broken set of **four standing stones** (✪ 56°35'12"N 6°10'24"W), one of which has been set into a dry-stone wall with a casual nonchalance to its history.

The attractive settlement of **Dervaig** is most memorable for **Kilmore Church**. Built around 1904 by the architect Peter Macgregor Chalmers (who also built Rhu Church on Canna; page 125), it has a tall white spire and colourful stained-glass windows. The Kilmore Cross, part of which is now protected inside the church, is also said to have been the grave of John Campbell, the 'grisly lad', and is made in the 14th or 15th century, Iona School style. The sheltered waters of **Loch a' Chumhainn**, on which Dervaig sits, have made Dervaig a popular settlement throughout history and are also a favourite haunt of otters. For the best chance of spotting one, spend some time quietly observing the grassy banks of the loch around dawn or dusk.

Calgary The tiny township of Calgary packs a punch in terms of nearby visitor attractions. Most visitors come here for **Calgary Bay**, an idyllic stretch of sand that has the reputation of being Mull's best beach; it's also one of the most accessible on the island.

Opposite Calgary Bay is the walled **Calgary Burial Ground** with an early Christian stone carved with crosses on both sides, one of which is upside down. The cross stone stands on a raised area, just in front and to the left of three modern gravestones and next to another well-weathered grave slab. The stone itself is simple and weathered, but shows that this site has had a religious significance for over 1,000 years.

Just north of Calgary Bay, **Calgary Art in Nature** (✆ 01688 400256; w calgaryartinnature.co.uk; ⊕ 10.00–17.00 daily) is an excellent art gallery with local pieces in clay, wood, mosaic, watercolour, oils, tapestry and mixed media. More famous is their open garden and woodland walk (£2 including map) with hidden sculptures, a zip line, rope swing, willow tunnels and plenty of artistic detail. There is also a great view over Calgary Bay.

The wild west coast The coastline from Calgary all the way down to the Ross of Mull is either a delight or a horror depending on how much of a hurry you're in. The scenery is sublime, with views out to the Treshnish Isles and then looking across Loch Tuath to Gometra and Ulva. Driving conditions are tricky, with deep pot-holes in parts, sharp turns and very few passing places along certain stretches. Near Kilninian is a deserted black beach, **Traigh na Cille**, which makes a beautiful spot for a picnic if you can find somewhere to park without blocking either gateways or passing places.

In **Ballygown**, a hamlet just northwest of Ulva Ferry, is **Lip na Cloiche** ✳ (✆ 01688 500257; w lipnacloiche.co.uk; ⊕ dawn–dusk all year; £2.50). This densely planted, layered garden winds around several levels. Flowers, specifically chosen to help the bees, and delicate scents of lemon balm follow you around the intricate paths and gardener Lucy's artistic touches are everywhere. Outdated farming implements frame the way and a wonderful circle of glass fishing floats reflects the sunshine (if you are lucky enough to have some). Lucy also has a small craft shop in her porch.

Opposite Ballygown, between Lip na Cloiche and the small headland called Rubha Leadaig, is a well-preserved broch called **Dùn nan Gall** (⊕ 56°30'36"N 6°10'26"W), although there isn't anywhere sensible to park very nearby. Shortly further south is a parking place for **Eas Fos Waterfall**; this pretty cascade is only 20yds away and much more impressive after rain. Further south, at the tiny township of **Ulva Ferry**, you can catch the passenger boat to Ulva (page 179).

As the road turns east, skirting around **Loch na Keal**, the scenery becomes even more spectacular. Those driving all the way along the western coast will quickly become familiar with the outline of tiny, uninhabited Eorsa in the middle of the loch; there is also a good selection of places to pull over in order to stop and admire the view. Those who are searching for eagles with binoculars should spend some time scouring the hilltops and coast here; both species live around this area.

Just after the small settlement of Gruline is **Macquarie's Mausoleum**. A small, stone structure of particular interest to Australians, Lachlan Macquarie was born on the Isle of Ulva in the mid 18th century. Because of his work as the Governor of New South Wales, he became a prominent figure in colonial times and is now nicknamed 'The Father of Australia'. The tomb is shared by the National Trust of Scotland and the National Trust of Australia, but it is important to note that you must walk the final section in order not to drive over private land.

Skirting the base of Beinn Bheag and Beinn a' Ghraig, the way becomes even more dramatic as it approaches Ben More (see below).

The Burg Estate, Ardmeanach Peninsula
The Burg Estate occupies 2 square miles at the most westerly tip of Ardmeanach, one of Mull's most untouched peninsulas. It is owned by the National Trust for Scotland (w nts.org.uk/visit/places/burg) and forms part of Ardmeanach's 'Special Area of Conservation', recognised for its exceptional plant life. Unusual species such as grass of Parnassus and delicate Iceland purslane thrive in the rich volcanic soil here, a habitat that supports notably colourful and interesting species of insect such as tiger beetles and the rare Scotch burnet moth, as well as larger animals: ravens, eagles and feral goats.

To reach the Burg Estate, take the side road that heads west at Killinichen Bay; you can park at Tiroran car park to continue on foot, following the main track that leads further west. The initial stages are good and would be manageable for pushchairs or wheelchairs with some assistance on steeper parts, but it gets much rougher after a couple of miles.

Several cleared townships also lie within the Burg Estate, including the ruined houses at **Salachry** (⊕ 56°22'13"N 6°07'51"W) and **Culliemore** (⊕ 56°22'18"N 6°08'30"W), which were both evicted in the mid 19th century. While the coastline is a glorious setting for an afternoon walk, life in these remote settlements would have been a struggle against the elements through the winter months.

Ben More
Distance: 5¾ miles; time: 6 hours; start/end: Dhiseig; OS Explorer map: 375 Isle of Mull East
Though this route is less than 6 miles, it ascends and descends 3,100ft, so hikers should prepare for a whole-day walk (page 34). While the views are incredible on clear days, in bad weather hiking without a GPS could be dangerous and, considering there will be nothing to see, for most people there is probably little point in attempting it.

THE FOSSIL TREE

In 1811 John MacCulloch, a geological cartographer, discovered an impressive phenomenon. When the volcanic rock of Ardmeanach was forming, a huge conifer was engulfed in molten lava and left behind its 39ft-tall shape, imprinted in a wall of basalt sculptures that now form the cliff.

In the far west of the Burg Estate, the imprint of this fossilised tree (✛ 56°22'16.1"N 6°12'28.7"W) can be reached on a rough 10-mile return walking route (w walkhighlands.co.uk/mull/fossil-tree.shtml). Though not a great idea for anyone with a fear of heights, the walk takes you along the clifftops, where you will notice the basalt formations below that were created by a series of lava flows. Eventual access to the shore is also tidal and via a long, rickety ladder. This coastal path is also prone to landslides, which might block the route; updates can be found on the National Trust for Scotland's website (w nts.org.uk/visit/places/burg).

If you have a car, park in the small car park (✛ 56°26'57"N 6°04'04"W) between the few buildings at Dhiseig and the shore at Traigh Doire Dhubhaig. There is a sign to read from Benmore Estate (✆ 01680 300229) with important information about deer stalking, which occurs between August and October. From here a side road leads up to Dhiseig; follow it for about 400yds before bearing right around the buildings and going through a small gate to find the path. Splitting occasionally, the correct path follows close-by the river, Abhainn Dhiseig, as it tumbles down small waterfalls and through gorges. An Gearna, a smaller hill on the flanks of Ben More, is above you and to the left, though this route aims directly for Ben More. Being the biggest mountain in the area, with the direct route also being the most sensible from here, it is quite easy to navigate to the top in clear weather. Around 2 miles into the walk, you will find that the path crosses Abhainn Dhiseig. As you begin to ascend more steeply, take some time to look back and admire the view of Ulva and northern Mull, and do not forget to keep checking the sky for eagles. Sometimes you might be lucky enough to see both white-tailed and golden eagles flying together.

Nearer the top of the Munro, there is some scree to navigate. Though this will slow you down, it should not be a problem for intermediate to experienced hillwalkers. Following the ridge southeast, there is a substantial and much-appreciated rock shelter at the summit, as even in calm weather this can be a windy spot. Looking down to A'Chioch in the northeast, with a backdrop of Beinn Fhada, Beinn Talaidh and other hills across central Mull behind, the view is truly spectacular. To the south are Islay and the Paps of Jura (page 243); the Treshnish Isles, Coll and Tiree are to the northwest; and Ireland is visible on a very clear day. Rùm and the Skye Cuillins are to the north, majestic as ever from every angle. There is no other place in the Inner Hebrides from which you can see the whole region so clearly. Retrace your steps to return to more sheltered ground and head back the way you came.

CRAIGNURE AND THE SOUTHEAST Receiving nearly all of Mull's visitors, but mostly only as they speed to and from the ferry, Craignure is a small, leafy village, down-to-earth and welcoming. Though the ferry is not particularly obtrusive, the port's mere presence seems to hurry people through. Ignoring the ferry terminal, Craignure has a pleasant shoreline, great for wading birds, and lovely views up Loch Linnhe.

Tours

Mull Eagle Watch Craignure PA65 6BA; ☎01680 812556; w mulleaglewatch.com; ⊕ Apr–Sep. Ranger-guided visits to view white-tailed eagles. A successful community-managed programme to encourage conservation, run as a partnership between Forestry & Land Scotland, the RSPB, Mull & Iona Community Trust, Scottish Natural Heritage & Police Scotland. Trips take 1½hrs & depart from Craignure.

Where to stay

🏠 **Pennygate Lodge** (6 rooms) PA65 6AY; ☎01680 812333; w pennygatelodge.scot; ⊕ Mar–Dec. Luxury accommodation in a 1831 old manse. House stands proudly at the end of a striped lawn with patches left wild for the bluebells, looking out over the bay. Good value. **££££**

🏠 **Craignure Inn** (3 rooms) PA65 6AY; ☎01680 812305; w craignure-inn.co.uk. Old-fashioned, cottagey rooms above 1800s village pub. **£££**

🏠 **Craignure Bunkhouse** (20 beds) PA65 6AY; ☎01680 812043; w craignure-bunkhouse.co.uk; ♿. Modern, small but well-equipped bunkhouse. Underfloor heating fuelled by biomass. Closed in daytime for cleaning. Paid laundry facilities & shower also open to non-residents after 16.30. **£**

⛺ **Sheilings Campsite** PA65 6AY; ☎01680 812496; w shielingholidays.co.uk. Large waterfront campsite on secluded peninsula. The 'Sheilings' (18 tents) are spacious, permanently erected tents with accommodation types ranging from dorm (£20 pp) to private en suite (2 people/£80), with basic self-catering facilities inside. Though there is bedding & the standard/en-suite options have burners, tents are not insulated & extra layers are recommended. Also space for caravans, campervans (book ahead) & tents. Free Wi-Fi. Effective covered drying tents for clothes. **£**

Where to eat and drink

✗ **Pennygate Lodge** (see above) ⊕ Mar–Dec evening meals booked in advance. Elegant meals cooked with local ingredients served in an attractive Georgian dining room. **£££**

✗ **Craignure Inn** (see above) ⊕ summer noon–21.00 daily, winter noon–15.00 & 17.00–20.30 daily; ♿. Decent pub food popular with locals & visitors alike. Manager Matthew, originally from Johannesburg, is welcoming & makes people feel at home. **££**

🍺 **Blazeys on Mull** Craignure; ☎01680 812471; ⬛; ⊕ Mar–Dec daytimes (works around ferry times) daily; ♿. Well-filled fresh sandwiches, hot pies, coffees, cakes & beer on tap. Bigger than it appears, clean & presented with pride. Outside seating. There's also a small shop selling local jams, inexpensive & impressive local wildlife photography. **£**

Shopping

The Craignure Stores & Post Office (Spar) PA65 6AY; ☎01680 812301; ⊕ 07.30–17.30 Mon, 08.00–17.30 Tue–Sat, 10.00–17.00 Sun. Relatively well-stocked local grocery shop with some fruit & veg, alcohol & essentials.

Invalussa Mussels Near Loch Spelve PA65 6BD; ☎01680 812109; w inverlussa.com/about-us/ mussel-farm; ⊕ when available. Self-service mussels in ice box 2/5kg £2/5.

The Old Post Office Lochbuie PA62 6AA; ☎01680 814153; w oldpostofficelochbuie.co.uk; ⊕ 09.00–17.00 daily. Small shop with self-serve tea/coffee (50p) & local produce. Local 'ready meals' can be pre-ordered from Lochbuie Larder (see website).

Other practicalities

Fuel The Craignure Stores & Post Office (Spar) (see above). Ask in Craignure Stores before filling.

➕ **Medical** Mull & Iona Community Hospital, Craignure PA65 6BG; ☎01680 300392

✉ **Post office** The Craignure Stores & Post Office (Spar) (see above).

What to see and do

Duart Castle (3 miles southeast of Craignure PA64 6AP; ☎ 01680 812309; w duartcastle.com; ⏰ Apr 11.00–16.00 daily, May–mid-Oct 10.30–17.00 daily; grounds open access; adult/child/family £7.50/4/19; combination tickets that inc transport from Oban or Craignure are available: see website) Of all the castle museums covered by this book, Duart is the most rewarding. A fortress rather than a turreted affair, it stands in a dramatic position between the Firth of Lorn and Sound of Mull.

An early MacDougall stronghold, Duart started its existence as a simple fortified dwelling. More complex additions were built later by the MacLeans who erected a tower house on four levels, incorporating one existing wall and utilising others to form a courtyard. They lost the castle in the 1670s, and it fell into disrepair over many generations until Sir Fitzroy MacLean finally bought it back in 1911.

The museum is spread across several of the (now restored) castle's floors, beginning in the courtyard with information on the restoration, before heading inside to the kitchens, original well and dungeons, with an atmospheric recording of seagulls and a prisoner vomiting. Upstairs, past the pantry, are a collection of fascinating Ordnance Survey diagrams from 1748, followed by the spectacular Sea Room and its unbeatable view. From here you can look out to 'Lady's Rock' where, in the early 16th century, one particular Lachlan MacLean, wishing to marry another woman, dropped off his wife and left her to drown: she was then rescued and the MacLean was murdered by her brother.

Next you will enter the banquet hall, with many generations of MacLean chief portraits observing your progress around the collection of historical swords and guns. Everything is labelled, sometimes with extensive anecdotes and often, endearingly, written out by hand in fountain pen. Despite the solid rock walls, the winds howls through the castle and you are unlikely to want to take off your coat.

Upstairs again is the state bedroom and dressing room, an outrageously tall, floral, four-poster bed, and a small, but wonderful collection of 18th- and 19th-century outfits. There is a portrait of Sir Charles MacLean, painted during World War II 'in exchange for a packet of cigarettes' and a huge number of family photos, which may be of interest to those with a hereditary connection.

Up a tight final staircase is a rather dated timeline of objects, including cannonballs that were found in the mortar during restoration and a key from the captain's chest of the Spanish galley that blew up in Tobermory Bay. From this level, you can access the battlements for a view of the dozens of chimneys, the Lismore Lighthouse and the mountainous mainland beyond. Once you have finished exploring the castle, take some time to visit Duart Point and look out for porpoises and dolphins, which are known to pass by. **The Tearoom** café serves sandwiches and soup at lunchtimes (⏰ noon–15.00 daily; £).

Lochbuie One of Mull's many beautiful, hidden corners, **Lochbuie** is at the end of a long single-track road. A small car park is indicated just before a bridge, from which white painted stones lead for around half a mile through several fields to the **stone circle** (⊕ 56°21'30"N 5°51'29"W). Though not quite comparable with Lewis's famous Callanish Stones, this site is the most impressive and atmospheric of its type in the Inner Hebrides. From here you can rejoin the track going south and follow it bearing right at the first building, before choosing to go either left or right at the fork around the farm buildings. Down at the shore is the imposing **Moy Castle**, another defensive post of the MacLeans, much of which was built in the 15th century. Hikers have infinite further possibilities from here. There are fallow deer living in this area and don't forget to check the sky for eagles.

Returning to the main road and heading west, you will travel along the Lussa River and through Glen More; this stunning stretch of road weaves through the mountains, passing a glorious view of Loch Airdeglais and Loch Sguabain and approaching Ben More (page 169) to the north.

A woodland walk from Craignure

Distance: 3 miles; time: 2 hours; start/end: Craignure; OS Explorer map: 375 Isle of Mull East
The woodland walk from Craignure to Torosay Castle is beautiful, with a great view across to Duart Castle, though note that Torosay is a private residence and cannot be visited. The return journey is via the coast.

Start on the road going south from Craignure; pass the garage on your left and continue until you see a track leading off to the left with white gate posts, a small house and a sign that says 'Private Road no unauthorised vehicular access' (✦ 56°27'59"N 5°41'53"W). You can follow this track through the woodland, with sunshine dappling through huge broad-leaved trees, the smell of wild garlic and startled red deer.

The track leads all the way to Torosay where, before you reach the 'castle' itself (more a large house), you can take the hairpin bend down to the left and head down to take a look at the old jetty (✦ 56°27'29"N 5°40'41"W), where thrift is growing and there is a spectacular view of Duart Castle across the bay.

From the jetty, you can continue along a path that leads around the coastline. It is a rougher walk than the woodland track, but you cannot get lost if you keep the sea on your right. You'll initially pass an outrageously sized memorial cross, followed by a strange structure thought to be an old explosives store; look out too for otters and wading birds such as curlews around the tiny tidal island of Eilean Bàn. The faint path eventually leads to the grass and rocky shoreline below Sheilings Campsite on the west side of Craignure; it's then a short stroll back to the village.

FIONNPHORT AND THE ROSS OF MULL
Samuel Johnson describes the journey to Iona on horseback across Mull as a great inconvenience, 'traversing this gloom of desolation', but today there's no doubting that the Ross is absolutely stunning. Like Johnson, most rush through on their way to Iona but, with great hillwalking and beautiful beaches, the Ross of Mull is a perfect place for outdoors people and nature lovers. In the far west, the village of Fionnphort is small but bustling; it has a lovely beach of its own, and many of the Ross's amenities.

Getting there and around
West Coast Motors (page 160) run a bus route from Craignure to Bunessan and Fionnphort.

Where to stay
Map, page 174
Considering its small size, Fionnphort has a reasonably large collection of quality B&Bs. Self-catering properties are more widely distributed, tucked away in beautiful corners of the Ross; Visit Scotland (w visitscotland.com/destinations-maps/isle-mull) have an extensive list of options.

🏠 **Staffa House** (4 rooms) Fionnphort PA66 6BL; 📞01681 700677; w staffahouse.co.uk. High-quality, comfortable B&B. Janice is welcoming & takes pride in looking after guests. Guest lounge with local info & maps. Chris used to be a chef & often puts on evening meals, which are

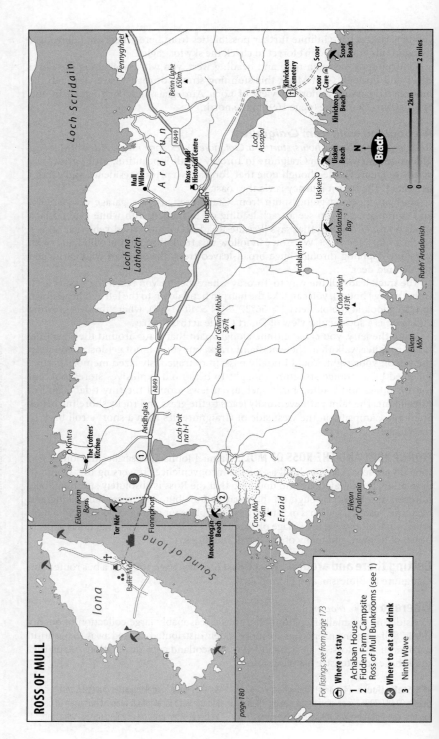

ROSS OF MULL

Iona

Baile Mòr

Sound of Iona

Erraid

Eilean a' Chalmain

Eilean Mòr

Eilean nam Ban

Loch Scridain

Loch na Làthaich

Loch Poit na h-I

Loch Assapol

Ardtun

Pennyghael

Beinn Lighe 650m ▲

Mull Willow ●

Ross of Mull Historical Centre ▥

Bunessan

Kintra

The Crofters' Kitchen ●

Ardghlas

Ardalanish

Uisken

Ardalanish Bay ↙

Rubh' Ardalanish

Benn a' Chaol-airigh 413ft ▲

Beinn a' Ghrìme Mhòir 367ft ▲

Cnoc Mòr 246m ▲

Tor Mòr ↙

Fionnphort

Knockvologan Beach ↙

Kilvickeon Cemetery ✝

Kilvickeon Beach ↙

Scoor Cave ⌂

Scoor ○

Scoor Beach ↙

A849

page 180

For listings, see from page 173

① Where to stay
- Achaban House
1 Fidden Farm Campsite
   Ross of Mull Bunkrooms (see 1)

✕ Where to eat and drink
3 Ninth Wave

Bradt

0   1   2km
0   2 miles

174

of exquisite quality, using the best, sustainable produce available. Good environmental principles with solar-panel hot water. They grow their own vegetables & make their own jam. Packed lunches can be provided. 2-night min stay in summer. **£££**

🏠 **Achaban House** (6 rooms) PA66 6BL; ☎01681 70005; w achabanhouse.co.uk. Somewhere between a B&B & self-catering accommodation, Achaban House conveniently offers en-suite private rooms with shared guest kitchen. Can be booked as a whole (min stay 2 nights). Light Continental b/fast. Stylish, but comfortable modern interior, lovely bay windows & standing stone in the garden. 5-bed family room available. Just east of Fionnphort. **££**

🏠 **Ross of Mull Bunkrooms** (2 rooms) Just east of Fionnphort PA66 6BL; m 07759 615200; w rossofmullbunkrooms.co.uk. 2 well-equipped rooms with USB charging & personal lights. Each room sleeps 4 & must be booked as whole. Good value. **£**

⛺ **Fidden Farm Campsite** Knockvologan Rd, PA66 6BN; ☎01681 700427; ☼ May–Sep; ♿. Beautifully situated but busy campsite on the beach near Erraid. Owner is a friendly farmer who started what was a small campsite & watched it grow exponentially. Dogs must be kept on leads. Phone in advance. **£**

Weekly rental

🏠 **Scoor House Holidays** (6 properties) Scoor, Bunessan PA67 6DW; m 07763 468300; w scoorhouse.co.uk. Range of simple, affordable self-catering properties (sleeping 4–6) in a great, secluded location. £370–530/week.

Where to eat and drink *Map, opposite*

With fishing boats bringing in their catch on a daily basis, Fionnphort is the perfect place to try some of Mull's excellent seafood. Bear in mind that most eating establishments are seasonal.

✕ **Ninth Wave** Bruach Mhòr, Fionnphort PA66 6BL; ☎01681 700757; w ninthwaverestaurant. co.uk; ☼ May–Oct 19.00–21.00 Wed–Sun; ♿. Award-winning restaurant. Fresh produce from own croft garden, local seafood. Perfectly presented. Children over 12 only. **£££**

✕ **The Creel Seafood Bar** Fionnphort pier, PA66 6BL; ☼ Apr–Oct 09.00–19.00 daily. Small shed selling fish & chips, scallop & black pudding rolls, fresh sandwiches & salads. Picnic tables. **£**

☕ **The Kiosk** Next to Fionnphort pier, PA66 6BL; ☼ summer 09.00–17.00 daily, winter 10.00–15.00 daily. Cheap teas, coffees, b/fast rolls & sandwiches with friendly service. Unappealing location next to public toilets, though. **£**

Shopping
Arts and crafts
Ardalanish Isle of Mull Weavers South of Bunessan PA67 6DR; ☎01681 700265; ☼ Apr–Oct 10.00–17.00 daily, Nov–Mar 10.00–16.00 Mon–Fri. Working farm & weaving mill with shop selling high-quality woven clothing & blankets, also own Highland beef & mature lamb. Walks on farm trail or to beach.

Fingal Arts & Crafts Fionnphort PA66 6BL; ☎01681 700470; w ferryshopmull.co.uk; ☼ 09.00–18.00 Mon–Sat, noon–14.00 Sun. Fingal Arts & Crafts has souvenirs & postcards, with also a bookshop attached. Good collection of local guides & maps.

South West Mull Makers Columba Centre, Fionnphort PA66 6BL; ☎07835 613589; 🟦;

☼ Apr–Oct flexible. A collection of 10 artists & artisans from the south of Mull who have not quite decided what their group is, but run this shop together. Wide collection of goods including paintings, hand-decorated shoes, clay-work, jams & adorable knitwear.

Food shops Grocery stores are
limited to corner shops & honesty box stalls. Consequently, it is probably a good idea to bring some essentials with you, especially if you are planning on self-catering.

The Crofters' Kitchen Dail an Inbhire, Kintra PA66 6BT; w ecocroft.co.uk; ☼ Apr–Oct 09.00–18.00 Mon–Sat. Fresh salad, help-yourself coffee, sourdough bread, local meat. Signposted from the main road to Kintra.

The Ferry Shop Fionnphort PA66 6BL; ☎01681 700470; w ferryshopmull.co.uk; ⊕ 09.00–18.00 Mon–Sat, noon–14.00 Sun. Basic grocery supplies & ATM.

Pennyghael Stores & Post Office Pennyghael

PA70 6HB; ☎01681 704229; w pennyghaelstores. co.uk; ⊕ 09.00–18.00 Mon–Sat. Small shop with groceries & gifts.

Spar Bunessan Post Office Stores, Bunessan PA67 6DB; ☎01681 700395; ⊕ 08.00–18.00 Mon–Sat, 10.00–16.00 Sun. Groceries, alcohol & coffee.

Activities

Mull Willow On a side road near Eorabus & Ardtun PA67 6DH; m 07742 611781; w mullwillow.com. Practical, sustainable & relaxing willow-weaving courses. Half- & full-day options include vegan/vegetarian

lunch & can be booked up to 4hrs in advance.

Staffa Trips ☎01681 700755; w staffatrips. co.uk; ⊕ Apr–Oct. Trips to Staffa & Fingal's Cave, with puffins present May–Jul.

Other practicalities

Fuel Ardfenaig Filling Station, Coach Hse, Ardfenaig PA67 6DX; ⊕ Jun–Sep 09.00–19.00 daily, Oct–May 09.00–18.00 Mon–Sat. Also sells delicious local tablet.

✚ **Medical** Ross of Mull & Iona Medical Service, Ulva Hse, Bunessan PA67 6DG; ☎01681 700261

✉ **Post offices** Bunessan PA67 6DB (⊕ 09.00–17.30 Mon–Tue & Thu–Fri, 09.00–13.00 Wed & Sat); The Ferry Shop, Fionnphort (see above; ⊕ 09.00–17.30 Mon–Tue & Thu–Fri, 09.00–13.00 Wed & Sat); Pennyghael Stores & Post Office (see above; ⊕ 09.00–13.00 Mon–Thu, 09.00–14.00 Fri)

What to see and do Though there is plenty of alternative hiking and exploration, the Ross of Mull is most spectacular for its beaches. The main road runs along the northern coast, with fantastic views across gentle Loch Scridain, with Ardmeanach and Ben More behind. However, most of the region's sandy shores are down long and difficult minor roads to the south, often with some amount of hiking needed to reach them.

Pennyghael Pennyghael is a peaceful village that looks over the muddy head of Loch Scridain. It was most likely named from 'Pennyland of the Gael', referring to a system where land was valued against the penny.

Bunessan From Pennyghael, the coastline continues quietly, eventually revealing views of the Treshnish Isles and Staffa. Shortly afterwards, you will reach the village of **Bunessan**, a small crofting and fishing community.

Ross of Mull Historical Centre (Ionad Eachdraidh an Rois Mhuilich; Millbrae Cottage, Bunessan PA67 6DG; ☎ 01681 700659; w romhc.org.uk; ⊕ Easter–Oct 10.00–16.00 Mon–Fri) This small, locally run heritage centre, set in an old mill building, has an archive, genealogy information and cultural exhibitions. The community volunteers who run it also provide visitor information, including a range of local information publications, internet access, hot drinks and a picnic area.

Kilvickeon and Scoor A junction between Bunessan Primary School and the village centre leads southeast towards the farm and beaches at Scoor. These 3 miles of badly surfaced road pass Loch Assapol and lead to several options for shorter walks to amazing beaches and interesting archaeological sites. The OS Explorer Map 373 (*Iona, Staffa & Ross of Mull*) and a compass will help you to navigate in this remote area of Mull. You can park at the junction near **Kilvickeon Cemetery** and the ruined 13th-century church for both Kilvickeon or Scoor (⊕ 56°17'53"N 6°11'05"W).

The cemetery and ruined church are well worth exploring in themselves, with several interesting grave slabs in the burial ground. Additionally, on the left of the church entrance at the west end of the north wall, about a foot above you, is a severely weathered carving believed to be a 'sheela na gig' (a figurative carving of a naked woman with an exaggerated vulva). They are found all over Europe, but their purpose or meaning is matter of much debate.

Kilvickeon Beach This double beach with a tidal island, slightly to the west of Scoor can be reached by following the arrow pointing along a track directly opposite the parking area; it runs in a generally southeasterly direction all the way down to the excellent, sandy beach. It is around 1½ miles return and suitable for families.

Scoor To reach Scoor, walk down the left-hand track from the junction by the cemetery, which leads generally southwest for half a mile to the cluster of buildings at Scoor Farm. There are three possible options from Scoor Farm: you can walk down to the beach; visit a cave with markings over 1,000 years old; or take an inland route to the abandoned village of Shiaba. The first two options are short but rough return walks of a mile or less (a total of 2 miles from Kilvickeon Cemetery car park), while to reach Shiaba is about 3 miles return (4 miles from the car park). Do watch where you are putting your feet as there are adders (page 32) in summer.

From Scoor Farm, the beach is accessed by walking about half a mile over fields, followed by a short, but steep section traversing down a muddy pathway to the sand. The view from the cliffs is spectacular. With lovely sand, and surrounded by cliffs, with skerries leading out into the water, **Scoor Beach** is completely worth the effort to get there. In summer months, you should look out to sea for basking sharks. The water is magically clear; if you have a wetsuit or are brave enough to stand the cold, you could bring a snorkel to make the most of it.

To reach the **cave** (⊕ 56°17'23"N 6°10'27"W), bear right from the farm and walk towards Ploughman's Cottage, the furthest south of the buildings at Scoor. There is a rough path to the southeast side of the cottage, which then bears south over grassland before following a stream down the gully to the shore. The cave is tucked into the east side of the gully. It has many carvings of crosses and other markings, probably dating from the 6th to 9th centuries. You will need a torch to explore it properly.

The abandoned settlement of **Shiaba** (⊕ 56°17'48"N 6°08'28"W; route & map: w walkhighlands.co.uk/mull/shiaba.shtml) can be reached from Scoor Farm by heading around the left-hand side of the largest building, Scoor House. The route, which heads about 1½ miles away to the northwest, is best navigated with an OS map and compass or GPS. It was here, in the mid 19th century, that more than 100 people were removed from their homes by the Duke of Argyll; around a dozen roofless houses are all that remains of their existence. With lush green grass leading down to a bay, and the cliffs of Carsaig to the east, Shiaba was once a thriving township, with a school, sheep and cows. Although some people were evicted to other areas of Mull, where they tried to scrape a living on less fertile land, many others went overseas. By the 1861 census there were only 18 people living at Shiaba, and by 1871 there was just one shepherd left. Lonely shepherds continued to live in Shiaba Cottage until the 1930s, when a storm finally blew the roof off.

Uisken Beach and Ardalanish Bay From beside the Argyll Arms Hotel in Bunessan, a side road (initially signposted to Ardachy House Hotel) leads towards the secluded beaches at Uisken and Ardalanish. With a place to park just yards from the sand, **Uisken** is one of the few beaches on Mull that doesn't require much of a walk to access. A gentle cove made of pale sand and sheltered by rocky, offshore islets, on a good day you can see as far as Jura.

Ardalanish, a small settlement and home to Ardalanish Isle of Mull Weavers (page 175), has its own beautiful bay, which is only 600yds from the car park. Stretching across the best part of a mile, smooth sand leads down to gloriously clear water with a few protruding strips of rock. Looking past the wilderness peninsula of Rubh Ardalanish, there's a view of Colonsay on the horizon.

Fionnphort In Fionnphort, the pretty port village where ferries arrive and leave for Iona (page 181), it's impossible to miss 'Fingal's Rock' in the middle of the beach. The story goes that it was thrown there in a temper by Fingal the giant on his way between Staffa and Ireland, which caused the crack that can be seen today. Numerous other stories and names for the rock abound but, regardless, it is almost certainly a glacial erratic.

From Fionnphort you can walk north along sheep tracks, keeping the sea on your left, for around half a mile to **Tor Mòr**. Best known as a quarry for the Ross of Mull's characteristic pink granite, signs of its history are only visible from the presence of a small pier. This beautiful sandy beach is sheltered by the tidal island of Eilean Eòin and it appears to be unknown to almost all of Fionnphort's visitors.

From here, you can continue along the coast for a pleasant 1½-mile walk to the hamlet of **Kintra**, where cows often roam the beach. You'll notice Iona is mostly hidden from view by the small, uninhabited Eilean nam Ban just off the coast.

Erraid The inhabited tidal island of Erraid was a signal station for the Dubh Artach and Skerryvore lighthouses. It has a row of cottages built for the

DUBH ARTACH LIGHTHOUSE

Dubh Artach is the name of a remote rocky islet at the end of a long and dangerous scattering of skerries, 15 miles southwest of Mull. This area was responsible for 30 shipwrecks between 1800 and 1854, and in 1863 the steamer *Bussorah* was wrecked on her maiden voyage; all 33 people aboard were lost. Finally, a huge storm in 1865 destroyed 24 boats within 48 hours.

Although a lighthouse here had previously been thought impossible, work began on one here in 1867. An iron barrack was erected to house the workers during construction. This sturdy structure turned out to be a well-chosen upgrade from previous wooden versions, when it saved the lives of engineer Alan Brebner and 13 other men trapped inside it for the course of a five-day storm in August. With 75ft waves crashing down above them, blocking out all light for several seconds at a time, water came in through the trap door and swept away all of their food. They managed to survive.

Standing at 144ft, Dubh Artach Lighthouse was completed in 1872. One hundred years later it was automated, ending an era and a romantic, lonely profession that had certainly saved hundreds of lives. It remains one of only four Scottish lighthouses situated more than 10 nautical miles from the shore.

keepers and was also used as the land base for building Dubh Artach Lighthouse (see box, opposite), 15 miles southwest of Mull, which was designed by David and Thomas Stevenson.

In the novel *Shipwrecked*, by Thomas's son Robert Louis Stevenson, the main character is marooned on Erraid and believes he is stuck there, before passing fishermen point out that he can just walk across at low tide. With forward planning, you can also walk across to the island at low tide, climb the highest point Cnoc Mòr (230ft) for wonderful views over many tiny islets and to the abbey on Iona.

ISLE OF ULVA (ULBHA)

The Isle of Ulva (w ulva.scot) – just 7½ miles long and 2½ miles wide – was bought in 2018 by the people of Ulva and a group from northwest Mull through the community 'Right to Buy' scheme. On Mull, depending on who you ask, this is either a great success or a huge waste of money, but at least the island's small population (which, at the time of writing, stands at six) now have some agency over the land they live on, which considering the island's history is a difficult concept to condemn.

In 1846, 500 people were cleared from Ulva in what was one of the largest forced clearances in Argyll; the island is still littered with the remains of their houses. The island's new ownership is still in its infancy, but it is a fascinating place to visit, with a successful restaurant, wonderful geology and signposted walks ranging from 1 to 6 hours; don't miss the spectacular basalt cliff in the southeast (OS Explorer 374: *Isle of Mull North & Tobermory* will help with navigation). Walkhighlands (w walkhighlands.co.uk/mull/isle-of-ulva.shtml) have maps and descriptions for several fantastic Ulva walks. Head to Sheila's Cottage, a reconstruction of a traditional thatched croft house just 100yds north of the ferry jetty, for information on both exploring Ulva and its heritage.

GETTING THERE AND AWAY A small passenger boat runs from Ulva Ferry (on Mull) to Ulva (Jun–Aug 09.00–17.00 Sun–Fri, Sep–Jun 09.00–17.00 Mon–Fri). Slide the panel left to reveal a red sign beneath to summon the ferry, but don't forget to replace it once the boat arrives. Queries can be made at the Boathouse restaurant.

WHERE TO EAT AND DRINK   *Map, page 156*
✗ **The Boathouse** ⬦01688 500241; w theboathouseulva.co.uk; ⏲ Apr–Sep 09.00–17.00 Mon–Fri, Jun–Aug also 09.00–17.00   Sun. Just a few steps from the ferry, this small restaurant serves excellent seafood including Ulva prawns. Book ahead. £

IONA

A small and magical place, at around 4 miles long and 1 mile wide, Iona has wonderful beaches, fields of wildflowers and makes a fascinating excursion for geologists owing to its Lewisian and Torridonian rocks. Far more important than those qualities, however, is its history as a centre for the spread of Christianity, of learning and as the base of one of the most important monastic systems in Great Britain.

Although Iona receives a great many visitors, the small island somehow manages to absorb them without losing the best of its character. The abbey is by far the island's main attraction, but a respectful silence is usually maintained inside, and the religious, spiritual and historical sites are large and well enough spread out that you need not fear the dense crowds of pilgrims found in the Vatican or more

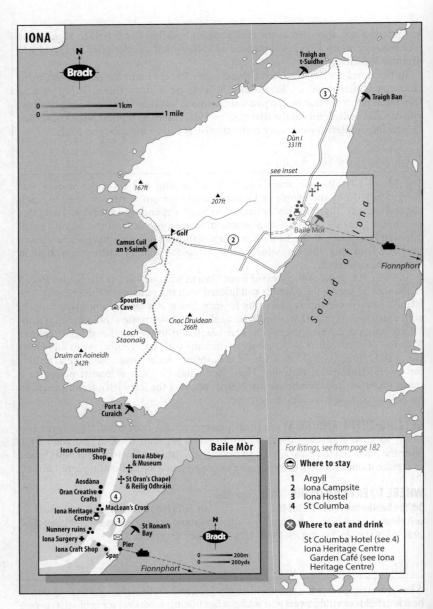

IONA

Bradt

N

0 ——————1km
0 ————————1 mile

Traigh an
t-Suidhe

③

Traigh Ban

Dùn I
331ft

167ft

see inset

207ft

Baile Mòr

②

Golf

Camus Cuil
an t-Saimh

Sound of Iona

Fionnphort

Spouting
Cave

Cnoc Druidean
266ft

Loch
Staonaig

Druim an Aoineidh
242ft

Port a'
Curaich

Baile Mòr

Iona Community
Shop

Iona Abbey
& Museum

St Oran's Chapel
& Reilig Odhráin

Aosdàna

Oran Creative
Crafts

④

MacLean's Cross

Iona Heritage
Centre

Nunnery ruins

St Ronan's
Bay

N

Bradt

Iona Surgery

Iona Craft Shop

Pier

Spar

Fionnphort

0 ——————200m
0 ——————200yds

For listings, see from page 182

Where to stay

1 Argyll
2 Iona Campsite
3 Iona Hostel
4 St Columba

Where to eat and drink

St Columba Hotel (see 4)
Iona Heritage Centre
Garden Café (see Iona
Heritage Centre)

accessible sites elsewhere. To leave other people behind, simply walk out of the village in any direction.

HISTORY After founding the religious centres of Kells and Durrow in Ireland, Columba, a scholar and warrior priest, was forced to flee from Ireland after the Battle of Cul Dreimhne in AD563. Along with his 12 companions, he is supposed to have sailed and landed at the southern end of Iona on a beach now named Port a' Curaic'. Once settled, they built their cells at Tor Abb, just west of the present-day abbey.

Over the following 200 years, Iona became an important centre of learning, producing carvings of a particular style, such as the Kildalton Cross on Islay (page 229), and invaluable historical documents, in addition to providing a base for converting the Picts to Christianity. It is probable that the beautiful Book of Kells was created on Iona in the 8th century. It wasn't long after that Iona's new Christian Celtic culture came under attack from the Norse. The community was raided by Vikings in 795, 802 and 806; in the wake of the 806 raid, where 68 inhabitants were killed, the Abbot of Iona fled across to Kells. From then on, a very small community of devout monks struggled on in Iona, ready to die for their cause. One, Blathmac, who deliberately came to the island with the hope of being martyred, succeeded in being so by hiding the shrine of St Columba and refusing to give up its location under interrogation. The small island was raided again in 845, 878 and 986, but a small group of monks survived until the 11th century when life was finally settled enough to build monastic buildings for the remaining few.

As a spiritual centre, many early kings of Scotland were buried on Iona and in 1203 a new Benedictine-style abbey was built, with the nunnery added five years later. Both were active until the Reformation when, in 1561, Iona was seen to be too close to Rome; it is thought that a reforming mob destroyed the buildings and crosses. Despite the destruction, the nunnery ruins are still the most complete example of a medieval nunnery in Scotland.

In 1609, a meeting was held on Iona to establish the authority of the reformed church. 'The Statutes of Iona' were agreed and it was decided that Scottish clan chiefs should send their heirs away to be educated in English-speaking Protestant schools. This was one of the roots of the disconnection between landowners and the people that worked for them, and ultimately could be blamed for some of the casual disregard of tenants when it came to the Clearances 200 years later. Gaelic was being lost.

Though work had already begun through the Duke of Argyll and Iona Cathedral Trust, much of the lengthy process of the abbey restoration was steered by a Reverend George MacLeod from 1938. Convinced that 'work is worship', he employed members of his newly founded 'Iona Community' to work on the project, which continued for many decades. Most of the members came from either Mull or Iona, speaking Gaelic and forming a new community on the island, which still survives in some form today.

GETTING THERE AND AWAY CalMac (℡ 08000 665000 or, from outside the UK, +44 1475 650397; w calmac.co.uk) run frequent sailings between Fionnphort and Iona, a route that takes around 10 minutes and is only open to foot passengers (unless you have a disability badge). Keep a lookout for porpoises as you sail.

GETTING AROUND Although most people can't bring a car, Iona is small and centred around the only village, Baile Mòr. For many people, walking is completely feasible, but a bicycle would allow you to reach the north end or western beaches more quickly, and there is also a local taxi service.

Bike hire
Iona Craft Shop Baile Mòr PA76 6SJ; ℡ 01681 700001; w ionacraftshop.com; ⏱ Apr– Oct 10.00–17.00 daily, Nov–Mar 10.00–15.00 Tue–Sat. Bike hire from £10 for 2hrs, £20 for a day.

Taxi
Iona Taxi m 07810 325990; w ionataxi. co.uk. Provides transport on Iona & can also pick up from Mull if required.

TOURIST INFORMATION

National Trust for Scotland w nts.org.uk/visit/ places/iona; ⏰ open access. An unstaffed shelter on the main road leading away from the pier, providing illustrated maps & local information.

🏠 WHERE TO STAY *Map, page 180*

Staying on Iona overnight or longer will give you an entirely different impression of the island; once the last of the day-trippers have left, you can absorb the same silence and sanctity appreciated by generations of monks. While St Columba Hotel collect your luggage and the Argyll Hotel is only a couple of minutes' walk from the ferry terminal, you will have to walk, cycle or hire a taxi (page 181) to reach the hostel or campsite.

🏠 **St Columba Hotel** (27 rooms) On the road from Baile Mòr to Iona Abbey PA76 6SL; ☎01681 700304; w stcolumba-hotel.co.uk; ⏰ end Mar–Nov; ♿. Peaceful location about ½ a mile north of the ferry terminal, from where your luggage will be collected. Shared sitting room with fireplace & wonderful sun lounge with huge windows & sea view. Substantial price difference between rooms with/without sea view. ££££

🏠 **Argyll Hotel** (17 rooms) Baile Mòr waterfront PA76 6SJ; ☎01681 700334; w argyllhoteliona.co.uk; ⏰ Mar–Oct. Historical hotel made of Ross of Mull pink granite, with oldest parts dating from the 1860s. In the centre of the village, only 100m north of the ferry terminal. Each room is different & sea/courtyard view is reflected significantly in price. £££–££££

🏠 **Iona Hostel** (22 beds) Lagandorain PA76 6SY; ☎01681 700781; w ionahostel.co.uk; ♿. In the peaceful north of the island is this lovely hostel on a working croft. Great sea views, wooden furniture & good environmental principles. Also private & secluded bothy with electricity that sleeps 2. About 1½ miles from the ferry terminal. ££

Ⓐ **Iona Campsite** Cnoc Oran PA76 6SP; m 07747 721275; w ionacampsite.co.uk. Basic campsite in beautiful location with sea view, southwest of Baile Mòr. £

🍴 WHERE TO EAT AND DRINK *Map, page 180*

There are a few good places to eat on Iona, with a great range of locally caught and grown produce. Eating establishments are mostly seasonal, however, and close for a few months in winter.

🍴 **St Columba Hotel** (see above) ⏰ Mar–Nov 11.00–20.30 daily; ♿. Quality local food, much grown on the island. Sea view from large restaurant & extensive outdoor seating. ££–£££

🍴 **Argyll Hotel** (see above) ⏰ Mar–Oct 10.00–20.00 daily. Freshly prepared food, much of which is grown on their 1-acre grounds, including strawberries, herbs & seasonal vegetables. Good vegan & gluten-free options. Best to book, for dinner especially. ££

🏠 **Iona Heritage Centre Garden Café** Iona Heritage Centre (see opposite), PA76 6SJ m 07754 371494; 📘; ⏰ 10.30–15.00 Mon–Sat. Soup, toasted sandwiches, cakes & hot drinks. Lovely leafy garden seating. £

SHOPPING Iona has a range of small, locally sourced gift shops selling crafts, artwork and other souvenirs.

Arts and crafts

Aosdàna St Columba Steadings, PA76 6SJ; ☎01681 700121; w aosdanaiona.com; ⏰ Easter–Oct 10.00–17.00 daily. ♿. See ad, 2nd colour section. Elegant, Iona-themed jewellery.

Iona Community Shop Across the road from the abbey, PA76 6SN; w ionabooks.com; 📘 ionacommunity; ⏰ Apr–Oct 10.00–17.00 Mon–Sat, noon–17.00 Sun; ♿. Although the Iona Community is a religious one, their large shop sells a good range of books, crafts & knitting to interest anyone, regardless of faith.

Iona Craft Shop (page 181) A good selection of high-quality knitwear, some of which is made from Iona wool.

Oran Creative Crafts St Columba Steadings, PA76 6SJ; w orancrafts.co.uk; ⊕ Easter–Oct 10.00–17.00 daily. &. A craftworkers co-operative of 8 members making/selling different art forms & crafts.

SPORTS AND ACTIVITIES

Golf

The Iona course (⊕ open access; free), towards the south of the island, has 18 holes & dates back to 1886. Free.

Sailing

🟊 **Alternative Boat Hire** \01681 700537; w boattripsiona.com. Mark Jardine, originally a sea kayaker, takes people on sailing trips in the *Birthe Marie*, a renovated traditional fishing boat with a gaff ketch rig. He runs trips to the Treshnish Isles, as well as less commonly visited islands such as Gometra, Inch Kenneth, Soa & Eilean a' Chalmain (Island of the Dove), among other places

Food shops

Spar Baile Mòr PA76 6SJ; \01681 700321; ⊕ 09.00–18.00 Mon–Sat, 11.00–18.00 Sun. Small grocery shop.

such as Traigh Geal on the south coast of Mull & even Dubh Artach Lighthouse (see box, page 178). Possibly even more exciting than the destinations themselves is the sailing; you are welcome to join in as much or as little as you feel comfortable doing. Your chances of seeing some of these waters' most exciting species are increased by the silent passage of the boat. Trips to see puffins on Lunga during nesting season cannot fail to impress, but there are also chances of spotting basking sharks, porpoises, dolphins & even minke whale, along with unusual seabird species such as shearwaters, razorbills, guillemots, skua & kittiwakes.

OTHER PRACTICALITIES

✚ **Medical** Iona Surgery, Baile Mòr PA76 6SJ; \01681 700261

✉ **Post office** 50yds northwest of ferry terminal, Baile Mòr PA76 6SJ; ⊕ 09.00–13.00 Mon–Tue & Thu–Fri, 09.00–12.30 Wed & Sat

WHAT TO SEE AND DO With so much to see within easy walking distance of the ferry terminal, even just a day trip to Iona is very worthwhile. As you land on the island you will notice lovely **St Ronan's Bay**, which sits directly in front of the main village of Baile Mòr and makes an admirable spot for a picnic.

The Nunnery ruins (⊕ open access) Two hundred yards northwest of the ferry terminal are the remains of an Augustinian priory. Founded in the early 13th century, it consisted of a church, chapter house and living quarters and is thought to have been in use until the nunnery was dissolved in 1574. Now largely roofless, it is an extensive and peaceful ruin that retains some of its pink-stone walls with archways, rounded windows and a section of vaulted ceiling, surrounded by grassy areas and plant borders with benches allowing you to stop and sit for a while.

MacLeans's Cross Passing the medieval St Ronan's Church, just north of the nunnery, and continuing 160yds further along the main street, you will come to MacLean's Cross. This elaborate 15th-century, free-standing cross is carved with intricate entwined foliage and a crucifix on its western face.

Iona Heritage Centre (PA76 6SJ; w ionaheritage.co.uk; ⊕ Easter–Oct Mon–Sat; donation requested) Once the manse for the church next door, both of which were designed by Thomas Telford. As the island's heritage centre, it now houses collections of photographs, which may be of interest to those with ancestral links to Iona, as well as local information about island life and geology.

St Oran's Chapel and Reilig Odhráin (⊕ open access) Between St Columba Hotel and Iona Abbey, sits the modest St Oran's Chapel and its burial ground, Reilig Odhráin. Some of the chapel is thought to be from as early as the 9th century, but other parts date from the 12th and the roof has been restored much more recently. It is the oldest relatively intact building on Iona. Kenneth MacAlpin, King of the Picts and, according to legend, the first King of Scotland, was buried here in the mid 9th century, along with the proceeding Scottish kings until Macbeth, who died in the mid 11th century. According to folk history, it was also the final resting place of many Irish, Norwegian and French kings, but nothing remains to tell us of these early burials. There is a good collection of West Highland grave slabs, impressive within the region, but somewhat diminished by the huge number kept in Iona Abbey.

Iona Abbey (PA76 6SQ; w historicenvironment.scot/visit-a-place/places/iona-abbey-and-nunnery; ⊕ Apr–Sep 09.30–17.30 daily, Oct–Mar 10.00–16.00 Mon–Sat, partially open Sun; adult/child/concession £9/5.40/7.20) Iona Abbey is the impressive modern restoration of a grand Benedictine abbey (page 181), the original of which was begun in the 13th century. A large stone building with slate roofs, the abbey was once home to a community of monks and is now a focal point for pilgrims who visit Iona for its connection with St Columba and the centre of Christianity he founded. Along with the abbey building itself and the historical artefacts it contains, the ticket also allows you entrance to the Abbey Museum and grounds, which encompass a number of additional interesting archaeological sites. The whole site is well maintained and explained through a comprehensive array of plaques, labels and signs, as well as the free audio guide.

In the grounds, **Tòrr an Aba**, a small hill to the left of the path just after the entry gate, is all that remains of what is thought to have been St Columba's cell, which was mentioned in writing by his contemporary Adamnan. The short climb also gives a rewarding view over the abbey and the large crosses standing in its grounds, with an ocean backdrop. Also within the grounds, the excavated **Sraid nam Marbh** (Street of the Dead) leads from the abbey to Reilig Odhráin burial ground, and is thought to have been part of a 1,000-year-old processional route for bodies to be carried from the landing place at Martyr's Bay (south of the modern pier) to their final resting place. It was 7ft wide and cobbled with Ross of Mull granite, but all that remains now is an indented track with some stones exposed between overgrown grass.

The abbey interior is usually silent apart from the echoes from visitors' careful footsteps. For pilgrims and other interested visitors, the Iona Community welcomes all to its **church services** (at the time of writing 09.00 & 21.00 Mon–Sat; communion: 10.30 & 'service of quiet' 21.00 Sun). Otherwise, you are free to wander and discover its hidden corners for yourself. **The Great Church** is the most grand of the abbey's interior spaces, with high, stone archways and mighty carved pillars.

Those with a greater interest in history than religion may find the huge collection of **West Highland grave slabs** in the **Cloister** of most interest; even the large collection on Oronsay (page 213) is diminished in comparison. In the Cloister, a covered walkway around a square, grass-covered courtyard, light streams through the pillars on to the swords, ships and intricate foliage carved into the stones. There is an engraving dedicated to Aonghus Óg, one-time 'King of the Isles' on Islay.

Around the back of the abbey is the small **Abbey Museum,** which holds delicate and invaluable artefacts, including the remains of the three mighty crosses of St

Matthew, St John and St Oran. There is also a tiny bronze head which, as the label suggests, has a striking similarity to the faces depicted in the Book of Kells.

North from the abbey Allowing at least a couple of hours, you can discover some of Iona's peaceful northern end. Continuing north along the road from the abbey, houses become scarce and the fields are sprinkled with wildflowers in spring and summer; soon you will be alone with the sound of corncrakes (in May), and views across to the tiny island of Eilean nam Ban and the west coast of the Ross of Mull. A mile northwest of the abbey, an indicated path leads up the 331ft hill **Dùn I**. A cairn at the top marks the end of a pilgrimage route, which is piled high with stones carried across Iona from a beach in the south. The vantage point gives you a good view across the whole island. Continuing north along the main track for another mile, you will reach the idyllic beaches of **Traigh an t-Suidhe** and **Traigh Ban**.

The south end Following the roads initially south from the ferry port and then west across the island for about a mile, you can walk past the campsite (page 182) to the machair and **Camus Cuil an t-Saimh** ('the bay at the back of the ocean') with thousands of colourful pebbles, corncrakes and the possibility of seeing basking sharks in summer months. To the south, the rocks around **Spouting Cave**, which shoots water into the air, are a good place to see rock-loving seabirds such as shags.

THE TRESHNISH ISLES AND STAFFA

The tiny islands between Mull and Coll are part of the **Loch na Keal conservation area**. Staffa, from the Old Norse for 'stave' or 'pillar', for obvious reasons, is best known for Fingal's Cave and its dramatic basalt columns. The small island is unique and has been admired by visitors since the 18th century.

The Treshnish Isles consist of: Lunga, known for its colonies of around 6,000 nesting puffins; Fladda (flat island); Am Baca Mòr (Bac Mòr), also known as the Dutchman's Cap owing to its distinctive shape; Bac Beag; Sgeir an Eirionnaich; Sgeir a' Chaisteil; Cairn na Burgh Mòr and neighbouring Cairn na Burgh Beag. Aside from the puffins, there are also colonies of guillemots, kittiwakes, razorbills and shags living across the islands and the waters are among the best in Scotland for seeing minke whale, porpoises, dolphins and basking sharks, along with the enormous colonies of grey seals that bob in the water or lollop on rocks.

While they are now uninhabited, this was not always the case. The remaining parts of Cairnburgh Castle, an important fortress for over 500 years, occupies the adjacent islands of Cairn na Burgh More and Cairn na Burgh Beg, at the northeast of the Treshnish string. The site was first mentioned in the 13th-century *Hákonar saga Hákonarsonar* (an Icelandic saga written about the Old Norse kings) as the property of an island king related to Somerled, before later being held by MacLeans and then Campbells. Other signs of habitation are strung along the chain; even the Dutchman's Cap, which has no obvious way up on to it, has the ruined remains of shielings.

There is an excellent exhibit about the islands in Hynish on Tiree (page 153), or you can arrange boat trips through Alternative Boat Hire (page 183), Turus Mara (page 166), Staffa Trips (page 176), Tiree Sea Tours (page 148) and various other operators based mostly on Mull or in Oban.

Finding a path running south more centrally through the island will bring you to tiny **Loch Staonaig** and, within another mile and a half, down towards **Port a' Curaich** or Columba Bay, where the man himself is thought to have initially landed. Regardless of your interest, it is a lovely place for a picnic with views across rocky skerries and islets to tiny Soa further south. OS Explorer map 373 (*Iona, Staffa & Ross of Mull*) is helpful for navigating the south end of Iona.

8

Lismore (Lios Mòr) and Kerrera (Cearara)

Those with a fascination for castles should head directly to Lismore and Kerrera: between them, these two small islands in the Firth of Lorn have three substantial ruins, one excellent broch and countless duns between them. Both islands are green and fertile, with plenty of sheep, interesting rocky coastlines and unusual hilly landscapes. Of the two, Lismore has a substantially bigger population and thus a lot more going on.

LISMORE

Curiously positioned halfway up the Firth of Lorn, Lismore is separated from the mainland Highlands and Mull by just a few miles of water in every direction. Although the island itself is low-lying, it is surrounded by mountainous scenery: Loch Linnhe cuts into the Great Glen in the northeast with the mighty Ben Nevis and Glen Coe in the distance; Ben Cruachan is on the skyline to the southeast; Mull lies to the southwest; and the wild coast of the Morvern Peninsula runs parallel to Lismore, only 3 miles to the northeast. The surrounding higher ground, particularly the hills on Mull, means that Lismore lies in a rain shadow, enjoying significantly better weather than much of its surroundings. The island is around 9 miles long and 1½ miles wide, with a limestone base that is unusual in the Inner Hebrides; thankfully this means that midges are not an issue on Lismore.

Green fields, interrupted by rocky protrusions, are separated by undulating dry-stone walls, and houses are scattered in a rather haphazard manner – the biggest settlement, Achnacroish, is barely more than a hamlet. The island's shop, church and heritage centre are somewhat sporadically dotted along the central main road with little else around them. In the north, Port Ramsay is picturesque but has no amenities whatsoever, while the south of the island is totally uninhabited. Despite its proximity to the mainland, Lismore feels very much like the island it is.

HISTORY The earliest evidence of humans on Lismore came in the form of a Neolithic polished stone axe head that has been dated to 3500BC. In addition, there are a number of Bronze-Age burial cairns, including the large and well-preserved Cnoc Aingeal (Fire Hill), where the later kings of the Picts are also said to have been cremated. Then there's Tirefour Castle (page 191), an imposing Iron-Age broch on the east coast, plus several less impressive remains from the same period.

From the 6th century AD, Lismore was an important centre of Celtic Christianity thanks to St Moluag. A contemporary of Columba (page 14), Moluag's legacy

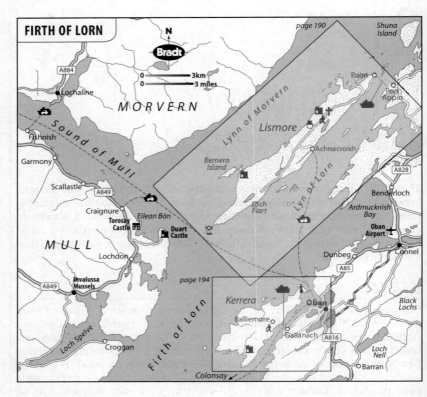

page 190

FIRTH OF LORN

N

Bradt

0 ———— 3km
0 ———— 3 miles

Shuna Island

MORVERN

A884

Lochaline

Fishnish

Sound of Mull

Garmony

Scallastle

A849

Craignure

Torosay Castle

Eilean Bàn

Duart Castle

MULL

Lochdon

Invalussa Mussels

A849

Croggan

Loch Spelve

Firth of Lorn

Lynn of Morvern

Lismore

Bernera Island

Loch Fiart

Bernera Island

Lynn of Lorn

Achnacroish

A828

Benderloch

Ardmucknish Bay

Oban Airport

Dunbeg

A85

Connel

Black Lochs

page 194

Kerrera

Balliemore

Gallanach

Oban

A816

Loch Nell

Barran

Colonsay

has been substantially less well documented, but he may have been even more consequential in the process of evangelising of the Picts.

Moluag's arrival on Lismore is a subject of much speculation: a folk tale describes St Moluag and Columba racing across the Lynn of Lorn to be the first to land on Lismore and found a monastery. The story goes that Moluag only won by cutting off his finger and throwing it ashore. An alternative version suggests that as he stood on a rock on the Irish coast it detached itself so he could drift across the ocean.

What is certain is that in 562 he founded a community on Lismore and went on to found two other important centres of Christianity in Scotland at Rosemarkie near Inverness and Mortlach (now known as Dufftown) in Moray. These three communities became the Roman Catholic diocese of the Isles, Ross and Aberdeen. A millennium later, Moluag was still stated to be the patron saint of Argyll. The island's Gaelic name, Lios Mòr, is ancient Gaelic for 'great courtyard' or 'garden' and is thought to be in reference to his monastery.

During the medieval period, the castles of Coeffin and Achadun were built on the island and the MacDougalls, who still own much of nearby Kerrera (page 193), were a powerful force in the region. Lismore was also the seat of the Bishop of Argyll until 1507 when it was moved to Kintyre on the mainland. The Duke of Argyll still owns most of Lismore today.

Following similar patterns to the rest of the region, Lismore's population fell dramatically in the mid 19th century. Cheaper imported food from the colonies undercut Lismore's once-thriving grain industry, fisheries failed and the kelp market crashed; there was a lack of employment and food, coupled with long harsh winters and bad summers between 1836 and 1838. The famine was felt severely and in around 1839 a public appeal was held to raise funds to prevent starvation; £50,000 was raised for food in the area. The 1840s held more severe winters and the cattle market subsequently collapsed. By 1880, the population had dropped from a peak of 1,500 to 621.

Today Lismore's population is only around 190, but steadily growing thanks to the occasional outsiders who fall in love with the island and cannot bear to leave.

GETTING THERE AND AWAY

By ferry CalMac (℡ 08000 665000 or, from outside the UK, +44 1475 650397; w calmac.co.uk) run ferries from Oban to Achnacroish (1hr; car/foot passenger £12.15/2.85) up to four times a day. **Argyll & Bute Council** (℡ 01631 730383; w argyll-bute.gov.uk/port-appin-point-lismore-ferry-timetable) operate a foot passenger ferry regularly throughout the day from Port Appin (on the mainland) to Point at the far north end of the island; it takes 10 minutes and costs £1.85.

GETTING AROUND

With very few allocated car parks, Lismore is hands-down the worst place to find a parking spot in the Inner Hebrides. There is also no filling station on the island, so make sure you fill up on the mainland if you are bringing your car over. Note that all but the smallest of campervans will struggle to fit in the infrequent passing places. Given the small size of the island, a bicycle is significantly more convenient for exploring.

Don't be alarmed if you see someone driving along missing a door – an interesting law states that an island without a mechanic should not require inhabitants' vehicles to have the standard yearly MOT check.

Bike hire

🚲 **Lismore Bike Hire** m 07376 425996; f

Taxis and tours

🚐 **Explore Lismore** m 07490 416255, 07578 646689; w explorelismore.co.uk. Land Rover tours with local food picnics, plus taxi & shuttle service.

WHERE TO STAY Map, page 190

The majority of Lismore's accommodation is self-catering; full listings are available at w isleoflismore.com/accommodation/self-catering.

🏠 **Lismore Bunkhouse & Camping** (12 beds) Baleveolan Croft PA34 5UG; m 07720 975433; f; ♿. Good green credentials, well-equipped kitchen, comfortable communal areas & plenty of books. There are resident Highland cows & chickens. With the help of volunteers, they have planted thousands of broad-leaved trees. Private & bunk rooms. A purple letter box marks the entry. **£**

🏠 **The Sailean Bothy** (sleeps 4) Sailean PA34 5UG; ℡ 01631 760282; w lismoregrassfedbeefandlamb.co.uk/stay-at-sailean; ◷ Mar–Sep. Beautifully basic self-catering accommodation in a remote location on Sailean Bay. Similar facilities to camping: compost toilet outside & no shower. Mattresses provided, but bring your own bedding. **£**

WHERE TO EAT AND DRINK Map, page 190

Options for eating out on Lismore are very limited. When ferry times are favourable, you could opt to take the short ferry to Port Appin (page 265) for evening meals.

LISMORE

For listings, see from page 189

Where to stay
1 Lismore Bunkhouse & Camping
2 The Sailean Bothy

Where to eat and drink
Taigh Bidh (see Lismore Gaelic Heritage Centre)

Lynn of Morven

Lynn of Lorn

Oban

Bernera Bay
Achadun Bay
Achadun Castle
Achinduin
Bernera
Lismore Lighthouse
Eilean Musdile
Dalnarrow
Dùn Chruban
Fiart Farm
An Dùn
Barr Mòr 417ft
Kilcheran
Kilcheran Loch
Loch Fiart
Eilean nan Gamhna
Eilean nan Cloiche
Sailean
Baligrundle
B8045
Achnacroish
Loch Baile a' Ghobhainn
Lismore Stores & Post Office
Lismore Gaelic Heritage Centre
Castle Coeffin
St Moluag's Cathedral
St Moluag's Chair
269ft
Tirefour Castle
Eilean Dubh
Port Ramsay
B8045
Point
Airds Bay
Port Appin
North Shian
South Shian
Eriska
Camas Nathais

0   2km
0   2 miles

N

Bradt

✖ Taigh Bidh Lismore Gaelic Heritage Centre, Port A Charron PA34 5UL; 📞01631 760020; 🟦; 🕐 Apr–Oct 11.00–16.00 daily; ♿. Hot drinks, sandwiches & burgers. Inside & outside seating with wonderful views. £

▭ Honesty Box Point PA34 5UN; 🟦 dutchbakerylismore; 🕐 Easter–Oct daily & occasional w/ends year-round. Excellent cakes from the Dutch Bakery are available at the ferry terminal. Honesty box payment. £

SHOPPING AND OTHER PRACTICALITIES

Lismore only really has one shop, which also provides other useful services. The nearest doctors' surgery is in Port Appin (page 265) and the nearest hospital in Oban (page 262). Note that you can't get fuel on the island.

Lismore Grass Fed Highland Beef & Shearling Lamb Sailean PA34 5UG; 📞01631 760282; 🌐lismoregrassfedbeefandlamb.co.uk. This small-scale farm offers same-day deliveries on the island. Call to check what's in stock.

✉ Lismore Stores & Post Office PA34 5UG; 📞01631 760272; 🕐 09.00–17.00 Mon–Tue & Thu–Fri, 09.00–13.00 Wed & Sat; ♿. Small but well-stocked & friendly shop selling hot drinks & groceries, plus free Wi-Fi & internet access (donations welcome). Ramp for access, but aisles are a bit narrow for many wheelchairs.

ACTIVITIES

Children are welcome to use the **play park** near the school in Achnacroish. Other activities offered on Lismore are somewhat unusual. The following options happen sporadically when the organisers have both time and participants. **Mairi Campbell** (🌐 mairicampbell.scot) hosts various musical retreats and workshops. You can go on **seaweed foraging walks** (🟦 lismoreseaweed) and the **Sailean Project** (Sailean; 🌐 lismoregrassfedbeefandlamb.co.uk) run **farm open days** as an introduction to regenerative agriculture (£35 pp). Crop rotation aims to put carbon back into the soil, they have Highland cows and Jacob sheep, and sometimes offer two-day **willow-weaving workshops** (£150).

EVENTS
Spring
Lismore Spring Fair Local produce; check local noticeboards.

July
Lismore Agricultural Show 🟦 lismoreshow1
Lismore Sports & Raft Race 🟦

September
Taproot Music and Literature Festival 🟦 lismoretaproot

December
Lismore Christmas Craft Fair Check local noticeboards.

WHAT TO SEE AND DO
The north At the north end of Lismore, Point is the location of the foot passenger ferry to the mainland. From here, it's possible to walk about a mile around the coast (with the sea on your right) to **Port Ramsay** (also reachable by road). This idyllic row of white workers' cottages overlooks tidal islands and out towards Movern on the mainland; the muddy flats support a rich ecosystem and are a favourite with herons and other wading birds.

Tirefour Castle (🕐 open access; free) On the east side of the island, a turning marked to 'Balure' leads to ruined Tirefour Castle. Despite its name, this substantial ruin is not in fact a castle but the best example of an Iron-Age broch (page 266) in the whole of Argyll. The grass-topped walls are almost 16ft tall in places and 13ft wide, enclosing a courtyard 39ft across. Complete, it may have been 49ft tall. One thing's for certain: it commanded a magnificent position over the Lynn of Lorn, tiny Eilean Dubh island and out towards the mainland.

Relics of St Moluag (page 14) Indicated by a wooden sign and visible from the road, **St Moluag's Chair** (✪ 56°32'24"N 5°28'00"W) is a natural seat in a rock, which sits in a field beside the road. The chair's arms were broken off by a roadman towards the end of the 19th century. It is said that St Moluag used to sit here and meditate; sitting on it used to be considered a cure for rheumatism.

A little further south is the pretty, whitewashed local church, also known as **St Moluag's Cathedral** (w isleoflismore.com/island-groups/parish-church). Visitors are welcome to join services and the door is always open at other times. This was the cathedral church of the medieval diocese of Argyll, built somewhere between the 12th and 14th century. Although it is dedicated to St Moluag, there are no remains here from the early Christian period, though it is likely that the building occupied the site of an earlier church dedicated to the saint. Despite its name, don't expect a cathedral – the church is rather modest in size, though there are some wonderful carved grave slabs from the 14th and 15th century outside.

Lismore Gaelic Heritage Centre (Port A Charron; ☏ 01631 760030; w lismoregaelicheritagecentre.org; ⊕ Apr–Oct 11.00–16.00 daily; ✦; free) This modern building has a well-presented museum with interesting information, archives and artefacts such as the 'Port Appin Head' (a Pagan Celtic carving), a Norse-era link plate made of gold, and coins from the 13th and 14th centuries. Outside is a replica 'cottar's house' (page 266), set out as it would have been in the late 19th century. There's also a café here (page 191).

🏃 Castle Coeffin ✳
Distance: 2 miles; time: 1–2 hours; start/end: St Moluag's Cathedral; OS Explorer map: 376 Oban & North Lorn

The moss- and grass-covered remains of Castle Coeffin (✪ 56°32'16"N 5°29'25"W) are some of the most atmospheric in the Inner Hebrides.

Around 220yds south of St Moluag's Cathedral you will see a minor crossroads; take the track on the right. Follow this track southwest for about 200yds before taking the left route when it forks. After another 380yds or so the track curves around to the right and begins to head north. Continue in this direction for just under a mile until you see Portcastle Farm and the castle on your left; a magnificent fish trap is visible on the shore at low tide, just a few yards to the south of the castle.

When you reach a junction, join the track leading left, downhill towards the sea and the castle, though be aware that horses are kept in these fields and try not to disturb them.

Positioned on a small promontory jutting out into the sea, the castle ruins are small, but atmospheric, next to a peaceful rocky bay. Castle Coeffin is named after Caifen, the son of a Norse king. Caifen's sister Beothail ('of the golden hair') is said to have lost her lover in a battle in Norway. Distraught, she died of a broken heart and they buried her at the castle. Beothail then haunted the castle until they dug up her body, washed her bones in the well and took them across to Norway. One finger bone was forgotten, however, and her spirit refused to rest until they found it, so Caifen and his men searched and were eventually able to take it across. It is said that you can still hear Beothail's sighs in the wind. What exists today of Castle Coeffin is not the Norse stronghold, but the severely ruined remains of a

13th-century hall-house and bailey, with some later additions, probably built by the MacDougalls of Lorn. Unsurprisingly, the naturally strategic position was popular throughout the ages.

To return to the cathedral, retrace your steps the way you came.

The south

Sailein and Achadun Castle Taking the minor road towards Achinduin on the west coast, you can turn off right to reach the farm and shoreline at **Sailean**, also known as Salen. Here you can see the remains of an impressive 19th-century lime quarry and kilns (✪ 56°30'54"N 5°31'06"W). The Sailean Project (page 191) is based here and you might have a chance to see their Highland cows. Further down the west coast is the 13th-century **Achadun Castle** (🕑 open access), probably built by the MacDougalls. It fell out of use in the 16th century, but the ruined walls are substantial, giving you some concept of its original scale.

From here, look out for the small tidal island of **Bernera**; it's possible to walk out there with careful planning – you'll need to check tide times (page 27) in advance. Bernera is said to have been settled by St Moluag and his monks in the 6th century. St Columba is also supposed to have used the island as a retreat and is said to have preached under a huge yew tree there. The tree was felled and the trunk turned into a staircase in Lochnell Castle near Oban; it is said that the staircase survived despite the rest of the building being burnt twice.

Exploring the far southwest Back on the island's main road, if you take the road that leads off to the right at **Baligrundle** it's possible to follow the coast to the south. Note, however, that the road deteriorates dramatically around **Loch Fiart** and it is easy to get a car stuck in the mud. Around 300yds southwest of the head of Loch Fiart are the grass-covered remains of **An Dùn** (✪ 56°28'49"N 5°33'22"W). Probably once a broch, the spot is possibly more interesting to most people for its glorious views over the loch and across the green surrounding landscape. From here there is a 6-mile return walk out to Rubha Fiart, at the far southwest point of Lismore.

Continuing along the track you will pass Fiart Farm, followed by a small pond in a pretty, green valley, before reaching the buildings at Dalnarrow. Choosing the track following nearest to the sea, you will soon come to the ruins of **Dùn Chruban** (✪ 56°27'51"N 5°35'06"W), the scant remains of a fortress set on top of a natural rocky outcrop. From here, it's only possible to continue for another mile further southwest; climb up the hill at the end for a vantage point with views out to the lovely 19th-century Lismore Lighthouse on the island Eilean Musdile, as well as across to Duart on Mull, the Movern Peninsula and to Kerrera in the south. The dramatic coastline, rocky crags and sheltered hollows were once used to hide a small-scale illegal distilling industry in the 18th and 19th centuries.

KERRERA

Just across the water from Oban, Kerrera's decision not to allow visiting cars makes it a totally different world from the mainland. Peaceful and green, it is a hilly island with a substantial 16th-century tower house, Gylen Castle, and lovely views of Mull and the mainland across the Sound of Kerrera. It is about 5 miles long and 2 miles wide. Aside from the sheep grazing quietly above the rocky shoreline, there are about 40 inhabitants.

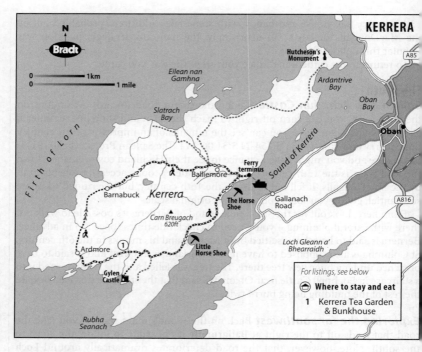

For listings, see below

🏠 **Where to stay and eat**
1   Kerrera Tea Garden
     & Bunkhouse

GETTING THERE AND AWAY

By ferry **CalMac** (📞 08000 665000 or, from outside the UK, +44 1475 650397;
w calmac.co.uk) run a Gallanach Road (southwest of Oban) to Kerrera foot-
passenger ferry regularly from 09.00 to 17.00/18.00; it takes only a few minutes
to cross and costs £1.60. Day visitors should check the last returning ferry time
carefully at the port or ask the ferry crew. Parking at Gallanach Road is quite limited.

Bus to ferry port   The 417 West Coast Motors bus service (📞 01586 552319;
w westcoastmotors.co.uk) runs from Oban to Kerrera Ferry/Gallanach Road twice
a day on school days. Times revolve around children getting to Oban for school and
are thus not very convenient for organising a day trip.

Moorings
Oban Marina Ardentrive Bay, Kerrera; 📞 01631
565333

WHERE TO STAY AND EAT   *Map, above*

🏠 **Kerrera Tea Garden & Bunkhouse** (sleeps
7) PA34 4SX; 📞 01631 566367;
w kerrerabunkhouse.co.uk; 🕐 Easter–Sep
10.30–16.30 daily. The bunkhouse is only booked
exclusively, so perfect for groups of friends or
family. They also rent out a bell tent (sleeps

2), weather permitting, & host unofficial wild
camping with use of the toilets. Inexpensive
café (£) serving hot drinks & cakes, as well as
international soups & stews in the colder months &
fresh salads in the height of summer. **£**

WHAT TO SEE AND DO   Unsurprisingly, given that it's a car-free island, the best
way to see the island is on foot. The walk described below is ideal for day visitors;

if you're staying longer, you can take the time to explore more widely and at a slower pace.

Gylen Castle and southern Kerrera

Distance: 7 miles; time: 4 hours, but a whole day is recommended; start/end: Kerrera ferry terminal; OS Explorer map: 359 Oban, Kerrera & Loch Melfort

From the port, turn left (you can check the telephone box here for local postcards, which you can buy on an honesty box system) before taking a lower track along the coast that passes the **Horse Shoe**, a gently curved bay. Ignore the minor turning up to the right here and the first white house. Some time later you will come to the **Little Horse Shoe**, a picturesque circular bay. At the next fork, follow the signs to the castle and Tea Garden, taking the turning bearing right inland and up the hill.

Once you reach the bottom of the hill, just before you get to the Tea Garden (see opposite), take the turning towards the left, past a small compost toilet and follow signs to the castle.

The imposing remains of **Gylen Castle** ('castle of fountains') have been preserved rather than restored, maintaining its venerable atmosphere without the danger of it collapsing on anyone's head. Free to enter and accessible up steps, you can actually (and unusually for the Inner Hebrides) climb inside and get a great sense of the original vantage point. An L-plan tower house, it consists of a square main block and stair tower, originally commissioned by Duncan MacDougall and completed in 1582. It is set strategically on a naturally high, rocky peninsula, situated to command the southern approach to Oban. The castle was besieged and burned by a Covenanter army led by General David Leslie in 1647 and subsequently left unoccupied.

If you are short on time, returning along the same route is the quickest and easiest way back to the ferry, but continuing to make a circular route is more rewarding. Return to the main track, which leads behind the Tea Garden and roughly west, then southwest to the couple of buildings at **Ardmore**. At the white house with the grey extension, you need to bear right up through the gorse. Accompanied by its coconut scent, a rocky path will lead you up to a large pond on a plateau. The path becomes faint and grassy as it heads on to open land, with views out to sea on your left. After some time, the grassy path returns to a more substantial track and you descend to the farmhouse at **Barnabuck**, which was once a larger settlement.

There are occasional signs indicating the way back to the ferry, which help you along the way. Passing the ruined buildings around Barnabuck, the path soon begins to climb up the hill again and over to the east side of the island. The views over the coast and small islets around Eilean nan Gamhna are spectacular, but it is not a pleasant climb if you are rushing for the last ferry.

Passing above a farm on your left, head straight on through the gate to return to the ferry or turn left to head up towards the north end of the island. You can find a description of this route (which is to the Hutchesons Monument obelisk – a memorial to one of the founders of CalMac) on Walkhighlands (w walkhighlands. co.uk/argyll/kerrera-hutcheson.shtml); the route is around 3 to 4 hours return.

SEND US YOUR SNAPS!

We'd love to follow your adventures using our *Inner Hebrides* guide – why not tag us in your photos and stories on Twitter (@BradtGuides) and Instagram (@bradtguides)?

9

The Slate Islands

Although the name of this group of four islands summons images of grey mining towns and industrial scenery, this in fact could not be further from reality. Centre of the Scottish slate industry in the 18th and 19th centuries, only Seil, Luing and tiny Easdale still have permanent communities, while Belnahua, now abandoned, makes a ghostly silhouette opposite Luing's biggest village Cullipool. Glasgow Cathedral, Lorn's Armaddy Castle, Appin's Castle Stalker and many other important buildings in Scotland are still roofed in Easdale slate. The abandoned quarries have weathered gently over time to form a unique landscape: their walls, caved in by winter storms, have left squared-off pools of glowing turquoise water, separated by thin bulwarks of rock. Owing to its small size, Easdale is the most defined by these features – aerial photos show a large percentage of the island's surface to be water rather than earth or rock. By contrast Luing, pronounced 'Ling', seems startlingly green, an emerald in the clear, clean waters rushing past it. With much of the islands' uninhabited, the further you get away from Clachan Bridge (known as 'The Bridge Over The Atlantic'), which connects Seil to the mainland, the more wild and peaceful the islands become.

The Firth of Lorn Marine Special Area of Conservation includes the Slate Islands, the north end of Jura and other, uninhabited islands such as the Garvellachs and Scarba. The area has been chosen for protection because of its rocky reef habitats; exposed or underwater depending on the depth and tide, they support colonies of sponges, brittle stars, sea ferns and cup coral, making the habitat among the most biodiverse in Europe. On a larger scale, these waters are one of the best areas in Europe to see porpoises, bottlenose dolphins (there's a resident pod of 30) and occasionally even minke whales. Otters also appear to be unusually common here, with locals reporting that they now see more of these elusive creatures than they did ten years ago. The area is also one of the only places in the UK where seal numbers are still increasing, with colonies of around 20,000 common seals and 110,000 grey seals. Additionally, these waters are also covered by the Loch Sunart to the Sound of Jura Marine Protected Area as the last stronghold of the flapper skate. The largest of all the European skates and rays, capable of reaching over 8ft long and over 6ft wide (across the wings), this curious-looking fish will never rival the fluffy panda as an appealing conservation poster child, but it is critically endangered.

Aside from history and natural heritage, possibly the most striking attribute of the Slate Islands is the notably friendly and welcoming attitude of local people.

GETTING THERE AND AWAY

Seil is attached to the mainland by a bridge (page 27), which makes it simple to get on to the island. From Seil there is a small passenger boat to Easdale (page 202) and a vehicle ferry across to Luing (page 203); neither of these crossings take much more than 5 minutes.

TOURIST INFORMATION

There is no official tourist information centre on the Slate Islands, but Luing's Atlantic Islands Centre (page 204), The Slate Islands Heritage Trust Centre (page 201) on Seil and the Easdale Island Folk Museum on Easdale are informative on the islands' history, sights and natural heritage. Online information is available about Luing (w isleofluing.org), Seil (w seil.oban.ws) and Easdale (w easdale.org), as well as from the more history-focused w slateislands. org.uk.

OTHER PRACTICALITIES

Despite being only a stone's throw from the mainland, the Slate Islands are lacking in some basic amenities: there is nowhere to fill up with fuel and network coverage is almost non-existent, so do not rely on online maps.

⊞ **Medical** Easdale Medical Practice, Seil PA34 4TL; ☏ 01852 300223; w www. easdalemedicalpractice.scot.nhs.uk

✉ **Post office** Balvicar Stores (page 200; ⏰ 08.30–17.00 Mon–Fri, 09.00–13.00 Sat); Luing Stores (page 204; ⏰ 09.00–11.00 Mon–Sat)

EVENTS

The **Atlantic Island Centre** on Luing (w isleofluing.org/what-do/events-calendar) hosts art exhibitions, talks and events through the year.

SEPTEMBER
World Stone Skimming Championships Easdale Island; w stoneskimming.com. By far the biggest event on the Slate Islands, over 300 people enter this competition every year, sometimes coming from as far away as Japan & Australia.

SEIL (SAOIL)

A curious crossover between mainland and island, Seil is accessibly close to Oban and day trips from here down to Ellenabeich or Easdale are a popular choice for those short on time. Away from the main settlements much of Seil is wild and uninhabited with plentiful walking opportunities – but you'll need a decent map.

GETTING THERE AND AROUND Only half an hour's drive south of Oban and without the need to catch a ferry, Seil is arguably the easiest of the Inner Hebridean islands to access. There is no fee for crossing the bridge and it can be walked, cycled or driven over.

BUS West Coast Motors (☏ 01586 552319; w westcoastmotors.co.uk; ♿) currently runs the 418/18 Oban–Clachan–Balvicar–Noth Cuan–Ellenabeich service several times a day from Monday to Saturday, making it easy to reach most of the island.

WHERE TO STAY *Map, page 198*
There's just a handful of places to stay on Seil. Choose to stay away from the bridge if you are after a more authentic island experience.

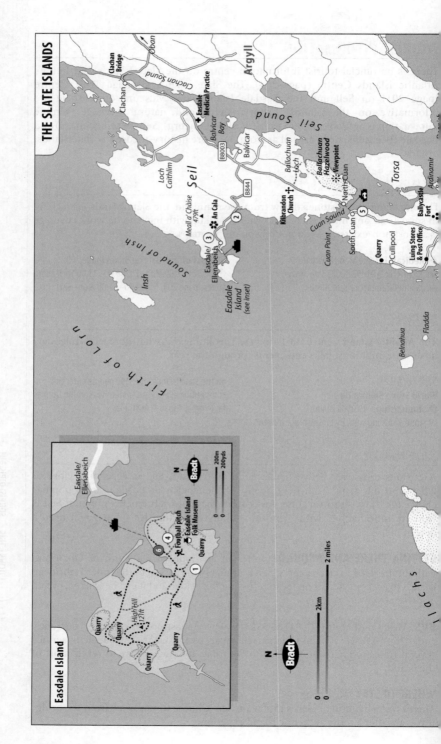

THE SLATE ISLANDS

Oban

Clachan Bridge

Clachan

Clachan Sound

+ Easdale Medical Practice

Argyll

Balvicar Bay

B8003

Balvicar

Loch Caithlim

Seil Sound

Seil

Ballachuan Hazelwood * Viewpoint

Ballachuan Loch

B844

Meall a'Chaise 479ft ▲

An Cala ❀

(3)

(2)

+ Kilbrandon Church

North Cuan

Easdale/ Ellenabeich

Easdale Island (see inset)

Cuan Point

Cuan Sound

South Cuan

(5)

Torsa

Ballycastle Fort

Ardinamir

Insh

Sound of Insh

Quarry

Cullipool

Luing Stores & Post Office

Firth of Lorn

Belnahua

Fladda

Luing

Easdale Island

Easdale/ Ellenabeich

Quarry

Quarry

Quarry

High Hill 125ft ▲

Quarry

Quarry

(4)

⚽ Football pitch

🏛 Easdale Island Folk Museum

Quarry

(1)

(5)

Bradt

0   200m
0   200yds

Bradt

0   2km
0   2 miles

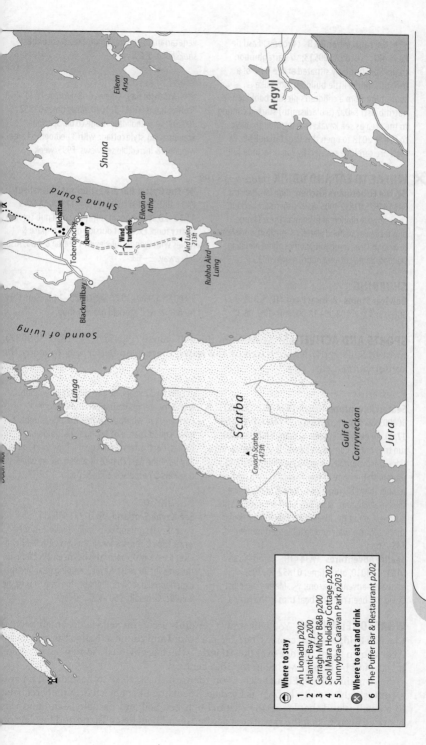

Where to stay

1 An Lionadh *p202*
2 Atlantic Bay *p200*
3 Garragh Mhor B&B *p200*
4 Seol Mara Holiday Cottage *p202*
5 Sunnybrae Caravan Park *p203*

Where to eat and drink

6 The Puffer Bar & Restaurant *p202*

🏠 **Garragh Mhor B&B** (4 rooms) Easdale PA34 4RF; 📞 01852 300513; **w** garraghmhor. co.uk. Spectacularly situated at the base of a cliff, this quirky little building looks like something from a children's picture book. Jan (a nutritionist) & Daz (a blacksmith) started coming to the area as sea kayakers & decided to move to Seil in 2018 to open this vegetarian B&B. B/ fasts are carefully curated by Jan & include full

vegetarian, buckwheat pancakes & coconut *shakshuka*. **£££**

Weekly rental
🏠 **Atlantic Bay** (sleeps 6–8) Easdale PA34 4RF; 📞 office hours 0631 571010, other times 01852 300203; **w** seilholidaycottage.co.uk. Spacious Scandinavian-style cottage with 3 bedrooms. Large windows & incredible sea views. £995/week.

✕ WHERE TO EAT AND DRINK   *Map, page 198*
✕ **The Fisherman's Kitchen** Tigh Ian, Balvicar PA34 4TF; 📞 01852 300578; **w** fishermanskitchen. co.uk. Private dinners at fisherman Drew's home, plus takeaway seafood platters & shellfish workshops to help you overcome your worries about handling seafood. Some advance notice required. **£££**

✕ **The Oyster Bar & Restaurant** Ellenabeich PA34 4RQ; 📞 01852 300121; 🕐 11.00–15.00 & 17.30–20.30, longer in summer. Local pub serving hearty food. Excellent outside decking space & tables with wonderful views of Scarba & Jura. Also takeaway. **£–££**

SHOPPING
Balvicar Stores Balvicar PA34 4TE; 📞 01852 300373; 📘 🕐 08.30–18.00 Mon–Thu, 08.30– 19.00 Fri, 09.00–19.00 Sat, 09.30–14.00 Sun. Very friendly & well-stocked grocery shop.

SPORTS AND ACTIVITIES   Apart from the **golf course** (Balvicar; 📞 01852 300087), most of Seil's activities are based on the water; there is no better way to enjoy the conservation area.

Boat trips
Seafari Adventures Easale PA34 4RQ; 📞 01852 300003; **w** seafari.co.uk/oban; 🕐 Mar–Oct 09.00– 17.00. An exhilarating ride in orange RIBs, Seafari run trips out to Corryvreckan whirlpool when spring tides are favourable, as well as wildlife-watching tours with the hope of seeing whales from mid-Jul to Aug. They also run trips to Iona & Staffa to see the basalt columns & puffins. Staff are enthusiastic & honest about the likelihood of seeing particular species. Warm/waterproof clothes recommended. £45–90pp.
Sealife Adventures PA34 4TR; 📞 office hours 01631 571010, other times 01852 300203; **w** sealife-adventures.com; ♿. Marine biologist David has been running boat trips in the Firth

of Lorn for 32 years; he also works as a wildlife & underwater photographer. Trips include Corryvreckan whirlpool (when the tide is right) & have a good chance of seeing seals, golden/sea eagles, deer, otters & wild goats. Trips from Jun to Sep have the best chance of seeing minke whales, dolphins & porpoises. £58–81pp.

Kayaking
Sea Kayak Scotland 📱 07771 918431; **w** seakayakscotland.com. Individually designed kayak trips & courses for all abilities with Kenny, a level 5 sea kayak coach who has been operating in the area for 20 years. Kayak/camping gear hire for experienced paddlers. Probably the best way to see wildlife. Generally £60–135 pp/day.

WHAT TO SEE AND DO   You will almost certainly arrive on Seil via the small, arched **Clachan Bridge**, which crosses the Clachan Sound and connects Seil to the mainland. Also known as the **'Bridge over the Atlantic'**, which is obviously somewhat of a joke, it was built by Robert Mylne in the 18th century.

Seil's main village, **Ellenabeich**, is on the west coast, close to Easdale Island and – confusingly – is also known as Easdale. The name Ellenabeich originally referred to a small island that lay in the channel between Seil and Easdale Island and was quarried away to just the rim. The space between Ellenabeich Island and Easdale on

Assuming that a service is not taking place, you can park at **Kilbrandon Church** and walk down the private road leading east that starts on the opposite side of the road. Less than a mile down this road a marked turning to the right will take you towards the small Ballachuan Loch and Ballachuan Hazelwood Nature Reserve (w scottishwildlifetrust.org.uk/reserve/ballachuan-hazel-wood).

The woodland is an important habitat for elusive pine martens and in autumn and winter you should come across interesting lichens and fungi, while butterflies live on the grasslands around the loch between May and July.

The area is maintained by the Scottish Wildlife Trust and there is a map and information near the beginning of the trail. Paths are quite overgrown, but the woodland is relatively small, so it should be easy enough to explore.

Seil was filled with waste material from the quarry until enough ground was created to build the rows of houses that still stand there today. Soil from Ireland, previously used as ships' ballast, was then added to make a little more land for the houses' gardens; these houses, built on Ellenabeich, became a small part of the village of Easdale. In 1881, a great storm filled the rest of the quarry with water, closing down its operations, and today's landscape is a confusing combination of land that was once part of the sea and water where there used to be land. To add a further layer of complication, the name Ellenabeich has recently evolved to mean the whole village (of Easdale), presumably because of the confusion between Easdale on Seil and Easdale Island, but you will still find the village on Seil referred to as Easdale by certain locals and on the front of buses.

To get a sense of local history, or for further information on the area, it's worth making your first stop **The Slate Islands Heritage Trust Centre** (13a Ellenabeich, PA34 4RQ; ☎ 01852 300307; w slateislands.org.uk; ⊕ 10.30–16.30 daily (variable in winter months); donation requested). This small but fascinating museum is almost as great a wealth of information as the volunteers who work there, with written notices mirroring their humour and all levels of society represented in their exhibits. There is a particularly interesting model of a working slate quarry.

Near the primary school are the beautiful 90-year-old gardens of **An Cala** (PA34 4RF; ☎ 01852 300237; ⊕ Apr–Oct 10.00–18.00; donation requested), full of quirky sculptures and water features. Ellenabeich is also where you can catch the small passenger ferry across to Easdale Island (page 202).

Further south, on the western side of the road, is **Kilbrandon Church**, most famous for its striking stained-glass windows designed by Dr Douglas Strachan. These show scenes from the Bible and particularly the Sea of Galilee. In the central window on the east wall, Jesus is shown quelling a great storm from a boat; the colours and sense of movement are very dramatic.

EASDALE ISLAND (EILEAN ÈISDEAL)

The smallest permanently inhabited Inner Hebridean island, Easdale is totally unique. Without any cars and accessed by a short passenger ferry journey from Seil, it is one of the few islands in this book that I can recommend visiting as a day trip, but you could easily stay for longer.

GETTING THERE AND AWAY It is not possible to take a car on to Easdale.

Ferry A small motorboat carries foot passengers from Ellenabeich (at least twice an hour: 07.15–12.45 & 14.00–21.00 Sun–Thu, 07.15–12.45 & 14.00–23.00 Fri & Sat; £2.10 return). The journey takes a couple of minutes and you pay on the boat.

Moorings Community-owned moorings in Easdale Sound are available adjacent to the old pier and a pontoon in Easdale Harbour (dries on spring tide). Please do not tie up on to walls as access is needed for the ferry. Pay £10 a night in the honesty box at the north end of Easdale Island ferry shed.

WHERE TO STAY, EAT AND DRINK   *Map, page 198*

Seol Mara Holiday Cottage (sleeps 6) 6 Easdale Island, PA34 4TB; `01852 300154; e ghalia.asaid@gmail.com. One of Easdale's tiny, white cottages, but deceptively large on the inside, this is a very good-value option in the centre of the village. Immediately welcoming & friendly owner Ghalia was originally from Syria but has lived on Easdale for decades & can tell you about the island. **££**

An Lionadh (sleeps 8–10) PA34 4TB; `01688 400388; w anlionadh.co.uk. This is a truly spectacular 4-bedroom house, right on the beach

with the feeling of an enormous beach hut. It has quite a few interesting nautical curiosities such as a huge model boat, telescope & old-fashioned diving helmet. Quiet location & unfenced lawn down to the sea. £920/week.

The Puffer Bar & Restaurant `01852 300022; f; ⏰ variable: lunch, dinner & evening bar most days. Easdale's only place to eat & drink is great for seafood with Firth of Lorn crab, langoustines, lobster, scallops & 'squatties' (squat lobsters). Venison from Seil & other local produce. Award winning. **£–££**

WHAT TO SEE AND DO In the east of the island, **Easdale Island Folk Museum** (4 Ellenabeich, PA34 4TB; ` 01852 300173; w easdalemuseum.org; ⏰ Apr–mid-Oct 11.00–16.00 daily) has displays on the slate industry, army volunteers, geology, boats and other aspects of Easdale Island life.

A walk around Easdale Island

Distance: 1½ miles; time: 1 hour; start/end: Easdale village; OS Explorer map: 359 Oban, Kerrera & Loch Melfort

This walk covers easy, flat terrain unless you decide to go up High Hill, which makes it marginally more difficult.

Disembark from the ferry and turn right just before the large collection of wheelbarrows; these are used for transporting heavy items around the island.

Follow the road into the village passing the modern-looking community hall and Puffer Restaurant & Bar on your left, and the play park on your right. When you reach the square football field, surrounded by small white cottages that were once lived in by quarry workers (now homes for islanders), turn right down towards the harbour.

Follow the waterfront until you reach a sign with an arrow pointing left for 'Quarries' and 'High Hill'. From here, take the indicated rocky path that leads through piles of slate splinterings, ruined buildings and out on to the rim between two large **quarries** filled with aquamarine-coloured water. They are a bizarre clash of industry and nature, more picturesque than you would imagine. Keep an eye out to sea for marine mammals such as porpoises and stay on the path as it turns left and climbs some steps.

To reach **High Hill**, Easdale's highest point, take an unmarked but obvious left-hand turning after a ruined building on your left, just before the L-shaped, water-filled quarry on your right. This path will take you to a small, green bench where you must bear right up to a grassy area with a picnic bench and trig point on top of the hill. Be careful to watch small children and dogs as there are sheer drops off the plateau. On a clear day, you can identify the surrounding islands and landmarks by reading the directions off the top of the trig point: Mull, Kerrera, Seil, Luing, Belnahua and parts of the mainland can all (potentially) be seen. Return the same way to the small, green bench and back down the steps to the main path.

From here, follow the path past the L-shaped quarry, then another larger quarry that's also full of water and some more dry and increasingly overgrown pits. The path soon passes a pretty pond on the left and through blackthorn bushes that are covered in white flowers in spring; this area is home to large hosts of sparrows that flock between perches as you pass.

Eventually you will come to a short alley between two walls and into the back of the village. Follow the sign for 'Ferry, Hall, Pub & Museum' and keep the sea to your right. Bear left to join with the main path through the village, and back to the football pitch.

LUING (LUINN)

Of the three substantially inhabited Slate Islands, Luing is the least visited. It is the biggest of the three and you can take a car there, making it less of a novelty than Easdale, but don't let that put you off: Luing is a beautiful island with its own pretty rows of white miners' cottages, aquamarine water-filled mines and slate scrap beaches. The main road leads along the raised spine: open grassy fields, rich with wildflowers in spring, end in rocky shores and glorious views of the sea, Torsa and mainland Argyll. It's a peaceful island with excellent walking routes and plenty of space for wildlife. Look out for glossy red-brown Luing cattle; originally bred in 1947 from beef cattle shorthorns and Highlanders for their hardiness, but now recognised as a separate breed.

GETTING THERE AND AWAY

Ferry **Argyll and Bute Council** (☏ 01852 300252; w argyll-bute.gov.uk/isle-luing-isle-seil-ferry-timetable) runs a regular and inexpensive car ferry between North Cuan on Seil and South Cuan on Luing (another example of settlements spanning across a stretch of water). You buy a ticket on the boat with cash or cheque and the journey takes only a few minutes (cars/foot passengers £8.30/2.05).

GETTING AROUND
All of Luing's roads are single track, but at less than 6 square miles it does not take long to get around the island by car. Travelling by bicycle can be even more enjoyable, allowing you to stop and admire the views more easily.

Bike hire
Sunnybrae Caravan Park South Cuan PA34 4TU; ☏ 01852 314274; w oban-holiday.co.uk/things-do/bike-hire. Bike hire (inc for children) from £10/day; e-bikes, trailers & tag-alongs also available. Group discounts.

WHERE TO STAY, EAT AND DRINK *Map, page 198*
Sunnybrae Caravan Park (6 caravans, 2 lodges) South Cuan PA34 4TU; ☏ 01852 314274; w oban-holiday.co.uk. Forget your preconceived notions of holiday parks, Sunnybrae is a breath of fresh air. Pale green caravans & grey roofs are absorbed into the shoreline, while interiors are spotlessly clean, new & well equipped with ovens & full-sized bathroom suites. Ask for one on the

water's edge & it's like having a personal bird hide. Seabirds float past in the current & otters live along the shoreline. The owners are environmentally conscious, let wildflowers grow for the insects, provide compost bins & sell local produce on site. Orchid Lodge (sleeps 4; &) is the most luxurious option. Caravan £590/week; Orchid Lodge £850/week.

SHOPPING

✉ **Luing Stores & Post Office** Fladda, nr Cullipool PA34 4TX; ☎01852 314276; ⊕ 11.00–16.00 Mon–Fri, 11.00–14.00 Sat. Decorated in blue & white stripes like a beach hut, this great little store sells bread from Luing Bakery & some groceries as well as slate-themed gifts, knitted accessories & coffee.

💻 **Atlantic Islands Centre** 23, Cullipool PA34 4TX; ☎01852 314096; w isleofluing.org/atlantic-islands-centre; ⊕ Apr–Oct 12.30–14.30 daily, 18.00–20.00 Sat, Nov–Mar 12.30–14.30 Mon & Fri–Sun; &. Modern café selling coffees, goods from Luing Bakery, sandwiches, soup & light bites such as breaded mushrooms. £

WHAT TO SEE AND DO Luing's main settlement, **Cullipool**, is a quiet, seaside village, dwarfed by a huge quarry in the north. It has pretty, white miners' cottages, similar to those in Easdale, and a jagged beach made of half-cut pieces of slate, some of which are studded with fool's gold. The prettier, water-filled quarries are said to be home to huge numbers of toads.

While in Cullipool, do not miss the **Atlantic Islands Centre** (☎ 01852 314096; w atlanticislandscentre.com; ⊕ Apr–Oct 10.00–17.00 Mon–Fri, 10.00–late Sat, 11.00–16.00 Sun, Nov–Mar 11.00–16.00 Mon & Fri, 11.00–late Sat, noon–16.00 Sun; &). Downstairs is the café (see above), while upstairs are changing exhibitions of local interest and information about Luing's history. There's also an excellent view across to Fladda Lighthouse and Belnahua.

Toberonochy Luing's second-largest settlement, Toberonochy mostly consists of a couple of rows of pretty whitewashed cottages, built in the late 18th and early 19th centuries for people working in the quarry. Walking down through the village, past the village hall, you will come to a large pier with lovely views across to the island of Shuna and along the coastline of Luing. Further south, there is a gently rotting boat and a couple of beaches. If you want to have a look at the mine, which is water-filled and curiously picturesque with sheer diagonally striped slate walls and twisted trees growing on top, go through a metal gate on the opposite side of the road from the pier and follow a path around past a few sheds for around 100yds.

Àird Luing The south of Luing is only really inhabited by birds and Ardlarach Farm's cattle. The farm is managed with biodiversity in mind and is home to flocks of Canada and greylag geese, swooping lapwings and long-beaked snipe.

Coming from the north, about 220yds after the turning to Toberonochy there are some large barns and farm buildings. Taking a right turn (on foot) just after the biggest barn should bring you to a cattle grid and the beginnings of a track that leads around 2 miles all the way down to Àird Luing – the southernmost point of the island. As the track sticks to higher ground, you have consistently great views of Scarba, Shuna, the mainland, as well as out to sea. The small islet in the wide bay at Eilean an Atha on your left is thought to have been an ancient dun.

At the end of the track, you should be able to see a trig point up on your right. The Garvellachs, Belnahua and Mull are off to the west; Scarba and the north end of Jura are south. Take some time to scan the water for porpoises and dolphins if it is a calm day.

Invaluable havens for wildlife, none of the other, somewhat mysterious, Slate Islands have more than a handful of inhabitants or a regular ferry connection. Looking out to sea, you will get to know their silhouettes on the horizon; some of the organised boat trips allow you a closer look as you pass them, while both Seafari and Sealife Adventures (page 200) can organise private landing tours.

BELNAHUA Northwest of Luing, Belnahua was the fourth of the main Slate Islands, but is now uninhabited. It was once home to 200 people who worked in the quarries, but now all that remains is the ruins of their cottages and a huge water-filled mine that takes up most of the interior.

FLADDA Fladda is dominated by its lighthouse and the lighthouse keepers' cottages, which were built in 1860 by the Stevenson brothers. It is also known to host a large colony of terns.

LUNGA Situated west of Luing, Lunga is privately owned and used to host an activity centre for schoolchildren, though it has now closed down.

SCARBA Relatively large and round, Scarba is now uninhabited and separated from Luing by the 'Grey Dogs' tidal race and from Jura by the Gulf of Corryvreckan with its famous whirlpool (page 247). You can sometimes see the wild boar that live here on boat trips.

SHUNA Shuna is privately owned with a working farm, several holiday cottages (✆ 01852 314244; w islandofshuna.co.uk) and lots of deer. On the northwest shore lies the wreck of an old ferry; it has a turntable for cars and was later used for transporting cows, before being beached here when it was no longer needed. Visitors that stay are picked up as foot passengers and given a small motorboat for the duration of their holiday.

TORSA Lying between Seil Sound and Cuan Sound, Torsa is very close to the shore of Luing's Ardinamir Bay. It has one house that is rented out as a holiday cottage (✆ 01852 314274; w torsa-island.co.uk) and the ruins of a 16th-century hunting lodge.

The coastline in this part of the island is wild and unpathed, lending itself to a more adventurous romp, with plenty of birds, such as little ringed plovers and herons, and chances of spotting otters.

Ballycastle Fort to Kilchattan
Distance: 2½ miles; time: 1½ hours; start: Ballycastle Fort, near Ardinamir; end: Kilchattan; OS Explorer map: 359 Oban, Kerrera & Loch Melfort

This is an easy walk, though it can get muddy in places. The route takes in two interesting archaeological sites and wonderful views along the coastline. To make it a 5-mile circular route, return from Kilchattan to Ardinamir along the road.

To reach **Ballycastle Fort** (✜ 56°14'51"N 5°37'47"W), now little more than rubble remains of an imposing dun, take the main road that runs south from the ferry terminal and follow the turning marked towards 'Ardinamir'.

The fort is half a mile down the road, up on a hill to the left, standing in a strategic position with a clear view across Ardinamir Bay to the island of Torsa and Seil Sound beyond.

Around 110yds further down the road is a turning on to a farm track on the right-hand side of the road; take this and choose the higher path at the fork you come to shortly afterwards. The track is easy to follow and leads above the shoreline for about 2½ miles, taking in glorious coastal views. The landscape is green and gently undulating with good chances of spotting smaller birds of prey such as kestrels, beautiful white and black male hen harriers, short-eared owls and buzzards.

When the track eventually meets the main road, turn left and walk a short distance to the ruins of the **old parish church of Kilchattan** and its **burial ground**. Although this building dates from the 12th century, the site is thought to have had religious significance for substantially longer. Careful inspection of the outer faces of the ruined building should reveal rudimentary carvings or graffiti of boats. They are thought to depict medieval galleys or birlinns, which are consistent with a style used in the 12th or 13th century. Contradictory arguments suggest that they refer to either a failed military expedition in 1249 by King Alexander II or King Haakon's fleet coming from Norway in 1263. There were of course many other boats passing Luing and thus there are a number of other suggestions as to the carvings' meaning.

Colonsay (Colbhasa)

At 10 miles long and 2 miles wide, Colonsay is a relatively small island, with a varied landscape that's dramatic in places, plus beautiful sandy beaches and some interesting pockets of archaeology. With a population of 135, there are plenty of wide-open spaces and its remote location makes the island a rewarding place to watch the night sky. To the south, neighbouring Oronsay (Oransay to some locals) is attached by a tidal sand bank and would be nothing more than a footnote if it were not for its wonderful Augustinian priory. With a large collection of carved grave slabs and two Celtic crosses, as well as the ruins of the buildings themselves, the priory is comparable to Iona Abbey in many ways, but with only a fraction of the visitors. Both islands are also notable for their birdlife, with Oronsay being an RSPB reserve and Colonsay's teeming seabird cliffs among the richest in birdlife of anywhere in the region.

GETTING THERE AND AWAY

BY FERRY CalMac (✆ 08000 665000 or, from outside the UK, +44 1475 650397; w calmac.co.uk) offers two options for getting to the island: **Oban to Colonsay** takes 2 hours and 25 minutes and runs five times a week in summer or three times a week in winter (cars/foot passengers £38.55/7.60); **Islay to Colonsay** takes 1 hour 10 minutes and runs twice a week in summer and sometimes once a week in winter (cars/foot passengers £17.75/4.25). Ferries arrive into the main settlement of Scalasaig; Colonsay Holidays (w colonsayholidays.co.uk) offer a pickup service for £20.

BY PLANE Hebridean Air Services (✆ 08458 057465; w hebrideanair.co.uk) fly from both Oban and Islay to Colonsay; the airfield is on the west coast; pickup is available from Colonsay Holidays (w colonsayholidays.co.uk; £20).

GETTING AROUND

All of Colonsay's roads are single track and several sharp corners and blind summits mean that extra care is needed when driving. The central 'ring road' is 8 miles long and many of the island's main highlights are long detours off this; the island is therefore too big for most people to get around on foot, but a bicycle could do the job nicely.

BIKE HIRE

🚲 **The Colonsay Hotel** West Scalasaig PA61 7YU; ✆ 01951 200316; w colonsayholidays.co.uk; ⏰ mid-Mar–Oct. £12/day.

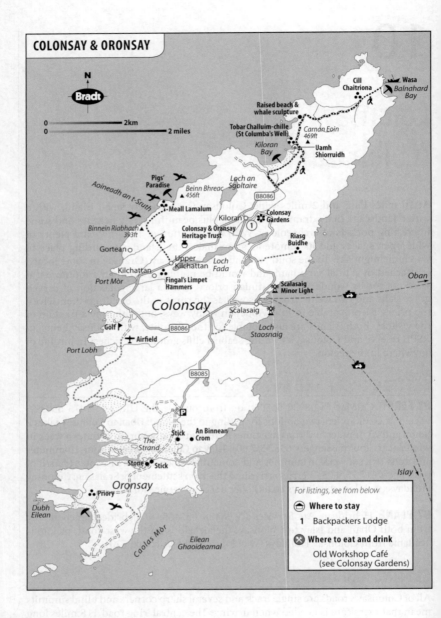

COLONSAY & ORONSAY

Bradt

N

0 ————— 2km
0 ————————— 2 miles

Cill Chaitriona
Wasa
Balnahard Bay

Raised beach & whale sculpture

Tobar Challuim-chille (St Columba's Well)

Carnan Eoin 469ft

Kiloran Bay

Uamh Shiorruidh

Aoineadh an t-Sruth

Pigs' Paradise

Beinn Bhreac 456ft

Loch an Sgoltaire

B8086

Meall Lamalum

Kiloran

Colonsay Gardens

Binnein Riabhach 393ft

Colonsay & Oransay Heritage Trust

Riasg Buidhe

Gortean

Upper Kilchattan

Loch Fada

Kilchattan

Port Mòr

Fingal's Limpet Hammers

Oban

Scalasaig Minor Light

Colonsay

Scalasaig

Golf

B8086

Loch Staosnaig

Airfield

Port Lobh

B8085

P

Stick

An Binnean Crom

The Strand

Stone   Stick

Islay

Oronsay

Priory

For listings, see from below

⊖ Where to stay

1 Backpackers Lodge

⊗ Where to eat and drink

Old Workshop Café
(see Colonsay Gardens)

Dubh Eilean

Caolas Mòr

Eilean Ghaoideamal

 WHERE TO STAY *Map, above*

The Colonsay Estate owns the majority of the island and runs most of its accommodation, including the following two excellent choices, which are at the top and bottom of the spectrum respectively. Most of Colonsay's other accommodation options are self-catering and you can find extensive listings and information on **w** colonsay.org.uk/accommodation and **w** colonsayholidays. co.uk/cottages.

🏠 **The Colonsay Hotel** (9 rooms) West Scalasaig PA61 7YU; 📞 01951 200316; w colonsayholidays.co.uk; 🕐 mid-Mar–Oct. Friendly & well run, the Colonsay Hotel occupies a proud historic building with stylish, modern interiors in a delicate colour scheme. Just 500yds west of the ferry terminal, with sea views out towards Jura. **££££**

🏠 **Backpackers Lodge** (16 beds) PA61 7YU; 📞 01951 200312; w colonsayholidays.co.uk/backpackers. An old-fashioned cottage in a very secluded location, 500yds southeast of Kiloran. **£**

WHERE TO EAT AND DRINK *Map, opposite*

There are only three places to eat out on Colonsay, two of which are open seasonally.

✖ **The Colonsay Hotel** (see above) 🕐 mid-Mar–Oct 18.00–21.00, bar until late; ♿. Hearty, locally sourced dishes such as Balnahard beef & Colonsay ale pie with mash. Drinks include 2 local gins & beer from the Colonsay Brewery. Choose between comfortable leather sofas & log fire in the bar or the more formal restaurant with stunning views. **££**

✖ **The Colonsay Pantry** Scalasaig PA61 7YW; 📞01951 200325; w thecolonsaypantry.co.uk; 🕐 summer 10.00–20.00 Mon & Wed–Sat, 10.00–15.00 Tue, 15.00–20.00 Sun, winter noon–16.00 on boat days (later on request); ♿. Family business open since 1988, serving good food served in the clean & attractive interior, though it appears rather uninspiring from the outside. Has small gift shop, serves alcohol & also does takeaway. **£**

📺 **Old Workshop Café** Colonsay Gardens PA61 7YU; 🕐 Apr–Oct noon–17.00 Wed & Fri, 14.00–17.00 Sat. Friendly service, filled rolls & hot drinks. **£**

SHOPPING

Colonsay has one place to buy groceries and a small, but varied selection of other shops.

ARTS AND CRAFTS

Christine's Den 4 Glen Oran, Scalasaig PA61 7YW; 🕐 variable: check on the door. Small local craft shop.

House of Lochar Scalasaig PA61 7YR; 📞01951 200232; w houseoflochar.com; 🕐 Easter–end-Oct 15.00–17.30 Mon–Sat. Specialist Scottish publisher & bookshop with a great selection of local titles, identification books & ID charts.

Old Waiting Room Gallery Scalasaig PA61 7YT; m 07850 230000; w balnahard.com/theoldwaitingroomgallery; 🕐 11.00–14.00 Mon–Tue & Sat, noon–14.00 Wed, 17.00–19.00 Fri. Arts, crafts & gifts, plus yarns from Colonsay Wool Growers.

FOOD SHOPS

Colonsay General Store Scalasaig PA61 7YW; 📞01951 200265; w colonsayshop.net; 🕐 summer 09.00–17.30 Mon–Fri, 11.30–12.30 Sun, winter 09.00–17.30 Mon, Wed & Fri, 09.00–13.30 Tue & Thu, 09.00–13.30 Sat, 11.30–12.30 Sun. Well-stocked shop with good assortment of loose veg. Pre-order & delivery service available including fresh fish delivered Sat.

Wild Island Distillery & Colonsay Brewery Dunoran, Scalasaig PA61 7YZ; 📞01951 200190; w colonsaybrewery.co.uk; 🕐 15.00–17.00 Mon, Wed, Fri & Sat. Brewing 3 core beers, including an IPA, which earn Colonsay the title of 'the smallest island in the world to have its own brewery'. Also gin infused with native botanicals.

SPORTS AND ACTIVITIES

Once you arrive on Colonsay, look out for posters around Scalasaig as local events and activities are often advertised this way. **Beach cleans** in company (often 10.00 Saturday) are a popular effort to clean the whole coastline of Colonsay, and visitors are welcome to join.

Golf Colonsay Golf Course, Traigh an Tobair Fhuair/Port Lobh PA61 7YW; w colonsay.org.uk/ things-do/golf. An 18-hole course on the machair, 'golf as it was first played'. Pay fees at Colonsay Hotel (membership/single round £60/10).

MacPhie Bagging w colonsay.org.uk/things-do/macphie-bagging. Colonsay might look like a small island on the map, while here you can conquer all of the island's 22 'peaks' at over 300ft (91.46m); the whole route is around 20 miles and involves lots of hillwalking over rough ground.

OTHER PRACTICALITIES

Fuel Colonsay General Store (page 209); community owned, cash only.
⊞ **Medical** Scalasaig PA61 7YW; ☎01951 200328; ⏰ 09.00–10.00 & 17.00–18.00 Mon–Wed & Fri. Doctor; call any time if urgent.

✉ **Post office** Scalasaig PA61 7YW; ⏰ 09.00–13.00 & 14.00–17.30 Mon–Wed & Fri, 09.00–13.00 Thu & Sat. This is also where you should check tides for the crossing to Oronsay.

EVENTS

APRIL/MAY
Colonsay Book Festival w colonsaybookfestival.com
Colonsay Spring Festival w colonsayspringfest. com. A 3-week celebration of nature, art, foraging, craft & heritage.

AUGUST
Colonsay International Open w colonsay.org. uk/things-do/golf

SEPTEMBER
Ceòl Cholasa w ceolcholasa.co.uk. Traditional music festival.

OCTOBER
Food & Drink Festival w colonsayfoodfest.co.uk

WHAT TO SEE AND DO

THE NORTH Colonsay's main settlement is **Scalasaig**, roughly halfway down the west coast. A small village of around 20 loosely scattered houses and shops, nestled at the base of low hills, this is where the ferry arrives and is home to most of the island's amenities. From here, a ring road of sorts traverses the middle of the island, with a road heading off north to Kiloran Bay, and another south towards Oronsay. North of Scalasaig is **Scalasaig Minor Light** (⊕ 56°04'16.3"N 6°11'02.1"W), a tiny white and red lighthouse that looks a lot like a baby's bottle. Originally built by David Stevenson in 1903, it has recently been moved from nearby Rudha Dubh and restored.

Around 1 mile further north, it's possible to do a 2-mile return walk out to the abandoned village of **Riasg Buidhe**. To start this, look for the track opposite a lay-by, which leads to a recycling centre and a small car park just before it (⊕ 56°04'47.3"N 6°11'15.7"W); walk around the left-hand side of the recycling centre fence, following a faint path and join a track that leads east towards the sea. Pass two ruined buildings on your left and follow the track, which is a little unclear in places, until you come to an abandoned village. The village was deserted in 1922, when the estate provided occupants with new houses nearer Scalasaig. The ruins are a desolate place and a reminder of harder times gone by. There is a terrace of houses that you would assume had been built as a block, but oral history reports that they were built one by one by the inhabitants themselves. Slightly elevated to the south are the remains of an early chapel, although little can now be distinguished. A wonderful 8th-century cross was found here, with

Celtic decorations and a face, suggesting a longstanding religious significance to the site. It has now been moved to the gardens of Colonsay House, while a small slab engraved with a cross is now in the National Museum in Edinburgh; unfortunately, nothing is left to indicate its existence.

Surrounded by woodland, just east of the road that heads towards Kiloran Bay, is the centre of Colonsay Estate. Belonging to Colonsay House, a private residence, **Colonsay Gardens** (⊕ Apr–Oct noon–17.00 Wed & Fri, 14.00–17.00 Sat; adult/child £2.50/1) has several historical gems among its lawns, mature trees and rose gardens; the previously mentioned **Riasg Buidhe Cross**, the lens from Rubh a Mhail Lighthouse on Islay (built in 1874), an old millstone and other objects of interest are hidden around the grounds.

Kiloran Bay to Balnahard Bay

Distance: 7 miles; time: 4–5 hours; start/end: Kiloran Bay; OS Explorer map: 354 Colonsay & Oronsay

This is a very rewarding walk with two stunning beaches, interesting archaeological sites and a varied coastline.

Begin by either walking north along the yellow sands of Kiloran Bay or following sheep tracks through the dunes. At the end of the beach there are the remains of a dead whale, likely to be there in some state for the next few years at least. It's possible to explore the caves at the northern end of the bay with a torch; **Uamh Shiorruidh** (⊕ 56°06'33"N 6°10'38"W) is deep and L-shaped.

From here, head back to the beach and up on to the grass, heading inland at the base of the cliffs until you reach a solid track; turn left on to it and begin to climb the hill.

About 200yds up this track you might notice a tooth-shaped rock (which has been placed here) on your right. On the opposite side of the track, around 40yds west and 5yds south, is **Tobar Challuim-chille** or St Columba's Well (⊕ 56°06'34"N 6°10'33"W). Covered with slab of rock, this stone-walled spring is initially difficult to spot as you walk down towards it, but quite unmistakable once found. Ferns grow from the cracks between rocks and layers of moss and lichen give a little indication to its age. The well is said to have been blessed with healing properties by St Columba himself.

Continue along the track for around another mile, passing a raised beach with pebbles that have been moved into the shape of an enormous whale – an art installation started by Julian Meredith – as the track bends around to the right, heading east past the impressive buildings at Balnahard Farm. This end of the island is a good place to spot wild goats (not to be confused with the Hebridean black sheep that are farmed here).

Eventually you will come to a small barn on your left and the end of the proper track. Bearing slightly left, head down through the dunes to Balnahard Bay. The severely rotten and rusted shipwreck here is what remains of the steamship *Wasa*, which caught fire off Colonsay in May 1920. It is now in two parts and only partially visible, poking out from the sand.

Once you have enjoyed the beach, head back to the barn; on its far side, follow a fence across to the right. In an enclosed field, where there is a small gate for access, are the remains of **Cill Chaitriona**, a chapel standing within its burial ground (⊕ 56°07'19.0"N 6°09'00.1"W), with a hollowed stone font and much-weathered early cross in the opposite corner to the gate.

From the ruined chapel, the easiest way back to Kiloran Bay is to return to the track; that said, now you will have your bearings, it is much more exciting to follow the high ground above the coast. There are wonderful views of the craggy coastline and, on a clear day, across to Mull in the north.

THE WEST COAST On the western side of the 'ring road', just before Kilchattan Primary School, is a white building with a grey slate roof that used to be the Baptist church and is now the **Colonsay and Oronsay Heritage Trust** (f; ⊕ daily; donation requested). This small museum has an eclectic mix of locally relevant exhibits and information, including the old telephone exchange, useful maps of archaeological sites, photos of what life was once like, and a few whale bones.

🚶 Pigs' Paradise and the seabird cliffs *

Distance: 5 miles; time: 3 hours; start/end: Upper Kilchattan; OS Explorer map: 354 Colonsay & Oronsay

This walk visits the most spectacular stretch of coastline on Colonsay – in fact, it's among the most impressive in the entire Inner Hebrides. Note, though, that it is very exposed and can be treacherous in bad weather.

In Upper Kilchattan, take the turning marked towards 'Alister Annie's' and walk up the track, passing a white house, a stone house and a green barn on your left.

Continue straight on, passing through a gate, until you are nearly at Gortean House (a white house with a red roof). Go around the house to the left and then carry on straight along grassy paths. After crossing over a stile, continue in the same direction until you reach the cliffs over the sea. There is already a spectacular view, but it is only a taste of what's to come.

Turn right and walk along the clifftops with the sea on your left. You can walk along narrow grassy paths until you reach a channel, at Aoineadh an t-Sruth, down to a wide platform of grass on a lower level. The route runs underneath one wall of cliffs with another set of cliffs below, bringing you closer to guillemot nesting sites above the sea.

You can walk northeast at this lower level for about 400yds before an easy way back to the top presents itself; you will need to clamber back up to the higher clifftops when the way runs out.

Shortly afterwards it's possible to get down closer to the sea again, past a memorial cairn and on to a large, grassy promontory called **Meall Lamalum** that is thought to have been a fort (⊕ 56°05'34"N 6°14'01"W). This naturally defensive position has tremendous views, allowing you to look back along the coastline to see layer upon layer of towering cliffs disappearing into the distance. Waves crash against the exposed rocks below and razorbills, shags, guillemots, gulls and fulmars fish in the surrounding waters.

Retracing your steps but up to the clifftops again you can walk about 500yds further to **Pigs' Paradise**, between the hill Beinn Bhreac and the small cove at Port Bán (⊕ 56°05'36"N 6°13'40"W); a sheltered area of grass surrounded by high cliffs, this is where pigs are rumoured to have been kept. The easiest way to return is along the higher coast path.

Back on the main road in Kilchattan, the standing stones known as **Fingal's Limpet Hammers** are on the left-hand side in a field beneath a grey house. Presumably this is yet another reference to the famous giant.

ACROSS THE STRAND TO ORONSAY The crossing to Oronsay (also known as Oransay, or Orasaigh in Gaelic) can only be attempted when tide times are favourable; these are displayed with an explanation in the post office (page 210) where you should also ask for advice before crossing. As the natural causeway is only exposed for a limited amount of time, which changes every day, it is sometimes not possible to cross at all. The best times to visit Oronsay are the two days following full moon and new moon; it's worth checking tide times in advance online (**w** tides.willyweather.co.uk: search for 'Colonsay – Eilean Olmsa' and then deduct 10 minutes for local conditions). As the Strand, the section of muddy sand between both islands, is covered in broken shells in some places, you might prefer to take wellies or water shoes, rather than cross in bare feet.

If you have a car, park at the Strand car park, at the end of the road that leads south; from the car park it is a 5-mile return walk to the priory. Visible to the southeast from the car park is a curiously jutting rock called **An Binnean Crom** (the crooked pinnacle), which is also known as Hangman's Rock. Walking along the shoreline with the sea and Oronsay on your right-hand-side, you will begin to see the hole in An Binnean Crom, which was supposedly used to loop a rope through for executions in the 17th century.

An Binnean Crom is directly inland from a stick on the shoreline that lines up with another stick and an upright stone (✪ 56°01'42.4"N 6°13'42.1"W) on Oronsay, marking the route across to the smaller island. The Strand is a good place to see twite, lesser redpoll, meadow pipit, linnet, stonechat and many other exciting species of bird.

In order to make the most of the time available, cross as the tide is still receding, while the water is ankle deep; some standing water usually remains over the way, even at low tide. As you walk across, scan the seabed for crabs, anemones, cockles and other sea creatures.

Once you reach Oronsay, an obvious track leads southwest and then south for about 1½ miles to the ruined **priory**. According to tradition, the site was originally a Celtic monastery founded by St Columba in 563 and the current Augustinian building was later refounded by John, Lord of the Isles in the 14th century. The priory first appears on record in 1353 and in the early 16th century it was home to an important school of monumental sculpture. There are two Celtic crosses outside: the Great Oronsay Cross from around 1510 with a crucifix and interlacing foliage, and a second, smaller cross that is more weathered, with a carving in relief of the Virgin Mary. Inside the prior's house, a building to the northwest of the priory, is a wonderful collection of carved grave slabs: swords, priests, stags, knights, ships and intricate patterns are all well preserved.

From the priory, if the tide times allow, you can return briefly along the track you came in on, before heading south through a field full of geese, lapwings or (usually invisible) corncrakes depending on the season, towards what appears at a distance to be a standing stone, but is actually a modern memorial. From here you can head down to a beautiful sandy beach. Look out for golden and ringed plovers, dunlin and oystercatchers.

Be sure to allow plenty of time to return back to Colonsay, rather than risk being stranded.

Islay (Île)

With a gentle landscape and a magical quality felt by many, Islay holds a special place in the hearts of locals, known as Ìleachs, and repeat visitors alike. Aside from the whisky (see box, page 220), which is world renowned, most visitors come to Islay for its beautiful, empty beaches and the wildlife. The island has plentiful grey and common seals; red, roe and fallow deer; ten pairs of golden eagles; an otter for every mile of coastline; and, incredible numbers of wintering geese (over 30,000 barnacle and 6,000 Greenland white-fronted). With only 50 pairs left in Scotland, around 90% of which live on Islay, the island is also one of the only places you have a chance of seeing red-legged choughs.

Rich in archaeology, Islay also has probably the most attractive collection of lighthouses in the region, some of which are truly remote, but with others easily viewed from the main roads. Although Islay's population of 3,200 is one of the Inner Hebrides' largest, drivers still wave to each other in passing and it's not unusual to come across two cars stopped in the middle of the road with their windows open for a chat.

HISTORY

At Port Na Seilich, on Islay's east coast, radiocarbon dating puts evidence of human activity as among the earliest known in western Scotland: sometime between 9000BC and 7700BC. This evidence would have been left by Ice-Age hunter-gatherers and, as the temperature began to rise and conditions became a little more favourable, people began to settle here; there are Mesolithic kitchen middens dating on the island from around 7000BC. From Neolithic times there were more permanent settlements. At least eight roundhouses from the late 2nd millennium BC have been found at An Sithean (page 236), and there are various other burial cairns and standing stones from the Neolithic and Bronze ages. There is a wealth of forts, duns and crannogs (page 266) dating from the Iron Age.

From the time we have written records, about halfway through the 1st millennium AD, up until the turn of the 18th century, Islay is portrayed as both prominent and bloody. Written history gives us the names of lairds and leaders, but not much detail about the ordinary inhabitants. Luckily, on Islay, there are strong folk traditions and, in the past few decades, these have begun to be recorded.

From the 6th century, during the time of Dál Riata, Islay was ruled by the family group of Cenél nÓengusa. According to the *Senchus fer n-Alban* (*The History of the Men of Scotland*), the island saw various battles including one in 627 between Uí Chóelbad (a branch of the Ulster kingdom Dál nAraidi) and an army of Dál Riata, which resulted in the death of the Irish king's son.

Dál Riata's dominion was eventually demolished by the Vikings, who began their raids as early as the end of the 8th century. From the island's Norse place names

– such as Nerabus (meaning 'nether' or 'lower farm') and Port Askaig ('ash tree harbour') – it's evident that, after the initial period of conquest, many of the Norse who settled here were not Vikings, but farmers happy to be left in peace. One of the most significant leaders of the Norse Kingdom of the Isles, Godred Crovan, is associated with Islay and is thought to have died of pestilence (the plague) on the island in 1095. According to folklore, the standing stone at Carragh Bhan near Kintra Farm marks his grave.

In 1156, there was a battle off the coast of Islay between Godred Olafsson, the unpopular grandson of Godred Crovan, and Somerled. Though this 'Battle of epiphany' ended in a bloody stalemate, it resulted in Somerled taking all of the southern Hebrides and subsequently even more territory. Building the sea fortress Claig Castle on the small island Am Fraoch Eilean between Islay and Jura gave Somerled control of the Sound of Islay which, due to the monstrous Corryvreckan whirlpool north of Jura, was effectively control of the route from the mainland to the Hebrides and, ultimately, the ocean.

In the 14th century, John of Islay, chief of Clan Donald and self-styled 'Lord of the Isles', controlled significant stretches of the west coast and all of the Hebrides apart from Skye as a semi-independent kingdom. Three small islands in Loch Finlaggan (page 225) were the centre of this kingdom until, one century later, the Lords of the Isles inherited more land, including Skye, and moved their control base from Islay of Aros and Ardtonish across the Sound of Mull.

Following this, John of Islay's son founded 'Clan MacDonald of Dunyvaig', using Dunyvaig Castle (page 231) as their naval power base. After the Treaty of Perth (page 14) the Lords of the Isles continued as crown dependencies until John MacDonald II made a secret deal with Edward IV of England in 1462. An interruption from the War of the Roses meant that James IV of Scotland did not discover the plot against him until 13 years later and even then John MacDonald II managed to quell calls for his lordship to be forfeited by giving up some of his territory on the mainland and Skye. Shortly afterwards, John's nephew was involved in launching a raid on mainland Ross and the exasperated James IV of Scotland finally removed the family's control, destroyed Finlaggan and placed their lands under the Scottish Crown. The Prince of Wales still holds the 'Lord of the Isles' title to this day.

Incredibly, Clan MacDonald of Dunyvaig's holdings in Islay were restored in 1545 but conflict arose as the MacLeans had been granted Dunyvaig Castle in the meantime and subsequently expanded their territory. In 1578 the MacLeans were besieged and ousted from Loch Gorm Castle and in 1598 they were defeated in the Battle of Traigh Ghruinneart; it's thought that those MacLeans who escaped then burnt to death in Kilnave Chapel (page 235).

In the early 15th century, the MacDonalds' power began to slip once again and in 1614 Islay was given to Sir John Campbell of Cawdor, who eventually succeeded in subduing them. When Campbell became Sheriff of Argyll, Islay was absorbed and the island's significance faded away. However, far from life settling down for the island's regular inhabitants, Islay was attached again in 1647 after branches of the Campbells chose different sides of the Civil War.

Life did finally begin to calm down for Islay in the latter half of the 17th century and improvements were made in transport infrastructure, while fishing, cattle and the kelp market grew. An official whisky industry (see box, page 220), rather than the previous illegal distilling, started to develop in the early 19th century and, as was the case on most of the islands, the population grew for the first half of that century until the crash in the kelp industry, the potato famine and the introduction of sheep. Mostly emigrations from Islay appear to have been voluntary; John

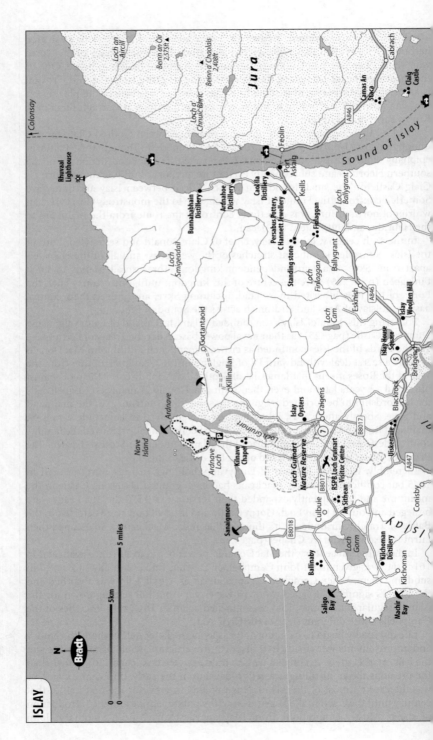

ISLAY

0   5km
0   5 miles

N

Bradt

Colonsay →

Loch an
Aircill

Beinn an Oir
2,575ft ▲

Loch a'
Chnuic Bhric

Benn a' Chaolais
2,408ft ▲

Jura

A846

Camas An
Staca

Claig
Castle

Cabrach

Sound of Islay

Feolin

Port
Askaig

Kells

Rhuvaal
Lighthouse

Bunnahabhain Distillery

Ardnahoe
Distillery

Caol Ila
Distillery

Persabus Pottery,
C Hannett Jewellery

Standing stone

Loch
Snigeadail

Finlaggan

Loch
Ballygrant

Loch
Finlaggan

Ballygrant

A846

Eskmish

Islay
Woollen Mill

Loch
Cam

Gortantaoid

Killinallan

Islay House Square

Bridgend

Blackrock

Ardnave

Nave
Island

Ardnave
Loch

Sanaigmore

Kilnave
Chapel

Craigens

Islay
Oysters

Loch Gruinart

Loch Gruinart
Nature Reserve

RSPB Loch Gruinart
An Sithean Visitor Centre

Culbuie

B8017

B8017

Uiskentuie

B8018

Ballinaby

Loch
Gorm

A847

Conisby

ISLAY

Saligo
Bay

Machir Bay

Kilchoman

Kilchoman
Distillery

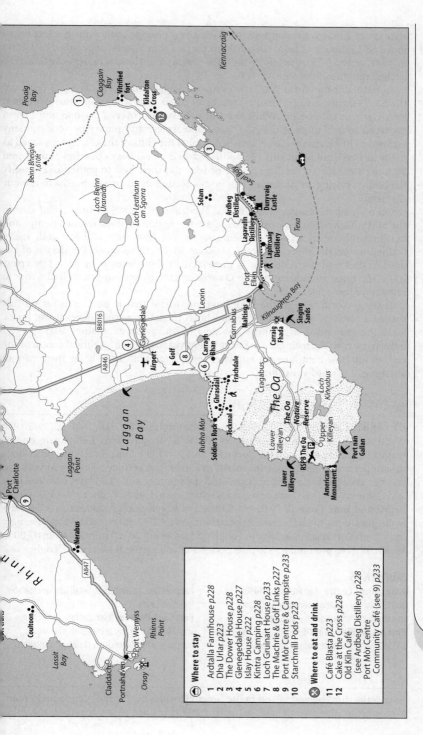

Proaig
Bay

Claggain
Bay

Vitrified
fort

Kildalton
Cross

①

⑫

Benn Bheigier
1,610ft

③

Loch Beinn
Uaraidh

Loch Leathann
an Sgorra

Solam

Seal Bay

Ardbeg
Distillery

Lagavulin
Distillery

Laphroaig
Distillery

Dunyvaig
Castle

Texa

Kennacraig

Kilnaughton Bay

Carraig
Fhada

Singing
Sands

Port
Ellen

Leorin

B8016

Glenegedale

A846

④

Airport

Golf

⑧

⑥

Carragh
Bhan

Frachdale

Cornabus

Maltings

The Oa

Cragabus

Ghrasdail

Tockmal

Rubha Mòr

Soldier's Rock

Lower
Killeyan

Loch
Kinnabus

Upper
Killeyan

The Oa
Nature
Reserve

RSPB The Oa

American
Monument

Port nan
Gallan

Lower
Killeyan

Laggan
Bay

Laggan
Point

Port
Charlotte

⑨

Rhinns

A847

Nerabus

Coultoon

Claddach

Portnahaven

Orsay

Port Wemyss

Rhinns
Point

Lossit
Bay

ⓘ **Where to stay**

1   Ardtalla Farmhouse p228
2   Dha Urlar p223
3   The Dower House p228
4   Glenegedale House p227
5   Islay House p222
6   Kintra Camping p228
7   Loch Gruinart House p233
8   The Machrie & Golf Links p227
9   Port Mòr Centre & Campsite p233
10 Starchmill Pods p223

ⓧ **Where to eat and drink**

11 Café Blasta p223
12 Cake at the Cross p228
    Old Kiln Café
    (see Ardbeg Distillery) p228
    Port Mòr Centre
    Community Café (see 9) p233

Ramsay of Kildalton is supposed to have given passage money for his tenants to move to Canada and later visited them there. From a peak population of 15,000 in 1841, only 7,375 were left by the 1891 census and these numbers continued to decline into the 20th century.

In 1918, during World War I, two ships were wrecked off the Oa. On 5 February the SS *Tuscania*, an old luxury liner being used as a troopship, was torpedoed by a German submarine. While the Royal Navy destroyers *Mosquito* and *Pigeon* managed to save most of the 2,397 crew and American military personnel, many escaped in lifeboats only to be smashed against the cliffs of the Oa. Ìleachs saved as many as they could, but still 126 bodies washed up on Islay's beaches and around 40 more were lost at sea. The people of Islay did their best to gather and identify the bodies, sewing an American flag from a picture in an encyclopaedia to honour the dead.

On 6 October, disaster struck again. The troopship HMS *Otranto* collided with the HMS *Kashmir* in a storm off the Oa and, despite another rescue attempt and hundreds of American soldiers being saved, 431 lives were still lost and, again, washed up on the shore. Sergeant Malcolm MacNeill recorded the details of the dead bodies and his notebook is preserved in the Museum of Islay Life (page 234). The huge monument on the Oa was erected by the American Red Cross to remember these lives lost.

During World War II, the RAF built an airfield that is now used for civilian planes, as well as using Bowmore and Loch Indaal as a base for its flying boats. Since the war ended, agriculture, fishing and whisky have remained Islay's largest industries, with tourism growing over recent years. Once the political centre of the region, life now continues on a quieter level. If present-day Islay is the centre of anything, it is whisky distilling.

GETTING THERE AND AWAY

BY FERRY CalMac (✆ 08000 665000 or, from outside the UK, +44 1475 650397; w calmac.co.uk; cars/foot passengers £34.40/6.90) sails from Kennacraig on the mainland to Port Askaig in the northeast and Port Ellen in the south five times daily in summer and around three times daily in winter. The journey takes 2 to 3 hours and can be cancelled/redirected in high wind. In summer you can travel between Islay and Colonsay or Oban once or twice a week or just to Colonsay once a week in winter. **Argyll and Bute Council** (✆ 01496 840681; w argyll-bute.gov.uk/port-askaig-islay-feolin-jura-ferry-timetable; cars/foot passengers £9.45/1.80) run a car and passenger ferry from Port Askaig on Islay to Feolin on Jura, every 30–60 minutes from 07.00 to 18.30 daily. No pre-bookings are necessary and you pay on the ferry, cash only.

MOORINGS
Islay Marine Centre Lagavulin; ✆ 01496 300129; w islay-marine-centre.com. Visitor moorings, chandlery & other facilities.
Port Askaig Pier Argyll & Bute Council; ✆ 01586 552552; w argyll-bute.gov.uk/ports-and-harbours/port-askaig-pier. Small harbour suitable for small boats.
Port Ellen Harbour Association Port Ellen; m 07464 151200; w portellenmarina.co.uk. Pontoons with electricity & facilities in showers.

GETTING AROUND

Islay is the third biggest island in the Inner Hebrides but, as the island's main roads take a more direct route and its main settlements are closer together, travelling around is significantly quicker than on either Skye or Mull. Taking a car is not essential as the bus network connects all of Islay's larger villages and ports.

BY BUS Argyll and Bute Council/Islay Coaches (☏ 01496 840273; w argyll-bute. gov.uk/isle-islay-portnahavenport-askaig-bowmore-port-ellen-ardbeg) runs the 450/451 service from Portnahaven/Port Askaig to Bowmore, Port Ellen and Ardbeg several times a day.

BY BIKE While the island is gently hilly, cycling is an unhurried way to see Islay, giving you access to some of its more remote attractions and, unless you get stuck in the ferry traffic, roads remain quiet enough to make it enjoyable.

Bike hire

ڼ **Bicycles for Hire** Port Charlotte PA48 7TU; ☏ 01496 850488. Opposite the Port Charlotte Hotel; day/extra day/week £15/10/75 paid in person or honesty box.

ڼ **Islay Cycles** 2 Corrsgeir Pl, Port Ellen PA42 7EJ; w islaycycles.co.uk; m 07760 196592; day/week £20/70.

CAR HIRE

🚗 **Islay Car Hire** ☏ 01496 810544; w islaycarhire.com. Supplies cars to airport & ferry terminals.

TAXI

🚗 **Bonnie Islay Taxi and Tour** m 07903 568724
🚗 **Bowmore Taxi Service** m 07899 756159

🚗 **Carol's Cabs** m 07775 782155
🚗 **Jim's Islay Taxi** m 07967 505991
🚗 **Lamb Taxi** m 07846 055399

HITCHHIKING Islay is a large island, but hitchhiking is usually very easy, safe and a good way to meet local people. During rainy walks along the road, there is a good chance that locals will stop to ask you if you want a lift, whether you put your thumb out or not.

ESTATES AND DEER STALKING

On the east side of Islay, the majority of the interior is split into several large estates. For the purposes of visitors, the estates offer self-catering accommodation, fishing permits and deer stalking on their lands. Deer stalking is traditional on Islay and remains an important part of the economy, with people visiting the island especially to take part.

Stalking generally takes place between July and February, during which time walkers should usually call the estates before walking across the hills or, in some cases, avoid doing so completely; signs giving specific instructions and phone numbers are usually attached to boundary gates. Accidentally disrupting stalking in progress is frustrating for gamekeepers and can be dangerous, so it is always best to call if you are unsure.

Some of the larger estates on Islay are: Ardtalla (w ardtallacottages.co.uk), Callumkill (w callumkill.com), Dunlossit (☏ 01496 840232; w dunlossitestate. com), Islay Estates (☏ 01496 810221; w islayestates.com) and Laggan (☏ 01496 810235; w lagganestate.com).

BOAT TRIPS AND WATERSPORTS

Islay Sea Adventures Lagavulin PA42 7DX; ☏ 01496 300129; w islay-sea-adventures.co.uk. Gus Newman has several small motorboats & offers tours for wildlife watching, Corryvrechan, fishing & foraging. Weather permitting, trips leave every day in summer.

Kayak Wild Islay Port Ellen PA42 7BY; m 07973 725456; w kayakwildislay.co.uk. Moving quietly through the water, kayaks are one of the best ways to see Islay's wildlife, coastline & hidden beaches.

Trips are weather permitting. Variety of Fat Bike routes to choose from, including riding along the beach.

GOLF

The Machrie PA42 7AN; ☏ 01496 302310; w campbellgrayhotels.com/machrie-islay-scotland/golf. Originally designed in 1891, the 18-hole links course has recently had a £40 million renovation & now has every facility you might desire.

WHISKY AND DISTILLERIES

Irish monks are probably responsible for first introducing the distilling process to Islay. The island is very rich in peat, ancient layers of partially decayed vegetation that forms in bogs and contains a lot of energy. Peatland is naturally a very efficient carbon sink, locking carbon dioxide out of the air in the same manner as a fossil fuel, and has been burnt on Islay for many generations. In remote locations you will notice that the water runs an orangey brown; this is also due to the peat. During whisky making, peat fires are used to dry malted barley, leaving a distinctive flavour. The peaty taste of whisky is calculated in ppm of phenol: Scottish whiskies generally have up to 30ppm; the Islay whiskies are often more than 50ppm.

In 1644, when the new Excise Act levied a tax on whisky, the operation went underground and illicit stills were hidden in remote corners of the island, in hidden coves and secret caves. The first official, recorded distillery was Bowmore, founded in 1779.

DISTILLERIES AND TOURS Today there are nine working distilleries on Islay, most of which are grand, whitewashed buildings with slate roofs, distinctive pointed pagoda chimneys and their names painted neatly in enormous black letters, allowing them to be identified from out at sea.

On the northeast are **Bunnahabhain** (page 226), **Ardnahoe** (page 226) and **Caol Ila** (page 225); **Bowmore** is central (page 224); **Bruichladdich** (page 235) and **Kilchoman** (page 237) are in the western Rhinns; and **Laphroaig** (page 231), **Lagavulin** (page 231) and **Ardbeg** (page 231) are along the southeast coast. All of these distilleries, apart from Caol Ila, run tours and tastings ranging from £5 for a quick look around (followed by a dram, of course) to a couple of hundred pounds for several hours of exploration and tasting some of the rarer expressions. Closed since 1983, Port Ellen has recently been bought by Diageo, one of the world's largest alcoholic drink producers, who are planning to reopen it soon.

You can also stock up on Islay whisky and other local spirits from Bowmore's Islay Whisky Shop (page 224). Look out for **High Road Rum** (⬛), who bought the old lemonade factory on the outskirts of Port Ellen and hope to be selling their new rum soon.

GUIDED WALKS

RSPB w rspb.org.uk. The RSPB runs 2 inexpensive weekly guided walks from Apr–Oct. For either, bring sturdy footwear, warm, waterproof clothing (coat & trousers) & binoculars if you have them. The first (🕐 10.00 Tue, meet at Upper Killeyan car park near the American Monument) is a circular route on the Oa with dramatic coastline & chances of seeing rare birds such as golden eagles or choughs, & feral goats & other species. There are no facilities at all on the Oa, so come prepared. The second (🕐 10.00 Thu, meet at Loch Gruinart Visitor Centre) explores Loch Gruinart woodland & moorland to see Islay's famous barnacle & Greenland white-fronted geese, as well as a great many other birds, hares, roe & red deer.

EVENTS

APRIL

Walk Islay Week w walkislay.co.uk. 8 organised walks across Islay, Jura & Colonsay, including 2 led by staff from the RSPB. They range from easy to strenuous & cover a wide variety of landscapes, including beaches, mountains & moorland, different types of geology & archaeology, & the hope of spotting exciting wildlife. £5/walk. Sensible hiking clothing & footwear is vital.

MAY

Fèis Ìle/Islay Festival of Music and Malt w islayfestival.com. Now intrinsically linked to whisky, Islay's fèis is the biggest in the Inner Hebrides. As well as the traditional cultural events, each distillery hosts an open day & visitors come from across the world to join the festivities. The island's accommodation gets booked-up well in advance.

JUNE

Islay Beach Rugby Port Ellen; [f]. Though cancelled in 2020, this will hopefully be up & running again in future years. Teams come across from other parts of Scotland to compete & socialise.

JULY

Cantilena Festival w cantilenafestival.co.uk. A week of chamber music in various venues across Islay.

JULY/AUGUST

Islay Half Marathon w islayhalfmarathon.co.uk

AUGUST

Islay Show Bridgend; w islayshow.co.uk. Agricultural Show.
Ride of the Falling Rain w rideofthefallingrain. net. Cycling race.

AUGUST/SEPTEMBER

Islay Book Festival w islaybookfestival.co.uk

SEPTEMBER

Islay Jazz Festival w islayjazzfestival.co.uk. Hosted by Lagavulin Distillery (page 231), this small festival sells out quickly with visitors coming to Islay especially to attend performances from a mix of creative jazz & blues musicians.
Islay Marathon w islaymarathon.co.uk

NOVEMBER

Islay Sessions w islaysessions.wordpress.com. Small folk festival.

BOWMORE, BRIDGEND AND THE NORTHEAST

Bowmore, Islay's capital, is surprisingly small. Its most striking features are the harbour and Kilarrow Church, which surveys the village from the top of the hill. Built in 1767, the building is circular – so the devil couldn't find corners to lurk in – and unique within the region. There are small villages at Bridgend, the junction between west, northeast and south; Ballygrant; Keills and at the ferry terminal at Port Askaig. The far north is wild and uninhabited with plentiful hiking and wildlife, but most people go to this part of Islay to visit Finlaggan, the ruined centre of the Lordship of the Isles, or one of the distilleries.

TOURIST INFORMATION For tourist information, visit **Bowmore iCentre** (The Square, Bowmore PA43 7JP; ☎01496 305165; ⏰ Apr–Jun 10.00–17.00 Mon–Sat, Jul & Aug 09.00–17.30 Mon–Sat, 10.00–16.00 Sun, Sep–Mar 10.00–15.00 Mon–Fri). Staff are friendly and helpful; there's also a small on-site shop.

🏠 **WHERE TO STAY** *Map, below, unless otherwise stated*

Though there are plenty of rather luxurious places to stay, this part of Islay is generally lacking in budget accommodation; look to the Rhinns (page 233) and around Port Ellen (page 227) for more affordable options.

✳ 🏠 **Islay House** [map, page 216] (11 rooms) Bridgend PA44 7PA; ☎01496 810287; w islayhouse.co.uk; ♿. Recently refurbished, but retaining its historic charm, Islay House is a Grade I-listed building, with origins in the 17th & 18th centuries. This impressive white & slate building came into existence when Sir Hugh Campbell of Cawdor first built a tower house, then

called 'Kilarrow House', in 1677. Daniel Campbell of Skipness & his family expanded the house in 1726 & moved the village of Kilarrow across Loch Indaal to form a new settlement: Bowmore. Plenty of original features remain, including a couple of ghosts. As a hotel, it is suitably luxurious with plenty of antlers & wonderful views of the gardens & loch beyond. Staff are welcoming,

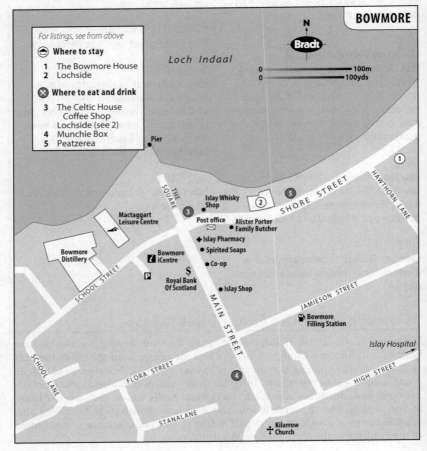

BOWMORE

For listings, see from above

⊖ **Where to stay**
1 The Bowmore House
2 Lochside

⊗ **Where to eat and drink**
3 The Celtic House
  Coffee Shop
  Lochside (see 2)
4 Munchie Box
5 Peatzerea

Loch Indaal

N

Pier

THE SQUARE

Islay Whisky Shop

3

2

5

SHORE STREET

HAWTHORN LANE

1

Mactaggart Leisure Centre

Post office ✉

Alister Porter Family Butcher

✚ Islay Pharmacy

Bowmore Distillery

🅿

ℹ Bowmore iCentre

$ Royal Bank Of Scotland

● Spirited Soaps

● Co-op

● Islay Shop

SCHOOL STREET

SCHOOL LANE

MAIN STREET

FLORA STREET

STANALANE

4

JAMIESON STREET

🅿 Bowmore Filling Station

Islay Hospital

HIGH STREET

✝ Kilarrow Church

0 —— 100m
0 —— 100yds

enthusiastic & more down-to-earth than you might imagine. Prices are heavily discounted in winter. **£££££**

🏠 **The Bowmore House** (5 rooms) Shore St; ☎ 01496 810324; **w** thebowmorehouse.co.uk. Set in an old bank building from 1898, this friendly B&B has large, comfortable rooms, 4 of which have sea views. Complimentary dram on arrival. **££££**

🏠 **Dha Urlar** [map, page 217] (4 rooms) Cruach PA43 7JQ; **m** 07967 505991; **w** dha-urlar-bed-and-breakfast.co.uk. In a peaceful location, 1 mile southwest of Bowmore, this welcoming B&B is surrounded by moorland with views of the Paps of Jura. Cosy guest lounge with wood burner. **££££**

🏠 **Lochside Hotel** (12 rooms) PA43 7LB; ☎ 01496 810244; **w** lochsidehotel.co.uk. Traditional Scottish interiors & great harbour views. **££££**

🏠 **Starchmill Pods** [map, page 216] (2 pods) High Rd, near Bridgend PA43 7LW; **m** 07494 173966; **w** starchmillpods.co.uk. An affordable self-catering option in a peaceful location off the 'High Rd' (B8016), which you'll need a car or bicycle to reach. 1 pod sleeps 4 & the other 6; 2-night min stay. **£–££**

WHERE TO EAT AND DRINK *Map, opposite, unless otherwise stated*

✕ **Lochside Hotel** (see above) ⏲ 19.00–01.00 daily. Dine in the conservatory with views over Bowmore Pier & Loch Indaal. Invalussa mussels from Mull are a popular choice. **££**

✕ **Peatzerea** 22 Shore St, Bowmore PA43 7LB; ☎ 01496 810810; **w** peatzeria.com; ⏲ noon–22.00 daily; ♿. Excellent pizza in a smart, modern restaurant with consistently friendly staff. **££**

☕ **Café Blasta** [map, page 216] Islay Gaelic Centre, P43 7LN; **m** 07585 699846; ⏲ Apr–Dec 10.00–15.30 daily, Jan–Apr 10.00–14.30 daily; ♿. Simple, good-value sandwiches & baked potatoes. Friendly service. Cash only. **£**

☕ **The Celtic House Coffee Shop** Shore St; ☎ 01496 810304; **w** theceltichouse.co.uk; ⏲ 10.00–16.30 daily. Quiet, friendly café, upstairs from the book & gift shop (see below). **£**

☕ **Labels** [map, page 216] Ballygrant PA45 7QL; ☎ 01496 840595; **f** Lynnlabels; ⏲ 09.00–16.30 Tue–Sat, 11.30–16.00 Sun; ♿. Owner Lynn is extremely friendly & fiercely down-to-earth; her café serves 'everything but chips', including paninis, cakes & coffee. **£**

☕ **Munchie Box** Main St, PA43 7JH; ☎ 01496 810669; ⏲ 08.00–14.00 Mon–Sat. Friendly, cheap takeaway food. **£**

SHOPPING
Arts and crafts
The Celtic House (see above) ⏲ 09.30–17.00. Bookshop, quality gifts & clothing.

C Hannett Jewellery On the road to Bunnahabhain PA46 7RB; **m** 07856 285290; **w** charlottehannett.co.uk; ⏲ noon–16.00/17.00 Tue–Sat. Charlotte sells her beautiful handmade silver, gold & platinum jewellery from this tiny workshop. She can also do repairs, remodelling & bespoke designs.

Islay Shop 47 Main St, Bowmore PA43 7JJ; ☎ 01496 810424; **w** theislayshop.com; ⏲ 09.30–17.00 Mon–Sat. An 'everything else' shop with stock ranging from make-up to lunch boxes.

Islay Woollen Mill Bridgend; ☎ 01496 810563; **w** islaywoollenmill.co.uk. Tweed designed & woven in-house. Their cloth designs have been used in films such as *Braveheart* & *Forrest Gump*.

Persabus Pottery PA46 7RB; ☎ 01496 840243; **w** persabus.co.uk; ⏲ flexible. Landscape, seascapes & floral design pottery, plus a small café.

Spirited Soaps Main St, Bowmore PA43 7HZ; ☎ 01496 810938; **w** spiritedsoaps.com; ⏲ 10.00–16.00 Mon & Wed–Fri, 10.00–14.00 Sat. Handmade transparent whisky soaps & toiletries using natural ingredients.

Food shops
There are a few great independent options for stocking up on either groceries or high-quality ingredients for special occasions. In addition to the shops listed below, look out for fresh free-range eggs along the High Rd & other small pop-up stalls selling local produce.

Alister Porter Family Butcher Bowmore PA43 7LB; ☎ 01496 810365; **f** A.S. Porter Family Butcher; ⏲ 08.00–17.00 Mon–Sat. Quality meat.

Bridgend Shop Bridgend PA44 7PQ; ☎ 01496 810335; **f**; ⏲ 08.00–19.00 Mon–Sat, 10.00–18.00 Sun. Grocery shop, much bigger than you might expect. Loose fruit & veg.

A turning off the A846, just 100yds north of Bridgend, leads to Islay House Square. First established by Walter Campbell in the 1790s, this large, open square is surrounded by the buildings that once housed servants working at nearby Islay House (page 222) and provided space for their workshops. Today it has an interesting collection of local businesses, including the **Islay Ales** brewery (01496 810014; w islayales.com; ⊕ Apr–Oct 10.00–17.30 Mon–Sat; Nov–Mar 10.00–16.00 Mon–Sat;), **Islay Quilters** (w islayquilters. org.uk; ⊕ 14.00–16.30 Mon–Fri, 11.00–16.30 Sat;), **Islay Gin Ltd Visitor Centre** (w islayginltd.com; ⊕ 11.00–16.00 Wed–Sat, noon–16.00 Sun), selling Islay-made Nerabus gin infused with Islay heather, **Eilzabeth Sykes Batiks** (01496 810147) and **MA MacKinnons Marmalade Shop** (01496 810695; ⊕ 10.30–16.30 Tue–Sat), which sells a lot more than marmalade.

Additionally, the **Toy Library** (01496 810450; w ijtoylibrary.co.uk; ⊕ 14.00–16.00 Mon–Fri) is a good option for families with limited luggage. You can borrow travel cots, highchairs and other children's necessities, but call ahead to check availability.

The turning for the square is just past Bridgend when heading northeast on the A846; the next left after the turning for Islay House itself.

Co-op Main St, Bowmore PA43 7JJ; 01496 810201; ⊕ 07.00–22.00 Mon–Sat, 10.00–19.30 Sun; . Biggest grocery store on the island.

Islay Oysters Craigens, Gruinart PA44 7PW; 01496 850256; ⊕ 13.00–16.00 Mon–Fri. Oysters grown on the east side of Loch Gruinart.

Islay Whisky Shop Shore St, Bowmore PA43 7LB; 01496 810684; w islaywhiskyshop. com; ⊕ 09.00–18.00 & 19.30–21.30 Mon–Sat, 12.30–17.00 Sun. Groceries & whisky.

Jean's Fresh Fish Jamieson St, Bowmore PA43 7HL; 01496 302609; ⊕ 09.00–16.30 Wed & Fri. Mobile fish van that visits Bowmore on Wed & Fri.

OTHER PRACTICALITIES

$ Bank Royal Bank of Scotland, Bowmore PA43 7JJ; 01496 810555; ⊕ 09.15–16.45 Mon–Tue & Thu–Fri, 09.30–16.45 Wed

Fuel Bowmore Filling Station, Jamieson St, Bowmore PA43 7HP (⊕ 08.00–17.30 Mon–Sat); Port Askaig Pump Stores, Port Askaig, PA46 7RD (ask at hotel if unattended)

＋ Hospital Islay Hospital, Gortonvogie Rd, Bowmore PA43 7JD; 01496 301000. Casualty Unit, GP, maternity, radiography, AHPs & community nursing.

Laundry Mactaggart Leisure Centre, School St, Bowmore PA43 7JS; 01496 810767; w mactaggartleisurecentre.co.uk; ⊕ Tue–Sun

＋ Pharmacy Islay Pharmacy, 42 Main St, Bowmore PA43 7JJ; 01496 301591; ⊕ 09.00–18.00 Mon & Wed–Fri, 09.00–13.00 Tue & Sat

✉ Post offices Ballygrant Village Hall, PA45 7QL (⊕ 09.30–11.30 Tue); Bowmore Shore St, PA43 7JH (⊕ 09.00–17.30 Mon–Sat); Bridgend PA44 7PQ (⊕ 09.00–17.30 Mon–Wed & Fri, 09.00–13.00 Thu & Sat)

WHAT TO SEE AND DO

Bowmore A simple Bowmore pleasure is strolling down to the end of the **pier**. This gives you an unusual perspective of the village and across Loch Indaal; there is occasionally a seal in the water or some small fishing boats.

You can also visit **Bowmore Distillery** (01496 810441; w bowmore.com; ⊕ Mar–Oct 09.30–18.00 Mon–Sat, noon–16.00 Sun, Nov–Feb 10.00–17.00 Mon–Sat; tours & tastings £10–130;), the oldest distillery on Islay, established in 1779 and home to the world's oldest whisky maturation warehouse. The distillery's bar,

Bowmore Whisky Tasting Bar (⊕ Mar–Oct 11.00–17.00 Mon–Sat, noon–15.30 Sun, Nov–Feb 11.00–16.30 Mon–Sat) is the perfect place to enjoy a special dram, with its fantastic view across Loch Indaal.

Around Bridgend
Heading along the coast northeast, you have lovely views over **Loch Indaal** and, in winter, many geese, before shortly reaching **Bridgend**. Easily bypassed completely, there is a short, circular walk around pretty **Bridgend Woods** from the village. It goes alongside the road via Nancy's Path in the direction of Bowmore for about 500yds, before turning off right into the mature woodland. You can follow the grassy track through tall trees down to the River Sorn, where you can either go left towards the loch or walk upstream back to the north end of the village. The woodland floor is stupendous for bluebells in spring.

Finlaggan
(w finlaggan.org; ⊕ open access; adult/concession/child over 12 £4/3/2) Just past Ballygrant, Finlaggan is the archaeological jewel in Islay's crown and one of the most important sites in western Scotland. Once the central power base for the Lords of the Isles (page 215), the small collection of ruined buildings here have a surreal location on the tiny islands of a loch. After crossing a wooden walkway over the water, visitors can wander around the ruins on **Eilean Mòr** (which means large island). The ruined buildings include the Lords' residence, the Great Hall and 14th-century chapel, as well as the remains of a stone jetty, food preparation area and grave slabs. Unusually for the Inner Hebrides, sites are well indicated and easily identifiable. There are no fences or cordoned-off areas, apart from the grave slabs which are protected with transparent perspex, and out of high season you are likely to have the place to yourself. There is an excellent, modern visitor centre (⊕ Apr–Oct 10.30–16.15 Mon–Sat), which is where you pay for your admission; if the centre is closed – put the money in the honesty box before the bridge.

This site seems to have been of high importance even before the Lords of the Isles. As you leave Finlaggan, notice the smooth, rounded **standing stone** of about 6ft. Mentioned by Martin Martin in 1695, it is thought to be one of a pair and, after a more recent geophysical survey, there is suggestion of it being part of a more complex 164ft-wide monument that has so far only been partially excavated.

North from Port Askaig
The ferry terminal at **Port Askaig** has an excellent view across to the Paps of Jura. From here you can travel further up the coast to the three distilleries: Caol Ila, Ardnahoe and Bunnahabhain. **Caol Ila** (✆ 01496 302769; w malts.com/en-gb/visit-our-distilleries/caol-ila) is not currently open for tours, but might be in the future.

TEACHING AN ISLAND TO SWIM

Although the 82ft pool at **Mactaggart Leisure Centre** (School St, Bowmore PA43 7JS; ✆ 01496 810767; w mactaggartleisurecentre.co.uk; ⊕ 09.00–20.30 Tue–Thu; 09.00–19.30 Fri; 10.00–17.30 Sat–Sun) might not look like much, it means a lot to the community. Growing up on an island without being able to swim is unthinkable, but up until the 1980s young Ìleachs had to take their lessons in the sea. In 1981 the Islay Swimming Pool Association was formed, Bowmore Distillery allowed them to use an empty building, and large sums of money were donated in order to finish the pool in 1990. Interestingly, the pool is kept warm with waste heat from the distillery next door.

Ardnahoe Distillery (✆ 01496 301430; w ardnahoedistillery.com; ⊕ 10.00–15.45 daily; tours & tastings £10–150; ♿) Established in 2018, Ardnahoe is Islay's newest distillery, established by the Scottish blenders and bottlers Hunter Laing. As Ardnahoe's first single malt will not be released for some time, its tastings focus on Hunter Laing's single cask bottlings from different regions of Scotland. The distillery is distinctly modern in its exterior appearance, though traditional techniques and equipment are used in the process. Tours provide an insight on Ardnahoe's use of unusual 'Worm Tub Condensors' in the production process. The on-site Illicit Still café (£) has a panoramic view across to the Paps of Jura.

Bunnahabhain and around (✆ 01496 840557; w bunnahabhain.com; ⊕ Apr–Oct 09.00–17.00 Mon, Wed, Fri & Sat, 09.00–19.00 Tue & Thu, 11.00–16.00 Sun, Nov–Mar 10.00–16.00 Mon–Sat, noon–16.00 Sun; tours & tastings £5–250) One of Islay's traditional distilleries, Bunnahabhain was established in the late 19th century and is known for its delicate, fresh-tasting whisky. Tour options include straight from the cask tastings of non-peated and peated drams, a chance to buy and fill your own bottle, and relaxed walks around the distillery with its views across the Sound of Islay.

From Bunnahabhain, you can walk just over 4 miles north along the coast to the elegant **Rhuvaal Lighthouse**. Most of the route has a grassy track, but you should go fully prepared for a day hike with an OS map (Explorer: 353 *Islay North*) for route finding. The whole walk has great views of Jura's wild and uninhabited west coast; there are deer and wild goats in the area, and you should keep an eye out for porpoises and dolphins in the Sound of Islay.

Killinallan Over on the northwest coast, Killinallan has a beautiful, seemingly endless beach. It is signposted from just east of Loch Gruinart Nature Reserve on the B8017. If you have a car, you can park it after Craigens Farm, at the end of the road just before a gate. From there, the beach is only 400yds north; starting out a little muddy on the banks of Loch Gruinart, it gets increasingly lovely towards Killinallan Point about a mile further north. Alternatively, a circular 7-mile walk from the car park begins by following the track past Killinallan Farm, heading northeast for 3 miles towards the abandoned settlement at Gortantaoid. You can then cut across to the beach just before the buildings and walk back to the start along 4 miles of sand.

Glorious in sunshine, this is a very exposed stretch in high winds, but good for beachcombing and watching seabirds. Cattle and bulls are usually kept here, so it might be more relaxing to walk along the beach rather than the track if you have a dog with you.

PORT ELLEN, THE OA AND THE SOUTHEAST

With picturesque white houses around a sandy bay, Port Ellen is Islay's second village. It is best known for its distillery, which is currently closed, making undrunk bottles extremely valuable. The village also has its own ferry terminal and is the start of the 'Three Distilleries Path'. To the southwest is the Oa Peninsula, with Islay's most spectacular cliffs and coastline, eagles, wild goats and an RSPB reserve. In the opposite direction, heading northeast from Port Ellen, the road becomes incrementally worse until it dwindles to nothing at Ardtalla.

WHERE TO STAY *Map, below, unless otherwise stated*

Some of Islay's most upmarket accommodation options are found in the south, but there are also quite a few B&Bs in Port Ellen and plenty of excellent, often remote, self-catering properties.

🏠 **The Islay Hotel** (13 rooms) Charlotte St, PA42 7DF; 📞 01496 300109; **w** theislayhotel. com; ♿. Comfortable bedrooms, luxury en-suite bathrooms & sea views. The 'Platinum' room has a jacuzzi bath. **£££££**

🏠 **The Machrie Hotel & Golf Links** [map, page 217] (47 rooms) Port Ellen PA42 7AN; 📞 01496 302310; **w** campbellgrayhotels.com/ machrie-islay-scotland; ♿. The most obviously luxurious hotel on Islay. Along with the golf course (page 220), it has a gym, sauna & spa. Views across the golf course & out to Laggan Bay. **£££££**

🏠 **Glenegedale House** [map, page 217] (4 rooms) Opposite the airport, PA42 7AS; 📞 01496 300400; **w** glenegedalehouse.co.uk. More personal than a hotel, this is a luxury B&B with every detail carefully considered: wallpaper is hand-printed in Glasgow, soft furnishings have touches of Islay Woollen Mill tweed & afternoon

tea is served on day of arrival. Great pride & care goes into ethically sourced dinner options, including local seafood platters. There is plenty of accommodation in this price bracket on Islay, but few offer quite such good value. **££££**

🏠 **The Trout Fly** (4 rooms) 8 Charlotte St, PA42 7DF; 📞 01496 302608; **w** troutfly-islay. co.uk. This friendly B&B has modern bedrooms, a communal dining/sitting room with TV & good information about Islay. Right at the bottom of this price range. **£££**

🏠 **Tigh Cargaman** (2 cottages) PA42 7BX; 📞 01496 302345; **w** selfcateringislay. com. Originally built for the manager of Port Ellen Distillery, Tigh Cargaman is a handsome self-catering house in extensive gardens with a small woodland of broad-leaved trees hosting a rookery. 2 small, simple & very affordable self-catering cottages, the Stables & Old Cottage, are

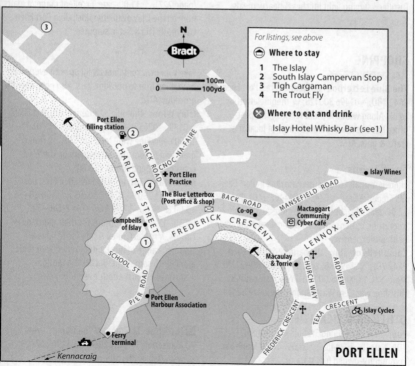

For listings, see above

🛏 **Where to stay**
1   The Islay
2   South Islay Campervan Stop
3   Tigh Cargaman
4   The Trout Fly

✖ **Where to eat and drink**
Islay Hotel Whisky Bar (see1)

PORT ELLEN

← Kennacraig

positioned in grounds with full use of the huge lawn overlooking the sea. Peaceful location, opposite Kilnaughton Bay & 5mins' walk from Port Ellen. 2-night min stay. ££

⚊ Kintra Camping [map, page 217] Kintra Farm, PA42 7AT; ☎01496 302051; w kintrafarm.co.uk; ⊕ May–Sep. On the dunes beside Laggan Bay, this is no-nonsense wild camping, with water taps, unisex disabled toilet & hot shower facilities. Both location & price are hard to beat. £

⚊ South Islay Campervan Stop Port Ellen Filling Station, PA42 7DF; ☎01496 302443. Facilities & accommodation for motorhomes. Also available for day guests. £

Weekly rental

⌂ Ardtalla Farmhouse [map, page 217] (sleeps 5) Ardtalla PA42 7EE; w ardtallacottages.

co.uk/accommodation/ardtalla-farmhouse. Without electricity, let alone Wi-Fi, Ardtalla is a perfect 'digital detox'. It has its own library with ancient books, a Rayburn for cooking & hot water, & gas lamps for evening lighting. The farm is at the end of a long & terribly maintained track; there are farm animals & a deserted beach is 10mins' walk away. £650/week.

⌂ The Dower House [map, page 217] (2 properties) Kildalton PA42 7EF; ☎01496 300038; w dowerhouseislay.com. 140-year-old house with a beach at the bottom of the garden. Split in 2 halves: one side (sleeps 8) is luxurious self-catering; the other is a small, accessible flat (sleeps 2; &.), owned by my parents. Various dogs, chickens & cat on site. House/flat £1,500/500/week.

✗ WHERE TO EAT AND DRINK

⚏ Old Kiln Café [map, page 217] Ardbeg PA42 7EA; ☎01496 302244; w ardbeg.com; ⊕ Jan–Oct 10.00–16.00 daily, Nov & Dec 10.00–16.00 Mon–Thu. High-ceilinged, modern café inside Ardbeg Distillery, serving light lunches & hearty meals. £–££

⚏ Cake at the Cross [map, page 216] Kildalton PA42 7EF. Honesty box coffee & cake next to Kildalton Cross. £

♇ Islay Hotel Whisky Bar [map, page 227] (page 227) ⊕ 11.00–late. Excellent range of malts from all the Islay distilleries, including Port Ellen. Live music Thu & Sat in summer.

SHOPPING

Arts and crafts

The Blue Letterbox 66 Fredrick Cres, Port Ellen PA42 7BD; ☎01496 300123; w theblueletterbox. co.uk. Along with the usual services, this post office has a carefully curated range of local arts, crafts & gifts. ATM.

Food shops

There is a small **Co-op supermarket** in Port Ellen (75 Frederick Cres; ☎01496 302446; ⊕ 07.00–22.00 daily; &.), but there are more sustainable & interesting options supporting the local economy; neither is expensive.

Campbells of Islay 19 Charlotte St, Port Ellen PA42 7DF; ☎01496 302264; ◼; ⊕ 08.30–21.00 Mon–Sat, 13.00–18.00 Sun. Previously Lauries, this shop was 'Zero Waste' before the craze began.

Take your own containers & fill up with everything from dried fruit to porridge oats. Also newsagent & groceries. ATM.

Islay Wines Dunollie, Mansfield Rd, Port Ellen; ☎01496 302353; w islaywines.com; ⊕ 10.00–18.00 daily. Free wine tastings. Scottish fruit & grain wines from 'the only winery on the West Coast of Scotland'. Bottles £3.80.

Macaulay & Torrie 102 Frederick Cres, Port Ellen PA42 7BQ; ☎01496 302053; ⊕ 08.30–13.00 & 14.00–17.30 Mon–Tue & Thu–Sat, 08.30–13.00 Wed. Famous for their giant, dirty carrots, Mrs MacCauley & Mrs Torrie have a seasonal range of local, unpackaged vegetables along with some other basics & a random assortment of just about everything else.

OTHER PRACTICALITIES

Fuel Port Ellen Filling Station, Charlotte St, PA42 7DF; ☎01496 302443; ⊕ 08.00–17.30 Mon–Sat. Community-owned fuel station.

▤ Internet Mactaggart Community Cyber Café, 30 Mansfield Pl, Port Ellen; ☎01496 302693; w www.islaycybercafe.co.uk; ⊕ variable

✚ Medical Port Ellen Practice, Geirhilda, Back Rd; 📞01496 302103; 🕐 08.00–18.00 Mon–Tue & Thu–Fri, 08.00–13.00 Wed

✉ Post office The Blue Letterbox (see opposite)

WHAT TO SEE AND DO

Port Ellen Sheltered in every direction apart from the southwest, Port Ellen has a perfect, horseshoe-shaped harbour, traditional cottages lining the bay and two lovely beaches. It's worth making time to walk the Three Distilleries Path while here (page 231).

Ardbeg to Ardtalla The road north from Ardbeg is a fun route to cycle. The beach at Loch an t-Sàilein, with its stretching skerries and tiny islets, is also known as **Seal Bay** for immediately obvious reasons. Along with Portnahaven (page 237) it is among the best places on Islay for *almost* guaranteed sightings of common seals. Depending on the tide, they are usually either lazing on the rocks or bobbing around in the sea. Unfortunately this beach collects a lot of rubbish from the tide, so if you have a car, please pick some up and dispose of it responsibly.

Around 4½ miles from Ardbeg, down a short road on the right-hand side, is the famous **Kildalton Cross**; part of the Iona group of ring crosses, with the only other examples being the three on Iona itself (page 184). Combining Irish, Pictish and Northumbrian features, it is carved with intricate reliefs including interlacing spirals, serpents, lions and birds, as well as biblical scenes: Mary, Jesus and angels together, David killing the lion, Cain murdering his brother Abel with the jawbone of an ass or camel, and Abraham preparing to sacrifice Isaac; all rather weathered. In common with those on Iona, it dates from the second half of the 8th century. The small ruined chapel here was built in the 12th or early 13th century, but has been subsequently restored. There are also around 17 West Highland grave slabs both inside the church and around the graveyard, showing Kildalton's importance from Early Christian times to the medieval period.

A little further along the road archaeology enthusiasts can walk through the field down to the shore and find a **vitrified fort** at Trudernish Point (✦ 55°42'04"N 6°01'54"W). Look out for otters among the rocks and seaweed. Just a little further is **Claggain Bay**, a long, peaceful pebbly beach in the shadow of Beinn Bheigier, Islay's highest hill.

From the north end of Claggain, a substantial track leads much of the way up 1,610ft **Beinn Bheigier**. Though it does not sound particularly high, there are stunning views from here across the whole island and out to Jura. The easiest route

---

THE LOST VILLAGE OF SOLAM

With use of an OS map (Explorer: 353 *Islay North*), you can walk up the track opposite the turning to Ardbeg Distillery (page 231) to find the traces of a township called Solam. According to legend, it was abandoned in the 18th century as a result of an outbreak of the plague. Shipwrecked sailors are thought to have brought the disease; leaving the villagers a pearl necklace as a thank you for their kindness and thus infecting them all. The wider community brought food for the villagers and left it on a rock to avoid infection. Once the food was no longer being eaten, the settlement was burned down. Callumkill Estate (see box, page 219), who now own the land, ask that you avoid walking there between mid-August and mid-February, while deer stalking is taking place.

down is to return the same way you came up; with proper equipment and navigation tools you can hike from the top down the northern slopes instead and then along old tracks above the coast to the old shepherds' cottage at **Proaig Bay**, now a bothy. From here, more serious adventurers can continue as far as the remote lighthouse at **McArthur's Head**, constructed in 1861 and automated 108 years later. This is unforgiving boggy terrain, with a bad reputation for ticks and adders. The walk can be dangerous in bad weather, so proper research and preparation is required (page 34). You would most likely have to camp somewhere. Keep an eye out for any instructional signs from Ardtalla Estate relating to deer stalking (see box, page 219) in the area.

Back on the 'main road' near Claggain Bay, you can continue north to the wild beach and skerries near the end of the road at **Ardtalla**. The road is so terribly surfaced that it is probably better to leave your car in the car park at the north end of Claggain Bay before making the final half a mile on foot. Before you reach the farmhouse, cut across the second field diagonally and walk down towards the sea, where there is a lovely, if rather seaweed-covered, beach with rocky islets offshore, resident swans and rock pools full of little fish and prawns at low tide. This secluded stretch of coastline provides a valuable marine habitat with lush kelp forests hidden under the water; look out for seals, otters and bottlenose dolphins, which pass occasionally.

West from Port Ellen
Pleasant and sandy **Kilnaughton Bay**, west of Port Ellen, is barely outside of the village. It looks back towards Port Ellen and out to **Carraig Fhada**, an attractive, square lighthouse built in 1832. It's possible to walk out and right around it, or turn off the track to the right just before the lighthouse along a path signposted for '**Singing Sands**', which is a short walk away. This perfect spot, with protruding lumps of rock emerging from the yellow sand, is a favourite with wild goats and otters. It is a lovely, sometimes sheltered, place for family picnics and diverting streams, so take along a couple of spades if you have children.

The Oa
My personal favourite part of Islay, the Oa Peninsula has spectacular cliffs, beautiful beaches and unique wildlife. The OS map for this area (Explorer: 352 *Islay South*) will help you find some of the more remote beaches.

The **RSPB reserve**, which covers the most southwesterly half of the Oa, was originally set up to preserve choughs, a type of crow with red legs; now that there are only 50 breeding pairs left in Scotland this work is more important than ever. More dramatic inhabitants are the birds of prey: golden eagles, especially in spring and summer, hen harriers and peregrine. Autumn and winter are a good time to see twite. A marked, 2-mile circular walk from the RSPB car park at Upper Killeyan visits the **American Monument** (page 218) and then follows the cliffs to the east, before heading north to return. Dogs should be kept on leads and greater care should be taken to stick to paths between March and June when ground-nesting birds are breeding.

You can also walk down to the spectacular rocky beach at **Port nan Gallan**, with the dramatic backdrop of cliffs and a slender waterfall. Beware, the path down is quite steep.

Like a scene from a fantasy novel, **Lower Killeyan Beach** has towering rocks emerging from the sea and seals sleeping on skerries. There is a small parking area at the settlement of the same name; the beach is less than a mile northwest.

The standing stone **Carragh Bhan** (✪ 55°39'00"N 6°14'54"W) stands on the west side of the road that leads to Kintra and, according to tradition, marks the grave of

King Godred Crovan who died in 1095, in exile from the Isle of Man. At the end of the road is Kintra Farm; go through the gate on the right to find the small car park (do not park in the farmyard). From here you can walk a couple of minutes down to **Laggan Bay** or 'The Big Strand'. Backed by dunes and machair, this windswept beach stretches 8 miles north and is the longest beach on Islay. It also collects a lot of plastic, so if you have a car, please take some away with you and dispose of it properly.

Three Distilleries Path

Distance: 4 miles; time: 2 hours, but allow all day to visit the distilleries; start: Port Ellen; end: Ardbeg; OS Explorer map: 352 Islay South; &

This easy walk, which visits the distilleries of Laphroaig, Lagavulin and Ardbeg, can be co-ordinated with the bus schedule; you could also choose to cycle or allow extra time to hitchhike back. There is an ongoing joke that this path is surfaced better than the car road; although it has been built to be accessible for someone using a wheelchair, note that there are steeper sections where some assistance might be required.

Start in the east of Port Ellen, pass the Co-op on your left and then take the left-hand turning just before Macaulay & Torrie's shop to go up the hill, passing the school. You will find the path (signposted) shortly afterwards on the right-hand side of the road. It meanders along the coastline, with rewarding views even for those who are not whisky enthusiasts.

After around 1½ miles, **Laphroaig** (☏ 01496 302418; w laphroaig.com; ⊕ 09.30–17.00 daily; tours & tastings £10–110), pronounced 'la-froyg', is the first distillery you will come to. Founded in 1815, Laphroaig is the only distillery in Scotland to hold the 'Royal Warrant', and uses traditional process methods such as floor maltings, hand-cut peat and a cold smoking process. The distillery offers a range of tours and tastings, ranging from 1 hour around the distillery with three whiskies to try afterwards, to a more extensive 'water to whisky' excursion, which includes a tour of the distillery, picnic lunch and a walk to visit the distillery water source and peat banks (Apr–Sep; adults only). You can also just pop into Laphroaig Lounge (⊕ 10.30–16.30 daily) for a dram.

A little further on is the small settlement and distillery of **Lagavulin** (☏ 01496 302749; w malts.com/en-row/our-whisky-collection/lagavulin; ⊕ May–Sep 09.15–18.00 Mon–Fri, 09.15–17.00 Sat & Sun, Mar, Apr & Oct 09.15–17.00 daily, Nov–Feb 10.15–16.00 Mon–Sat; tours & tastings £8–35). Traditional in appearance and one of Islay's oldest distilleries, Lagavulin officially dates from 1816, but it is thought that, like in many remote spots in the Hebrides, illicit distilling was carried out on the site from as early as 1742. The modern distillery is owned by the British multinational company Diageo, who also own Caol Ila (page 225). Lagavulin is known for its full-bodied, smoky tasting whisky, rich in the peaty flavours that Islay is famous for.

Continuing a little further along a section of the route with no pavement, you will notice a turning to the right, just as you come out of the village. This steep side road leads down 500yds to the remains of **Dunyvaig Castle**. Standing on a rocky promontory, overlooking the sea, this strategically defensive spot was the namesake and stronghold of the MacDonalds of Dunyvaig intermittently from the end of the 14th century. It is a curious and overgrown ruin, surrounded by small, pebbly beaches, with an excellent view back to Lagavulin across the bay.

Returning to the path that follows the main road, it is a further half a mile to reach the final distillery of the walk: **Ardbeg** (☏ 01496 302244; w ardbeg.com; ⊕ Apr–Oct

09.30–17.00 daily, Nov–Mar 09.30–17.00 Mon–Fri; tours & tastings £5–130; ♿). From the Gaelic An Àird Bheag, meaning 'a small promontory', Ardbeg Distillery is an extensive collection of attractive white buildings. It produces distinctly smoky whiskies, known for their light and complex flavours, which have won a range of awards including *Whisky Magazine*'s 'World's Best Single Malt Whisky' for their Galileo expression at the World Whiskies Awards in 2013.

From Ardbeg, you can either hitchhike, walk or catch a bus back to Port Ellen, or continue along the ever-deteriorating road north. If you are walking back in the evening, look out for owls and bats.

🚶 Abandoned settlements and Soldier's Rock

Distance: 5 miles; time: 4 hours; start/end: Kintra; OS Explorer map: 352 Islay South

This triangular walk starts on a good track and visits the ruined settlements of Frachdale, Ghrasdail and Tockmal; the path eventually dwindles to lumpy grassland as it approaches the coast. The majestic Soldier's Rock sea stack is just part of the dramatic scenery to be found as the route follows the rough coastline in this part of north Oa.

Walk along a track from the car park that initially heads west towards the sea before it curves around to the left; follow it in a generally southerly direction for roughly a mile until you reach the ruins at **Frachdale**. Once bustling with communities living off its fertile lands, the Oa was cleared in the 1860s. This is the remains of a farmstead; the curious round building on the eastern side is a kiln (⊕ 55°38'29.7"N 6°15'59.3"W).

The track turns a corner here and runs roughly west, through a gate and then begins to disintegrate as the next set of ruins comes into view. Head towards the ruins; you will come to another kiln (⊕ 55°38'43.0"N 6°17'00.2"W), this one thought to have been used for lime and now overgrown with heather and nettles inside, though it is well preserved, like a rocky igloo. This first set of buildings is thought to have been called Cnoc Mor Ghrasdail, with Grasdale some 700yds up ahead, towards the sea, and Tockmal across from it on the other side of the valley to the south. Take some time to look around the ruins of the first settlements, before continuing to Grasdale where the path dwindles away to almost nothing. From there, it is easy to walk the 300yds across the small valley to reach Tockmal.

Some 40yds east of Tockmal is a large boulder with cup markings (⊕ 55°38'37.1"N 6°17'25.5"W), small bored holes thought to have been from prehistoric times, but of unknown purpose. From **Tockmal**, head about 150yds northwest to a pile of stones that show where a small chapel once stood, of which very little remains. Cross the stream around this point and find the easiest sheep path down through the valley, following the stream northwest towards the sea. Look out for choughs and golden eagles as you pick your way through the heather and grassy tussocks, and in summer you can admire the orchids.

Less than a mile from Tockmal, the stream begins to hurtle down a chasm into the sea. Cross carefully where you can find a sensible option (⊕ 55°38'52.5"N 6°18'06.5"W) and walk a few yards around the coast to the south to see the towering sea stack of Soldier's Rock. There are guillemots and fulmars nesting on the cliffs here around May and June, along with shags on rocks further out and the possibility of spotting basking sharks or porpoises. The coastline is a splintered series of grassy pinnacles, natural arches and towering cliffs of pink and white Dalradian schist, colonised by thrift and lichens.

To return to Kintra, you can follow the coast north and then east, keeping the sea on your left. Intermittent goat trails will help you along the way and you have a good chance of bumping into a herd. The going is rough and boggy in places, with clumps of willow to find your way through and plenty of bracken. After about a mile and a half you will come to a couple of beautiful sandy beaches, good places to stop for your picnic. Following the higher ground, you should come across a sporadic gravel track, which eventually leads you back to the more substantial track you started the walk on.

THE WEST

The Rhinns Peninsula, Islay's western lung, is an undeniably picturesque part of the island with arguably some of the best beaches. The Rhinns are a delight for archaeology enthusiasts and could be a good starting place for anyone searching for their Ìleach ancestors. **Port Charlotte** is the main hub, with good provisions for visitors as well as a thriving local community. It is considered to be the most attractive village on the island (although I would make an argument for Portnahaven), and it is probably the best base for budget travellers.

WHERE TO STAY   *Map, page 217*
Most of Islay's affordable accommodation options are in this part of the island.

🏠 **Port Charlotte Hotel** (10 rooms) Port Charlotte PA48 7TU; 📞 01496 850360; w portcharlottehotel.co.uk. Right on the seafront, with tastefully traditional Scottish finishings & luxurious bathrooms. **£££££**

🏠 **Anchorage B&B** (4 rooms) Bruichladdich PA49 7UN; 📞 01496 850540; w theanchorage. squarespace.com. Built 200 years ago by a sea captain, at a time when rich merchants came to Islay to play golf on the Strand, this well-kept white building looks over Loch Indaal. Owners are friendly locals & good people to ask about the area. Cosy living room has open fire. Option of small self-catering wooden cabin outside (sleeps 2/3). **££**

❋ 🏠 **Loch Gruinart House** (4 rooms) Gruinart PA44 7PW; 📞 01496 850212; w lochgruinart.co.uk. Catherine & Jack, who also works for the RSPB, run this down-to-earth bed & 'get your own breakfast'. It is a smart, white building at the head of Loch Gruinart & within the

boundaries of the nature reserve. A great option for birdwatchers, outdoor people & anyone on a budget who would like a private room. Jack makes fresh bread every morning & is a wealth of information. **££**

🏠 **Port Charlotte Youth Hostel** (30 beds) Port Charlotte PA48 7TX; 📞 01496 850385; w hostellingscotland.org.uk/hostels/port-charlotte-islay; ⏱ end Mar–Sep. Housed in a former distillery warehouse, this Hostelling Scotland accommodation is the only one of its type on Islay & thankfully great. Near a beach, with views out to sea, it has large communal areas & kitchen, board games & laundry. Karl & Lorna have been running the hostel for 12 years & are friendly & helpful. **£**

⛺ **Port Mòr Centre & Campsite** Port Charlotte PA47 7UE; 📞 01496 850441; w islandofislay. co.uk; ⏱ Mar–Nov; ♿. Modern & well-equipped community-owned campsite with access near to the shore for people using wheelchairs. **£**

WHERE TO EAT AND DRINK   *Map, page 217*
✕ **Lochindaal Hotel** Main St, Port Charlotte PA48 7TX; 📞 01496 850202; w lochindaalhotel. co.uk; ⏱ Mar–Oct noon–01.00 daily, mid-Oct–Feb 15.00–01.00 daily. Excellent local seafood platters. Rare & unusual whiskies. **£££**

✕ **Port Charlotte Hotel** (see above) ⏱ noon–14.00 & 17.00–20.30. Choose between bar meals or à la carte. Light conservatory with view of Port Charlotte Lighthouse. Favourites include local

scallops & salt marsh lamb. Live traditional Scottish music every Wed & Sun. **£££**

✕ **Port Mòr Centre Community Café** South of Port Charlotte PA48 7UE; 📞 01496 850121; w port-mor-community-cafe.co.uk; ⏱ Mar–Nov 10.00–14.30 Mon–Thu, 10.00–19.30 Fri–Sun; ♿. Good-value, tasty food such as haddock & chips or steak pie. **£**

SHOPPING
Arts and crafts

Outback Art Gallery Sanaigmore; **f**. Wonderful art gallery in a remote location, also serves hot drinks & cake. **£**

Tormisdale Croft Crafts South of Kilchiaran PA48 7UE; ☏01496 860239; ⏲ Feb–Nov 09.30–17.00 daily. Hand-spun wool & knitwear, plus staghorn sticks.

Food shops

Mini Market Bruichladdich PA49 7UN; ⏲ 09.00–18.00 Mon–Sat, 11.00–18.00 Sun. A little of everything including groceries & small café.

Port Charlotte Store Main St, Port Charlotte PA48 7TL; ☏01496 850232; **f**; ⏲ 09.00–17.30 Mon–Sat, 12.30–15.00 Sun; **♿**. Groceries & bakery.

OTHER PRACTICALITIES

Fuel Port Charlotte (see below)

✚ Medical The Rhinns Medical Centre, Port Charlotte PA48 7UD; ☏01496 850210; ⏲ 08.00–18.00 Mon–Wed & Fri, 08.00–13.00 Thu

✉ Post office Mini market, Bruichladdich (see above); 23 Shore St, Portnahaven PA47 7SH (⏲ 10.00–noon Mon); 10 Main St, Port Charlotte (⏲ 08.30–17.30 Mon–Tue & Thu–Fri, 09.00–12.30 Wed, 08.30–14.30 Sat)

WHAT TO SEE AND DO

Port Charlotte Port Charlotte is a pretty village made up of several terraces of traditional white cottages overlooking Loch Indaal. You cannot fail to notice the lovely **Port Charlotte Lighthouse**, but there are a couple of less obvious attractions.

Islay Nature Centre (Main St, PA48 7TX; ☏01496 850288; **w** islaynaturalhistory. org; ⏲ Apr–Sep 10.00–16.00 Mon–Fri; adult/child/concession/family £3.50/2/2.50/8, valid for 1 week) Run by the Islay Natural History Trust, this small but informative centre is of interest to both adults who wish to know more about Islay's natural heritage and children, who might enjoy the fish tanks with various rock pool creatures and the owl pellets filled with tiny bones that they are allowed to dissect and examine.

Museum of Islay Life ✳ (PA48 7UA; ☏ 01496 850358; **w** islaymuseum.org; ⏲ May–Sep 10.30–16.30 Mon–Sat, 13.00–16.30 Sun, Apr & Oct 10.30–16.30 Mon–Fri; adult/child/concession/family £4/1/3/8) Housed in the restored Kilchoman Free Church, which was bought in 1976 for £100 and restored by the community, the Museum of Islay Life is a treasure trove of archaeological artefacts and historical information.

I had expected to find a cramped and dusty ensemble of traditionally dressed mannequins with threadbare eyebrows and gormless expressions, the men holding scythes and the women sat down sewing, but I was very much mistaken. With 3,000 objects and 5,000 photos, the carefully selected exhibits are arranged in a logical and eye-pleasing manner. There are sections for a late 19th-century croft house, a well-to-do Victorian bedroom and tools. A substantial exhibit on the tragic US shipwrecks *Otranto* and *Tuscania* includes both ships' bells, which were recovered by divers.

Toothache Stone (⊕ 55°44'23"N 6°24'36"W) Of unknown antiquity, the Toothache Stone is found in a small valley below the pump house at the back of Port Charlotte, about 1½ miles from the village. You will know you are approaching the right place when you notice a small white shed, which is located some yards behind the rock itself. Toothache sufferers are said to have gone (or maybe go?) to visit this boulder and hammer nails into the cracks on its surface. Whether effective or not, the action must have been cathartic as there are countless rusty nails jammed into every perceivable crack. Some recent coins are also stuck into the rock but, as nails rust quickly and eventually disappear, it is difficult to tell how long this site has been used.

Bruichladdich and around
In the small township of Bruichladdich is **Bruichladdich Distillery** (✆ 01496 850190; w bruichladdich.com; tours & tastings £5–£25). Bruichladdich distills three single malts: an unpeated Bruichladdich, the heavily peated Port Charlotte and the super heavily peated Octomore, as well as The Botanist (w thebotanist.com) dry gin, which is made using 22 locally hand-foraged botanicals.

A little further, above the main A847 road, at **Uiskentuie** (⊕ 55°47'15"N 6°19'06"W) is a gigantic, 9ft-tall standing stone presiding over Loch Indaal. It is visible for miles around, but its original purpose isn't known; a navigation tool is one seemingly sensible suggestion. If you want to look more closely, there is easy parking on the A847 across from a building with a caved-in roof, and a gate in the fence for access.

West of Loch Gruinart
RSPB reserve at Loch Gruinart
(✆ 01496 850505; w rspb.org.uk/reserves-and-events/reserves-a-z/loch-gruinart; visitor centre ⊕ 10.00–17.00 daily; ♿) This RSPB reserve is 6 square miles and includes a working farm. Cows and sheep are used to manage the land, demonstrating how farming and wildlife can coexist successfully; choughs, for example, rely on cowpats in order to find worms to eat. Roughly a third of the reserve comprises farmland; the rest is mostly heather moorland with an additional square mile of mudflats and salt marsh. It is a rewarding place to visit at any time of year, but especially in late April and May when the corncrakes are making their distinctive calls.

Towards the end of October, tens of thousands of barnacle geese and thousands of Greenland white-fronted geese fly in from further north and rest on the mudflats before dispersing elsewhere. Around this time, whooper swans and Brent geese also drop by on their way from Iceland to Ireland. Autumn is a good time to see birds of prey such as hen harriers, sparrowhawks, merlin and peregrine. You can still see the geese throughout winter, especially in the evening as they come back to roost on the flats. Looking out from the bird hide between flooded fields, you can spot exotic-looking ducks such as teal, goldeneye and shoveler.

In spring, all the animals are having young. Roe and red deer are raised on the reserve as well as young wading birds and hen harriers. Lapwings and redshanks dive-bomb intruders to keep them away from their nests. By late summer, the migrating birds are ready to leave again. The **visitor centre** has more information and there is wheelchair access from the car park to a viewing platform over the reserve.

Kilnave Chapel
In a desolate location, overlooking the sands of Killinallan, Kilnave Chapel dates from the 12th century. The MacLeans are thought to have been burnt to death here by the MacDonalds after the Battle of Traigh Gruineart in 1598. The chapel is more or less complete, apart from the roof, and there are several interesting artefacts around the site. Missing part of its arms and so thin that it seems likely that it'll be worn away completely by the rain over the next few hundred years, the 8th-century **Kilnave Cross** is older than Kildalton Cross by around half a century, but still impressive and decorated with patterns on its

eastern side. By the door of the chapel is a prehistoric saddle quern and stone for grinding grains.

👣 Ardnave

Distance: 4–5 miles; time: 2 hours; start/end: Ardnave Loch; OS Explorer map: 353 Islay North

At the most northerly point of the Rhinns is Ardnave, which has an easy circular walk from Ardnave Loch to Ardnave Point. The track follows easy ground, which becomes muddy after rain, while the coastal route is slightly longer and less well defined. It is one of the best places on Islay to spot choughs and there are lapwings and skylarks singing in summer.

Starting in the car park at Ardnave Loch, make your way along the track leading away on the right-hand side of the farm buildings. Keep right at the next fork; this track leads most of the way to Ardnave Point. The final section is pathless, but you can make your way down to the beach opposite tiny Nave Island; look out for seals and otters, and there is also a good view out to Colonsay in clear weather.

From the point, follow the coast, with the sea on your right, until you reach the old, concrete lobster pens on the shore, before heading inland and rejoining the track. It will bring you to the farmyard; walk past a cow barn before continuing back to Ardnave Loch and the car park.

The northwest On the B8017, just after the turning to Culbuie, **An Sithean** (⊕ 55°48'47.3"N 6°23'14.5"W) is an unexcavated archaeological site showing evidence of an ancient settlement. Thought to be over 3,000 years old, there are at least eight roundhouses between 29ft and 49ft wide; at least four of these are easily distinguishable in the brown or purple heather by the bright, green turf growing on top of them.

Travelling west along the B8017, **Loch Gorm** soon comes into view. One of the tiny islands is a crannog (page 266), with the now severely ruined remains of a later castle built on top. This is also a good spot to look out for golden eagles.

Turning right on to the B8018 at the T-junction and continuing to the north coast, **Sanaigmore** is a beautiful sandy beach surrounded by rocks, delicate machair and wildflowers. If you prefer, you can take the turning heading southwest past Loch Gorm to visit **Ballinaby** (⊕ 55°49'03"N 6°26'33"W), Islay's tallest standing stone, before reaching **Saligo Bay**, a small sandy beach with handy rocks to picnic on around its edges. Then there is **Machir Bay**, over a mile of sand dunes and clean, empty beach: another great place to spot choughs. Exposed to the full force of the Atlantic, it can get pretty windy down there and you should watch out for the currents if you're brave enough to go swimming.

The derelict church in the small village of **Kilchoman** is striking in the distance, but has the air of a crumbling tower block up close. The approach is distinctly unwelcoming, with nowhere to park and a sign on the gate saying 'DANGEROUS BUILDING KEEP OUT'. I asked around and was assured that I was allowed to go into the graveyard, but must definitely not cross the second fence close to the church. Saying that, there is plenty of interest in the graveyard, which can still be viewed safely at the time of writing. Around the back of the church is a large cross from the 14th or 15th centuries. It has carvings of Mary, angels, saints and below are figures of the doctor Patrick and his son Thomas of the Beaton family, who were physicians to the Lords of the Isles. There are hollows in the base of the cross; one of these has a stone in it that, if turned, is said to bring pregnant women better chance of having a boy. . . There is also the snapped shaft of another decorative medieval cross and several interestingly carved grave slabs including priests, swords and those with skull and crossbones. More archaeological artefacts are preserved in the Museum of Islay Life (page 234). The site was once the residence of Lord of the Isles and is thought to be the burial place of Lachlan MacLean of Duart, who died in the Battle of Gruineart.

To the southwest of the church is a later cemetery where the victims of the shipwrecked *Otranto* (page 218) were initially laid to rest, before many of the bodies were taken home across the Atlantic by their families.

Also in Kilchoman, but accessed more directly from the B8018, **Kilchoman Distillery** (✆ 01496 850011; w kilchomandistillery.com; ⊕ Apr–mid-Oct 09.45–17.00 daily; mid-Oct–Mar 09.45–17.00 Tue–Sat; tours & tastings £5–35) is the only independently owned distillery on Islay. Established in 2005, it was the island's first new distillery since 1881, as well as Islay's only farm distillery; Kilchoman has a distinctly different aesthetic from the historic coastal buildings of other distilleries. They also have a café serving lunches, cake and hot drinks (£).

To travel further down the west coast by car, you need to return to Port Charlotte to find a turning marked to Kilchiaran. Just after Kilchiaran Farm, on the coast overlooking Kilchiaran Bay, **Kilchiaran Chapel** has been somewhat restored to showcase a medieval font and grave slabs. One has a cross entwined in intricate foliage, two kneeling figures and a large sword; there should also be a small man and barrel, but this is difficult to make out. Outside, some 25yds closer to the sea on the southwest, is a slab with round, prehistoric cup markings, one of which has been ground right through to form a hole (⊕ 55°45'11.7"N 6°27'26.3). The dramatic and rather exposed **Kilchiaran Bay** would make a lovely lunch stop on a calm day. In 1826, 25 families were removed from Kilchiaran by Walter Frederick Campbell in order to make room for a larger-scale farm and steading thought to be more profitable.

Four miles further south, oval in shape and 115ft wide at its narrowest point, **Coultoon** (⊕55°43'31.5"N 6°28'05.7) would be one of the most formidable Bronze-Age sites in the United Kingdom, if only they had managed to stand the stones up. Excavation in the 1970s reported that although sockets had been dug, most of the rocks were never actually erected and only a couple are still standing now. Though the rocks are horizontal, their placement is still alien in the landscape and the sheer scale of the site makes for mind-boggling further consideration as to what purpose these prehistoric people had in mind.

At the most southerly point of the Rhinns are the conjoined townships of **Portnahaven** and **Port Wemyss**, looking out to the island of Orsay and its attractive lighthouse. With the feeling of a storybook beach town, small, white cottages line the harbour; this is one of the easiest places on Islay to see common seals.

Returning northeast, at **Nerabus**, there is a group of five medieval West Highland grave slabs including one of a priest and four with claymores. There is parking down a small track opposite Nerabus Farm, towards the graveyard. Find the medieval site beyond the far side of the modern graveyard, following signs to 'Ancient Burial Ground of Clan Donald'.

12

Jura (Diùra)

Studying the map, it's easy to assume that Jura could be Islay's sibling; similar in size and separated only by the narrow Sound of Islay. But while Islay has the Inner Hebrides' second largest population, Jura is predominantly a wilderness.

Dwarfed by its Paps – the three mountains that dominate the skyline of the southern Hebrides – Jura is well known for having more deer than people. Though it's one of Scotland's largest islands (at 142 square miles it ranks eighth in size), it has a population of just under 200. Historically, along with the exposed mountainous areas, much of the island has always been uninhabitable due to vast swathes of blanket bog. Where humans struggled to settle, nature has thrived and the entire north and west coasts, as well as the interior moorland and forests, have been left entirely for wildlife.

In 1695, Martin Martin described the island as 'perhaps the wholesomest plot of ground either in the isles or continent of Scotland, as appears by the long life of the natives and the state of their health, to which the height of the hills is believed to contribute in a large measure'; one such long-lived islander was Gillour MacCrain who apparently lived to 180. Though Martin's claim that the constant air flow blew away diseases and kept the population healthy is now viewed rather dubiously, there is no doubt that Jura is rich in wide-open spaces and there is still something to be said for the mental and physical benefits of battling high winds across exposed moorland.

GETTING THERE AND AWAY

BY FERRY Outside of the summer months, you will most likely have to travel via Islay. **Argyll and Bute Council** (☎ 01496 840681; w argyll-bute.gov.uk/port-askaig-islay-feolin-jura-ferry-timetable) run a year-round car and foot passenger ferry from Port Askaig on Islay to Feolin (every 30–60mins 07.35–18.30 Mon–Sat, with some later sailings; 6–7 sailings Sun; vehicle/foot passengers start at £9.45/1.80). No pre-booking is necessary unless you are travelling after 18.30 or on certain Sundays, in which case you must call before noon one day in advance. Otherwise, just queue up and pay on the ferry (cash only). Campervan drivers should contact the ferry office to check if their vehicle will clear the ramp. **Jura Passenger Ferry** (m 07768 450000; w jurapassengerferry.com; ⊕ Apr–Sep Wed–Mon) runs from Tayvallich on the mainland to Craighouse in under an hour (twice daily Mon–Sat, 1 sailing Sun; £20 pp; bikes free).

MOORINGS

Craighouse Bay 16 swing moorings for boats up to 15 tonnes. £10/night paid to Jura Development Trust ☎ 01496 820161; w juradevelopment.co.uk/about-jura/getting-to-jura) in advance or at shop/hotel (page 240) on the day.

BY CAR Jura is 29 miles long and, as its single track A road wins the prize as the worst in the Inner Hebrides, journey times should not be underestimated. As you drive further north, there are savage pot-holes and the sides of the roads are sunken from the tyres of previous travellers; at a certain point, grass starts to grow in the middle. In many places, the road is quite unsuitable for large vehicles, especially those with low clearance; note that there are no facilities for campervans. The nearest car hire is on Islay (page 219) or in Lochgilphead (page 38).

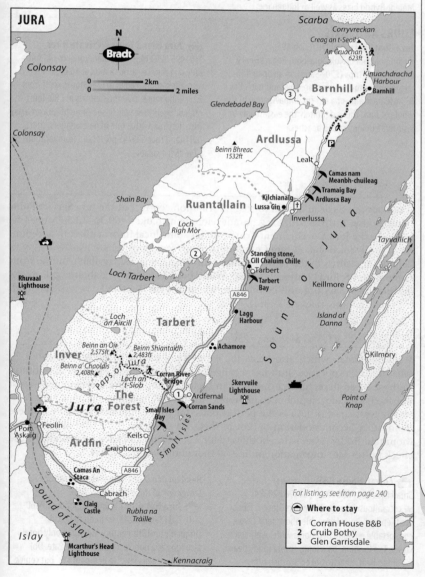

BY BUS Garelochhead Coaches/Argyll and Bute Council (w garelochheadcoaches.
co.uk; ☎01436 810200) operate the 456 bus (Feolin–Craighouse–Inverlussa) several
times a day from Monday to Saturday.

BY BIKE
Bike hire

🚲 **Jura Cycles** Craighouse (can deliver for small fee); m 07436 886621; e juracycles@outlook.com. Friendly local Gerry hires out a variety of Ridgeback Meteor Hybrid bikes as well as Ridgeback

Dimension bikes for children (day/week £20/100). He also has helmets, some panniers & provides a puncture-repair kit with every hire.

TOURS AND TAXIS

Jura Boat Tours m 07976 280195; w juraboattours.co.uk. Jura-born Robert Henry offers various trips (£20–50pp) on an open RIB, including out to Corryvreckan, Lowlandman's Bay & Brosdale Island, or a 4hr circumnavigation of the whole of Jura. This is definitely the easiest way to visit Jura's unique raised beaches.

🚗 **Jura Island Tours & Private Hires** ☎01496 820314; w juraislandtours.co.uk. Jura's only taxi service carries a max of 16 passengers & also offers tours. Feolin to Craighouse costs from £25; Craighouse to Ardlussa starts at £80. Tours offer a hassle-free way to see some of Jura on a day trip. They run with a min of 6 passengers; short/full island tour £35/45 pp. Pickup from locations on Islay also available.

TOURIST INFORMATION

Jura does not have an official tourist information centre, but the **Jura Service Point**
(Craighouse; ☎01496 820161; w juradevelopment.co.uk; ⊕ 09.30–12.30 Mon–Fri)
is run by the Jura Development Trust and has some local information. In addition,
the friendly local staff at **Jura Community Shop** (see opposite) are usually happy to
help point visitors in the right direction. Information is also available online from
Explore Islay & Jura (w islayjura.com); **Wild About Argyll** (w wildaboutargyll.co.uk/
destinations/islay-jura-and-colonsay/jura); and **Visit Scotland** (w visitscotland.
com/destinations-maps/isle-jura).

WHERE TO STAY *Map, page 239*

With one hotel, which also hosts the campsite, a couple of B&Bs and about 20
self-catering properties, Jura has a range of accommodation options. In addition
to those listed here, further options can be found on the Jura Development Trust
website (w juradevelopment.co.uk/about-jura/where-to-stay).

The west coast of Jura is the perfect place for **wild camping** (especially as there
is no other accommodation option in this part of Jura). The island also has two
Mountain Bothy Association bothies (page 111): **Cruib** and **Glen Garrisdale**. Please
check up-to-date information online (w mountainbothies.org.uk).

🏠 **Corran House B&B** (2 rooms) Small Isles Bay PA60 7XZ; ☎01496 820374; w corranhousejura.co.uk. Owners Steve & Fiona are friendly & knowledgeable about Jura. Large, comfortable en-suite bedrooms with lovely sea views. The location, on a long, empty sandy beach, is hard to beat. Hearty cooked Scottish b/fast.

Resident dog & cat. Dogs welcome, call ahead. Lower end of this price range. **£££**

🏠 **Jura Hotel** (17 rooms) Craighouse PA60 7XU; ☎01496 820243; w jurahotel.co.uk. Originally an 18th-century inn, Jura's only hotel also runs as a pub, restaurant & campsite. Dbl rooms have sea view. No bedroom TVs, but copies of Orwell's *Nineteen Eighty-Four* & photography books. **£££**

⚊ Camping at Jura Hotel Craighouse PA60 7XU; ☎ 01496 820243; w jurahotel.co.uk; ♿. Cheap camping on grassy field, right on the seafront with plenty of space for tents, but no car park. Toilets, showers & laundry. Disabled access to facilities. **£**

WEEKLY RENTAL

🏠 Barnhill Estate (2 properties) ☎ 01786 850274; w escapetojura.com. Almost entirely a wilderness, the Barnhill Estate makes up the northern 7,000 acres of Jura, with miles of rugged coastline & hills. The estate run 2 self-catering properties: Barnhill (sleeps 6) & Heather Cottage (sleeps 5). An adventure in itself, Barnhill, where George Orwell

(see box, page 248) wrote *Nineteen Eighty-Four*, remains largely as it once was with extremely basic facilities: coal-fired Rayburn & gas cooker, a generator for limited electricity & cool box instead of a fridge. Access is via 4 miles of rough track only accessible to off-road vehicles. Further south Heather Cottage, overlooking the River Lussa & beach, is accessible by road & has normal facilities such as a washing machine & microwave. Linen £10 pp extra. Barnhill £1,000/week, Heather Cottage £400/week.

🏠 Torr na Faire & Tulach Ard (2 houses, each sleeps 4) Ballard, Craighouse; ☎ 01496 820396; w juraselfcatering.com; ♿. Clean & new, these 2 identical houses are surprisingly spacious & comfortable inside. The best thing about them is their elevated position & great view over the Small Isles Bay. £450/week.

WHERE TO EAT AND DRINK

There are only two places to get a main meal on Jura and both are in Craighouse; the Jura Hotel is open for longer hours, while the Antlers is closed in winter.

✗ Jura Hotel (see opposite) ⊕ summer noon– 14.30 & 18.00–20.30 daily, winter noon–14.00 & 18.30–20.30 daily. Hearty food & seasonal seafood including local langoustines & Islay crab, as well as Jura's famous venison. **££**

⊑ The Antlers Craighouse PA60 7XS; ☎ 01496 820496; 🻲 antlers.jura; ⊕ Apr–Sep 10.00–16.00 daily, plus 18.00–19.00 Fri (takeaway). Relaxed, community-run place with outside seating in good

weather, serving warm drinks, b/fasts, hot lunches & cake. Fish & chips available for takeaway on Fri evening. **££**

⊑ Tea on the Beach Inverlussa Beach, Ardlussa PA60 7XW; ☎ 01496 820053; 🻲; ⊕ Apr–Aug flexible daytime hours. Help-yourself hot drinks & cakes from the back of a horse box. It is run by 11- to 16-year-olds, with payment/ donations via an honesty box.

SHOPPING

Jura Community Shop Craighouse; ☎ 01496 820231; w juracommunityshop.co.uk; ⊕ 09.00– 13.30 & 14.30–17.00 Mon–Sat. This community-owned shop has all the basics including groceries, toiletries & cleaning products. There is a decent selection of fresh fruit & veg (mostly unpackaged) & a small bookshop upstairs with a good range of

local-interest books, OS maps & map sections of the Paps of Jura. Cashback also available.

Craft Fair Village Hall; ⊕ 10.30–16.00 most Wed in summer (when possible). Local crafts, framed photos & home-baked cakes. Check noticeboards or ask locally to confirm dates.

OTHER PRACTICALITIES

Fuel Pier Garage Filling Station, Craighouse PA60 7XF

🌐 Internet The Jura Service Point (see opposite). Public-use computers.

✚ Medical Jura Medical Practice, Glencairn Surgery, Craighouse PA60 7XG; ☎ 01496 820218;

m 07753 040699 for urgent care. Also has a small dispensary.

✚ Pharmacy Basic painkillers & over-the-counter medicines, first-aid supplies & cold remedies can be bought in the shop (see above).

✉ Post office Jura Community Shop (see above)

There's nearly 6,000 red deer on the island, which means you only need to leave Craighouse in order to see some of them. Not just a noble part of the island's fauna, these deer actually account for the majority of Jura's economy. Jura's seven estates own and manage most of the island's land and, counting them as one employer, they are also the biggest provider of jobs. Deer populations are managed and people travel from far and wide to take part in stalking. It is important for hikers and wild campers to be aware of the deer stalking season and the island's estates. Stalking runs annually from 1 July to 15 February, and during these months it is respectful and sensible to call the estate whose land you want to walk over in advance. For the Paps of Jura, call the Hillphone service (01496 820151). Otherwise, these are the phone numbers for each estate; their boundaries are marked on the map on page 239.

Ardfin 01496 820198
Ardlussa 01496 820321
Barnhill 01496 820327
The Forest 01496 820217

Inver 01496 820223
Ruantallain 01496 820287
Tarbert 01496 820207

EVENTS

MAY

Isle of Jura Fell Race Craighouse; [f]. This event has been going since 1973. Only for serious fell runners, this 28km race includes 7 summits, including the Paps of Jura, & an intimidating 7,775ft of ascent. Unmarked & over rough terrain, in addition to fitness & fell-running technique you'll also need navigation skills. It is said to be one of the toughest challenges in British hill racing; regardless, the 250 places fill up fast.

JULY

Ardlussa Sports Day Contact Ardlussa Estate: 01496 820323; e enquiries@ardlussaestate.com. Visitors are welcome to just turn up & join in with sports & games on Ardlussa lawn field. Last Sat afternoon of the month.

AUGUST

Jura Regatta Stone pier, Craighouse. On the 1st Sat of the month this event includes sailing & swimming races. Spectators & visiting competitors are welcome, just show up on the day & put your name down if you want to join in. Concert & dancing in the village hall afterwards.

SEPTEMBER

Jura Music Festival Craighouse; 01496 820362; w juramusicfestival.com. Now in its 25th year, this is a well-established favourite for traditional music lovers. From the locals' Fri night cèilidh right through to the Sun night concert in the distillery, it's a weekend packed with fantastic performances & workshops. Tickets £8–45 depending on which events you attend & can be bought online or at the door; book in advance for the Sat night Grand Concert.

WHAT TO SEE AND DO

FROM FEOLIN TO CRAIGHOUSE From Feolin, where there is a very small ferry terminal and one house, the road runs perilously along the bottom of the cliffs as it follows the rocky shoreline, which is frequented by otters. Look out for your first red deer as the view opens up to bleak moorland. After about 3 miles, just after a patch of woodland, 300yds southwest of the road, is a huge, intentionally placed upright rock. At over 11ft tall **Camas An Staca**, a Gaelic name relating to the bay, is the tallest standing stone on Jura. Looking to the southwest from here, you can just about see the remains of **Claig Castle**, a sea fortress defended by the MacDonald Lords of the Isles until they were crushed in the 17th century. McArthur's Head Lighthouse (page 230) and its complex array of white walls can be seen clinging to the cliffs over on Islay.

CRAIGHOUSE Jura's tiny capital is home to most of the island's amenities, including its only shop, pub and campsite. Also setting it apart from the island's other small villages is the wonderful view over **Small Isles Bay**.

From north to south these uninhabited Small Isles, not to be confused with the ones detailed in *Chapter 5*, are Eilean Bhride (Bridget's Island), Pladda (Flat Island), Eilean nan Coinein (Rabbit Island), Eilean Diomhain (Useless Island) and Eilean nan Gabhar (Goat Island). The last of these, appropriately, is home to a herd of wild goats that was running amok in Craighouse around 15 years ago – rather than shoot them, they were relocated to Eilean nan Gabhar. There were originally just five goats but they have subsequently (and unsurprisingly) tripled in number.

Too far offshore to make out properly, the Small Isles' presence lends a mystical element to the bay. If conditions are favourable and you have some experience, it is possible to rent a small rowing boat from Robert who runs Jura Boat Tours (page 240), otherwise some of his trips run past the islands, allowing you to get a closer look.

Jura Distillery (Craighouse; ✆ 01496 820385; w jurawhisky.com; ⏲ Apr–Oct 10.00–16.30 Mon–Sat, Nov–Mar 10.00–16.00 Mon–Sat) Originally founded by the Laird of Jura, Archibald Campbell, in the early 19th century, Jura Distillery could reportedly produce 720 gallons of whisky each week when it was first built. The establishment has gone through several long spells of disrepair before being rebuilt in its present form in 1963, with some subsequent editions. Tours start from £6 for 45 minutes – for £25 you can learn about some of Jura's 'rarer expressions'.

Jura Picture Collection Attached to Craighouse Village Church, towards the northern end of Craighouse, this historical photo collection shows life on the island from as early as 1854. The space is tiny, but the exhibition is particularly notable for its unusual inclusion of photos showing normal village life. There is 'Kate Buie at her spinning wheel' and 'Off to Islay' – depicting women on a small boat going for a 'cruise' and men heading over to the neighbouring island for a drink. There are also many labelled images of Jura's older houses, which make for an interesting comparison with the modern day. The door is left open and the exhibition is free, but donations to the church are welcome.

CORRAN SANDS At the northern end of Small Isles Bay is the idyllic Corran Sands, arguably Jura's finest beach. Once the island's main deep-water anchorage, this was where emigrants waited for ships to take them away in the 18th and 19th centuries. (The island's population had dropped to just a few hundred by the 1900s – not due to forced evictions as elsewhere but rather most of Jura's residents seemingly left by choice, with hopes of escaping their impoverishment.) These days, if winds are favourable, it is a lovely place for a picnic.

PAPS OF JURA Visible on the horizon from as far afield as Mull and even Northern Ireland, the Paps of Jura are three mountains: **Beinn an Òir** (Mountain of Gold; 2,575ft), **Beinn Shiantaidh** (Sacred Mountain; 2,483ft) and **Beinn a' Chaolais**

(Mountain of the Sound; 2,408ft). Climbing them is undoubtedly one of the main reasons people come to Jura and, on a clear day, the views are difficult to beat.

To climb all three takes about 10 hours and is a serious expedition that should only be done after checking the weather forecast and with proper equipment, including navigation tools. The scree slopes are relentless and, with weather likely to change fast, you must be prepared for all conditions. As winter sees more extreme weather conditions (including the possibility of snow) and shorter hours of daylight, it's generally better to attempt the Paps between April and September. Climbing just Beinn an Òir, the highest of the peaks, is a more manageable hike of around 5 hours, but the same preparation instructions apply.

🅰 Climbing Beinn an Òir

Distance: 8 miles; time: 4½–6½ hours; start/end: Corran River Bridge; OS Explorer map: 355 Jura & Scarba

This hike has an ascent and descent of 2,487ft. There is not a lot of scree to tackle, but the ground is very boggy for the first few miles. These instructions are only meant for general route finding; you must also have a proper map and compass or GPS device (and know how to use them).

Start just over 3 miles north of Craighouse at Corran River Bridge, a three-arched structure over the Corran River, built by Thomas Telford in 1810. If you have a car, park on the north side and then walk back across the bridge to find a stile and path leading northwest. The path starts near the river before climbing up to higher ground across the corner of a hill. Soon you will have an excellent view of all three Paps: Beinn Shiantaidh is the closest and largest looking of the three, with Beinn an Òir behind it and Beinn a' Chaolais on the left. When you see Loch an t-Siob, head towards the river running off it to find the substantial stepping stones and cross it.

The path then runs around the northern side of the loch, below Beinn Shiantaidh. Begin to climb up when you are level with the gap between Beinn Shiantaidh and Beinn an Òir; here the path disappears. You should soon find yourself on a beautiful triangular plateau (obvious from the contour lines on your map). From here, head west for a few hundred yards, towards the south of Beinn an Òir, where you should be able to find a path leading up directly north, before it heads northwest for the final ascent.

The remains of stone buildings at the top were once Colby Camp, used for triangulation and mapping of the area. The summit is a little further south, with superlative views across to Islay and over to Beinn Shiantaidh and Beinn a' Chaolais. Don't forget to look out for eagles. Return along the same route.

FROM CORRAN RIVER BRIDGE TO ARDLUSSA Heading north from Corran River Bridge, after about a mile the road passes **Lowlandman's Bay**, where the old cottages of Skervuile Lighthouse's keepers occupy the headland that reaches around to the east. The lighthouse itself, a small white tower, was constructed in the mid 19th century to mark dangerous rocks near the southern end of the Sound of Jura.

A little further north, **Achamore** (between ⊕ 55°55'01.4"N 5°52'34.3"W and ⊕ 55°54'59.9"N 5°52'28.9"W) is the remains of a small settlement of stone-walled huts on the edge of a ravine. One for real archaeology enthusiasts, they are on the opposite side of the road from a patch of woodland and the small hill Cnoc na Fritheilt. Not particularly easy to find, once you have spotted the remains of one house you will realise that there are many in the same area. The origin of the buildings is something of a mystery as they are smaller than permanent residences usually are, but the rig and furrow, lazy beds and field walls suggest that farming

EASGA BHUIDHE NA FÈIDH

A story recounted by Heather Dewar in *Seanchas Ìle: Collecting, Recording and Preserving Islay's Gaelic Heritage* (page 270) refers to the postal route, from a time when mail had to travel through Jura before being delivered to Islay. Two women had gone from Islay to Jura to collect whelks, when one asked the other to look after her baby while she worked. Returning, she immediately noticed something was wrong; not only would her friend not tell her where the baby was, but there was also a terrible smell coming from the fire. Going to check in the pot, she was terrified to discover her baby had been cooked and ran away as fast as she could – but the cannibalistic woman caught her and ate her too. Thrown into a rage, the mad woman fell to all fours; her nails grew long like the 'claws of an eagle' and her hair grew long like a beast. Anyone who went too close was also killed and eaten.

Too scared to travel their normal route through Jura, the Islay mail came to a halt until one day when two Ìleach men with dogs and guns decided to find and kill her. One of the men climbed Beinn an Òir and, after some struggle, managed to kill her with the stock of his gun. Sgrìob na Caillich ('the scrape of the old woman'), a geological feature on the southwest flank of Beinn an Òir known as a medial moraine, is supposed to have been where she fell down and died. This woman, recorded in folk tales as 'Easga Bhuidhe na Fèidh' was used for generations as a scare tactic to stop young islanders from staying out late. Kelp on the beaches was said to be her hair and Clach an Daormunn, a huge stone close to Ardnahoe on Islay, is said to be a stone she threw across in rage.

While the majority of this folk tale is fantastical, it probably reflects to some extent an unfortunate woman with mental health problems who was villainised by the community and considered to be a witch.

definitely took place here. A post-medieval settlement, it was already abandoned by the end of the 18th century. This peaceful spot seems idyllic in good weather, but it would have been a tough and exposed place to grow crops. Although the ruins are not far from the road, an OS map or GPS device is probably needed to locate them.

Lagg Harbour The well-preserved pier and walled cattle slipway in Lagg Harbour were both built around 1810; the farmhouse at Lagg was built around the same time as an inn for the cattle drovers to drink in while they waited for (frequently delayed) ferries – it is now a private residence. For the nearby islands of Islay and Colonsay, Jura was often used as a stepping stone to the mainland. This ferry carried incoming and outcoming cows for all three islands, in addition to being the official postal route for Jura and mail on its way to Islay. This was a hazardous crossing, made in open boats with both livestock and drovers vulnerable to large waves and currents. You can walk down the track to the curved pier and slipway, which remains an impressive site with an interesting perspective over the bay. Be very careful if you walk on either as there are many loose rocks, holes and algae to potentially slip on.

Tarbert About 2 miles north of Lagg Harbour, and easily recognisable by a standing stone next to the road, is the small settlement of Tarbert, which overlooks Tarbert Bay. Meaning 'a place to carry your boat across the land from sea to sea', you will find Tarberts and Tarbets all over the west coast of Scotland, something that can cause major confusion on the mainland. Here, the name refers to the short distance between the settlement of Tarbert and Loch Tarbert, which cuts into Jura from the opposite (west) coast. At this point, Jura is nearly cut in half and the walk across the island from Tarbert on the east coast to Loch Tarbert on the west is only 1 mile.

Eighty yards after the standing stone is a parking place on the right-hand side of the road; you can follow the track leading east towards Tarbert and Tarbert Bay on foot from here. After about 200yds, cutting across the field south towards the bay, you will reach **Cill Chaluim Chille** (✦ 55°58'23"N 5°50'01"W), a walled graveyard that stands conspicuously in an otherwise clear grassy field, surrounding the remains of a medieval chapel. As well as the lower walls of the chapel, there is also a tall stone, which, underneath the crusty lichen, has sunken Latin crosses on both faces. This stone may be prehistoric, but believed to have been moved, with the cross a later addition.

If you would like to walk across the island to **Loch Tarbert**, an easy 2-mile return route begins on the opposite side of the main road, 150yds southeast of the standing stone. A track (✦ 55°58'23"N 5°50'21"W) leads all the way across to the loch. The shore of Loch Tarbert is a peaceful place with a small boathouse. Look out for wading birds and sit quietly for a while in the hope of seeing otters.

INVERLUSSA AND ARDLUSSA Five miles north of Tarbert are the small settlements of Inverlussa and Ardlussa, named after the Lussa River. Just south of Ardlussa a turning to the right, marked for Inverlussa, follows the river down to **Inverlussa Beach**, passing the graveyard at **Kilchianaig** where Mary MacCrain, a descendant of the even longer-lived Gillour MacCrain (page 238), was buried after dying at the grand age of 128 in 1856. Inverlussa and its sandy, grass-bordered bay, is just 400yds further; you can get 'Tea on the Beach' (page 241) in summer months. Signs of human habitation in the form of small flint artefacts from over 8,000 years ago have been found here. Today, you are just as likely to share the beach with cows.

Lussa Gin (The Stables, Ardlussa; ☎ 01496 820196; w lussagin.com) Lussa Gin, north of Inverlussa, is distilled and bottled by Jura residents Georgina, Alicia and Claire. What started in a kitchen has now grown into an award-winning business. Their giant copper contraption, Hamish, makes a smoother version of the same recipe they first crafted five years ago. The gin is distilled with 15 botanicals, giving it a pleasantly complicated taste with hints of citrus from the lemon thyme and balm. They grow 11 of the plants themselves, while some, such as water mint, are picked wild from the island (they are working on self-sourcing the other four). Tours are free and, as the space is small, relatively concise; call ahead or email e tours@lussagin.com to book.

NORTH OF ARDLUSSA The road, steep in places, continues along the coast, past small beaches and ancient oak woods until eventually you will come to **Lealt**, where in order to proceed you will have to open a gate before driving a further ¾ mile to the end of the public road. Those wishing to walk to see Corryvreckan and the very north end of Jura should find somewhere to park here: don't attempt to drive down the track at the end of the road, as it isn't suitable for vehicles, even those with 4x4 capability.

Corryvreckan The name Corryvreckan comes from the Gaelic Coire Bhreacain ('cauldron of the speckled seas'). As the flood tide enters the gulf between uninhabited Scarba and Jura, it speeds up to 8½ knots and races through various underwater rocky features to create the third largest whirlpool in the world. Corryvreckan is at its best during spring tides: these occur during times when there is a full or new moon and are nothing to do with the seasons. You can check the dates at w tides.willyweather.co.uk.

To Corryvreckan The walk to see the very northern end of Jura and Corryvreckan is a long and boggy, but not particularly difficult, 13 miles return – though it can take more than 7 hours. You should be prepared for hiking in wet weather, and have the means of navigation for the final stretch as there is no path. A good track runs as far as the turning to **Barnhill**, where George Orwell wrote *Nineteen Eighty-Four*. In not too dissimilar a condition from how it was in 1948, the lonely cottage is now

THE TRAGIC TALE OF PRINCE BRECKAN

A natural phenomenon as impressive and intimidating as Corryvreckan has its fair share of folk stories. One of these tells the tale of a Scandinavian prince called Breckan, who wanted to marry a daughter of one of the local lords. The latter agreed on the condition that Breckan would anchor his galley in the Hag, as the whirlpool is also called, for three days and three nights. Breckan went home to make ready his galley, and was advised by wise men to take three anchor ropes: one of the best wool, one of hemp grown in a graveyard, and one of pure maidens' hair. He followed the instructions, but as you might expect, the first night the wool rope broke. During the second night the hemp rope also gave way, and finally on the third night the maidens' hair rope broke too, because one of them had lied about her virginity. Breckan was drowned. He was pulled ashore by his dog, and buried in Breckan's Cave (Uamh Bhreacain), in Bagh Gleann nam Muc, north Jura. The dog died in the sound to the north of Scarba, which is now called the Grey Dogs Race.

Once known to Jura locals by his real name, Eric Blair, George Orwell lived on Jura from 1946 to 1948. During this time he was seriously ill with tuberculosis but, with a typical writer's stubbornness, insisted on living in the badly equipped, damp house at Barnhill until he was no longer physically able to. Government surveillance, propaganda and the perpetual war suffered by the characters in his dystopian novel *Nineteen Eighty-Four* may seem far away from life on Jura, but it would be hard to find a more isolated spot to find the time and concentration required to write such a masterpiece. In the charming booklet *Jura and George Orwell*, written by Gordon Wright in 1983, Mrs Nelson of Ardlussa explains how Orwell was a 'tall, gaunt and sad-looking man' who she worried would not manage on his own. In fact, he did not live alone for long and, reading between the lines, was only able to concentrate on his great novel through the tireless efforts of his sister Avril who dug the garden, cooked and kept the house going. There were also several other people around to help, as well as his three-year-old son, who he nearly lost in the Gulf of Corryvreckan on a camping trip. A booklet with more information and Mrs Nelson's personal account is available in several places on Jura including from Fiona, Gordon Wright's daughter, at Corran House B&B (£2.50; page 240).

available as holiday accommodation (w escapetojura.com/Barnhill.html). Located a couple of hundred yards from the walking track, the owners ask that you observe from afar as it is not otherwise open to the public.

Just north of Barnhill the track meets a junction, where you should choose to go left, following the track north for about half a mile. Passing through some protected woodland, you will reach a junction with a short sidetrack to to **Kinuachdrachd Harbour** and its small jetty, which once served a ferry route to the mainland. Returning to the main path and continuing north past the bay, take a fork on to a grassy path going left just before the last house at Kinuachdrachd.

Keeping on higher ground, with the coast on your right, the path begins well, but soon disintegrates into bog and sheep tracks for the final mile and a half. The flat rock platforms between **An Cruachan** and **Creag an t-Seoil** (⊕ 56°08'48"N 5°42'29"W) make a good spot for a picnic and are the best place to observe **Corryvreckan** when the whirlpool is swirling. Look out for gutsy porpoises or dolphins, swept along in the current of the channel. Return along the same route.

13

Gigha (Giogha)

Gigha (pronounced 'Gee-a') sits at a jaunty angle off the Kintyre Peninsula and is the most southerly of the Inner Hebrides. Owned by the community, the island is run by the Isle of Gigha Heritage Trust. With just 165 residents, and at just 6 miles long and no more than 1½ miles wide, Gigha is the epitome of small-island life; literally everybody knows everyone and, if you are friendly, it will only take a few days for a lot of them to know you too. The community holds meetings to decide the best way forward for the island, whether it's a serious discussion about finances or to debate the fate of the island's peacocks. As the new fire engine whizzes up and down Gigha's only road, trying to rack up the 200 miles of practice required for the island's voluntary firefighters to be fully qualified to use it, it becomes obvious why mainland logic doesn't and shouldn't always apply here.

Ardminish is the only settlement that can be defined as a village on the island and, approaching on the ferry, it's hard to believe that this is Gigha's 'capital'. Adapted very little over the last 100 years, with whitewashed walls and grey slate roofs, the township is barely a sprinkling of houses, the grandest of which is Gigha Hotel. Ardminish is where you will find all the island's amenities, places to eat and much of its accommodation. Though it has a pleasant beach of its own, to visit Gigha without exploring further than Ardminish would be doing yourself and the island a great disservice. The wild, uninhabited north coast has an iconic, double-sided beach and a wealth of ancient sites to be discovered among the heather, while the cliffs and bays to the south are home to many seals and squawking seabirds.

As on many islands, the range of mammals is smaller than on the mainland and the introduction of new, innocuous-seeming animals can cause real havoc to Gigha's ecosystem. Invasive hedgehogs, for example, are captured and taken to a mainland sanctuary before they devour the eggs of native ground-nesting birds. Gigha's warm microclimate, due to the surrounding Gulf Stream and a lack of any large mountains, encourages an unusual array of plants, though larger mammals such as deer are absent and you'll find a better variety of bird species on neighbouring Islay. Around Easter, the whole island bursts into colour with a profusion of wildflowers. Thrift, orchids, bluebells, yellow iris and grass of Parnassus are all widely distributed across Gigha's plentiful wild areas. Both the air and surrounding bodies of water, coming straight from the Atlantic, are refreshingly clear and clean.

HISTORY

Rev R S G Anderson, writing in his 1939 book *The Antiquities of Gigha* describes Gigha's history as: '… the scattered links of a broken chain, most of which are lost and the others mixed.' However much you try to smooth it over, there is no

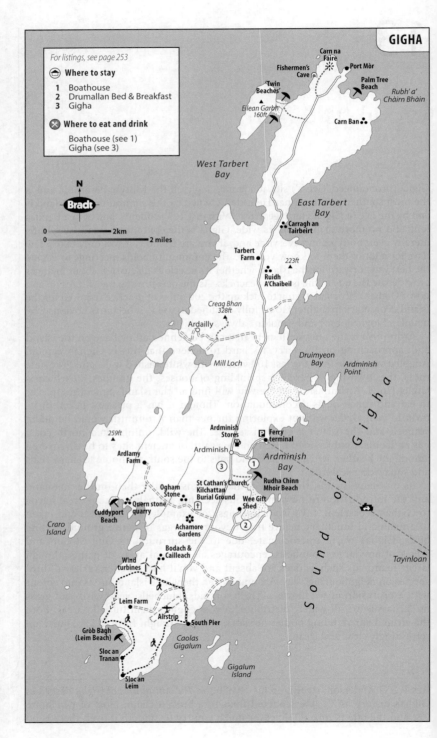

GIGHA

For listings, see page 253

Where to stay

1　Boathouse
2　Drumallan Bed & Breakfast
3　Gigha

Where to eat and drink

　　Boathouse (see 1)
　　Gigha (see 3)

N

Bradt

0 ———— 2km
0 ———— 2 miles

Carn na Faire
Port Mòr
Fishermen's Cave
Palm Tree Beach
Twin Beaches
Rubh' a' Chàirn Bhàin
Eilean Garbh 160ft
Carn Ban

West Tarbert Bay

East Tarbert Bay

Carragh an Tairbeirt

Tarbert Farm
223ft
Ruidh A'Chaibeil

Creag Bhan 328ft
Ardailly

Mill Loch

Druimyeon Bay
Ardminish Point

259ft

Ardlamy Farm

Ardminish Stores
Ferry terminal
Ardminish
3　1
Ardminish Bay

Ogham Stone
St Cathan's Church, Kilchattan Burial Ground
Rudha Chinn Mhoir Beach
Wee Gift Shed
2

Cuddyport Beach
Quern stone quarry
Craro Island
Achamore Gardens

S　o　u　n　d　　o　f　　G　i　g　h　a

Bodach & Cailleach
Wind turbines
Leim Farm
Airstrip
South Pier
Gròb Bàgh (Leim Beach)
Sloc an Tranan
Caolas Gigalum
Gigalum Island
Sloc an Leim

Tayinloan

getting away from the fact that the island's written history is very sporadic; before Clan MacNeill came on the scene in the 15th century, we have mostly only place names and archaeology to rely on. In some ways this makes exploring the island more intriguing; it feels like there is something left to discover and plenty more on the verge of being lost. Prehistoric archaeological sites on Gigha, including Bronze-Age burial cists (page 255) and mysterious standing stones like the small but distinctive Bodach and Cailleach (page 257), are inconspicuous, sometimes hidden in the undergrowth.

The Vikings started their raids on the southern Hebrides at the end of the 8th century and the name 'Gigha' itself most likely comes from the Old Norse Guðey meaning God or possibly 'good island'; there are various other place names and some archaeological sites left by the Norse. Evidence for Viking visits include a grave that was found in East Tarbet Bay, which hoarded held treasures including a bronze weighing balance from the 10th century. Additionally, one of the first written references to Gigha comes from the Icelandic book *Haakon's Saga*, which mentions King Haakon IV of Norway visiting the island, after bad weather delayed his 100 ships in Gigalum South, on his way to the Battle of Largs in 1263 (where he was defeated).

In the 14th century, Gigha came under the control of the Lords of the Isles who, in 1449, granted part of Gigha to Torquil MacNeill of Taynish, a clan chief from the mainland; by 1493 the MacNeills had control of the whole island. Excluding a few short periods, the MacNeills kept control of the island for the next 372 years. Seemingly consistent in retrospect, it was not a peaceful time and though the following history reads like the squabbles of petulant children, clan warfare wreaked havoc, massacre and destruction on the people of Gigha. The best surviving archaeological relics from these times can be found at St Cathan's Church and Kilchattan Burial Ground (page 256).

In 1792 Gigha's population peaked at 614 but, like most of the Inner Hebrides, was almost halved over the following century owing to the economic hardships around the time of the Clearances (page 15). The MacNeills sold up the island in 1865 and in the 20th century Gigha saw several owners including Sir James Horlick, 4th Baronet and chairman of Horlicks Ltd, the malted-milk drink company. Although some lairds showed generosity, the people of Gigha saw their lives and property passed from one man to the next. The community lacked agency and the quality of social housing was poor; some houses still had dirt floors in the 1970s. By the turn of the millennium Gigha's population had dwindled to around 90 people.

On 15 March 2002, after being put on the market again, the community voted to buy out the island. With the help of grants and loans from the National Lottery and the Highlands and Islands Enterprise, the Isle of Gigha Heritage Trust purchased Gigha for £4 million. Through selling Achamore House, although not the gardens, and huge fund-raising efforts from the people themselves, the Trust then managed to pay off the short-term loan of £1 million they had taken from the Scottish Land Fund within two years of purchasing the island.

At the time of writing, the Isle of Gigha Heritage Trust is still in debt, but their population has risen to 165, the school has doubled in size and many small businesses have sprung up on the island. Perhaps their most inspiring success has been in setting up Gigha Renewable Energy. Their wind turbines, known locally as the Dancing Ladies, produce three times what the island needs in electricity and the community is further supported by selling the excess to the National Grid. While it is always important to support the local economy as you travel, on Gigha the argument is particularly compelling.

GETTING THERE AND AWAY

Only a short ferry ride from the mainland, Gigha is surprisingly accessible in comparison with many of the Inner Hebrides' islands. The ferry over to the island is an enjoyable trip and the only plausible option for the vast majority of visitors, but those with their own boat or aircraft are also catered for; for the latter, contact the **Trust Office** (✆01583 427300; w gigha.org.uk). Caravans are not permitted, but campervans are.

BY FERRY CalMac (✆ 08000 665000 or, from outside the UK, +44 1475 650397; w calmac.co.uk; cars/foot passengers £7.80/2.70) runs services from Tayinloan on the mainland. The journey takes around 20 minutes, with ferries running between six and ten times a day. In contrast to other routes, visitors with cars can just show up and drive on to the ferry (as directed) without purchasing a ticket in advance. There is a small ticket office on the lower car deck. If you are lucky enough to see dolphins, the captain might even stop to give you a better view.

MOORINGS The island has 22 moorings and a new pontoon. It costs £15 per night for a mooring, £20 per night for the pontoon or £5 for the day, and payment can be made at the honesty box at the top of the pontoons, a moorings operator if you find one, the Trust Office in Ardminish (⊕ 09.00–17.00 Mon–Fri) or by card over the phone (✆01583 427300). Water and showers are available at the Boathouse during the summer and fuel and other supplies can be bought at Ardminish Stores.

GETTING AROUND

ON FOOT For fit and enthusiastic hikers with a generous time frame, Gigha is very rewarding to discover on foot. Away from the main tracks, most paths are overgrown, poorly marked and often dwindle out of existence, but with sturdy walking boots and a sense of adventure, this is the best way to explore the island. You should always carry a map (OS Explorer: *357 Kintyre North*) and compass and/or GPS device and know how to use them, but a rudimentary awareness of the island's landmarks makes it relatively easy to find your bearings from the top of the nearest hill. Hitchhiking up or down the main road should also be relatively easy and safe. There are promising plans for a coast path to be built around Gigha's 30 miles of coastline, which would be a very inviting two- or three-day prospect if followed through.

BY CAR Gigha's main road is single track and is regularly used by tractors and trucks, so be careful not to park blocking passing places or gates.

BY BIKE In calm weather cycling is a perfect way to get from one end of the island to the other. Bike hire is available from Ardminish Stores (½/whole day £10/15; see opposite).

TOURIST INFORMATION

There's no official tourist information office, but the Gigha Heritage Trust website (w gigha.org.uk) is a helpful source of information.

Gigha has a handful of accommodation options. For self catering, contact The Gigha Community Trust (01583 427300; w gigha.org.uk), which owns five cottages, sleeping two–six people. A stay in one of these is a great way to contribute to the island's community.

Gigha Hotel (8 rooms) Ardminish PA41 7AA; 01583 505254; w gighahotel.com. Standing proudly above the village, and its largest white building, Gigha Hotel is difficult to miss. Genuinely welcoming, with comfortable bedrooms & beautiful views out towards the Kintyre Peninsula, the hotel balances great service with an effortlessly relaxed atmosphere. Along with the restaurant & bistro, there is also a small pub in one corner downstairs, which is an interesting place to meet locals. Ask early for a sea view & be sure to try the Loch Fyne Kipper for b/fast. Dogs welcome. Arriving from the ferry, follow the road up to a T-junction & turn left; the hotel is about 200yds further. **£££**

Yurt (sleeps 4) Post Office Hse, Ardminish PA41 7AA; 01583 505251; e tealejc@yahoo. co.uk; late Mar–Sep. With a sea view & wood-burning stove, this 20ft-wide Mongolian yurt is an off-grid glamping experience. Separate toilet & shower facilities. No dogs. **£££**

Drumallan Bed & Breakfast (3 rooms) Drumallan, just off the Gallochoille rd, PA41 7AD; 01583 505241. Though not born on Gigha, Mary Allan has lived on the island for most of her life & her B&B is a local 'home from home' experience. There is a separate communal dining/sitting room for guests, with comfortable sofas & a lovely sea view. Resident cats, but dogs are also welcome. **££**

Boathouse Ardminish; 01583 505123; e sharon@boathouseongigha.com; May–Sep. Run by the Boathouse restaurant (see below), this basic campsite is right beside the sea. It's a good idea to call ahead & book a space as the site is small & popular in summer months. **£**

Boathouse (see above) w boathouseongigha.com; May–Sep 10.00– 22.00 daily. High-quality restaurant with excellent local seafood, right on the beachfront. Book in advance. **££–£££**

Gigha Hotel (see above) Mar–Nov 10.00–13.00 & 17.30–19.30, Dec–Feb pre-booked lunchtime or from 18.30 daily; . While head chef Adam cooks for both, the Bistro is cheaper & more casual, while more elaborate dishes are served as a fine-dining experience in the Arches Restaurant.

The butternut squash & wild mushroom tagliatelle in the restaurant is excellent. **££**

Pottery Tea Room Gigha Gallery, Ardminish PA41 7AA; 01583 505150; gighagallery; e henri.smashingglass@gmail. com; 10.00–16.00 Mon–Sat, noon–16.00 Sun (flexible). Run as a co-operative, this cosy art gallery cum café serves hot & cold drinks, smoothies, homemade cakes & ice cream. Local produce where possible & good vegan options. **£**

SHOPPING

In addition to the places listed below, it's worth checking out the Gigha Gallery, which is also home to the Pottery Tea Room (see above) and hosts different local-interest art exhibitions.

Ardminish Stores 01583 505251; ; e tealejc@yahoo.co.uk; summer 09.00–18.30 Mon–Sat, noon–16.00 Sun, winter 09.00–17.15 Mon–Tue & Thu–Sat, 09.00–13.00 Wed, noon–14.00 Sun. All your absolute essentials under 1 roof, Joe & Hannah sell groceries & gifts, a post office, ATM, petrol/diesel filling station & bicycle hire. Though stock is limited, there is a good range of local products. On the corner of the T-junction between the main road & the ferry port.

Gigha Crafts Next to the Gigha Gallery, Ardminish PA41 7AA; ⏲ 10.00–16.00 Mon–Sat, noon–16.00 Sun (flexible). This is a small but carefully curated shop with an emphasis on local handiwork. In addition, owner Henri plays traditional local tunes & offers mandolin or fiddle lessons at £10 for 30mins.

Gigha Natural Skincare Upstairs from Gigha Crafts, Ardminish PA41 7AA; m 07881 426616; w gighas-naturalskincare.co.uk; ⏲ 10.00–16.00 Mon–Sat, noon–16.00 Sun (flexible). This shop sells a large range of natural oils & creams. The owner, Movern, works at the school, but is also enthusiastic about natural therapies & offers ear candling & reiki sessions by appointment. She hopes to expand the business to include massage in the future.

Wee Gift Shed Calag Ruadh, North Drumachro PA41 7AB; ✆01583 505151; e caroline_mcvean@ yahoo.co.uk; ⏲ Apr–Oct 10.30–17.30 daily. Whether you're looking for a knitted chicken, woolly hat or handmade necklace, Caroline's Wee Gift Shed has souvenirs & presents crammed into every inch of available space. She makes many of the things herself.

OTHER PRACTICALITIES

✚ **Medical** Nurse on call m 07876 132130; ⏲ 08.30–15.00 Mon–Fri

EVENTS

APRIL
Gigha Challenge m 07881 426616; ⎑; e gighachallenge@yahoo.co.uk. Walk, run or cycle 11 miles up & down the island or join the 5km run.

JUNE
Isle of Gigha Music Festival ✆01583 505160; w gighamf.org.uk. Intimate traditional Scottish music festival held on the last w/end in Jun.

JULY
Gigha Raft Race Contact the Boathouse restaurant (page 253). Competitors race home-built rafts. Usually held on the last Sat of Jul, this is entertaining to watch even if you haven't had time to sculpt your own craft.

LOCAL PRODUCE

As a visitor, choosing to buy local produce is a positive contribution to Gigha's economy, plus the carbon footprint of your food will be small and the quality is excellent.

Emma, of the **Wee Isle Dairy** (✆01583 505400; ⎑), calls her 200 free-range cows the Liquorice Allsorts – a mixture of breeds for the best-quality milk. The dairy produces rich, unhomogenised whole milk that is pasteurised in a less intensive, old-fashioned method and sold in glass bottles. Ron started making ice cream in the kitchen of Achamore House and has now expanded into a small range of sauces. Tarbet Farm, where the milk is produced, is not open to visitors, but you can try some of their dairy products in the Pottery Tea Room (page 253) or from Ardminish Stores (page 253).

With a focus on welfare and sustainability, **Gigha Halibut**'s (w gighahalibut. co.uk) land-based aquaculture system uses fresh seawater without polluting the ocean. The farm is not open to the public, but you can try the fresh fish in the Boathouse restaurant (page 253) and Gigha Hotel (page 253), or buy it smoked in Ardminish Stores.

Gigha's clean water is perfect for oysters and in high season, **Gigha Oysters** can be found on the menu in both of the island's restaurants.

ACHAMORE GARDENS The Gigha Heritage Trust decided to sell the mansion at Achamore, but keep possession of the garden, which is open to visitors (\01583 505390; w gigha.org.uk; adult/child/family £6/3/15). The house is private but was back on the market at the time of writing, so it will be interesting to see what happens in the future. More of a Hebridean jungle exploration than the finely manicured grounds one might imagine of a stately garden, the 54-acre Achamore Gardens were created in 1944 by the laird Colonel Sir James Horlick and his gardener Kitty Lloyd Jones. The Trust are doing their best to restore them with a limited budget. Gigha's warmer microclimate has ensured the survival of many plants that would not usually be found in Scotland. Keep an open mind as you explore; the vast collections of rhododendrons and camellias are not diminished by their overgrown state, and the pathways' mossy carpets are pleasant to feel underfoot.

WALKING, BEACHES AND ARCHAEOLOGY Owing to Gigha's small size, extensive coastline and wealth of archaeology, it is difficult to walk anywhere without passing something of interest; actually locating historical sites among the undergrowth can sometimes be a different matter. Gigha's beaches are much more easily located and, as you are never far away from the turquoise water, one of the greatest pleasures to be had is in discovering your own secluded patch of sand.

Easily found at the summit of Gigha's most northerly point is **Carn Na Faire** (the 'Watch Cairn') (⊕ 55°43'42.5"N 5°43'22.4"W). There is a clear (though possibly very muddy) path, marked with yellow sticks, which leads off to the left just after the small ruined building on the other side of the road. This spot was used for centuries during clan times, and probably by the Vikings, as a smoke-signalling beacon. Anderson suggests that it is 'practically certain' to be late Bronze Age and that excavations would uncover burial cists. In its current state, there is not a lot to see other than a large pile of rocks, but it is a fantastic viewpoint for the surrounding coastline, with the possibility of seeing large marine mammals such as seals or occasionally dolphins, and well worth the short walk in any weather conditions.

At the very northern end of the island's road is **Port Mòr**, the old ferry port; it's possible to park here. To reach **Palm Tree Beach** (⊕ 55°43'27.4"N 5°43'01.7"W) – just one of a long string of remote sandy beaches without any sign of human habitation in sight – walk east from here, keeping the sea on your left. This beautiful, low-lying stretch of coastline is home to many species of seabird, including oystercatchers and cormorants.

It's possible (though perhaps something for the more committed archaeology enthusiasts) to search for the late Bronze-Age **Carn Ban** (the 'White Cairn') (⊕ 5°43'17.6"N 5°42'48.3"W) by tramping roughly a mile further south along an intermittent path around the coast. Note, though, that it is not easy to find and there is a lot of spiky heather to battle through. The burial site was discovered accidentally by dyke builders in 1792, who found chambers, a complete skeleton and 'an intolerable stench'. The whole cairn was apparently a complicated structure of 49ft diameter, with four cists. What is visible now is even less than during Anderson's time and anyone not looking carefully would be forgiven for mistaking Carn Ban for yet another group of protruding boulders. On closer inspection, however, large cover stones, which would have formed the tops of the graves, are obvious and it is easy enough to peek into one of the chambers. There are a couple of bones inside, but it seems unlikely they are Bronze Age.

Around 2 miles south from Port Mòr, there is a walking track that leads from the main road off to the west coast, which is indicated to the **'Twin Beaches'**. This tombolo, a double stretch of sand separated by a few yards of coastal grasses, connects Gigha to the tied island of **Eilean Garbh**. With turquoise water and white sand the beach is a truly unique sight but unfortunately, as with so many places in the Hebrides, its exposed location means the sand can collect a lot of plastic debris after storms (please take some back to the mainland with you if you have a car). The rocky island has unparalleled views down Gigha's western coastline and across to Islay and Jura.

From here, it's possible to walk a mile further north to **Fishermen's Cave** (✦ 55°43'35.5"N 5°43'30.1"W), located between a small inlet called Bàgh Beag and the hill Cnoc An Itch, which has been inhabited at several times throughout history. This must have been a miserable existence as the only truly sheltered, dry area here is extremely small. Bored inhabitants have carved the walls and reportedly there is an engraving that dates from 1735, but the oldest I could find were from the 1800s.

Continuing south along the main road brings you to **Carragh An Tairbeirt** (the Stone of Tarbert) (✦ 55°42'25.8"N 5°43'56.1"W), on the left-hand side. Also known as the Hanging Stone, Druid's Stone or Spitheag an Fhamhair (the Giant's Chip/Pebble), this is a distinctive cleft standing stone, which you will most likely recognise from the Gigha Heritage Trust's logo. Horrifically, it was once used for hanging people condemned at the nearby Hill of the Assembly, but this was not its original purpose, which has now been forgotten.

About 600yds further south, in the field opposite Tarbert Farm, is **Ruidh A'Chaibeil** (Field of the Chapel) (✦ 55°42'03.9"N 5°44'02.3"). Though this is an ancient burial site, which once had stones to mark the graves, the battered remains of a Celtic cross are all that is now distinguishable to an interested novice. Apparently the graveyard had originally been larger but was destroyed by a farmer who wanted to make more use of his field. The graveyard's date is unknown, but it certainly pre-dates Kilchattan (page 206).

In the centre of the island, it's an easy clamber up to **Creag Bhan** (✦ 55°41'40.0"N 5°44'35.4"W), Gigha's highest hill at 328ft, which is a good vantage point to spot hen harriers and provides unrivalled views across the island. To get there, take the rough road up towards Ardailly (west off the main road); opposite Mill Loch, on the right-hand side, you'll find the well-marked track that leads to the summit. There is a small place here where it is possible to park without blocking the passing place.

Back in Ardminish, **Rudha Chinn Mhoir Beach** is signposted from the main road just south of the Gigha Hotel. It only takes a couple of minutes to walk there and, although it's small, the sand and water look as tropical as anywhere on the island.

Half a mile south of the Gigha Hotel is a turning to the right marked to Achamore Gardens (page 255). Just 300yds up the track, past the village hall (on your right), **St Cathan's Church and Kilchattan Burial Ground** is the perfect place to ponder on previous generations of island inhabitants. Now an atmospheric ruin with some elaborate window frames intact, the church is thought to have been built in the 13th century. Most of the graves are unidentifiable under layers of moss and lichen, but among the more obvious and interesting are those of Malcolm MacNeill (in a walled enclosure to the east of the church), who died in 1493 and is depicted as a warrior, and an elaborately carved grave slab in the southeast corner of the church, thought to be from the 14th century.

Continuing along the track, at its highest point, before you reach the houses, there is a small gate and path up to the **Ogham Stone** (✦ 55°40'10.8"N 5°44'56.7"W).

This proud pillar, presiding over the burial ground, is inscribed in Ogham, an early medieval alphabet from Ireland. The translation is disputed and the stone is currently coated in crispy lichen, making it difficult to distinguish anything at all. It's thought to be a gravestone of around 1,400 years old and mentions the name of the man buried there and his father.

Cuddyport Beach and the **quern stone quarry** (✪ 55°40'07.7"N 5°45'49.9"W) are further along the main track that passes the burial ground and the path to the Ogham Stone; the bay is best reached on foot or by bike as parking is very limited once you pass the Ogham Stone. Follow the track and bear left past a couple of houses at the top of the hill, heading towards Ardlamy Farm. When you reach a small junction you'll see that 'Cuddyport Beach, Quern Stone Quarry' is signposted at the beginning of a path leading northwest through the fields.

Stop some 200yds before you reach the farm to pass through the gate on your left. Follow this next track southwest until it dwindles to nothing around a gateway where you should bear right and head diagonally across the field (southwest) towards the small white house, 250yds away. Just before reaching the house turn left through double gates to follow a short path down beside the house to the shore.

Arriving at the shore, Cuddyport Beach is just 50yds to the west (on your right-hand side). Sometimes referred to as Ardlamey Bay by locals and Port Na Cathrach on the OS map, this is an attractive sandy beach with an old rocky pier and a small boathouse; it would make a perfect spot for a picnic. The quern quarry, with its many distinctive 20-inch-wide, round marks, can be found on the western side of the headland, though it is generally best approached from the other side. The site probably dates from the 18th century; quern stones were used for grinding corn. The picturesque sands of Cuddyport Beach are 150yds west of the headland and definitely worth a visit even if you have no interest in history.

South coast circle with Bodach and Cailleach

Distance: 3 miles; time: 3 hours; start/end: South Pier; OS Explorer map: 357 Kintyre North
This magnificent hike covers some fairly arduous ground, encompassing ancient stones and most of the south coast.

Starting at South Pier (the very southern end of the main road; parking is possible here), begin by walking back up the road, past the grassy airstrip on the left, until you reach a gravel track that heads towards the wind turbines.

Follow this track until you are level with the turbines; here you will see a gateway on the right, marked with a small sign for 'Bodach and Cailleach, Eun Eilean'. Go through this gateway, then through the wind turbines and head 200yds north to the very small, rocky hill **Cnoc A'Bhodaich** ('Hill of the Old Man').

At the top of the small hill are **Bodach and Cailleach** ('the old man and woman', or 'hag' to be more precise; ✪ 55°39'41.8"N 5°45'19.5"W), two very curiously shaped stones that appear to be linked to other sites in Scotland. For example, Tigh nam Bodach ('house of the old man') in central Scotland has a Cailleach, Bodach and a whole family of their smaller stones. On Gigha itself, a folk tale talks of how they prowl the moorland after dark.

Return the way you came, back to the wind turbines and the gate on the far side of the field. This time, turn right on the gravel track, go through another gate, pass the third turbine and go through a final gate on to the open moorland along the coast. Follow an overgrown path that bears to the left and head southwest towards the sea.

From this point onwards you will roughly be making your way around Gigha's southern coastline anticlockwise. The next section of the walk is boggy and unclear. To follow the coast, cross a stile in the fence to a small beach or you can just keep to the drier ground above, but you may miss some wildlife. Along the coast, look out for boulders of white quartz, basking seals, seabirds and more elusive otters.

Eventually you will come out on to the wide, sandy **Gròb Bàgh** (known locally as **Leim Beach**), with Leim Farm on your left. On the far side of the bay, climb a stile over the wall and head straight uphill towards the highest ground and a small cairn.

The higher ground is easier but, if you are interested, there are several sensible ways to get down to the natural rocky features of **Sloc an Tranan** ('the Snoring Pit'; ✪ 55°38'55.2"N 5°45'42.3"W) and/or the larger and more impressive blow hole **Sloc an Leim** (Jumping Pit/Squirting Cave; ✪ 55°38'47.6"N 5°45'42.5"W) slightly further south. Be careful of your footing. Depending on the conditions, you will find the caves by the intimidating sounds or the jets of seawater they project. From the pits you can return to higher ground by making your way along the coast for about 200yds, then turning left and walking up the grassy slope, before turning right at the top to head roughly northeast.

Having now reached the most southerly point of Gigha, the route heads along the southeast coast; follow a stone wall roughly northeast along the clifftops. Looking out to sea you will see Cara Island, the smaller Gigalum Island, further north, and, beyond them both, have a good view out towards Kintyre.

Continue to follow the wall down to where it meets a fence and pass through the gateway there. You can walk along the beach or grassy area beside it all the way back to **South Pier.**

14

Gateway Towns

OBAN

Oban is by far the biggest and most exciting of the ports serving the Inner Hebrides. Home to around 9,000 people, a population that more than doubles with visitors in the summer months, the waterfront town maintains its charm through a thriving community and the historic buildings and characterful boats of its harbour. Ferries leave from here to Mull, Coll, Tiree, Lismore, Colonsay and Islay; and, with a train station, bus connections and even an airport, the town is well connected to the rest of the mainland. There is plenty to detain you in Oban for a couple of days, which is particularly fortunate in bad weather when you might not have any other option. Those doing extended trips in the Hebrides might be pleased to have a break from the restrictions of remote island life; of all the places featured in this book Oban has by far the best shopping and eating opportunities. For information and listings beyond what is included here, check w oban.org.uk.

GETTING THERE AND AWAY

By bus or rail Oban is well connected to Glasgow; those wanting to travel to/from Mallaig will usually need to change in Fort William or Crianlarich. Oban Station Square bus stop and the train station are just 350yds from the ferry terminal. For route planning and connecting bus and train services, use w traveline.info.

By ferry CalMac (☎ 08000 665000 or, from outside the UK, +44 1475 650397; w calmac.co.uk) run services between Oban and the islands of Mull, Coll, Tiree, Lismore, Colonsay and Islay. The ferry terminal is near the centre of town.

By air **Oban and the Isles Airport** (North Connel PA37 1SW; ☎ 01631 572910; w obanandtheislesairports.com) is a small airport, and only open during the daytime. Services from here are operated by the equally small **Hebridean Air** (☎ 08458 057465; w hebrideanair.co.uk), which runs flights to Coll, Colonsay, Tiree and Islay, as well as charter flights.

GETTING AROUND Oban is easy to wander around on foot. There are a few outlying attractions, such as Dunollie Castle, which are quicker to reach on the bus (see w westcoastmotors.co.uk/timetables/oban-isle-of-mull for route map & times), or by cycling or driving. Note that parking (mostly pay and display in the centre) in Oban is in high demand during the busy summer season and as a result can be difficult at times.

Gateway Towns OBAN

14

259

OBAN

Oban & the
Isles Airport

CORRAN ESPLANADE

*Dunollie Castle &
1745 House Museum
(1 mile)*

Bradt

N

| 0 | | 100m |
| 0 | | 100yds |

DUNOLLIE RD

DUNOLLIE ROAD

BREADALBANE STREET

ALBERT LANE

NURSERY LANE

CORRAN ESPLANADE

GEORGE STREET

① ②

For listings, see opposite

🛏 **Where to stay**
1 Backpackers Plus
2 Oban Backpackers
3 Perle
4 Whisky Vaults

🍴 **Where to eat and drink**
5 Baab Meze & Grill
6 Ee.usk
7 George Street Chip Shop
8 Nories
9 Piazza
10 The Pokey Hat
Whisky Vaults (see 4)

Oban Phoenix
🎬 Cinema

Post office
Oxfam ✉
Books ●

Oban War &
⚓ Peace Museum

*Oban
Bay*

Oban
Cycles
🚲

⑧

⑩

⑥
⑨

*Lismore, Mull,
Colonsay, Coll,
Tiree*

🚢

Millets ●

GEORGE STREET

CRAIGARD ROAD

ALBERT ROAD

DALRIACH ROAD

ARDCONNEL ROAD

ARDCONNEL TERRACE

LAUREL ROAD

McCaig's
Tower

DUNCRAGGAN ROAD

ARDCONNEL ROAD

TAYLOR'S BRAE

ROCKFIELD ROAD

ARGYLL ST

Boots ✚
Royal Bank $
of Scotland

TWEEDALE STREET

④

HILL STREET

Waterstones ●

⑤ Jackson
③ ⑦ Butchers
$ TSB

QUEEN'S PARK PLACE

STATION ROAD

Oban Station
Square bus stop 🚌

Railway
station

AIRD'S PLACE

AIRD'S CRESCENT

STEVENSON STREET

Argyll
Square
$
Clydesdale

● Ferry
terminal

SHORE STREET

ALBANY STREET

CAMPBELL STREET

CREAG AN AIRM

GLENSHELLACH STREET

DRIMVARGIE RD

HIGH STREET

COMBIE STREET

LOCHSIDE STREET

McConechy's Tyre
🔧 & Auto Centres

SOROBA LANE

SOROBA ROAD

GLENCRUITTEN ROAD

Tesco

Ⓟ

Lidl
Oban

*Lorn & Islands
Hospital (½mile)*

Ⓟ

Ⓟ

Bike hire

Oban Cycles 87 George St, PA34 5NN; w obancyclescotland.com; ⏰ 10.00–17.00 Tue–Sat. Hires, sales & repairs.

WHERE TO STAY *Map, opposite*

Whether you're looking for luxury on the seafront or a lively backpackers' hostel, Oban has a full range of accommodation options and good choices to make within each. Should you need them, free toilets and showers are available behind the white buildings with red roofs on the harbour.

🏠 **Perle** (59 rooms) Station Sq, PA34 5RT; ☎ 01631 700301; w perleoban.com. A grand old building, built in 1882 as the first hotel for the railway, it has gone under various names such as 'The Station' & 'The Caledonian'. It is now a listed building, right in the centre of town. Some rooms have great sea views, which is reflected in the pricing structure. **£££££**

🏠 **Whisky Vaults** (10 rooms) 3 Tweeddale St, PA34 5DD; ☎ 01631 566722; w obanwhiskyvaults. co.uk. Newly renovated old town house in a striking but tasteful colour scheme of turquoise & gold. Friendly owners & special rates for stranded islanders when ferries are cancelled. **£££–££££**

🏠 **Backpackers Plus** (47 beds) Breadalbane St, PA34 5PH; ☎ 01631 567189; w backpackersplus. com. Large hostel in an old church. Dorms & private rooms (with & without private bathroom): rooms with shared bathrooms recommended as they are cheaper & more spacious with windows. Shared computer. B/fast inc. **£–££**

🏠 **Oban Backpackers** (55 beds) Breadalbane St, PA34 5NZ; ☎ 01631 562107; w obanbackpackers.com; ⏰ Apr–end Oct. Colourful hostel with wonderful painted map on the wall in communal area. Kitchen would be rather lively if fully booked, but communal seating is pleasant & relaxed. **£**

WHERE TO EAT AND DRINK *Map, opposite*

✕ **Baab Meze & Grill** Station Rd, PA34 5RT; ☎ 01631 707130; w baabgrill.co.uk; ⏰ 17.30–21.30 daily. Eastern Mediterranean theme with dishes from Greece, Turkey & the Levant. Golden light streams in at sunset. **££**

✕ **Ee.usk** North Pier, PA34 5QD; ☎ 01631 565666; w eeusk.com; ⏰ noon–14.30 & 17.45–21.00 daily; ♿. This modern white building with a red roof on the harbourfront serves reliably good local seafood, including lobster from Luing. Surrounded by glass for harbour views. **££**

✕ **Piazza** North Pier, PA34 5QD; ☎ 01631 563628; w piazzaoban.com; ⏰ 10.00–14.30 & 17.30–20.30/21.00 daily; ♿. Spacious family restaurant serving pizza & pasta. Next to Ee.usk, with views over harbour. **£**

✕ **George Street Chip Shop** 13–15 George St, PA34 5RU; ☎ 01631 566664; w georgestreetfishrestaurant.co.uk. Fish & chips with crispy batter, plus a great vegetarian haggis. Takeaway only. **£**

✕ **Nories** 86 George St, PA34 5NN; ☎ 01631 563736; ⏰ noon–22.30 daily. Fish & chips with very friendly service; sit inside or takeaway. **£**

🍦 **The Pokey Hat** 13 Stafford St, PA34 5NJ; 🅵. Pink building with lime green sign & model cows outside serving Italian ice cream that's homemade on the premises daily. **£**

🍷 **Whisky Vaults** (see above) ⏰ summer 15.00–midnight daily, winter 18.00–quiet daily. As the name suggests, this hotel's bar is the go-to place for whisky enthusiasts. Having worked in the trade for most of his life, John has built up a lot of knowledge as well as his enormous whisky collection. A dram costs anything from £3.60 to £380 (a Macallen 30-year-old Speyside), so best ask first if you are on a budget! The furnishings in the bar are made from recycled whisky barrels, with coopers' tools & copper trimmings. John hosts whisky-tasting evenings every month for up to 40 people (£25–50 pp).

SHOPPING Oban has a decent range of standard high-street shops for clothing and other things you might have forgotten.

Food shops Although most of the islands have grocery stores & it is good to support the local economy there, it's generally worth taking at least some food across with you for self-catering holidays, & Oban is by far the best place to stock up.

Food from Argyll at the Pier The Ferry Terminal, The Railway Pier, PA34 5DB; ☎01631 563636; w foodfromargyllatthepier.com; ⏰ 09.00–16.00 Mon–Sat. Shop, café & takeaway (£) with a good selection of local produce.
Jackson Butchers 2 George St, PA34 5RX; ☎01631 562016; ⏰ 07.30–17.30 Mon–Sat. Traditional butchers established in 1932.
Lidl Oban Soroba Rd, PA34 4HY; w lidl.co.uk; ⏰ 08.00–22.00 Mon–Fri, 08.00–20.00 Sat & Sun. Probably the cheapest & best value for money of the large supermarkets.

Tesco Lochavullin Rd, PA34 4HP; w tesco.com; ⏰ 06.00–midnight Mon–Sat, 08.00–20.00 Sun. Jarringly enormous supermarket.

High-street shops
Millets George St, PA34 5NN; ☎01631 571122; w millets.co.uk; ⏰ 10.00–17.30 daily. Affordable outdoor gear, but choose carefully for quality products.
Oxfam Books 107/109 George St, PA34 5NT; ☎01631 566465. Notably large selection of secondhand books, including local interest.
Waterstones 12 George St, PA34 5SB; ☎01631 571455; w waterstones.com; ⏰ 09.00–21.00 Mon–Sat, 11.00–17.00 Sun. Oban branch of the nationwide bookshop chain.

OTHER PRACTICALITIES
$ Banks Clydesdale Bank, 6 Argyll Sq, PA34 4AZ; ☎0800 345 7365; ⏰ 09.15–16.30 Mon–Fri); Royal Bank of Scotland, 26 George St, PA34 5SB; ☎03457 242424; ⏰ 09.15–17.00 Mon–Tue & Thu–Fri, 10.00–17.00 Wed, 09.00–12.30 Sat); TSB, 31–35 Airds Cres, PA34 5SQ; ☎01631 399998; ⏰ 09.00–16.30 Mon–Fri)
🎬 Cinema Oban Phoenix Cinema, 140 George St, PA34 5NZ; ☎01631 562905; w obanphoenix.com; ♿. Independent & community owned.
Fuel Tesco Petrol Filling Station, Lochavullin Rd, PA34 4HP; ☎03456 779519; ⏰ 06.00–20.00 Mon–Sat, 07.00–20.00 Sun
Mechanic McConechy's Tyre & Auto Centres,

21 Lochside St, PA34 4HP; ☎01631 570047; ⏰ 08.30–17.00 Mon–Sat
✚ Hospital Lorn & Islands Hospital, Glengallan Rd, PA34 4HH; ☎01631 567500; w obanhospital. com
✚ Pharmacy Boots, 34–38 George St, PA34 5NL; ☎01631 562517; w boots.com; ⏰ 09.00–17.30 Mon–Sat, noon–16.00 Sun
✉ Post offices There are 2 conveniently located post offices in Oban: one at 128 George St, PA34 5NT (⏰ 06.00–22.00 daily) & the other in the Tesco on Lochside St, PA34 4HP (⏰ 08.00–20.00 Mon–Sat, 10.00–16.00 Sun).

EVENTS Check **Oban What's On** (w obanwhatson.co.uk) for event listings around the time of your visit.

June
Oban Live w obanlive.com. Argyll's largest music event.

WHAT TO SEE AND DO There's plenty to fill a day or two in Oban. This is just a small selection, but pick up a copy of the *Oban Times* or find more on w oban.org.uk.

The **Oban War & Peace Museum** (Old Oban Times Bldg, Corran Esp, PA34 5PX; ☎01631 570007; w obanmuseum.org.uk; ⏰ Mar–Apr & Nov 10.00–16.00 daily; May–Oct 10.00–18.00 Mon–Sat, 10.00–16.00 Sun; free) is a good introduction to Oban's history, including the town's role in World War II.

Just a little north of the town is **Dunollie Castle** and the **1745 House Museum** (PA34 5TT; ☎01631 570550; w dunollie.org; ⏰ Apr–Oct; adult/child £6/3; ♿). While the ruined castle itself is small, it is spectacularly positioned with views across to Kerrera (page 193). The museum, set in an 18th-century house about 100yds away, gives a more balanced account of history than most castle museums, with space and consideration given to servants and normal people from the 18th century. The restored Dunollie weaving loom is a real highlight. The castle has wonderful leafy grounds with mature deciduous trees. The on-site **Kettle Garden Café** sells soup, proper coffee, homemade cakes and ice-cream floats to be eaten outside or under a marquee.

MALLAIG

The only other substantial port town serving the Inner Hebrides is Mallaig, which has ferries running to Skye and the Small Isles. Little more than a village, it is mostly made up of B&Bs, fish 'n' chip shops, fishing boats and seagulls, with a backdrop of pretty hills and an interesting boatyard. There are limited shopping opportunities, but they are still probably more extensive than those on the Small Isles or Sleat.

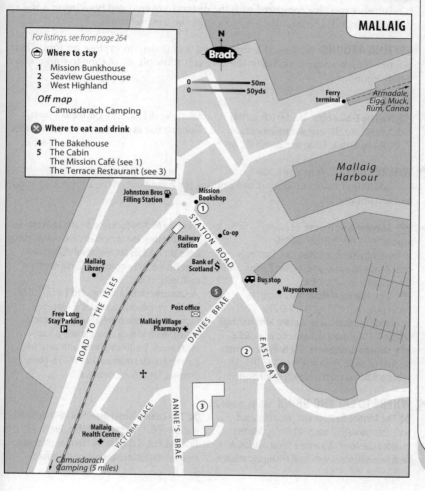

MALLAIG

For listings, see from page 264

Where to stay
1 Mission Bunkhouse
2 Seaview Guesthouse
3 West Highland

Off map
Camusdarach Camping

Where to eat and drink
4 The Bakehouse
5 The Cabin
The Mission Café (see 1)
The Terrace Restaurant (see 3)

0 ____ 50m
0 ____ 50yds

Ferry terminal — Armadale, Eigg, Muck, Rùm, Canna

Mallaig Harbour

Johnston Bros Filling Station
Mission Bookshop

Railway station
Co-op
STATION ROAD
Mallaig Library
Bank of Scotland
Bus stop
Wayoutwest
Free Long Stay Parking
ROAD TO THE ISLES
Post office
Mallaig Village Pharmacy
DAVIES BRAE
EAST BAY
VICTORIA PLACE
ANNIE'S BRAE
Mallaig Health Centre
Camusdarach Camping (5 miles)

GETTING THERE AND AWAY By both rail and road the journey to Mallaig follows two of the most beautiful routes in Scotland. **The West Highland Line** runs arguably the most picturesque railway journey in the UK, crossing the unforgettable Glenfinnan Viaduct, famous for its appearance in the *Harry Potter* films. Travelling by road, the A830, which starts just north of Fort William, forms part of the well-known **Road to the Isle**s, passing mountainous scenery, lochs and parts of the coast.

By ferry CalMac (08000 665000 or, from outside the UK, +44 1475 650397; w calmac.co.uk) runs services to Armadale on Skye (page 56), the Small Isles (page 108) and South Uist in the Outer Hebrides. The ferry terminal is on the western side of the harbour.

By rail or bus The easiest and quickest journeys from the rest of the UK to Mallaig usually pass through Glasgow. Check w traveline.info to plan all connecting rail/bus journeys on the mainland. **West Coast Railways** (08448 503131; w westcoastrailways. co.uk) run the picturesque *Jacobite* steam train from Fort William to Mallaig; the fare is relatively expensive compared with the distance covered and booking in advance is recommended. The train station is opposite the ferry terminal.

GETTING AROUND Mallaig is a small town and is easy to explore on foot. There is a free long-stay car park, but make sure you allow plenty of time to find a space before your ferry.

By bike
🚲 **Mallaig E-bike Hire** The Pier Office, PH41 4QD; 01687 462233; w mallaigebikehire.co.uk; ⏲ 09.30–16.00 daily. E-bike hire: hour/half day/ full day/week £10/25/35/150. Useful if you're looking to take an e-bike to Skye or the Small Isles.

WHERE TO STAY *Map, page 263*
For additional accommodation and options for eating out, have a look at w road-to-the-isles.org.uk.

🏠 **Seaview Guesthouse** (8 rooms) Main St, PH41 4QS; 01687 462059; w seaviewguesthousemallaig.com. Spotlessly clean & tastefully decorated in greys & blues. 5 of the rooms are en suite. **£££**

🏠 **West Highland Hotel** (41 rooms) Davies Brae, PH41 4QZ; 01687 462210; w westhighlandhotel.co.uk. A grand hotel with high ceilings & a large guest lounge. Good value. **£££**

🏠 **Mission Bunkhouse** (12 beds, inc 3 private rooms) Station Rd, PH41 4QA; m 07765 013817. Chavdar & Darina run this friendly little hostel above the Mission Bookshop & Café. Bedrooms are small, but there is a comfortable communal lounge & the kitchen does not feel crowded. Door on to large flat roof gives extra space & is a novelty in good weather. **£**

🏕 **Camusdarach Camping** PH39 4NT; 01687 450221; w camusdarach.co.uk; ⏲ Apr–Sep. Located 5 miles south of Mallaig on the way to Arisaig, this is a lovely campsite near a huge sandy beach. Small café & shop with no tables, but proper coffee machine. Free Wi-Fi & phone charging. Kettle & microwave. **£**

✕ WHERE TO EAT AND DRINK *Map, page 263*
✕ **The Terrace Restaurant** West Highland Hotel (see above); ⏲ noon–21.00; ♿. Waiters in tweed waistcoats & a terrace to eat outside. A fresh, seasonal menu with local Arisaig mussels & Mallaig cod. **££–£££**

✕ **The Cabin** Davies Brae, PH414PU; 01687 462207; 📘; ⏲ noon–20.00 Mon, Tue & Thu–Sat. Fish & chips to takeaway or sit-down meals in restaurant, specialising in seafood. **£–££**

The Bakehouse The Old Quay, PH41 4QF; 01687 462808; ⏱ 09.00–15.00 Tue–Sat. Coffee, fresh bread & excellent pastries. No tables, but decking outside on the harbourfront. £

SHOPPING

Co-op Station Rd, PH41 4PY; 01687 462240; w coop.co.uk; ⏱ 07.00–20.00 daily. Medium-sized grocery store.

Mission Bookshop Station Rd, PH41 4PU; 01687 460105; 🔲; ⏱ from 08.00 Mon–Sat, from 09.00 Sun; ♿. Old history books including some local & of the isles, also fiction. Proceeds to local charities.

Wayoutwest Main St, PH41 4QS; 01687 460006; 🔲. Outdoor gear.

OTHER PRACTICALITIES

$ Bank Bank of Scotland, Main St, PH41 4PZ; 01687 462265; ⏱ 10.15–15.45 Mon–Tue & Thu–Fri, 10.15–13.00 Wed

Fuel Johnston Bros Filling Station, PH41 4QD; ⏱ 09.00–17.00 Mon–Fri, 10.00–16.00 Sat

🔲 Internet Mallaig Library, Mallaig & Morar Community Centre, West Bay, PH41 4PX; 01687 460097; ⏱ 10.30–14.00 Tue, 13.00–17.00 Wed, 17.00–20.00 Thu, 10.00–14.00 Fri, 10.00–noon Sat

✚ Medical Mallaig Health Centre, Victoria Rd, PH41 4RN; 01687 462202

✚ Pharmacy Mallaig Village Pharmacy, Davies Brae, PH41 4QY; 01687 462209; ⏱ 09.00–13.00 & 14.00–17.30 Mon–Fri, 09.00–13.00 Sat

✉ Post office 1 Davies Brae, PH41 4PU; ⏱ 08.00–22.00 Mon–Sat, 09.00–21.00 Sun

OTHER PORTS AND CONNECTIONS

Although Oban and Mallaig serve the majority of the Inner Hebrides, there are several other small ports. The following port towns have small villages and a couple of limited amenities: **Kyle of Lochalsh** for the Skye Bridge (page 56); **Arisaig** for the Small Isles (page 107); **Kilchoan** for Tobermory on Mull (page 159); **Lochaline** for Fishnish on Mull (page 159); and **Tayinloan** for Gigha (page 252).

Port Appin, where you can catch a short passenger ferry to Lismore (page 189), has certain amenities that are missing on Lismore: a doctor (Port Appin Surgery, PA38 4DE; 01631 730271) and somewhere to get evening meals (Pier House Hotel, PA38 4DE; 01631 730302; w pierhousehotel.co.uk; ⏱ 12.30–14.30 & 18.30–21.30 daily). Nearby **Castle Stalker** (PA38 4BL; w castlestalker.com), a spectacularly positioned fortress on a tiny island, could also technically be counted as one of the Inner Hebrides.

Kennacraig, where ferries leave from for Islay (page 218), and **Gallanach**, for Kerrera (page 194), are both just ferry ports with nothing else around them.

Appendix 1

GLOSSARY

Gaelic, Scottish and regionally specific archaeological terms used in the text.

Bard A poet. Historically, bards were employed by Clan chiefs to tell their family history; they were professional storytellers, oral historians and genealogists who composed poems and songs.

Broch A specific term for a round Iron-Age fortification with wide, double dry-stone walls that contained galleries, cells and a stairway.

Cairn Referring to a stony mound, this word comes from the Scottish Gaelic *càrn*. While more modern cairns can be used as waymarkers or are the result of collective efforts to indicate the end of a journey, often to the top of a hill or mountain, in archaeology these piles of stones often conceal deliberately deposited human remains dating from prehistoric times. They are often found in dramatic positions and sometimes have individual chambers.

Cenél An Old Irish word meaning kinship or family group in the time of Dál Riata (page 214).

Cist A burial method; generally rectangular and formed from stone slabs, set on an edge and covered by one or more horizontal slabs or capstones to make a coffin shape. They might be above or below the ground and can be from as early as Neolithic times.

Clan A Scottish group whose leaders claim descent from a common ancestor. Following Dál Riata, various family groups established territories across the islands. Lower-class people who lived on the ruling families' lands were also considered to be part of the clan.

Corrie A bowl-shaped geographical feature found among hills, usually formed by glaciation.

Cottar Relating predominantly to the 17th and 18th centuries, this is a Scottish term for a tenant on a farm who occupied a cottage, which may or may not have had a small piece of land attached. Comparable in meaning to the word peasant.

Crannog A small artificial or partially artificial island built within a loch or wetland and dating from anywhere between prehistoric and medieval times.

Croft In the Highlands, islands and west coast of Scotland, a croft is a small piece of agricultural land, which often has an accompanying dwelling and access to grazing rights in an area of common land. Subject to special protective legislation since 1886, crofts were originally a form of rented land; however, since 1976 tenants have had the option to buy and become owner-occupiers. Working crofts are common in certain parts of the Inner Hebrides, most noticeably on Tiree.

Cup-marked stones Somewhat mysterious, this term is used in archaeology to describe a rock bearing one or more obviously artificial, small, round depressions. In certain cases this is thought to be prehistoric art, but other examples seem more likely to indicate some sort of grinding for practical or superstitious reasons.

Dùn/Dun A Scottish Gaelic word meaning fort; often Anglicised to 'dun'. In archaeology, it refers to a rounded building or settlement enclosure with a thick dry-stone wall, often found in an elevated position. Generally, they are small structures that would have been able to protect a family group.

Firth A coastal inlet similar to a fjord, but with a less constrained definition; generally the result of glaciation and often associated with a large river.

Fish trap In the context of this book, a fish trap is an archaeological term relating to a substantial ring of rocks intended to catch fish as the tide goes out.

Fort A fort is a defensive enclosure, often in an elevated position, with one or more banks, ditches, ramparts or walls. Generally distinguished from a dun by being big enough to house a small community.

Hut circle An archaeological term to describe the remains of a roundhouse, often only visible as a raised circle with an indented centre.

Lazy beds Parallel banks of rig and furrow dug by spade for cultivation purposes.

Loch Scottish Gaelic and Scots word for a lake or a sea inlet.

Machair A Gaelic word for a fertile low-lying area of grass; used more specifically to describe the place where sand and shells have been colonised by plants along the edge of a beach.

Malt Germinated grain that has been dried in a process called 'malting'.

Midden An ancient rubbish dump, which can be as old as the Mesolithic era.

Mill stone Large, disk-shaped stones used in a mill for grinding grain. They originally would have come as a pair.

Pictish stone Decorative stones engraved by the Picts.

Ppm phenol Often used as a measure of the 'peatyness' of whisky, this term specifically refers to the parts per million of phenols, a group of aromatic chemical compounds, found in malted barley after they come out of the kiln and before being used in the rest of the whisky-making process.

Quern stones, saddle querns and quern quarries Quern stones are rocks used for grinding food such as corn from Neolithic times up until the 19th century. A saddle quern is usually thought to be the earliest incarnation, later being replaced by round rotary quern stones. At various points in the 18th and early 19th centuries, landowners banned quern stones and built mills with the intention of charging tenants to use them. Quern quarries are easily distinguished by their obviously artificial succession of roughly 60cm circular indentations; often in difficult-to-access locations, begging the question as to whether they were made in secret.

Roundhouses In Britain, circular or oval-plan roundhouses were the standard type of dwelling between the Bronze and Iron ages.

Saga Icelandic literature written in the 12th and 13th centuries to record the historic or legendary figures and events of Norway and Iceland.

Shielings Upland pastures used for grazing in summer; shieling huts are usually smaller than regular houses and were often inhabited by women and children or used for storing dairy. Most common in the 16th, 17th and 18th centuries.

Skerry A word originating from the Old Norse *sker*, meaning a small rocky island or reef.

Souterrain An underground chamber or passage, not found to contain human remains and often associated with an above-ground structure such as a roundhouse. There is some speculation that they were used for storing food. Generally thought to be from the Iron Age.

Standing stone Stones that have been deliberately set upright in the ground. These are of mysterious origin, but usually thought to be prehistoric, often Neolithic or Bronze Age.

Stone circle A circular or oval formation of multiple standing stones.

Ungulate A zoological term for a large group of hooved mammals.

Appendix 2

FURTHER INFORMATION

Many works, both factual and fictional, have been written about the Inner Hebrides. While the list below is far from exhaustive, the following publications are valuable in their specific areas of expertise and have been instrumental in the research for this guide. For literature, including children's books, see page 21.

GEOGRAPHY, GEOLOGY AND NATURAL HISTORY   The following books and websites are essential for identification and, in some cases, developing a wider understanding of the Inner Hebrides' natural environment.

Buczacki, Stefan *Collins Fungi Guide* HarperCollins, 2013
Chinery, Michael *Collins Complete Guide to British Insects* HarperCollins, 2009
Horne D J *The Geology of Jura* D G B Wright, Craighouse. Part of a series of booklets available to buy on Jura (page 241).
Oldham, Tony *The New Caves of Scotland* 2004. A *very* extensive record of Scotland's caves.
Sterry, Paul *Collins Complete Guide to British Coastal Wildlife* HarperCollins, 2012
Streeter, David *Collins Wild Flower Guide* HarperCollins, 2016
Svensson, Lars *Collins Bird Guide* HarperCollins, 2015
Tolman, Tom *Collins Butterfly Guide*, HarperCollins, 2009
Watson, Jeff *The Golden Eagle* T & A D Poyser, 2010

Websites

Hebridean Whale and Dolphin Trust w hwdt. org
Lochaber Geopark w lochabergeopark.org.uk
Royal Society for the Protection of Birds w rspb.org.uk
Scottish Geology w scottishgeology.com
Scottish Natural Heritage w nature.scot
Scottish Raptor Study Group w scottishraptorstudygroup.org

HISTORY, ARCHAEOLOGY AND HISTORICAL TRAVELOGUES   Many of these books or publications are more suited to academic research and would be a good starting point for anyone interested in studying the islands' history in more depth.

Anderson, R S G *Antiquities of Gigha* The Galloway Gazette, Newton Stewart, 1936. A dated but extensive guide to Gigha's archaeological sites.
Argyll: An Inventory of the Monuments, Volume 5: Islay, Jura, Colonsay & Oronsay The Royal Commission on the Ancient and Historical Monuments of Scotland, Glasgow, 1984. An enormous tome of a book, full of invaluable archaeological information.

Boswell, James *The Journal of a Tour to the Hebrides with Samuel Johnson* (4th edition) The Temple Classics, 1903. Boswell's account of his journey with Johnson in 1773. Johnson's book (see below) is more informative and easier to digest.

Caldwell, D H *Islay, Jura and Colonsay: A Historical Guide* Birlinn, 2001. Useful guide for discovering archaeological sites.

Caldwell, D H *Islay: The Land of the Lordship* Birlinn, 2008. An exploration of Islay's history.

Cameron, Archie *Bare Feet and Tackety Boots: A Boyhood on Rhum* Luath Press, Edinburgh, 1988. A valuable first-hand account of social history on Rùm before World War I.

Campbell, J L *Canna: The Story of a Hebridean Island* Oxford University Press, 1984

Hardy, K and Wickham-Jones C R (eds) *Mesolithic and Later Sites around the Inner Sound, Scotland: the Scotland's First Settlers project 1998–2004* SAIR 31 (Scottish Archaeological Internet Reports), 2009

✳ Hunter, John *The Small Isles* Historic Environment Scotland, Edinburgh, 2016. The most in-depth study of Small Isles' archaeology, this book is also full of incredible aerial photographs and is aesthetically pleasing enough to keep on the coffee table.

Hutchinson, Roger *Calum's Road* Birlinn, 2008. The incredible story of Calum MacLeod, resident of northern Raasay.

Johnson, Samuel *A Journey to the Western Islands of Scotland* Cassell & Company Ltd, London, 1886. Johnson's account of his and Boswell's trip in 1773.

Lamont, W D *The Early History of Islay* Burns & Harris Ltd, Dundee, 1966

Macaulay, Margaret *The Prisoner of St Kilda – The True Story of the Unfortunate Lady Grange* Luath Press Ltd, Edinburgh, 2009. An interesting revised history of Rachel Chiesley (see box, page 79).

Macculloch, J A *The Misty Isle of Skye: Its Scenery, its People, its Story* Oliphant, Anderson & Ferrier, Edinburgh, 1905

Maceacharna, Domhnall *The Lands of the Lordship: The Romance of Islay's Names* Argyll Reproductions Ltd, Port Charlotte, 1976

Martin, Martin *A Description of the Western Islands of Scotland, circa 1695: A Voyage to St Kilda* Birlinn, 1999

McDonald, Andrew *The Kingdom of the Isles: Scotland's Western Seaboard, c 110 – c1336* Tuckwell Press, East Lothian, 1997

Meek, Donald *Seanchas Île: Collecting, recording and preserving Islay's Gaelic heritage* Argyll Publishing, 2007

Miers, Mary *Western Seaboard: An Illustrated Architectural Guide* The Rutland Press, Edinburgh, 1998

Omand, Donald (ed) *The Argyll Book* Birlinn, 2004. An introduction to Argyll with sections written by different experts covering history, folklore, literature and a range of other topics.

Wilson, Les *The Drowned and the Saved: When War Came to the Hebrides* Birlinn, 2018. A history of the shipwrecked SS *Tuscania* and HMS *Otranto* during World War I.

Wright, Gordon *Jura and George Orwell* D G B Wright, Craighouse, 1993

Wright, Gordon *Jura's Heritage: A Brief History of the Island* D G B Wright, Craighouse, 1994

Website

Historic Environment Scotland Canmore
w canmore.org.uk. This amazing resource contains more than 320,000 records & 1.3 million catalogue entries for archaeological sites across Scotland.

WALKING AND GENERAL GUIDEBOOKS

Fairweather, Nick *Exploring Raasay: 20 Walking Routes* Thirsty Books, Edinburgh, 2015

Orr, Willie *Discovering Argyll, Mull & Iona* John Donald Publishers, Edinburgh, 1990. A dated guidebook full of fascinating anecdotes.

Welsh, Mary *Walks on the Isle of Islay* Clan Walk Guides, Perthshire, 1996

Youngson, Peter *The Long Road: A Driver's Guide to Jura* D G B Wright, Craighouse, 2005

Website

Walkhighlands w walkhighlands.co.uk.
Extensive website dedicated to Scottish walks (see box, page 65).

OTHER SCOTLAND GUIDES   For a full list of Bradt guides, visit w bradtguides.com/shop.

Greig, Donald and Flint, Darren *Slow Travel: Dumfries and Galloway* Bradt Travel Guides Ltd, 2020

Le Vay, Benedict *Scotland from the Rails: A Window Gazer's Guide* Bradt Travel Guides Ltd, released 2021

Rowe, Mark *Orkney* Bradt Travel Guides, 2019

Rowe, Mark *Outer Hebrides: The Western Isles of Scotland, from Lewis to Barra* Bradt Travel Guides Ltd, 2020

TOURIST INFORMATION WEBSITES AND BLOGS

Argyll w wildaboutargyll.co.uk
Canna w theisleofcanna.com
Coll w visitcoll.co.uk
Colonsay w colonsay.org.uk
Easdale w easdale.org
Eigg w isleofeigg.org
Gigha w gigha.org.uk
Iona w welcometoiona.com
Islay w islayinfo.com
Islay & Jura w islayjura.com
Jura w juradevelopment.co.uk
Kerrera w visitkerrera.co.uk
Lismore w isleoflismore.com
Luing w isleofluing.org
Muck w isleofmuck.com

Mull w isle-of-mull.net
Mull & Iona w visitmullandiona.co.uk
Oban w oban.org.uk
Raasay w raasay.com
Road to the Isles (inc Mallaig & the Small Isles) w road-to-the-isles.org.uk
Rùm w isleofrum.com
Seil w seil.oban.ws
Skye w isleofskye.com
Slate Islands w slateislands.org.uk
Sleat w visitsleat.org
Tiree w isleoftiree.com
Ulva w ulva.scot
Waternish w visit-waternish.co.uk

INNER HEBRIDES ONLINE

For additional online content, articles, photos and more on the Inner Hebrides, why not visit w bradtguides.com/innerhebrides?

NOTES

Page numbers in bold indicate main entries; those in italic indicate illus...

Index

Page numbers in **bold** indicate main entries; those in *italics* indicate maps

1745 House Museum (Oban) 262–3

A' Chill (Muck) 131
Abbey Museum (Iona) 184
accommodation 40
  see also individual islands
Achadun Castle (Lismore) 193
Achamore (Jura) 245–6
Achamore Gardens (Gigha) 255
adders 32
air travel 30
Àird Luing (Luing) 204–5
Àird nan Uan (Muck) 132
amphibians 11
An Àird peninsula (Skye) 62
An Corran (Skye) 53
An Corran beach (Skye) 69
An Iodhlann Museum (Tiree) 149
An Sithean (Islay) 236
archaeology 13
architecture 20
Ardalanish Bay (Mull) 178
Ardbeg Distillery (Islay) 231–2
Ardlussa (Jura) 246
Ardmeanach Peninsula (Mull) 169
Ardminish (Gigha) 249
Ardnahoe Distillery (Islay) 226
Armadale Castle (Skye) 93
Aros Castle (Mull) 167
art 20
assisted passage 15, 159
Atlantic Islands Centre (Luing) 204

Baird, William 97–8
Balamory 21, 161
Balephuil Bay (Tiree) 153
Balevullin (Tiree) 151
Ballachuan Hazelwood Nature Reserve (Seil) 201
Ballygown (Mull) 168
Battle of the Braes 56
bees 12
Belnahua 205
birds 10–11
  eagles 10, 214, 215, 244 *see also* white-tailed eagles *and* golden eagles

Manx shearwater 114
  puffin 11, 23, 26, 67, 83, 87, 126, 132, 148, 166, 176, 183, 185 *see also* tours, puffin
blackhouses 20, 135, 149
boat trips *see individual islands*
Bonnie Prince Charlie 15, 56, 88
Bonnie Prince Charlie's Cave (Skye) 88
bookshops 163, 175, 209, 223, 241, 262, 265
Book of Kells 181
bothies **42**, 71, 111, 120, 230, 240
Bowmore (Islay) 221–5, *222*
Bowmore Distillery (Islay) 224–5
Braes, the (Skye) 62
Breachacha Bay (Coll) 143
Bridgend (Islay) 225
Broadford and Elgol (Skye) 85–8
Brochel Castle (Raasay) 102
brochs 78, 80, 81, 82, 150, 169, 187, 191–2, **266**
Bronze Age 13, 158
Brothers' Point (Skye) 68
Bruichladdich Distillery (Islay) 235
budgeting 36
Bunessan (Mull) 176
Bunnahabhain Distillery (Islay) 226
Burg Estate (Mull) 169
buses 28
butterflies 11

Caisteal An Duin Bhain (Muck) 131
Caisteal Uisdean (Hugh's Castle; Skye) 73
Calgary (Mull) 168
Calgary Art in Nature (Mull) 168
Calum's Road (Raasay) 102
Camas Daraich (Skye) 94
Camas Mòr (Muck) 133
Cameron, Archie 112
campervans 38
camping 41–2 *see also individual listings*
Canna (Canaigh) 105, 122–9, *124*
Canna (Canaigh) and Sanday (Sandaigh) 122–9, *124*
Canna Harbour 125
car hire 38–9
Carbost (Skye) 84
Carn Ban (Gigha) 255
Castle Coeffin (Lismore) 192–3

Castle Maol (Skye) 92
cattle 47
caves 71, 88, 89, 119, 120, 177, 185, 256
cèilidhs 22, 46, 91
Cenél Loairn 14, 158
Cenél nGabráin 14
Cenél nÓengusa 14
Charles Edward Stuart *see* Bonnie Prince
    Charlie
Chiesley, Rachel *see* Lady Grange
children 33–4
cinema 46
Clach Ard (Skye) 78
Clachan (Raasay) 100
Clachan Bridge (Seil) 200
clan rule 15
climate 5, 23
climate change 5
coastguard 32
Coire Dubh (Rùm) 113
Coll 137–44, *138*
Coll (Cola) and Tiree (Tiriodh) 134–54
Colonsay (Colbhasa) 207–13, *208*
Colonsay and Oransay Heritage Trust 212
Colonsay Gardens 211
conservation 5
Coral Beach (Skye) 81
Corran Sands (Jura) 243
Corryvreckan whirlpool (Jura) 247, 248
Coultoon (Islay) 237
crafts 20–1
Craignure (Mull) 170–3
Cranachan 42
crannogs 121, 143, 236, **266**
Crofters' Act 1886 56
crofting 17
Crossapol Bay (Tiree) 154
Crovan, Godred 14, 215
Cuillin Ridge (Rùm) 116
Cuillins 8
Cullipool (Luing) 204
cultural etiquette 49
culture 19–22
cycle routes
  A loop around Sleat 93–4
  Cycle to Harris (Rùm) 114
  Cycle to Kilmory Bay (Rùm) 113
cycling 39

Dál Riata 13–14, 53, 158, 214–18
dancing 22
deer, red 9
deer stalking 219, 242
Dervaig (Mull) 168
dinosaur footprints 68, 69
disability, travelling with a 33
distilleries 43, 164, **220**
  Ardbeg (Islay) 231–2
  Ardnahoe (Islay) 226

Bowmore (Islay) 224–5
Bruichladdich (Islay) 235
Bunnahabhain (Islay) 226
Caol Ila (Islay) 225
Jura (Jura) 243
Kilchoman (Islay) 237
Lagavulin (Islay) 231
Laphraoig (Islay) 231
Lussa Gin (Jura) 247
Raasay (Raasay) 99, 101
Talisker (Skye) 84
Tobermory (Mull) 164
Torabhaig (Skye) 92
Whitetail Gin Distillery (Mull) 166
distillery tours (Islay) 220
doctors 30
dogs 34
dolphins 7, **9**, 196
dragonflies 12
drink driving limit 38
drinking water 31
driving 32, 36–9, 57
Duart Castle (Mull) 172
Dubh Artach Lighthouse (off Mull) 178
Duirinish peninsula (Skye) 74, 81
Dùn Beag (Skye) 81–2
Dùn Borrafiach (Skye) 79
Dùn Cana (Raasay) 101–2
Dùn Fiadhairt (Skye) 81
Dùn Grugaig (Skye) 88
Dùn Hallin (Skye) 78–9
Dùn Mòr Broch, Vaul (Tiree) 150
Dunollie Castle (Oban) 262
Duntulm Castle (Skye) 71
Dunvegan (Skye) 80
Dunvegan Castle (Skye) 80–1

eagle, golden 8, **10**, 214, 244 *see also* tours,
    eagle
eagle, white-tailed (sea) 8, **10**, 115 *see also*
    tours, eagle
Easdale (Seil) *see* Ellenabeich
Easdale Island (Eilean Èisdeal) 201–3
  Folk Museum 202
eating out 42–3
economy 17
Edinbane (Skye) 78
Edinbane, Dunvegan and the Duirinish and
    Waternish peninsulas (Skye) 74–82
education 19
Eigg (Eige) 105, 107, 116–22, *117*
electric charging points 39
Elgol (Skye) 87–8
Ellenabeich (Seil) 200
embassies 27
emergency telephone numbers 30
entertainment 46
Erisco (Skye) 71
Erraid (Mull) 178–9

Ewan's Tower (Skye) 72
Eyre Point (Raasay) 101

Fairy Bridge (Skye) 78
Fairy Glen (Skye) 72
Fairy Pools (Skye) 84
farming 43
Feall (Coll) 144
ferries 28–30, 29 see also individual islands
festivals and events 44–5
Fingal's Cave (Staffa) 185
Finger of God (Eigg) 122
Finlaggan (Islay) 225
Fionnphort (Mull) 173–6, 178
Firth of Lorn 188
Firth of Lorn Marine Special Area of Conservation 196
fish farms 17
Fishermen's Cave (Gigha) 255
fishing 17
Five Pennies (Eigg) 122
Fladda (Raasay) 97, 103–4
Fladda (Slate Islands) 205
Fladda (Treshnish Isles) 185
flora and fauna 8–12
Fossil Tree (Mull) 170
freedom to roam 47
fuel 38

Gaelic language 14, 18, 19, 135
Gallanach Beach (Muck) 132
gardens, Achamore (Gigha) 255
  An Cala (Seil) 201
  Canna House (Canna) 125
  Colonsay Gardens 211
  Lip na Cloiche (Mull) 168–9
geese, barnacle 10, 214
  Greenland white-fronted 10, 214
genealogy 18
geography 3
geology 4
Giant MacAskill Museum (Skye) 80
Gigha (Giogha) 249–58, 250
Glenbrittle (Skye) 84
Glengorm Castle (Mull) 167
Gliori, Debi 21
government 16
Gylen Castle (Kerrera) 195

habitats 6–8
haggis 42
Harmonie (Coll) 143
health 30–2
Hebridean Whale & Dolphin Trust Discovery Centre (Mull) 164
Hebridean Whale Trail 7
Hedderwick, Mairi 21
Highland Clearances 15, 56, 97, 107, 159
highland games 22, 45, 58

hiking see walking
history 13–16 see also individual islands
hitchhiking 39, 219
Hogh Bay (Coll) 142
Hogmanay 45
hospitals 30, 87, 171, 224, 262
Hynish (Tiree) 153

internet 48
Inverlussa (Jura) 246
Iona 155, 179–86, 180
Iona Abbey 184
Iona Heritage Centre 183
Iron Age 13, 158
Islay (Ìle) 214–37, 216–17
  accommodation 222–3, 227–8, 233
  eating out 223, 228, 233
  events 221
  history 214–18
  other practicalities 224, 228, 234
  shopping 223–4, 228, 234
  sports and activities 220
  tourist information 222
  transport 218–19
Islay House Square 224
Islay Nature Centre 234
Isle of Rum Heritage Centre 113
Isle of Rum Red Deer Project 115
Isle of Ulva (Ulbha; Mull) 179
Isleornsay (Skye) 92
itineraries 25

Jura (Diùra) 238–48, 239
Jura Distillery 243
Jura Picture Collection 243

kelp forests 6–7
kelp industry 15
Kerrera 193–5, 194
Kilbrandon Church (Seil) 201
Kilchattan Church (Luing) 206
Kilchianaig (Jura) 246
Kilchiaran Chapel (Islay) 237
Kilchoman (Islay) 236–7
Kilchoman Distillery (Islay) 237
Kildalton Cross (Islay) 229
Kildonnan Historic Graveyard (Eigg) 118–19
Killinallan (Islay) 226
Kilnave Chapel (Islay) 235–6
Kilt Rocks (Skye) 69
Kilvaxter Iron-Age farmstead and souterrain (Skye) 72
Kilvickeon (Mull) 176–7
King of Norway's Grave, the (Canna) 128
Kinloch (Rùm) 111–12
Kinloch Castle (Rùm) 112
Kirkapol chapels (Tiree) 150
Kyleakin (Skye) 92

Lady Grange 79
Lagavulin Distillery (Islay) 231
Lagg Harbour (Jura) 246
language 18
Laphraoig Distillery (Islay) 231
Lealt Falls (Skye) 68
LGBTQ travellers 33
Lismore (Lios Mòr) and Kerrera (Cearara)
   187–95
Lismore 187–93, *190*
Lismore Gaelic Heritage Centre (Lismore) 192
literature 21
livestock 47
Loch a' Phuill (Tiree) 152
Loch Bhasapol (Tiree) 151
Loch Gruinart RSPB reserve (Islay) 235
Lochbuie (Mull) 172–3
Lords of the Isles 14, 15, 56
Luing (Luinn) 203–6
Lump, the (Skye) 63
Lunga 205
Lussa Gin (Jura) 247

MacDonald clan 15, 56, 79, 119
MacDonald, Flora 56, 71
MacDougall clan 158, 172
machair 6
MacInnes clan 56
MacKinnon clan 15, 56
MacLean clan 107, 135, 158, 172
McLean, Allan Campbell 21
MacLean, Sorley 22
MacLean's Cross (Iona) 183
MacLeod clan 15, 56, 79, 97, 119
MacNeacail clan 56
Macquarie's Mausoleum (Mull) 169
Mallaig 263, *263*
mammals 8–9
maps 26
Mary Stewart wreck (Tiree) 149
Massacre Cave (Eigg) *see* Uamh Fhraing
Maze, the (Tiree) 152
Mealt Falls (Skye) 69
media 48
medical services 30
Megalithic burial cist (Raasay) 101
Mendelssohn, Felix 22
Mermaid's Pool (Muck) 132
Mesolithic era 13
midges 31
Minginish and the Cuillin Hills (Skye) 82–5
money 35–6
moths 11–12
mountain rescue 32
Muck (Muc) 105, 129–33, *130*
Mull 155–79, *156–7*
   accommodation 161, 165, 171, 173–5
   eating out 161–2, 165–6, 171, 175, 179
   entertainment 162, 166

events 160–1
history 155–9
other practicalities 163, 166, 171, 176
shopping 163, 166, 171, 175–6
sports and activities 160, 163, 166, 170, 176
tourist information 160
transport 159–60, 179
Mull (Muile) and Iona (Ì Chaluim Chille)
   155–86
Mull Aquarium 163
Mull Museum 159, 164
Museum of Crofting Life (Eigg) 122
Museum of Islay Life 234
music 22

natural history 5–12
Neist Point (Skye) 81
Neolithic era 13
newspapers 46, 48
Norse language 14
Norse, the 14, 53, 135, 158, 215
North Bay (Camus Alba; Raasay) 101

Oa, The (Islay) 230–1
Oban 259–63, *260*
Oban War & Peace Museum 262
Ogham Stone (Gigha) 256–7
Old Man of Storr (Skye) 67
opening times 49
orca (killer whales) 9
orchids 12
Ord (Skye) 93
Oronsay 207, *208*, 212–13
Orwell, George 22, 247, **248**
otters 196
outdoor activities 46–7 *see also individual*
   islands

packing 34
Paps of Jura 243–4
parking 38
peat bogs 7
Pennyghael (Mull) 176
Pennygown Chapel (Mull) 166–7
people 18
pharmacies 30
Pictish stones 13, 78, 101, 121, 229, 267
Picts 13–14, 53, 78
Point of Sleat (Skye) 94
politics 16
pollution 5
pony trekking (Mull) 166
population 3, 15
porpoise 7, 9, 196
Port Appin 265
Port Charlotte (Islay) 233, 234–5
Port Ellen (Islay) 226, *227*, 229
Port Mòr (Muck) 131
Port Ramsay (Lismore) 191

Portree (Skye) 58–62, *61*
post offices 48
potato blight 15, 135, 159
public holidays 44
puffin tours *see* tours, puffin
Punishment Stone (Canna) 126

Quiraing, the (Skye) 69

Raasay (Ratharsair) *96*, 97–104
Raasay House (Raasay) 100
Raasay Distillery 101
red deer 115
red tape 27
religion 18–19
Rhinns peninsula (Islay) 233
Riasg Buidhe (Colonsay) 210–11
Ringing Stone (Tiree) 150
RNLI Shop and Visitor Centre (Mull) 164
Ross of Mull 173–9, *174*
Ross of Mull Historical Centre (Mull) 176
Rubh' an Dunain (Skye) 84
Rubha Sgorr nan Ban-naomha (Canna) 128–9
Rùm 105, **109–16**, *110*
Runrig 22
Rural Centre (Tiree) 154

safety 32–3
Sailean (Lismore) 193
St Cathan's Church (Gigha) 256
St Columba 14, 134, 149, 155, 181, 186, 188, 193, 211
St Columba's Isle (Skye) 77–8
St Donnán 118–19
St Maol-luag's Chapel (Raasay) 100
St Moluag 14, 100, 187–8
St Moluag's Cathedral (Lismore) 192
St Moluag's Chair (Lismore) 192
St Oran's Chapel (Iona) 184
salmon 17
Sanday (Sandaigh) 122–3, *124*, 125–6
Scalasaig Minor Light (Colonsay) 210
Scarba 205
Scoor (Mull) 176–7
Scottish independence referendum 16
Scottish Land Reform Act, 2003 16
seafood 42
seal, common *see* seal, harbour
seal, grey 9, 196
seal, harbour 196
Seil (Saoil) 197–201
sharks, basking 7, 10
sheep 47
Shiaba (Mull) 177
shopping 45–6 *see also individual islands*
Shuna 205
Skerryvore (band) 22
Skerryvore Lighthouse (Tiree) 148, 153, 178
Skye (An t-Eilean Sgitheanach) 53–94, *54–5*

Skye history 53–6
  accommodation 59, 65–6, 74–5, 82–3, 85–6, 89–91
  eating out 60, 66, 75–6, 83, 86, 91
  entertainment and nightlife 60, 76, 91
  events 58
  history 53–6
  other practicalities 62, 67, 76, 84, 87, 92
  shopping 60–2, 66–7, 76–7, 83, 83, 87, 91–2
  sports and activities 58, 62, 65, 67, 76, 87, 92
  tourist information 57
  transport 56, 63, 74, 82, 85, 88–9
Skye bridge 30, 56
Skye Museum of Island Life 72
Skye Trail 94
Skyeskyns (Skye) 78
Slate Islands 196–206, *198–9*
Slate Islands Heritage Trust Centre (Seil) 201
Sleat (Skye) 88
Sleat, Kyleakin and the Southeast (Skye) 88–94, *90*
Small Isles 105–33, *106*
snakes 32
Soa 149
Solam (Islay) 229
Somerled 14, 135, 215
souterrains 53, 128, **268**
Spar Cave (Skye) 89
sport 22
Spouting Cave (Iona) 185
Square, The (Canna) 125
Staffa 185
Staffin Dinosaur Museum (Skye) 69
standing stones 13, 79, 129, 143, 158, 168, 212, 215, 225, 230, 235, 236, 237, 243, 246, 251, 256, 257, **268**
Stein (Skye) 78
Stephenson, Commodore Sir Gilbert 159
Storr mountains (Skye) 67
Suisnish (Raasay) 101
surfing 48

Talisker Bay (Skye) 84
Talisker Distillery (Skye) 84
Tarbert (Jura) 246
Teangue (Skye) 92
telephone 48
  emergency telephone numbers 30, 32
ticks 31
tides 27
Tiree 144–54, *146*
Tirefour Castle (Lismore) 191
Tobar Challuim well (Eigg) 122
Tobermory (Mull) 158, **161–5**, *162*
Tobermory Distillery (Mull) 164
Tobermory Lighthouse (Mull) 164–5
Toberonochy (Luing) 204
Toothache Stone (Islay) 234–5
Torabhaig whisky distillery (Skye) 92

Torsa 205
Totronald (Coll) 143–4
tour operators 25
tourism 17
tourist information 26 *see also individual islands*
transport 27–9
tours, eagle 26, 163, 200
tours, puffin 26, 67, 83, 87, 148, 166, 176, 183
Treshnish Isles 185
Trumpan Church (Skye) 79
Turner, J M W 20

Uamh Chrabhaichd (Cathedral Cave; Eigg) 120
Uamh Fhraing (Massacre Cave; Eigg) 119
Uig (Skye) 65–7, 72, 73
Uig and the Trotternish peninsula (Skye) 63–74, 64
Uig Tower (Skye) 72
Uig Wood (Skye) 72
Uisken Beach (Mull) 178
Ulva *see* Isle of Ulva
Upper Grulin (Eigg) 120

venison 42
Vikings *see* Norse, the
visas 27

Walkhighlands 65
walking 47–8
walks
  A loop around Sleat (Skye) 93
  A walk around Easdale Island 202–3
  A woodland walk from Craignure (Mull) 173
  A'Chill (Canna) 126
  Abandoned settlements and Soldier's Rock (Islay) 232–3
  An Sgùrr (Eigg) 120–1
  Ardnave (Islay) 236
  Balephuil Bay, St Patrick's Temple and Kenavara seabird cliffs (Tiree) 152
  Ballycastle Fort to Kilchattan (Luing) 205–6
  Beaches between Sorisdale and Eileraig (Coll) 141
  Beinn Airein and Camas Mòr (Muck) 132–3
  Ben More (Mull) 169–70
  Black Sand Beach and Compass Hill (Canna) 126–7
  Brae to Inver Beach (Raasay) 103
  Caisteal An Duin Bhain and the Mermaid's Pool (Muck) 131–2
  Castle Coeffin (Lismore) 192–3
  Climbing Beinn an Òir (Jura) 244–5
  Coire Lagan (Skye) 85
  Dùn Skudiburgh (Skye) 73–4
  Gylen Castle and southern Kerrera (Kerrera) 195
  Hallaig (Raasay) 102–3
  Hike up to Coire Dubh (Rùm) 113
  Hough Bay, Beinn Hough and the remains of the World War II RAF station (Tiree) 151–2
  Lookout over Rubha Hunish and Erisco, The (Skye) 70–1
  Pigs' Paradise and the seabird cliffs (Colonsay) 212
  Quiraing loop (Skye) 69–70
  Rubha nam Brathairean (Brothers' Point; Skye) 68–9
  St Columba's Isle and Clach Ard (Skye) 77–8
  Sgorr an Fharaidh (Eigg) 121–2
  Souterrains, the King of Norway's Grave and Canna's western coastline (Canna) 127–8
  South coast circle with Bodach and Cailleach (Gigha) 257–8
  Three Distilleries Path (Islay) 231–2
  To Corryvreckan (Jura) 247–8
  To Fladda at low tide (Raasay) 103–4
  Two secluded sandy beaches in the far north (Mull) 167–8
  Uamh Fhraing and Upper Grulin (Eigg) 119–20
Waterloo Beach (Skye) 87
Waternish peninsula (Skye) 78–80
Waternish Point (Skye) 79–80
weather 23–4, 27
whales 7, 9
whisky 17, **219**
whisky distilleries *see* distilleries
Wi-Fi 48
wildlife activities 111
wildlife watching 25–6
women travellers 33
World War II 15–16, 98–9, 159

INDEX OF ADVERTISERS

Aosdana 2nd colour section
CalMac 50
Elgol Bistro 95
Otter Lodge 95
South Skye Sea Kayak 2nd colour section
Wanderlust 268